i

NEW TRANSNATIONALISMS IN
CONTEMPORARY LATIN AMERICAN CINEMAS

Traditions in World Cinema

General Editors
Linda Badley (Middle Tennessee State University)
R. Barton Palmer (Clemson University)

Founding Editor
Steven Jay Schneider (New York University)

edinburghuniversitypress.com/series/tiwc

NEW TRANSNATIONALISMS IN CONTEMPORARY LATIN AMERICAN CINEMAS

Dolores Tierney

EDINBURGH
University Press

Edinburgh University Press is one of the leading university presses in the UK. We publish academic books and journals in our selected subject areas across the humanities and social sciences, combining cutting-edge scholarship with high editorial and production values to produce academic works of lasting importance. For more information visit our website: edinburghuniversitypress.com

Edinburgh University Press Ltd
The Tun – Holyrood Road
12 (2f) Jackson's Entry
Edinburgh EH8 8PJ

First published in hardback by Edinburgh University Press 2018

Typeset in 10/12.5 pt Sabon by
Servis Filmsetting Ltd, Stockport, Cheshire
and printed and bound by CPI Group (UK) Ltd, Croydon, CR0 4YY

A CIP record for this book is available from the British Library

ISBN 978 0 7486 4573 2 (hardback)
ISBN 978 1 4744 3113 2 (paperback)
ISBN 978 1 4744 3111 8 (webready PDF)
ISBN 978 1 4744 3112 5 (epub)

Note: *The Introductions to the different national film industries offered in this book endeavour where possible to quote the most up-to-date figures using available publications.*

CONTENTS

ACKNOWLEDGEMENTS

This book would not have been possible without the help and support of many individuals and institutions. I would like to thank Sussex University for two terms and one part-time semester of leave, and in particular the chairs of Media, Film and Music, Sue Thornham and Tim Jordan, and also the subject heads in film, Thomas Austin and Frank Krutnik. I would also like to thank the Center for Latin American and Latino Studies (CLALS) at American University (Washington DC) where a Research Fellowship in Autumn 2016 helped me with writing the final chapters of the manuscript and also Jeffrey Middents for help in organising the Fellowship. Some of the research for this book has also been conducted as part of the research project: 'Transnational relations in Spanish-American digital cinema: the cases of Spain, Mexico and Argentina' (CSO2014-52750-P), funded by the Spanish Ministry of Economy and Competitiveness. I thank José Cerdán Los Arcos and Miguel Fernández-Rodríguez Labayen for incorporating me into the project. Additionally, initial research for this book, in Mexico City in 2005/2006, was helped by funding from the Arts and Humanities Research Council.

I am eternally grateful to all those who have helped in some way by answering questions, providing information, materials and/or contacts, and friendship and positive energy which have helped in the book writing process: Misha MacLaird (in particular), Rielle Navtiski, Tamara Falicov, Olivia Cosentino, Ignacio Sánchez Prado (Nacho), Antonio Lázaro-Reboll, Hoi Lun Law, Gabriela Copertari, Gilberto Blasini, Christina Sisk, Carolina Rocha, Rosalind Galt, Victoria Ruétalo and again Jeffrey Middents. I thank Misha MacLaird,

Pedro Butcher and Natalia Ames Ramello who gave me their expert answers on different aspects of filmmaking in Mexico, Brazil and Peru.

I would also like to thank those who have read and offered advice on parts of the manuscript or helped shape it in some way: Misha MacLaird, Ana López, Catherine Grant, Ilene Goldman, Erica Segre, Rob Stone, Alex Marlow Mann, Niall Richardson, and my wonderful co-editors on *The Transnational Fantasies of Guillermo del Toro* Deborah Shaw and Ann Davies who, in addition to offering feedback on my writing about del Toro, helped me push forward and finish this book.

I am also deeply thankful for my great and supportive academic community who in different ways have helped foster my research including: the best mentor in the world Ana López, my colleagues past and present in Film at Sussex (Catherine Grant, Niall Richardson, Thomas Austin, Glenn Ward, Frank Krutnik, Michael Lawrence, Pam Thurschwell, Matilda Mroz, Luke Robinson, Lawrence Webb, Alisa Lebow and Rosalind Galt) and the different scholars in Latin American film studies and beyond in the broader areas of transnational filmmaking in the US and Europe whose work is a constant source of inspiration including everyone in the SCMS Latino/a Caucus (Luisela Alvaray, Laura Podalsky, Victoria Ruétalo, Isabel Arredondo, Elissa Rashkin, Catherine Benamou, Kathleen Newman, Nacho Rielle Navitski, Laura Isabel Serna, Sergio de la Mora, Gilberto Blasini, Iain Robert Smith, Jamie Sexton, Lúcia Nagib) to name just a few stellar individuals, as well as other cherished colleagues in Ibero-American cinema (Antonio Lázaro-Reboll, Miriam Haddu, the late and great Andrea Noble, Rob Stone, Sarah Barrow, Deborah Shaw, Stephanie Dennison, Lisa Shaw, Tiago de Luca, Tom Whittaker, Niamh Thornton, Belén Vidal, Christian Wehr and Friedhelm Schmidt-Welle) who have organised conferences, symposia or other venues that have enabled me to present and get valuable feedback for this research. I thank the participants of an Alejandro González Iñárritu symposium held at Sussex in May 2016, and in particular the presenters, Deborah Shaw, Niamh Thornton, Catherine Grant and especially Paul Julian Smith and Geoffrey Kantaris, my first two tutors in film who continue to inspire me with their work. I also thank my colleagues Michael Lawrence and Catherine Grant for help in organising and recording the day. Similarly, I would like to thank Catherine Grant for organising a Lucrecia Martel symposium at Sussex in June 2011 where part of this research was also presented and the participants of that symposium: Deborah Martin, Joanna Page, and Jens Andermann.

I also thank my mother for practical and research help scouring the British broadsheet newspapers for articles about Latin American cinema, my brother-in-law David for bringing my dead computer back to life, and my brothers Patrick and Richard for some great ideas. I thank my students on several iterations of my courses in Latin American Cinema, Spanish Cinema, Race and Ethnicity in Popular Cinema, and Gender and the Cinema at Sussex and Tulane Universities for their enthusiasm and their insights. I am extremely grateful to the series editors, Linda Badley and R. Barton Palmer, for their faith in the project from its proposal stage and their help throughout, and to Richard Strachan at Edinburgh University Press, and Jill Laidlaw for close reading and wonderful editing.

I thank Routledge, Palgrave and Intellect for permission to reprint the parts of this book which have already been published. An early version of Chapter One appeared in *New Cinemas: Journal of Contemporary Film* 7.2 (2009), a shorter version of Chapter Three appeared in *The Transnational Fantasies of Guillermo del Toro* (2014) and a part of the Introduction to the book appears in the *Routledge Companion to World Cinemas* (2017). I thank Natalie Foster at Routledge and also the co-editors of the *Routledge Companion to World Cinemas*, Rob Stone, Alex Marlow Mann, Paul Cooke and Stephanie Dennison. Table 1 is reproduced from the article 'National, Regional, and Global: New Waves of Latin American Cinema' by Luisela Alvaray from *Cinema Journal: The Journal of the Society for Cinema and Media Studies*, 47:3. I also thank the national film institutes of Mexico (IMCINE), Brazil (ANCINE) and Argentina (INCAA) and the website filmb.br.com for permission to reprint tables from their publications.

Finally, this book was written over several years during which I lost my dad and had three little girls. I dedicate the book to Dennis Tierney, to my children (Nancy, Dulcie and Elise) who are the best, and to Eddie for all his help but mostly for successfully navigating the challenging task of living with someone writing a book.

FIGURES

TABLES

TRADITIONS IN WORLD CINEMA

General editors: **Linda Badley** and **R. Barton Palmer**
Founding editor: **Steven Jay Schneider**

Traditions in World Cinema is a series of textbooks and monographs devoted to the analysis of currently popular and previously underexamined or under-valued film movements from around the globe. Also intended for general inter-est readers, the textbooks in this series offer undergraduate- and graduate-level film students accessible and comprehensive introductions to diverse traditions in world cinema. The monographs open up for advanced academic study more specialised groups of films, including those that require theoretically-oriented approaches. Both textbooks and monographs provide thorough examinations of the industrial, cultural, and socio-historical conditions of production and reception.

The flagship textbook for the series includes chapters by noted scholars on traditions of acknowledged importance (the French New Wave, German Expressionism), recent and emergent traditions (New Iranian, post-Cinema Novo), and those whose rightful claim to recognition has yet to be established (the Israeli persecution film, global found footage cinema). Other volumes concentrate on individual national, regional or global cinema traditions. As the introductory chapter to each volume makes clear, the films under discussion form a coherent group on the basis of substantive and relatively transparent, if not always obvious, commonalities. These commonalities may be formal, sty-listic or thematic, and the groupings may, although they need not, be popularly identified as genres, cycles or movements (Japanese horror, Chinese martial arts cinema, Italian Neorealism). Indeed, in cases in which a group of films is not already commonly identified as a tradition, one purpose of the volume is to establish its claim to importance and make it visible (East Central European Magical Realist cinema, Palestinian cinema).

Textbooks and monographs include:

- An introduction that clarifies the rationale for the grouping of films under examination
- A concise history of the regional, national, or transnational cinema in question
- A summary of previous published work on the tradition
- Contextual analysis of industrial, cultural and socio-historical conditions of production and reception
- Textual analysis of specific and notable films, with clear and judicious application of relevant film theoretical approaches
- Bibliograph(ies)/filmograph(ies)

Monographs may additionally include:

- Discussion of the dynamics of cross-cultural exchange in light of current research and thinking about cultural imperialism and globalisation, as well as issues of regional/national cinema or political/aesthetic movements (such as new waves, postmodernism, or identity politics)
- Interview(s) with key filmmakers working within the tradition.

INTRODUCTION: THE CULTURAL POLITICS OF TRANSNATIONAL FILMMAKING

In the late 1990s and early 2000s, a group of Latin American films – *Amores perros* (*Love's a Bitch* 2000), *Y tu mamá también* (*And your mother too* 2001), *Cidade de Deus* (*City of God* 2002), *Central do Brasil* (*Central Station* 1998), *Nueve reinas* (*Nine Queens* 2001), *El hijo de la novia* (*Son of the Bride* 2001) – enjoyed an unprecedented level of critical and commercial success in world film markets. At the time, these films were often talked about as part of a newly 'transnationalised' Latin American cinema wherein the term 'transnational' pointed towards the multiple ways they had benefited from capital or creative input or influences from *outside* their country of production (Baer and Long 2004; Deleyto and del Mar Azcona 2010; Poblete 2004; Sampaio 2011). Some of these influences included: engaging with aesthetic global trends or with popular genre templates *more* commonly found in Hollywood filmmaking; receiving script development support from US-based institutions such as the Sundance Institute or US- or partially US-owned companies such as Disney, Miramax, Patagonik; whole or fractional funding from transnational or multinational corporations or bodies; innovative marketing campaigns funded by US-based global distribution networks, and global distribution through these same networks.[1] When these films were followed in the 2000s by a series of equally critical and/or commercially successful 'deterritorialised' films, films that were shot and/or co-produced outside their directors' national industries and most often, but not always, in English (*21 Grams* [2003], *Babel* [2006], *Biutiful* [2010], *Children of Men* [2006], *The Constant Gardener* [2005], *Blindness* [2008], *Hellboy* [2004], *Hellboy II: The Golden Army* [2008], *El espinazo del diablo* [*The Devil's Backbone* 2001] *El laberinto del fauno* [*Pan's Labyrith* 2006], and *Diarios de motocicleta* [*Motorcycle Diaries* 2004]) the terms of a transnationalised Latin American cinema (including any notion of continental specificity) were much less frequently evoked to describe them and their connection to a sense of the nation or national cinema rarely made (Boyle 2009; Udden 2009; Mafe 2011; King 2004).[2]

In some academic criticism the first group of films was collectively hailed as the poster films of a Latin American cinematic renaissance (Hart 2004: 13) whilst other criticism downplayed the films' significance in relation to broader continental trends (Page 2009: 10). Indeed, the scale and size of these films' international distribution and box office takings (Table 1) and the displacement of (some of) their directors to the film industries of the Global North were atypical for a continent where the material conditions of film production and distribution remained and continues to be difficult and challenging. Nevertheless, it is the contention of this book that, although unusual in their level of success, both groups of films and other films of the late 1990s and the first decade or so of the 2000s are the highly visible representatives of a multiplicity of transnational modes of filmmaking which have since become more common in the continent's filmmaking practices, and that the subsequent deterritorialised films can also be connected to significant issues of national and continental specificity.

As Ana M. López points out, from the 1940s and 1950s, due to 'a series of important transcontinental forces and exchanges' Latin American cinema was already, 'and perhaps had always been a transnational phenomenon' (1998: 6). Transnational production continued in Latin America as an eagerly sought out option and an increasing necessity through the 1970s, 1980s and early 1990s (García Canclini 1997: 256). Then, as this book argues, over the last twenty years, what has made the transnational mode even more integral to Latin American production has been a shift in the way Latin American states fund and organise national industries. As the state has lessened and for a time completely withdrawn financial support and protectionist measures for the different national filmmaking endeavours, filmmakers have had to seek funding opportunities privately and often abroad from Europe and the United States. At the same time, transnational media conglomerates and quasi-state cultural organisations in Europe and the US, as well as individual auteurs such as Pedro Almodóvar, have looked to Latin America to develop and expand into new markets and to seek out cultural renewal (D'Lugo 2003a: 104; Donoghue 2014a).[3] This dismantling of state protection for national filmmaking and exposure to global market forces has had both detrimental and beneficial effects on its major national industries. On the one hand, these measures initially decimated production numbers and further increased the hold of Hollywood films on the domestic box office. On the other hand, these measures have facilitated both the distribution and circulation of *some* films and

Table 1 Latin American box office successes 1998–2004 (Alvaray 2008: 53, © 2008 University of Texas Press. All rights reserved. Courtesy of the University of Texas Press)

Film	Production	Distribution in US	Distribution Companies US and local	US Box Office	Worldwide Box Office
Central Station	Brazil, 1998	1998–1999	Sony Pictures Classics	$5,595,428	Approx. $21,000,000
Amores Perros	Mexico, 2000	2001	Lions Gate Films, No Vision	$5,383,834	$20,908,467
Y tu mamá también	Mexico, 2001	2002	IFC, 20th Century Fox	$13,622,333	$33,616,692
Nine Queens	Argentina, 2000	2002	Sony Pictures Classics, BVI	$1,221,261	$12,413,888
The Son of the Bride	Argentina, 2001	2002	Columbia Tristar, Argentina VH	$624,153	N/A
The Crime of Father Amaro	Mexico, 2002	2002–2003	Sony Entertainment, Samuel G	$5,709,616	$26,996,738
Real Women Have Curves	US, 2002	2002–2003	Home Box Office	$5,844,929	$7,777,790
City of God	Brazil, 2002	2003–2004	Miramax, Buena Vista International	$7,563,397	$27,387,381
Carandiru	Brazil, 2003	2004	Sony Classics, Columbia	$213,954	$10,781,635
Maria Full of Grace	US/Colombia, 2004	2004	Fine Line Features	$6,517,198	$9,383,264
The Motorcycle Diaries	Argentina et al., 2004	2004	Focus Features, Buena Vista International	$16,756,372	$57,641,466

creative and technical personnel both domestically and across borders and into global film markets and metropolitan production venues and initiated a series of artistically innovative but also commercially successful films. Although the state has in the course of these twenty years, returned to a position of support for filmmaking in the three major national traditions (Brazil, Mexico, Argentina), and production numbers have recovered, in the present moment, state support (via a system of grants, loans, subsidies, tax incentives and screen quotas) only accounts for a *part* of a film's complex financial structure. As a result, many Latin American films require a form of financial support that comes from outside their national borders at some point in their development, production, post production or distribution. This support comes in the form of funding from a European or US institution (Ibermedia, Hubert Bals, Fonds Sud, Sundance and others) or from a Motion Picture Association member company (Focus Features, Miramax, Disney). These institutions and corporations prove essential in securing distribution both domestically and abroad. These differing forms of transnational support are actively encouraged and sought out by the state.[4] Prominent filmmakers have also emerged as key players in this transnationalised cinematic sphere. Acting as mediators between the art and commerce of filmmaking, and using the leverage their transnational careers have afforded them, Latin America's most famous transnational auteurs (Alejandro González Iñárritu, Alfonso Cuarón, Guillermo del Toro, Fernando Meirelles, Walter Salles, Juan José Campanella) and their production companies (Esperanto Filmoj, VideoFilmes, Tequila Gang, Cha Cha Chá, O2Filmes, 100 Bares) have played an active role in fomenting the film cultures in their respective nations (D'Lugo 2003a: 103).

New Transnationalisms in Contemporary Latin American Cinemas argues for the importance of understanding the region's contemporary filmmaking output within this framework of transnationalism. The book analyses the internationally distributed Latin American blockbusters of the late 1990s, early 2000s and the 2010s and their world-renowned auteurs (Iñárritu, Cuarón, del Toro, Meirelles, Salles and Campanella), choosing to focus on them rather than the many other Latin American directors who have been in the past, and are in the present moment working transnationally most often but not always in the US and Latin America's different national and film industries.[5] The book puts forward the idea that Iñárritu, Cuarón, del Toro, Meirelles, Salles and Campanella in particular represent key aspects of this newly transnationalised Latin American cinema. It has been suggested that an excessive amount of attention has already been paid to these auteurs. This book argues that although their initial transnational successes may have been written about at length, their subsequent deterritorialised films have been much less written about, nor has there been sufficient focus on how all their work connects to significant issues of national and continental specificity.

To better understand how contemporary transnational Latin American cinemas work across the region, this Introduction begins by tracing the concept of transnational cinema as it has emerged in film studies and in particular how it is situated within broader discourses around Latin American national cinemas (the political, the postcolonial and the auteurist). It goes on to explore the cinema in which these discourses are more frequently employed – art cinema – looking at films from Latin America's art cinema resurgence and arguing that these also exemplify (in a different way) how transnational flows of capital and creativity impact on Latin American cinemas. It focuses in particular on two films by Peruvian director Claudia Llosa – *Madeinusa* (Perú/Spain 2006) and *La teta asustada* (*The Milk of Sorrow* Perú/Spain 2009) – as representatives of a key paradigm of transnational cinema: the 'festival funded film'. Centering on Llosa's films, but also drawing in other art cinema films from Latin America, this section lays out the histories and cultural politics of the funding bodies that finance films from the Global South. It explores what the links are between these films' transnational funding structures and their aesthetic features and what the study of Llosa's films and the broad art cinema resurgence brings to the exploration of transnational cinemas in Latin America and the industrial and/or deterritorialised cinema of Iñárritu, Cuarón, del Toro, Meirelles, Salles and Campanella. The Introduction concludes by laying out and explaining the rationale behind the organisation of the book.

THE CONCEPT OF TRANSNATIONAL CINEMAS IN LATIN AMERICA

A core point of enquiry of a new journal from Intellect (*Transnational Cinemas*, Higbee and Lim 2010), and the subject of several prominent recent anthologies (Lefere and Lie 2016; Ďurovičová and Newman 2010; Ezra and Rowden 2006), the concept of cinematic transnationalism has gained increasing currency in contemporary studies of global and postcolonial cinemas particularly in the way it offers a means of theorising the movement, and displacement, of cinemas, directors, actors and film personnel across national and regional borders as well as a way of describing 'production and distribution practices, sources of funding, casting decisions, [and] thematic concerns' (Hjort 2010: 12). In Latin American film scholarship, the concept of cinematic transnationalism has become central to contemporary theorisations of the region's cinemas which explore cinematic practices, cycles, particular films, or periods that in some way 'exceed' the aesthetic, geographical and political borders that have historically defined its national cinemas. These have included a recent *Transnational Cinema* dedicated to Latin American transnational cinema (Barrow and Dennison 2013), work on inter-American filmmaking in the classical era (Fein 1998; Tierney 2011); work on the transnational careers of the classical era's film personnel between Latin America, Hollywood and Europe

(López 1998, 2000; Tierney 2012), a focus on the contemporary 'transatlantic traffic' of co-productions between Latin America and Spain/Europe (Smith 2003a; Villazana 2008, 2009; MacLaird 2008–2009; Hoefert de Turégano 2004; Falicov 2007a; Triana-Toribio 2013) and the transnational filmmaking of individual filmmakers between Latin America, the US and Europe (Shaw 2013a; Davies, Shaw and Tierney 2014) and several recent anthologies which explore both the transnationality of the Mexican classical era (Irwin and Ricalde 2013) and the diverse transnationality of individual films (Bermúdez 2011; Dennison 2013).

As these examples illustrate, the transnational is a hold-all term, capable of describing a range of complex extra-national practices in contemporary and earlier modes of funding, production and distribution of films. It is precisely its multivalence however, which presents problems for some theorists. Firstly, as such an elastic concept in an industry that has always 'operated on a regional, national and transnational basis,' (Higson 2000: 67) the concept of the transnational risks the kind of plurality where it can simultaneously 'mean anything and everything' (Hjort 2010: 12) *and* consequently, nothing in particular. Secondly, its expandability threatens to homogenise the very important diversities between national cinemas, flattening out differences between them, whilst simultaneously seeking to connect them in a globally networked film economy. It is precisely the political and cultural displacement of the nation that the use of the term transnational suggests which is at the core of some Latin American film scholars' objection to it.

Whilst critics in Europe and other parts of the world have identified a number of difficulties with the concept of a national cinema (Higson 2000; Ďurovičová 2010), some scholars of Latin American cinema make the case for its continued relevance (Page 2009: 9; King 2000: 255; 2004: 304). John King, for instance, argues that 'the nation remain[s] the principle site for both the production and the reception of movies' (2004: 304) but does not take into account how, because of the piecemeal funding that most films involve, the nation itself becomes a multiply determined and transnational site, crisscrossed by currents of global commerce and international funding. What is at stake in the retention of the national as the only valid paradigm for exploring Latin America's national cinemas, is an anti-colonial and nationalist stance *against* the colonising tendencies of Hollywood and other cinemas of the Global North. What is understandably problematic about the transnational for these theorists is that it seemingly emphasises the few films – the blockbusters with evident transnational pedigree – at the expense of the many – the small art cinema films that are more overtly 'national' but which struggle to get production funding, and, once completed, to find distribution in their own national markets and internationally (Page 2009: 9–10, King 2004: 304), and that it celebrates the transnational capital, which is so often a prominent feature of these films, and its continued exploitation of Latin America's (cultural) resources.

For these critics, the transnational is masking the very real difficulties of film production in Latin America and creating an apolitical form of criticism that finds value in commercial success and ignores the very specific conditions of economic exploitation currently threatening Latin American national film-making endeavours. Whilst these critics are wholly correct about the problems faced by Latin American filmmakers, what they perhaps do not fully take into account in their drawing up of a national/transnational dichotomy is that those 'national' films focused on in scholarship that are 'state supported' in their respective countries have simultaneously also benefited from, and are in fact highly dependent on, several sources of transnational funding and, as the rest of this Introduction will argue, these transnational funding bodies are not insignificant in determining the aesthetic and cultural identities of the films. It is worth noting that many of the films Joanna Page (2009) explores in her excellent monograph *Crisis and Capitalism in Contemporary Argentine Cinema* have benefited from transnational funding too – in the form of monies from film festivals, cultural institutions, television stations and funding agreements located in Europe, the US or transatlantically between Spain and Latin America.[6]

The insistence on the concept of national cinemas espouses a familiar critical framework that privileges a certain narrative about Latin American cinema. This narrative focuses on film texts which may offer cultural (and economic) resistance and national autonomy in the face of (usually) Hollywood international domination (Higson 1989: 37). This in turn is linked to the privileging of an art cinema model of filmmaking and the denigration of commercial or popular filmmaking equated with the Hollywood 'mass entertainment film' (Higson 1989: 41). Correct as these scholars are to acknowledge the difficulties of the concept of the transnational, and the potential distortions it can bring to the overview of Latin American productions, these points also need to be situated alongside the shifting focus in Latin American and Global (previously Third) Cinema scholarship, away from 1960s paradigms of resistance to a Hollywood-based cultural hegemony and towards a more complex understanding of the relationship between Hollywood, popular cinema and the rest of the world (Alvaray 2008: 48; Thanouli 2008: 5).

Similarly, problematic for the political and postcolonial paradigms of Latin American film scholarship is the English language (and most frequently US or UK produced) cinema of Latin American directors (*21 Grams, Babel, Children of Men, The Constant Gardener, Blindness*, and most recently *On the Road, Pacific Rim, Gravity, Birdman, Crimson Peak, The Revenant*, and *360*). These English-language films and their potential transnationality have, in the past, been considered beyond the remit of most scholars of Latin American cinema.

This is potentially because of the perception that the US aesthetic and industrial practices within which these films are made put this cinema beyond the boundaries of national, and indeed 'serious', film criticism by necessarily absorbing, and often neutralising the authorial sensibility of, directors who work within its structures.[7] These critical approaches to the global film economy emphasise directorial moves between peripheral film-making nations and regions (such as Latin America) and the West (most often the United States, but also the United Kingdom) as a one-way process. In this model, the 'imperialist' nation (the United States) co-opts, depoliticises and commodifies the cultures of the smaller nations into its own system of ideology, meaning and production. Hence, directors such as Iñárritu, Cuarón, del Toro, Salles, Meirelles and Campanella who 'go to Hollywood',[8] make 'Hollywood style action films' (Bentes 2013: 104) or 'classical Hollywood style melodrama' (Andermann 2011: 41) are often presumed to be abandoning their authorial vision and their own national cinema when they work within, or in a way that is implicated in, Hollywood's 'imperialist' hegemonic system.[9] In the case of Campanella who, although not physically displaced from Argentina (in his feature film production – he does work in US 'quality' television), and still making films in Spanish is marginalised in scholarship on Argentine film as an 'industrial auteur' who works within Hollywood-influenced aesthetic and genre categories.

Less problematic for the political and postcolonial paradigms of Latin American film scholarship are the Latin American directors' deterritorialised films made in Spanish. Indeed, *Diarios de motocicleta, El espinazo del diablo*, and *El laberinto del fauno* have been excellently written about at length by scholars of Spanish and Latin American cinema (Thornton 2007; Williams 2007; Bueno 2007; Podalsky 2011; Davies 2006, 2008; Acevedo-Muñoz 2008; Lázaro-Reboll 2007). With these deterritorialised Spanish-language films, there is less of a preoccupation with assumed commodification and depoliticisation. This is partly to do with the sense of a shared language and history with Spain (Triana-Toribio 2013: 102) – which more often than not is the co-producer of these films – and also the sense that the Spanish film industry is equally invested in contesting Hollywood hegemony. It also has to do with assumptions made based on language and audience. As Spanish-language films, it is presumed that they are made on a smaller budget, circulate on the art cinema circuit and are therefore less circumscribed by mainstream industry norms and ideologies. They are consequently 'free' from the kinds of obstacles to auteurist expression faced by English language, industry projects. Yet these assumptions are also countered by the fact that del Toro's *El laberinto del fauno* circulated on mainstream circuits (and made a mainstream-sized box office of $80 million) and, although reflective of auteurist and political concerns (memorialising the forgotten Republican victims of the Spanish civil war and its aftermath) was *also* considerably informed by industry trends (fantasy elements) that reflect the renewed popularity of the fantasy genre – the success of *The Lord of the Rings*, *The Hobbit*, the *Harry Potter* and *The Chronicles of Narnia* franchises (Tierney, Shaw and Davies 2014: 3).

Taking a cue from a recent essay by Eleftheria Thanouli, this book proposes a critical approach to Latin America's current national cinemas and to its transnational filmmakers other than that of (a resistance to) American cultural hegemony. Rather than adopt the imperialist/peripheral model, or in Thanouli's terms, a model of 'Hollywood cinema [vs] the rest of the world' (2008: 5), this book thinks about Latin America's deterritorialised directors as 'interstitial authors' (Naficy 1996: 119) negotiating between their own national cultures and that of geographically dispersed Hollywood. Through this approach this book plans to contest the commonly held belief that auteurs from peripheral nations (and in this case Latin American directors in particular) are necessarily 'effaced' when they work within Hollywood (understood as a 'network of production, distribution and exhibition situated around the world'), one of its independent subsidiaries, or within mainstream parametres associated with classical Hollywood filmmaking (Naficy 1996: 120; Behlil 2016: 14).This book argues that what is going on with these travelling Latin American directors is much more complex than a simple 'effacement' or one-way journey towards a supposedly 'imperialist' United States, and that there are benefits to examining their US (or in the case of Cuarón his UK) work *alongside* their Latin American films. This book will show how, in a comparative analysis, between the locally made and deterritorialised films, these texts can be seen to share many of the same visual, stylistic and narrative strategies as well as a marked ideological coherence.

This book will argue against the unproblematic co-opting of these directors' deterritorialised films into the artistic production and ideological mind-set of a US or European mainstream. It will suggest that the concerns of Latin America's different national cinemas and their own authorial specificity *can* survive the multiple moves back and forth between their own cultures and those of the United States and Europe. In making these arguments, this book wishes to suggest alternative boundaries in the analysis of Latin American cinemas than those of geographical nation states,[10] and also offer a means of exploring the cultural politics of a globalised film economy. However, in analysing these directors' deterritorialised films in relation to their locally made films, what this book does not wish to do is to argue for the latters' purity in relation to a national style or the former's lack of purity. Instead this book argues that the work these directors have produced both locally and abroad problematises the notion of industrial and national borders by sharing many of the same radical and alternative aesthetic strategies.

To this end, *New Transnationalisms in Contemporary Latin American Cinemas* borrows from theorists of globalisation (Appadurai 1996; Naficy

1996, 2001) who emphasise in different ways how transnational cinematic forms from peripheral nations may actually contest 'stor[ies] of cultural homogenisation' (Appadurai 1996: 11)[11] and challenge the notion of an easy *appropriation* of Western models with a model of dynamic 'cinematic exchange' (Newman 2010: 4). It also takes into account Hamid Naficy's model of exiled and diasporic filmmaking by focusing as Naficy does on directors from peripheral and postcolonial nations making films across national boundaries and mostly in the West. Like Naficy, the book argues that these directors produce an 'accented' cinema that differs from what some consider (Hollywood's) dominant and 'accentless' cinema, in as much as it bears the trace of the directors' displacement (2001: 4). This book works with the ways Naficy's 'accented filmmaking' connects with the films of Meirelles, Cuarón, del Toro, Iñárritu, and Salles, who like those Naficy writes about, have at some point in their career shifted from peripheral nations to the West or who move back and forth between different filmmaking venues.

New Transnationalisms in Contemporary Latin American Cinemas also points out the difficulties of Naficy's model for the present generation of transnational and in some cases deterritorialised Latin American filmmakers. A previous generation of Latin American deterritorialised filmmakers (Glauber Rocha, Fernando Solanas, Jorge Sanjinés, Miguel Littín, Raúl Ruiz and others) exiled to the West by the military dictatorships of the 1960s and 1970s and the films they made in exile fit explicitly within Naficy's accented model in which directors work in an artisanal mode and in the interstices of film production institutions.[12] However, the directors this book focuses on, (del Toro, Cuarón, Iñárritu, Meirelles, Salles, Campanella) working often within Hollywood, or semi-Independent Hollywood, or industrial structures within their own countries and making films within mainstream aesthetic formula are less of an easy fit within the accented model. The 1960s and 1970s generation of directors were making films that were aesthetically and politically committed within their own countries and as part of the continental project of New Latin American Cinema (*Deus e o Diabo na terra do sol/Black God, White Devil* [Rocha 1964], *La hora de los hornos/The Hour of the Furnaces* [Solanas and Getino, 1968], *Yawar Malku/Blood of the Condor* [Sanjinés 1969], *El jackal de Nahueltoro/The Jackal of Nahueltoro* [Littín 1969]) and continued making these kinds of films in exile (*Der leone have sept cabeças/The Lion has Seven Heads*, [Rocha, Congo/France/Italy 1971], *Tangos el exilio de Gardel/Tangos, the Exile of Gardel*, [Solanas France 1985]). The present generation (as this book will emphasise) began by making films in their own countries which were less overtly political and engaged and played with popular and mainstream forms. Furthermore, whereas the 1960s and 1970s displacement was politically motivated or compelled, the present generation's displacement to metropolitan filmmaking venues is mostly financially, artistically and industrially motivated – by both the lack of filmmaking possibilities in their own countries and greater possibilities elsewhere – and only indirectly politically motivated in cases where the government controls access to the filmmaking infrastructure.[13] Additionally, the book argues against Naficy's assertion that 'Hollywood' is a necessarily accentless cinema and for the political potential of the Hollywood genre film, suggesting that it is sometimes from the politically progressive elements of some genres that these transnational auteurs take their cues.

This book takes a self-conscious, auteurist approach to Latin America's transnational cinemas. It takes into consideration how the model of auteurism itself must be adapted to the mobile careers and multiple collaborators of these different filmmakers and to the transnational systems of funding, production and distribution in which they operate (Grant 2000: 101). It suggests, following Catherine Grant, a 'commercial take on auteurism' (2000: 101) arguing that what makes it possible for these films to circulate globally is, in part, their 'constructed status as author cinema' (D'Lugo 2003a: 109). This commercial take on auteurism is very much at odds with the history of auteurism in Latin America. Brazilian filmmaker/critic Rocha saw 'commerce' and the 'auteur' as antithetical, writing in 1963 that 'if commercial cinema is the tradition, auteur cinema is the revolution' (Miller and Stam 2000: 5). Other New Cinema filmmaker/theorists rejected auteurism altogether considering it to be complicit with bourgeois cinema and its cult of the individual. Cuban filmmaker/critic Julio García Espinosa argued that the category of the individual artist (filmmaker/auteur) becomes defunct in a revolutionary society in which the goal is for everyone to be creators of a popular art (1997 [1969]: 76). Argentine filmmakers/theorists Getino and Solanas rejected auteur cinema (along with Hollywood cinema) as trapped inside a capitalist system of production, that allows only personal, but not political aesthetic freedom (1997 [1970]: 42). The model of transnational auteurism this book proposes represents a challenge to these continental new cinema ideals, as well as a pragmatic response to the material realities of contemporary filmmaking on the continent.

For example, as the analyses of these films will show, although Latin American film studies has moved on from the narratives of dependency and neocolonialism which marked the new cinemas of the 1960s, 1970s and early 1980s, the transnational texts of the deterritorialised filmmakers and their transnationalised filmmaking practices still engage with globalisation and its attendant issues and problems. These films therefore represent a political and ideological continuity with the new cinemas but not militantly so. Like other transnational cinematic texts (*Dirty Pretty Things* Stephen Frears 2002) these directors' films share a thematic similarity in their engagement with and critique of the processes of globalisation and neocolonialism (Ezra and Rowden 2006: 7); *Cronos, Babel, Biutiful, Children of Men, Y tu mamá también, The Constant Gardener, Diarios de motocicleta* and *On the Road* produce narratives which dramatise in different ways the processes of transcultura-tion, migration, displacement and loss. Meirelles, Salles, Cuarón, Iñárritu and Campanella make films about migrants, travellers, or characters who are often de-racinated, or separated in different ways from their history or place of origin or exploited/defeated by the nefarious practices of multinational companies or by neoliberal capitalism.[14] And by dealing with such politically charged themes, rather than posit a threat to Latin America's nationalist cinemas, transnational practices (at the level of production, distribution, funding and the film texts) have made possible the exploration of localist concerns in these films in ways which subsequently extend into regional, hemispheric and more global per-spectives in the wave of deterritorialised films: *21 Grams, Children of Men, Blindness, Babel, Biutiful, Diarios de motocicleta*, and *The Constant Gardener*.

When theorists dismiss the concept of the transnational and its utility in thinking about current production in Latin America, or limit the scope of the transnational to official co-productions and successful blockbusters, they fail to take into account the full extent of transnational practices in play in the region. There are other transnational practices including transnational funding structures which play an influential role in both the production of the much smaller, and often minimalist 'festival funded film' (Smith 2008a) and the sustaining of smaller national filmmaking endeavours. Two Peruvian films (*Madeinusa* and *La teta asustada*) reflect both how these funding structures work and offer a means of exploring the cultural politics of transnational film-making. Out of the crop of transnationally funded recent art cinema successes, what is particularly useful about Llosa's films to the aims of this chapter and indeed this book is that their narratives thematise the processes of cultural transformation and transculturation at the heart of critical debates about transnational funding.

THE CULTURAL POLITICS OF TRANSNATIONAL FILMMAKING: FUNDING THE FESTIVAL FILM

Transnational filmmaking in Latin America has historically and contempora-neously taken on a multiplicity of forms. In one of its most frequently cited forms, the official state-backed co-production between European cultural institutions (or television stations benefiting from grants given by the state) and producers from Latin America, two or more countries 'collaborate in the process of financing and producing a film' (MacLaird 2008–2009: 51).[15] International co-productions have produced some of Latin America's great-est critical and commercial successes. *El crimen del padre Amaro* (*The Crime of Father Amaro* Carlos Carrera 2002) was a Mexico, Spain, Argentina, and France co-production which grossed $27 million and was the third-highest grossing film in Mexico between 2000 and 2015. International co-productions have equally produced some of its worst failures; *El coronel no tiene quien le escriba* (*No One Writes to the Colonel* Arturo Ripstein 1999), based on the novella by Gabriel García Márquez, was a co-production between Mexico, France and Spain and was a commercial flop. In another of its most frequently cited forms transnational cinema is equated with the Latin American block-busters which have overt transnational status because they are either directly financed, developed or distributed by companies/cultural institutions from beyond the geospatial limits of the continent: *Amores perros*, *Diarios de moto-cicleta*, *Y tu mamá también* and *Cidade de Deus*.

Whilst theorists most commonly frame and sometimes judge co-productions and the continents' blockbusters as properly transnational, they tend to frame art cinema films as national in as much as they fit within the prescrip-tive textual and ideological features of national cinema (an auteurist, realist 'quality' cinema) (Higson 1989: 37, 41). They are however, in some ways, not that dissimilar. Latin America's most well-known art cinema directors (Llosa, Lucrecia Martel, Lisandro Alonso, Fernando Eimbcke, Amat Escalante, Carlos Reygadas) are similarly involved in a transnational dynamic. Their films add another critical dimension to the idea of transnational cinema in Latin America, presenting an alternative form of transnationalism not strictly reliant on a straight commercial transaction but on something else instead. How we understand the dimensions of this transnationalism is still, nevertheless, dependent on the funding structures of these art cinema films and the national situation of filmmaking in their respective industries.

Until the early 1990s, the category of film most commonly funded by Latin America's different national film institutes was a realist, auteurist, art cinema. But since the depletion of state monies given over to funding cinema, independent Latin American filmmakers, if they cannot raise money from private sources, are often in need of transnational support whether it is from a European institution, funding body, multilateral agreement or televi-sion station, or from the US, via the Sundance Institute or a Motion Picture Association member company.[16] Most frequently a film is funded from a com-bination of all these sources, including the state. This patchwork of funding, with or without state support, has become a typical scenario for the most suc-cessful recent Latin American art cinema films (Table 2).[17]

Funding initiatives, most of which are linked to European and US festivals, have increasingly become part of the financial structures of Latin American art cinema films and, in some cases, such as that of *el nuevo cine argentino* (the New Argentine Cinema), have actually played a role in developing and sustaining key movements.[18] Established in the 1980s, 1990s and early 2000s, many of these funding initiatives, particularly the European ones – Rotterdam Film Festival's Hubert Bals award, Fonds Sud Cinema award, Fribourg Film Festival's Visions Sud Est, the Sundance Institute, its awards

Table 2 Funding structures of selected art house cinema successes 2002–2015

		Festival Funding						
	Gov. Funding	Visions Sud Est	World Cinema Fund	Sundance/ NHK	Hubert Bals	Fonds Sud	European TV	Ibermedia
Perú								
Claudia Llosa								
Madeinusa (2006)	√			√			√ Canal+, TVE	
La teta asustada (2010)	√	√	√				√TVE	√
Mexico								
Fernando Eimbcke								
Lake Tahoe (2008)	√			√				
Carlos Reygadas								
Japón (2002)	√				√			
Batalla en el cielo (2005)	√				√	√	√ Arte France	
Stellet Licht (2007)	√		√				√	
Post Tenebras Lux (2012)	√					√	√ Arte France	
Amat Escalante								
Los bastardos (2008)	√					√		
Heli (2013)	√			√		√	√Arte	

| | Festival Funding | | | | | | | |
	Gov. Funding	Visions Sud Est	World Cinema Fund	Sundance/ NHK	Hubert Bals	Fonds Sud	European TV	Ibermedia
Argentina								
Lucrecia Martel								
La ciénaga (2001)				√				√
La niña santa (2004)						√		√
La mujer sin cabeza (2008)						√	√ Arte France	
Lisandro Alonso								
La libertad (2001)	√postprod.					√		
Liverpool (2006)		√			√			√
Jauja (2015)	√		√					

and its screenwriters lab, the Global Film Initiative, the Berlin Film Festival's World Cinema Fund, Cine en construcción (jointly organised by the San Sebastián Film Festival and the Latin American Film Festival of Toulouse), and the Cannes Film Festival's Cinéfondation[19] – are Government supported, usually by monies earmarked for foreign aid (Falicov 2010: 3; MacLaird 2011; Ross 2011: 261; Campos 2013: 15).[20] Awards are made to facilitate development, production, postproduction and distribution, and usually range from €10,000 or $10,000 up to $200,000, with average production awards ranging from €50,000 to €100,000 per film. Given that the average Latin American art cinema film costs around €1,000,000[21], the winning of multiple funding awards is required to successfully realise any single production. For instance, Eimbcke's *Lake Tahoe* (2008), Reygadas's *Batalla en el cielo* (*Battle in Heaven* 2005) and Escalante's *Los bastardos* (*The Bastards* 2008), were all funded by a system of support which included both funding from the Mexican state (through IMCINE, its funding bodies FOPROCINE or FIDECINE and in the case of *Lake Tahoe*, the tax incentive law, previously known as el EFICINE) and funding from a variety of festivals and their funds. *Batalla en el cielo* received funds from Hubert Bals and Fonds Sud whilst *Los bastardos* received funds from Fonds Sud. *Lake Tahoe* was developed through the Sundance/NHK screenwriting lab.

What is so significant about the financial assistance offered by foreign institutions, film festivals and their related competitions is not necessarily the amount: Fonds Sud's award for Martel's *La mujer sin cabeza* (*The Headless Woman* 2008) was €90,000 of a total budget of €1.71 million.[22] World Cinema Fund's award for Alonso's *Jauja* (2015) amounted to €50,000. What is important about this assistance is the 'access [it affords] to other economic resources' (Aguilar 2011: 12). Winning one funding competition singles-out scripts or incomplete features as attention-worthy for other festivals and ultimately distributors (MacLaird 2011: 3). Ironically, in Argentina in particular, these 'other [...] resources' whose interest is often piqued by foreign financial assistance has included its national film institute (INCAA) itself. The story of how Alonso's *La libertad* (*Freedom* 2001) was completed is illustrative of this particular process; although in its case it wasn't the funding of the 'other source' that proved crucial, just the other source's interest in the project. Not being able to even apply to INCAA because of its script-based funding application (which is the same with most funding competitions in Europe and North America) during pre production or production, Alonso made the film with $30,000 of family money and only received state support (of $70,000 post-production funds) when a Cannes' delegate (on a scouting trip to Argentina) expressed interest in showing the film in 'Un Certain Regard' section of the Festival (Matheou 2010: 293). In the case of Argentina it is not just foreign funding which has nudged its national institute towards greater support of its small art cinema circuit. As Aguilar points out, the state was forced into it 'in light of the impact of these movies on the festival circuit and their prestige among critics' (2011: 12). Similarly, in Mexico, its national film institute (IMCINE) was nudged towards greater support of its independent sector by the 'positive reception [on the funding and festival circuit]' of directors such as Reygadas (*Japón* 2002, *Batalla en el cielo*, *Stellet licht/Silent Light* 2007, *Post Tenebras Lux* 2012), who was 'originally turned down for state support' (MacLaird 2011: 2).

Multilateral agreements made between national film institutes is also a key source of funding. The largest of these is Programa Ibermedia. Ibermedia is the main co-production film fund between Spain and Latin America. Established by CAACI (Conference of Ibero-American Audiovisual and Film Institutes) and the heads of national film institutes in 1997, Ibermedia has historically included Spain, Portugal and twelve other member countries (Perú, Bolivia, Brazil, Chile, Colombia, Cuba, Mexico, Panamá, Argentina, Puerto Rico, Uruguay, and Venezuela) (Falicov 2007a: 21–22). Additionally, from October 2016, Italy has become a new member country (De Marco 2016). Each country makes a minimum contribution of $100,000 with some countries making larger contributions.[23] In 2007 these country contributions stood at: Mexico – $500,000, Brazil – $300,000, Perú, Argentina, Colombia, Cuba, and Portugal each – $100,000 (Falicov 2007a: 22). Until the economic crisis, Spain's contribution to the Ibermedia fund was as much as $3,500,000 a year (Anon. 2015). Since 2007, the minimum contribution has risen to $150,000 with some of the larger Latin American economies increasing their contribution beyond that in 2015: Brazil – $800,000, Argentina – $500,000 and Venezuela – $600,000 (Anon. 2015). Between 2015 and 2016 other countries have increased their contributions – Perú, Colombia and Chile each now contribute $225,000 (Ames Ramello 2017). Despite its ongoing economic crisis, Spain remains marginally the largest contributor, giving $850,000 in 2015 (Anon. 2015). All the member countries can compete via production companies to receive monies from a pot that was worth in 2015 $4,700,000 from Ibermedia's different funds (Falicov 2007a: 21–22; Anon. 2015). The only grants currently available are for co-production and development (the distribution and the training grants were eliminated some years ago and replaced by international workshops and distribution intitiatives like Ibermedia TV) (Ames Ramello 2017). Ibermedia has supported the production of many films of the art cinema renaissance including *La ciénaga* (*The Swamp* Martel, Argentina/France/Spain 2001) and *Liverpool* (Alonso, Argentina 2008) and more recently *Boi Neon* (*Neon Bull* Brazil/Netherlands/Uruguay, Gabriel Mascaro 2015) and *Zama* (Mexico/Argentina/Spain/Brazil Martel 2017). It has also supported the distribution of films within Latin America. Macondo Cine Video was awarded funds to distribute *Whiskey* (Uruguay/Argentina, Juan Pablo Rebella and Pablo

Stoll 2004) in Mexico and Atlanta Films was funded to distribute *La niña santa* (*The Holy Girl*, Martel, Argentina/Spain 2004) (Falicov 2007a: 22).

From the 1980s onwards European television companies have also played a large role in funding co-productions with Latin America. Between 1986 and 1992 Spanish television invested more than $20 million in co-productions with Latin American countries (Hoefert de Turégano 2004: 17). Coinciding with the withdrawal of state support across the region, this represented a sum larger than all the 'Latin American governments combined' (Hoefert de Turégano 2004: 17). The publically owned TVE (Televisión Española) has been the most active in co-productions with Latin America. Canal+ España, the second most important television network for Spanish film production, has also been active in co-productions in the region (Campos: 2013: 15–16). In France, in addition to public channels France 2 and France 3's participation in co-productions with Latin America, the work of the (Franco-German) private cable channel Arte France and its subsidiaries also stands out (Campos: 2013: 15–16). It has given partial funding to three of Reygadas' films; *Batalla en el cielo*, *Stellet Licht* and *Post Tenebras Lux*, to Martel's *La mujer sin cabeza*, and to Escalante's *Heli* (2013). As Minerva Campos points out, the support films receive from these television channels is more than direct investment and promotion – it also includes exhibition and distribution (2013: 16). Currently in Spain, film funding from television (or telecommunications companies) is mandated by Government quotas obliging television operators to 'buy or coproduce Spanish and European movies' (Hopewell 2013). These quotas benefit projects co-produced with Latin America (Hopewell 2013). Since the economic crisis, and with Spain producing fewer big films, Spanish companies are looking to other industries to co-produce with (Hopewell 2013). In 2012 this policy was under review because in addition to helping national products as well as co-produced Latin American projects it also resulted in help for some films (*Wrath of the Titans* Jonathan Liebesman 2012, *Fast and Furious 6: The Game* Scott Blackwood 2013) co-produced with Hollywood majors such as Warner Bros. and Universal (Hopewell 2012).

Filmmaking in Perú: *Madeinusa* and *La teta asustada* as Festival Films

Perú is one of Latin America's smaller national filmmaking endeavours in which production has been sporadic and only really began in earnest in the late 1970s (Middents 2009: 1–2). As in Brazil, Mexico and other countries in the region, in the early 1990s, as part of neoliberal economic and social measures, the state withdrew all support for the film industry, replacing its *ley de cine* (cinema law) (Ley No. 19327) from the 1970s – which had guaranteed exhibition for locally produced films and limited the exhibition of foreign films

through quotas (Martínez 2008: 10; Fowks 2016) – with a new law Ley No°
26370, which remains the current law (Ames Ramello 2017). This law 'establishes competitions for film grants' but does not ensure any other mechanism
for film preservation, distribution or international promotion. Although these
grants give money towards production and screenwriting, the small amounts
they represent mean that many contemporary films can only be made on an
artisanal basis; shooting with digital cameras, small production crews and
sometimes non-professional actors (Martínez 2008: 18; Ames Ramello 2017),
and can often take five years to reach completion (Fowks 2016). *Madeinusa*
and *La teta asustada* as well as other Peruvian successes of the last fifteen years
(Josué Méndez' *Días de Santiago* (*Days of Santiago* 2004) Daniel and Diego
Vidal Vega's *Octubre* (*October* 2010)), which were all partially funded by these
grants, were made following some if not all of these artisanal modes (Matheou
2010: 383; Ames Ramello 2017). In May of 2011 CONACINE, the state directory body for film, was absorbed into the Ministry of Culture and the office
DICINE (Dirección de Industrias Culturales) was created (Bedoya 2011; Ames
Ramello 2017).[24]

Madeinusa takes place over one Easter weekend in an isolated Andean
village, Manayaycuna, where during the time period of 'Tiempo Santo' (Holy
Time) God is dead and therefore sin does not exist. The villagers are hence free
to do whatever they want; steal, drink or have sex with whoever they like, even
if it is, in Madeinusa's father's case, his own daughter. The film follows the
eponymous protagonist (Magaly Solier) through her weekend of duties as the
Virgin Mary and her encounter with Salvador, a young engineer from Lima
trapped in the village on his way to another town

La teta asustada takes place in a *pueblo joven* (slum) outside Lima. It tells
the story of Fausta (Solier), a migrant from an Andean village, who is afflicted
with the 'milk of sorrow' (or more literally 'the frightened breast'), a psycho-
somatic illness believed to be passed through breast milk to the children of
women raped during the violence of the 1980s.[25] Fausta is so fearful of life,
of men and of sexual attack that she will not go out alone and has, as a pre-
cautionary measure, inserted a potato into her vagina. At the beginning of the
film, when her mother Perpetua dies and she needs money to bury her, she is
forced to take a job as night housekeeper at the house of a reclusive pianist and
composer, Aída (Susi Sánchez).

Like many prominent films of the recent art cinema resurgence, Llosa's films
reflect the multiple funding sources that have become typical and necessary in
Perú and across Latin America. For instance, in addition to money it received
from CONACINE ($100,000), *La teta asustada* received awards from two
European funds – Berlin's World Cinema Fund (€50,000) and Fribourg's
Visions Sud Est (CHF50,000) – as well as majority (80 per cent) funding
from Ibermedia, which was divided equally between two Spanish production

companies – Wanda Visión and Oberón. It also received support from the Departement de Cultura del la Generalitat de Catalunya and Televisió de Catalunya.[26] *Madeinusa* similarly received $10,000 from the Sundance/ (Japanese television network) NHK screenwriting competition, which facilitated the script's development at a screenwriting lab[27] (Matheou 2010: 377). TVE (Televisión Española) provided funding and/or support for both *Madeinusa* and *La teta asustada*. Canal+ España awarded a $125,000 prize to *Madeinusa* for best script at the Festival of New Latin American Cinema in Havana in 2004 (Matheou 2010: 376).

In addition to *Madeinusa*'s and *La teta asustada*'s transnational funding structures making them useful objects of study for the purposes of this Introduction, the narratives of their productions typify the difficulties and problems of filmmaking for Latin American filmmakers and illustrate the processes by which transnational funding may alleviate some of these problems. *Madeinusa* and *La teta asustada* both took several years to make and despite critical acclaim (high profile awards including the Golden Bear for *La teta asustada* at the Berlin International Film Festival) received poor theatrical distribution in the US. They circulated mainly in Perú where, thanks to a grassroots screening tour run by Llosa herself, *Madeinusa* was a 'smash hit' (Barrow 2013: 211) and *La teta asustada*, which was re-released after its Oscar nomination (the first ever for a Peruvian film), attracted 250,000 spectators (Middents 2013: 158), and on what Piers Handling, Director of the Toronto Film Festival, has called the 'alternative distribution network': the festival circuit (qtd in Turan 2002: 8; Ames Ramello 2017).

Madeinusa and *La teta asustada*'s narratives, extrafilmic conditions and aesthetics are also useful to the aims of this Introduction because they offer a means of scrutinising the same processes of cultural transformation and transculturation that are central to critical debates about transnational funding. These debates acknowledge the utility of festival funds in particular to cash-strapped Latin American filmmaking endeavours, particularly in the variety of filmmaking activities they fund and facilitate (talent campuses, script development, preproduction, completion, striking prints, exposure and, in the case of those with markets attached, distribution deals) (Falicov 2010: 4–6; Triana-Toribio 2013: 90–92). They also point out how the funds are potentially and sometimes inevitably characterised by a neocolonial power dynamic (Campos 2013: 16). As Tamara Falicov suggests, these festival funds are effectively 'exploiting the cultural resources of the South' to enrich the global festivals of the North' particularly because the awarding of completion funds is often about 'producing [innovative] content for [what are essentially competing] festival[s]' (Falicov 2010: 5). Significantly, Llosa's films premiered at the festivals which funded them; *Madeinusa* at Sundance in 2006 and *La teta asustada* at Berlin in 2009. Falicov further suggests that the neocolonial power dynamic is redoubled when these festival funding bodies make prescriptive demands of scripts from the Global South or influence the content and style of these films by only funding films that fit aesthetic criteria that appeals to Western audiences (2010: 5).

Llosa has never suggested she experienced any direct prescriptive demands on content from the various bodies who funded her films (Matheou 2010: 377), though other directors such as Martel have.[28] It is therefore important to think about whether the style of the films Llosa and other directors of Latin America's art cinema renaissance are producing under the guise of these festival-/European-funded films may not be indirectly prescribed. It has, after all, been suggested that 'a transnational aesthetic' is effectively produced in the film festival circuit, through funding and a larger 'system' of facilitation and encouragement (Falicov 2010: 5).

To date how this 'transnational aesthetic' might translate cinematographically has not been the focus of academic study. Instead, scholars have looked at the festival prescribed content in these films. Miriam Ross, for instance, writing about the Hubert Bals Fund usefully suggests the framework offered in festival funded films 'adheres to what film festival audiences have come to expect of developing world modes of being: poverty and limited social structures' (2011: 264).[29] But if we consider this 'transnational aesthetic' in cinematographic terms what is striking is that Llosa's *Madeinusa* and *La teta asustada* and other favourites of the festival circuit – Alonso's *La libertad* and *Liverpool*, Caetano's *Bolivia*, Eimbcke's *Lake Tahoe* and Escalante's *Sangre* (*Blood* 2005), *Los bastardos,* and *Heli* – all share a common use of neorealist modes (location shooting, non-professional actors, an artisanal mode of production, a focus on the quotidian). This realism as a project can be connected both with a broader realist revival in world cinema of which Latin America's transnational cinema is a part, and a 'historical chain of film cycles' starting from neorealism but continuing through the European new waves, into the Latin American new cinemas of the 1960s and the Dogme '95 movement (Nagib and Mello 2013: xiv).

There is of course, a broad spectrum of approaches and realisms within these and other festival funded successful art cinema directors, ranging from the transcendental realism of Reygadas to the haunting realism of Llosa and Martel who both explore the repressed/not-yet-come-to-terms-with histories of their respective countries: in *La teta asustada* the violent conflict between the Peruvian Army and the terrorist group *El sendero luminoso/The Shining Path,* and in *La mujer sin cabeza* the Dirty War of Argentina's dictatorship (1976–1983).[30] Given that realism is an important constitutive element of these and many other films of the continent's festival funded art cinema renaissance it is perhaps possible that it has become an 'unspoken' prescriptive demand determining which films get funded by these European and US funding bodies. In this way realism (as opposed to other aesthetic modes which have previously trended in Latin American cinemas such as allegory) becomes the favoured mode not just because it fits within the norms of European art cinema (Bordwell 2002a) and of national cinema (as described by Higson [1989]) but also because it is the most effective means for communicating the 'poverty' and 'limited social structures' which Ross argues is what audiences and the festivals which wish to attract them 'have come to expect of developing world [films]' (Ross 2011: 264; Wolf 2010: 16).[31]

For instance, in *La teta asustada* many scenes in the *pueblo joven* play out in realist master shots which enable the signaling of the very overcrowded living conditions Fausta and her family experience. In one of these scenes Fausta's cousin, Máxima (Maria del Pilar Guerrero) argues with her mother and father about the length of the train on her wedding dress. Pairing the master shot with another key realist technique, the framing in depth, other characters, including her brother Jonatan and mother, move from background into foreground and in and out of the composition as they too participate in the discussion and the holding up of the dress. The tableau framing and depth of field emphasise that the 'room' in which this scene plays out is in fact the dusty yard in front of the very small house in which the family live (Figure 1).

In *Madeinusa,* a similarly realist master shot is also used to point towards the insanitary conditions in which Madeinusa and the other villagers in Manayaycuna live. Early on the camera focuses on Madeinusa's necessary daily ritual of spreading rat poison around the house. When she finds a dead rat and throws it away we cut to a long shot, which frames Madeinusa beside the house and the rat in the extreme foreground (Figure 2). A similarly composed long shot of the house, with a still living but evidently poisoned rat in

Figure 1   *La teta asustada* (Claudia Llosa 2009)

Figure 2   *Madeinusa* (Claudia Llosa 2006)

the foreground appears towards the end of the film. The rat's death throes, its stomach rising and falling rapidly, foreshadow Madeinusa's revenge, when she poisons her father for raping her and breaking her mother's earrings.

Seeming confirmation about the neocolonial influences these festival funded films may reflect, and concerns that they are really addressed to western (festival) audiences are evident in some responses to Llosa's films by Peruvian critics. For instance, as Peruvian scholar Natalia Ames Ramello points out, the film's wholly invented central conceit of 'Tiempo Santo,' particularly the variety of bacchanalian festivities that villagers can take part in between 3pm on Good Friday (the hour of Christ's 'death') and dawn on Easter Sunday (his 'resurrection') results in the depiction of Perú's indigenous peoples and Andean culture through the stereotypes of the dominant Eurocentric discourse: drunkenness, crime and incest.[32] 'Tiempo Santo' involves mixing 'real local traditions' such as 'floral carpets' and Catholicism with fictional rituals such as 'the human clock' and the permission to misbehave. Ames Ramello suggests that the representation of the village is therefore much less a realist depiction and much more the reflection of Perú's dominant classes' anxieties about the perceived 'backwardness' of Andean culture (2012: 4, 6; Matheou 2010: 380). Local criticism like that of Ames Ramello's emphasises Llosa's position as part of the social class (of white Peruvians) that is critiqued in both films (César Hildebrandt qtd by Middents 2013: 158). This criticism of Llosa is potentially redoubled by the fact that her film education, like that of some of her filmmaking compatriots (e.g. Méndez), was acquired 'in the West.' She studied for a Masters degree in scriptwriting in Madrid.

However, Llosa mitigates these criticisms of her films through narratives that are self-consciously constructed to show awareness of the dominant classes' colonialist gaze and its problematic representational tropes and, by doing so, offer a counter perspective. For instance, both *Madeinusa* and *La teta asustada* dramatise and critique the encounter between an indigenous Peruvian (Solier) and a white Peruvian of European descent; Salvador the *limeño* engineer who is trapped in Manayaycuna during the Easter weekend festivities and Aída, Fausta's employer. Madeinusa sees Salvador as a manifestation of the Europeanised/Americanised culture she fantasises about – the trinkets of which she keeps in a box, including a magazine called *Maribel* and some beaded earrings which had belonged to her mother. She tells her sister that Salvador 'has light eyes, like in the magazines'. When she has sex with Salvador, she points out that he has her name on his T-shirt (misrecognising the label, which is ironically the likely origin of her name 'Made in USA'). His response to her observation 'You shouldn't be called Madeinusa, but Rosa or Carmen' shows his ignorance of the fact that these Spanish names are equally 'inauthentic' for her and a marker of the country's original colonisation.

La teta asustada also emphasises the Eurocentric impulse to (mis)name (control/map) indigenous Perú. Aída (played by Spanish actress Sánchez, which heightens the film's postcolonial critique) continually gets Fausta's name wrong, calling her a variety of names other than her own. She is inspired to compose again by the Quechua melodies Fausta sings around the house. She gets the very shy Fausta to sing these songs to her by promising to give her the pearls from a broken necklace. Fausta (who is aptly named) agrees to this pact because she needs money to transport her mother's dead body back to their Andean village for burial. However, at the film's denouement, Aída performs one of Fausta's Quechua melodies at a concert and then afterwards, when Fausta comments on the performance (in a way which oversteps prescribed class and ethnic boundaries) Aída puts her out of the car, refusing to pay her the promised pearls.

With narratives about cultural encounters and cultural theft both films are self-conscious parables about the tensions between an already hybridised indigenous Perú and a Europeanised Perú; both dealing in different ways with transculturation. The narrative of *La teta asustada* in particular gestures towards an awareness of the problems of transnational (festival) funding because it also involves a narrative which is about the exploitation of indigenous cultural capital (Fausta's Quecha songs) for the benefit of a(n ethnically) European (local) elite (Aída's piano concert). On the grounds of their own self-consciousness, *Madeinusa* and *La teta asustada* in many ways anticipate the criticisms that were made in Perú about the films and its director. Llosa's awareness of the neocolonised gaze and its problematic desire to folklorise

Perú's indigenous and mestizo population (Salvador's comments on what Madeinusa should be called, Aída's continual inability to remember Fausta's name) in part redeem the films, in that they acknowledge the problematic nature of their own representations.

These considerations aside, it is ultimately on their realist credentials that Latin American art cinema films like *Madeinusa* and *La teta asustada* present cultural capital to the film funds, television stations and festivals of the North which provide the monies for their development or completion. This cultural capital is often referred to in the mission statements of the various funding bodies as cultural 'expression' or 'diversity' (Fonds Sud 2016). In addition, Llosa's films offer what (European) film festival audiences expect – 'poverty and limited social structure' (Ross 2011: 264) – in a mode (art cinema realism) designed to appeal to those same audiences. However, as self-conscious meditations on the transnationalised cultural sphere that highlight both the advantages (the enabling of Perú's struggling cinematic culture, the circulation of Peruvian culture across borders) and the drawbacks (the re-ification of local narratives within tropes and stereotypes of art cinema) of these transnationalised funding structures *La teta asustada* and *Madeinusa* maintain a stance that is importantly political and critical in their realism.

The Structure of the Book

This Introduction's focus on Llosa and Latin America's art cinema resurgence has outlined the financial and aesthetic aspects of transnational Latin American cinema from a transatlantic perspective: looking at how funding and cultural imperatives operate between mostly Europe and Latin America (and sometimes the United States). In addition to its own research, it has drawn on the very compelling contemporary accounts of cinematic transnationalism by Falicov, Ross, Núria Triana-Toribio, Campos, and others to elucidate the extent to which these films are part of a transnational Latin American cinema. Adding to and expanding on the notion of a transnational Latin American cinema, this book looks mostly to the North and to what it argues is the other significant, but underexplored and, in some cases, underappreciated axes of transnationalism in Latin American cinema, the United States' film industry in its diverse and geographically dispersed forms.

New Transnationalisms in Contemporary Latin American Cinemas brings new perspectives to both transnational auteurs who work in the US industry (Hollywood and its independent environs) and also at those who engage with its genre conventions from somewhere else (Mexico, Brazil, Argentina, Spain, and the United Kingdom). It places these auteurs' initial transnational successes, written about at length by one group of (mostly Ibero-American focused) scholars alongside their subsequent deterritorialised (and often English language) films, written about by another group (of mostly Hollywood/European cinema focused) scholars. In this juxtaposition, the book fills some of the gaps in approaches to both groups of films: in the case of the analysis of deterritorialised productions, the lack of awareness of the broader, transnational and non-Eurocentric position in which they are rooted and, in the case of the initial, locally made, transnational successes, the lack of consideration for, or in some cases the critical disdain of, the mainstream parametres (of commercial and genre filmmaking) within which these auteurs are also working. With respect to the latter, the book intervenes in the polemics surrounding these transnationalised texts which are focused precisely on the directors' use of mainstream filmmaking conventions and language.

The book takes a variety of auteurist approaches to its six transnational directors arguing that it is the auteurist nature of many of these director's transnational films which play a key role in their ability to engage in political and postcolonial debates. In accordance with previous misgivings about some auteurist approaches however (Tierney 2007), and following the concerns laid out by noted film scholar V. F. Perkins in his seminal article 'Film Authorship: The Premature Burial' (1990), this book examines some continuities across the oeuvres or partial oeuvres of these directors without obsessively insisting on those 'continuities and coherence[s]' (1990: 57).

Additionally, although this book wants to suggest alternative boundaries in the analysis of Latin American cinemas than those of the geographical nation state, it also acknowledges the importance of the nation as a site of identity politics, and the national industries as the location of these directors' initial successes and hence situates these directors within three sections each named for the national industries in which they began and in different ways continue their filmmaker careers – Mexico, Brazil and Argentina. Each of these sections is prefaced with brief accounts of these national industries including descriptive chronologies of; the industry and/or legislative shifts which facilitated these directors' initial domestic successes, the industry and legislative shifts that have taken place alongside their deterritorialised successes, as well as accounts of the directors' ongoing relationship(s) to filmmaking in their own countries.

Chapter 1 analyses the cinematic transnationality of Iñárritu through a strictly auteurist lens suggesting that his Mexican-produced *Amores perros*, US-produced *21 Grams*, and *Babel*, and Spanish/Mexican co-produced *Biutiful*, problematise the notion of industrial and national borders and (for the deterritorialised productions) the assumption of political co-optation by sharing the same radical and alternative aesthetic strategies and ideologies. The chapter traces these continuities and critiques across the production contexts of Iñárritu's films from Mexican independent (privately funded) cinema in *Amores perros*, to a complex institutional position including US independent distributors, European Government bodies, Spanish and Mexican production companies and Spanish and Catalan television companies in *Biutiful*. The chapter argues that the films' 'independent', non-hegemonic funding structures and presence of a mostly unchanging core creative team facilitates the singular vision at the heart of the auteurist endeavour. The chapter's analysis of Iñárritu's first four transnationalised film projects (*Birdman* and *The Revenant* are analysed in the Epilogue) suggests that rather than purely imitate Hollywood or US traditions (as some scholarship has suggested) his films embody a perspective aligned with Mexico, Latin America and more broadly the peoples of the Global South.

Chapter 2 explores the cinematic transnationality of Alfonso Cuarón arguing that genre is a key element in understanding the ways in which his avowedly personal films – *Sólo con tu pareja* (*Love in a Time of Hysteria* 1991), *Y tu mamá también* and *Children of Men* – intervene in, and counter Mexican/Latin American mainstream politics. The chapter begins by analysing Cuarón's first feature *Sólo con tu pareja* with respect to how it defines the sexy *comedia/comedia light*/romantic comedy genre. It goes on to look at *Y tu mamá también*, exploring how the film adopts and adapts two Hollywood genres – the road movie and the teen or youth movie – to the moment of Mexico's political and social transition. Finally, it explores *Children of Men*, analysing how it subverts the narrative and textual conventions of the Hollywood disaster film and critiques the geopolitical ideologies which underpin the genre's presentation of disaster and destruction. Throughout the chapter's analysis of *Sólo con tu pareja*, *Y tu mamá también* and *Children of Men* (*Gravity* is explored in the Epilogue) it focuses on his contestatory use of genre as a key marker of auteurist practice. The chapter also complicates a non-commercial perspective on auteurism by looking at how, in the case of Cuarón, the auteur as a commercial category is most firmly underlined.

Chapter 3 looks at Guillermo del Toro's horror trilogy *Cronos* (1993), *El espinazo del diablo* and *El laberinto del fauno*. Using Feminist, Freudian and Marxist frameworks it explores how horror and horrific tropes function in these films on a political level to address particular issues relevant to Mexico (the impact of NAFTA) and Spain (the recovery of historical memory of Francoist repression). It traces how these three films respond to and reproduce a shared Hispanic imaginary, history and politics by adapting and adopting Hollywood horror conventions as these have been read in political terms by Robin Wood (1985), Tanya Modleski (1999), Linda Williams (1989) and Barbara Creed (1999). Ultimately, it suggests that *Cronos*, *El espinazo del diablo* and *El laberinto del fauno* (*Crimson Peak* is analysed in the Epilogue) speak not only to local/national issues but also to transatlantic political concerns enabled by the progressive discourse at the heart of horror cinema.

Chapter 4 looks at Fernando Meirelles' English language films *The Constant Gardener* and *Blindness* alongside *Cidade de Deus* and connects them to a sensibility that it not solely Hollywood or 'world cinema' but transnational and rooted in a Brazilian, postcolonial perspective. As with the English language films of other Latin American transnational auteurs, the chapter aligns *The Constant Gardener* and *Blindness* within continental notions of identity and politics as well as within those which radiate from the Global South. The chapter begins by analysing *Cidade de Deus* rehearsing the terms of the critical arguments ignited by the film's commerciality, 'foreignness' and mainstream depictions of violence, and reconciling them with the critical realism and political engagement which it suggests the film also displays. The chapter continues with a look at the key features of Meirelles' deterritorialised films exploring how these fit within normative concepts of the transnational and global, auteur and goes on to argue that aspects of the cinema novo-inspired ideological critique of *Cidade de Deus* are carried into these films – the UK/US co-produced *The Constant Gardener* and the international co-production *Blindness* (Brazil/Canada/Japan).

Chapter 5 explores how Walter Salles' *Diarios de motocicleta* and *On the Road* use the conventions of the road movie to forward different but not unrelated political agendas. Defending the political potential of mainstream formats like the road movie, the chapter argues that the films use the political strategies of the genre to (re)explore the beginnings of their related social, cultural and political revolutions.

Chapter 6 explores Juan José Campanella's *El secreto de sus ojos* (*The Secret In Their Eyes* 2009) and the ways in which it engages with the legacy of Argentina's dictatorship (1976–1983) and the twenty-year period of immunity which followed it. Using cultural studies paradigms, the chapter problematises the marginalisation of Campanella's 'transnational' and industrial genre filmmaking in scholarship on Argentine cinema in favour of the more 'national' *nuevo cine argentino*. Through the analysis of *El secreto de sus ojos*, it argues that melodrama and film *noir* can be an effective means both to self-consciously stage the past and also pose key issues of historical memory and accountability of the crimes committed during Argentina's 'Dirty War'.

The Epilogue briefly analyses some of these auteurs' recent films – Cuarón's *Gravity*, Iñárritu's *Birdman* and *The Revenant,* and del Toro's *Crimson Peak*. In the case of the wholly studio productions, it explores the extent to which it remains possible to conceive of these directors as 'interstitial auteurs' and whether the political and postcolonial concerns examined in this book remain as salient in these more recent films, embedded as they are in the larger ideological, institutional and industrial complex of contemporary studio filmmaking and located narratologically and in production and financing terms for the most part in the Global North (or off planet) and with no overt or symbolic peripheral Ibero-American narratives or links. It asks, amongst others things, whether it's possible to talk about Iñárritu's *The Revenant*, a western set in the

American North East, or Cuarón's *Gravity*, a (space) disaster film, in terms of a political position rooted in Mexico, Latin America or the Global South.

NOTES

1. *Central Station* and *Cidade de Deus* both received support from the screenwriters Labs run by the Sundance Institute. *El hijo de la novia* and *Nueve reinas* were funded by Patagonik, (a transnational conglomerate that involves media group Clarin, which includes the production company Artear, the newspaper *Clarín* and the cable channel Cablevision), by Buena Vista International (a subsidiary of Disney Studies) and by Spanish Telecom (Falicov 2008; Alvaray 2008). *Amores perros* and *Y tu mama también* were funded privately by CIE and Omnilife, companies with a transnational reach (Smith 2003a).
2. A part of this Introduction appears in *The Routledge Companion to World Cinema* (2017). I thank the book's co-editors Rob Stone, Stephanie Dennison, Paul Cooke, and Alex Marlow Mann and also Natalie Foster at Routledge for permission to reprint those parts here.
3. From 2000 onwards, through his production company El Deseo, Pedro Almodóvar has been co-producing what could be termed a 'transnational Hispanic identity' (García Canclini 1995: 130) in various Latin American projects, including Guillermo del Toro's *El espinazo del diablo* (*The Devil's Backbone* 2001), Lucrecia Martel's *La niña santa* (*The Holy Girl* 2004) *La mujer sin cabeza* (2008), and most recently two Argentine blockbusters *Relatos salvajes* (*Wild Tales* Damián Szifrón 2014) and *El clan* (*The Clan* Pablo Trapero 2015).
4. See the three country introductions, which detail the efforts of the three national film institutes of Mexico (IMCINE), Argentina (INCAA) and Brazil (ANCINE) to attract co-production funding and/or showcase their national cinemas through festivals and film markets.
5. In a list that is by no means exhaustive we could include Mexicans: Alfonso Arau (*Como agua para chocolate* 1992, *A Walk in the Clouds* 1995), Rigoberto Castañeda (*KM 31* 2006, *Blackout* 2008), Luis Mandoki (*When a Man Loves a Woman* 1994, *Message in a Bottle* 1998, *Voces Inocentes* 2004, *Fraude* 2007), Rodrigo García, whose work straddles Mexico and Los Angeles and both TV and film including *Things You Can Tell Just By Looking at Her* (2000), *Revolución* 'La Séptima y Alvarado' (*Revolution* 'La 7th Street and Alvarado' 2010), and *Albert Nobbs* (2011), Patricia Riggen (*La misma luna* 2007, *Lemonade Mouth* 2011, *Girl in Progress* 2012, *The 33* 2015); Argentine Alejandro Agresti (*Boda Secreta/ Secret Wedding* 1991, *Buenos Aires Vice Versa* 1996, *The Lake House* 2006); and Brazilians: Héctor Babenco (*Pixote* 1981, *Kiss of the Spider Woman* 1985, *At Play in the Fields of the Lord* 1991, *Carandiru* 2003), José Padilha (*Ônibus 174/Bus 174* 2002, *Tropa de Elite/Elite Squad* 2007, *Tropa de Elite 2: O Inimigo Agora é Outro/Elite Squad: The Enemy Within*, 2010, *RoboCop* 2014), seasons 1 and 2 of *Narcos* 2015, 2016, and Heitor Dhalia (*Gone* 2012, *Serra Pelada/Bald Mountain* 2013).
6. *Los guantes mágicos* (*The Magic Gloves* Martín Rejtman 2003) received funds from Hubert Bals Fund, Fonds Sud and Franco-German television station Arte. Albertina Carri got support for *Los Géminis* (*The Twins* 2005) from Fonds Sud. *Bolivia* (Adrián Caetano 2001) and *Rapado* (*Skinhead* Rejtman 1992) also received funds from Hubert Bals. Indeed, Gonzalo Aguilar in his *New Argentine Cinema: Other Worlds* (2011) points out that 'almost all' of the significant films of the *nuevo cine argentino* received sponsorship from one of these sources (2011: 12).

7. Take for instance the pronouncement of Mexican cultural critic Carlos Bonfíl, for whom success in terms of Oscar nominations and the presence of Iñárritu, Cuarón, del Toro, and others previously involved in Mexican cinema, including cinematographer Rodrigo Prieto, outside Mexico, points to a commensurate failure and gap back home in the Mexican film industry where, for him, they should be working (2007). Equally relevant are the more recent perspectives of noted film scholar Jorge Ayala Blanco who suggested in a CNN en Español, post-Academy Awards interview that it was a good thing that *The Revenant* had not won the Best Picture Oscar 'Afortunadamente no ganó *The Revenant*' ('Fortunately *The Revenant* didn't win') because it was essentially a 'hollow' 'empty' film. (See the full interview at <http://cnnespanol.cnn.com/2016/03/01/critico-de-cine-que-bueno-que-no-gano-the-revenant/> (last accessed 10 January 2017).)

8. By Hollywood I refer to a system of production, financing and institutional practice that for some time has not been located solely in Los Angeles. Take *Gravity* for instance, a 'British' Hollywood film or *Blindness*, a co-production between Japan, Canada and Brazil that while circumventing the industrial and financial control of Hollywood, still engages with it aesthetically in terms of genre (the contagion film) and star casting (Mark Ruffalo, Julianne Moore).

9. Guillermo del Toro suggests such a presumption was made about Cuarón when he made *Great Expectations* (1998) (Wood 2006: 97).

10. See López (1996) for an analysis of exiled Cuban directors in the United States and Europe as part of Greater Cuban Cinema. She conceives of the Cuban National Cinema as existing beyond the geospatial limits of the island of Cuba.

11. Arjun Appadurai for instance, focuses on the ways in which transnational communities may consume first world culture in such a way that 'often provokes resistance, irony, selectivity, and, in general, *agency*' (1996: 7).

12. Indeed Naficy analyses Solanas (2001: 106–110, 133, 240–232) and Littín (2001: 279–282) as exiled and accented filmmakers and refers to Rocha and Ruiz in the same terms.

13. I refer here to the system of government patronage which was the only way to make films in Mexico in the early 1990s. See the introduction to Mexico, and Chapters 2 and 3 for more on this.

14. As a later chapter will explore, Campanella both is and is not a part of this narrative. He makes films within an industrial cinema in Argentina and has not (since a couple of English language films early in his career) taken on the same kind of deterritorialised, English language production of the other five transnational auteurs explored in this book. However, some of his films (*Luna de Avellaneda/Avellaneda's Moon* 2004, *El hijo de la novia*) engage with similar themes.

15. The story of Latin American international film co-production begins with and is most insistently characterised by Spain. Co-productions between Spain and different Latin American countries began in the 1940s and have increased exponentially from one film in the 1940s to 201 between 2000 and 2006 (Villazana 2008: 66).

16. In 2013, *¡Asu mare!* (Ricardo Maldonado 2013) was the exception to this rule. A domestic film, it broke box office records in Perú beating the 'Hollywood' competition to win an audience of 3.1 million (Ames Ramello 2017; Gutiérrez 2013). A movie adaptation of the stand up show of popular comedian Carlos Alcántara, the film was distributed by New Century films, the local subsidiary of Warner Bros., but 'funded by Tondero, a local production company, through private investment and product placement advertising' (Ames Ramello 2017).

17. This table is designed to illustrate the patchwork of state, film festival, European television and Ibermedia funding that have gone into key art cinema successes. For

reasons of space, not all agents involved in these films' production are mentioned including both public funding bodies – Ministère des Affaires étrangères et du Développement Internationale and Netherland Filmfund for instance, which both funded *Post Tenebras Lux* – and private producers – Deseo. S.A., which funded *La niña santa* and *La mujer sin cabeza*. Additionally, it should be noted that, although state entities (such as Mexico's IMCINE) might be listed as supporting certain films, in some cases (Reygadas, Alonso) this support has been nominal or has been awarded because of interest in the film from festivals abroad.

18. Significantly, in the case of the New Argentine Cinema, foreign institutions and their attached film festivals have played a key role in the promotion and funding of the movement with '[a]lmost all' of its films receiving 'sponsorship from one of these sources'(Aguilar 2011:12). When Rejtman's *Rapado*, an early masterpiece of New Argentine Cinema, was turned down by the INCAA (Argentina's national film institute) funding from the Hubert Bals fund ensured it was completed (Falicov 2007b: 116; Aguilar 2011: 12).

19. Hubert Bals' website <https://iffr.com/en/professionals/blog/hubert–bals–fund–fall–2015–and–nffhbf–selections> (last accessed 10 April 2016). World Cinema Fund's website <www.berlinale.de/en/das_festival/world_cinema_fund/wcf_pro fil/index.html> (last accessed 10 Aug 2011). Cinefondation's website <http://www.cinefondation.com/en> (last accessed 10 April 2016). Visions Sud Est's website <http://www.visionssudest.ch> (last accessed 10 April 2016). Global Film Initiative's website <http://www.globalfilm.org> (last accessed 10 April 2016). Cine en construcción's website. <http://www.cinelatino.fr/contenu/cinema–en–construc tion–presentation> (last accessed 10 April 2016). Sundance Institute opportunities website <http://www.sundance.org/create/overview/#workshops> (last accessed 10 April 2016).

20. Fonds Sud, for example, is administrated directly through the French Ministry of Foreign Affairs. The World Cinema Fund is financed by the German Ministry of Culture (Campos 2012: 174).

21. This figure is based on the reported budgets for a handful of representative films: *La teta asustada* – $1.4m (Eu 1m) ('Screendaily, 20 September 2007, <http://www.screendaily.com/claudia–llosa–the–scared–breast–teta–asustada/4034742. article>). The reader should also bear in mind that the reported $30,000 budget for Alonso's *Libertad* is very much the exception and take note of the fact that the film needed additional monies spent on it to make it suitable for exhibition at Cannes (Matheou 2010: 293).

22. Source: Fonds Sud website <http://www.filmfrasor.no/no/search?query=La+mujer+ sin+cabeza> (last accessed June 2011).

23. As Falicov points out, other Latin American members of CAACI, particularly those from Central America, have been excluded from participating in Ibermedia as the annual contribution (of $50,000) proved financially prohibitive. An alternative, Central American funding body (CINERGIA) was been established in 2004. Based in Cuba, its other member countries are Costa Rica, El Salvador, Guatemala, Panamá, Nicaragua, Belize, and Honduras (2007: 28).

24. See 'Ministerio pretende "dissolver" Conacine', 2 May, 2011. Available at <http://www.cinencuentro.com/2011/05/02/ministerio–cultura–pretende–disolver–conacine/> (last accessed 20 September 2011). From 2012, approximately $2 million per year has been given over to implementing Law 26370 and awarding film production monies through an increased number of competitions. In 2016, fifteen competitions were organised, giving approximately seventy awards to film projects. In 2013 DICINE changed its name to 'Dirección del Audiovisual, La Fonografía y los Nuevos Medios' (DAFO) (Ames Ramello 2017).

25. Llosa's film draws on the study of US anthropologist Kimberly Theidon (2012) on the traumatic effects of the civil war.
26. The film's official website lists the production shares as: Wanda Vision (40 per cent), Oberón Cinematográfica (40 per cent) and Vela Producciones (Perú) (20 per cent) http://www.milkofsorrow.com/#/production–information [Link now dead].
27. The Sundance/NHK award as advertised in 2007 was equal to a '$10,000 award and a guarantee from NHK to purchase the Japanese television broadcast rights upon completion of their project. In addition, the Sundance Institute will work closely with the award recipients throughout the year, providing ongoing resources and support in seeking out opportunities to finance and distribute their projects.' <http://www.sundance.org/pdf/press–releases/2007NHKFinalists.pdf> (last accessed 22 July 2011).
28. There is evidence that Martel has had this experience. At the Sundance screenwriters Lab it was suggested that she pare down the screenplay of *La ciénaga* to include one or two characters (Oubiña 2009: 21). From the finished film with its 'labyrinthine plot and erratic qualities' we know that Martel did not follow these suggestions (Oubiña 2009: 2).
29. That this is a 'transnational' rather than a 'national' aesthetic is underlined by the fact that many other Latin American art cinema directors (Reygadas, Eimbcke, Alonso, Martel) who find success (and indeed exhibition) on the festival circuit find little exhibition or indeed audience in their home countries, where lack of access to distribution means they are prevented from reaching a national audience. Llosa's films are representative in this sense in that they did well on the festival circuit but also exceptional in that they were able to reach significant numbers in Perú (Matheou 2010: 385), although this local reception was mixed.
30. The film displaces its representation of the victims of the dirty war onto ghostly or hallucinatory images of a young indigenous boy that the protagonist may or may not have run over and killed in a hit and run accident. Hand prints on the window of her car are pulled into sharp focus in the moments after the collision. Later on in the film, just as the old aunt suggests that the house is full of ghosts, a young indigenous boy appears seemingly from under the bed, looks at the protagonist, and exits. In another instance, a young indigenous boy at the door is backlit so that he appears in spectral silhouette.
31. As Jens Andermann and Alvaro Fernández Bravo have noted, the 'resurgence of national cinemas' or the art cinema boom, has been very much about a 'return to the real' (2013: 2).
32. In one scene a laughing woman is chased around a fire by a man holding a huge *papier maché* phallus. In others Madeinusa's father and several other men are seen to get so drunk they are incapacitated. In yet another scene two men steal a pig from a woman, despite her tearful protestations.

MEXICO: INTRODUCTION

In March of 2016 at the International Guadalajara Film Festival (IGFF), Mexico's National Film Institute, IMCINE (*Instituto Mexicano de Cinematografía*) presented its *Anuario Estadístico del Cine Mexicano/Statistical Yearbook of Mexican Cinema* outlining the key achievements of Mexican Cinema in 2015 as well as its aims for the future (IMCINE 2016). Figures from the 2015 report suggest that in production terms Mexican cinema is booming. Feature film production for 2015 was up on the previous year at 140 films, a number greater than the previous record-breaking 135 films in 1958. Four Mexican films attracted over a million spectators at the box office, including another film in the hugely successful animated comedy series *Un gallo con muchos huevos* (Gabriel y Rodolfo Riva Palacio Alatriste), which achieved audiences of over 4 million. Three new public digital platforms for Mexican cinema – FilminLatino, Plataforma Digital Cinema México and Pantalla CACI – were launched. Ten national films, including recent releases such as the box office success *No se aceptan devoluciones* (*Instructions Not Included* Eugenio Derbez, 2013) exceeded 25 million spectators on television including public and pay-per-view channels. Government support for the industry was also at a high, with 70 per cent of the films produced in 2015 receiving government monies (IMCINE 2016: 43).

The presentation of the 2016 yearbook, in March 2017, brought a similar round of good news for the Mexican industry. Feature film production was up to 162 films (IMCINE 2017: 13), and the Mexican comedies *¿Qué culpa tiene el niño?* (*Don't Blame the Kid* Gustavo Loza) and *No manches Frida* (*WTH*

Table 3 Top Mexican releases 2016 (IMCINE 2017: 94)

Película / Film	Fecha de estreno Release Date	Pantallas Screens	Asistentes Attendance	Ingresos (pesos) Revenue (pesos)
¿Qué culpa tiene el niño?	12/05	3031	5893885	277784904
No manches Frida	16/09	2318	5099744	222269875
Treintona, soltera y fantástica	7/10	2093	2956978	135655092
La leyenda del Chupacabras	21/10	2032	2593427	100106478
Compadres	31/03	1699	1968129	80275359
Busco novio para mi mujer	12/02	1360	1288352	52779950
Un padre no tan padre	21/12	1749	1119100	50147668
KM 31-2	4/11	1574	929723	38369501
Qué pena tu vida	2/12	1018	900458	40534847
Macho	11/11	807	875200	37510745

Frida Nacho G. Velilla) were the highest grossing national films attracting 5.9 and 5.1 million spectators respectively (IMCINE 2017: 92) (Table 3).

The reality for Mexican cinema is however less rosy than many of these figures suggest. Although annual production numbers are higher than six decades ago, many commentators continue to point out that the Mexican film industry, in terms of a structure that ensures the production, distribution and consumption of its own product, no longer exists (Vargas 2005: 16; MacLaird 2013a: 1–2). The Mexican market is dominated by US-owned multiplexes and US films filled all ten of the top box office slots in 2016 (Table 4). Other figures in the *anuario* recount a rise in the annual domestic cinema's share of the box office from 6.1 per cent in 2015 to 10 per cent in 2016. *Captain America, Civil War* (Anthony and Joe Russo) was the highest grossing film, attracting audiences of 14.5 million and making $728 million pesos at the Mexican box office (IMCINE 2017: 84, 91). The number of releases of Mexican films was 90 films and even this figure actually glosses over how little Mexican cinema is exhibited theatrically in Mexico given that all releases including those with limited launches, even on just one screen are counted (IMCINE 2017: 96). Indeed, the inclusion of television audience figures for national films in the 2015 and 2016 *anuarios* is likely meant to counteract the low figures of theatrical exhibition and to signal shifts in viewing practices more generally; shifts that are acknowledged by the three institutionally funded digital platforms launched in

Table 4 Top ten box office films Mexico 2016 (IMCINE 2017: 84)

Película Film	Director Director	Distribuidora Distributor	País Country	Fecha de estreno Release Date	Complejos cinematográficos Theater Complexes	Pantallas Screens	Clasificación Rating	Asistentes Attendance	Ingresos (pesos) Revenue (pesos)
Capitán América. Civil War / Captain América. Civil War	Anthony Russo Joe Russo	Walt Disney Int'l	EU/US	29/04	730	5422	B	14 523 084	728 156 354
Batman vs. Superman. El origen de la justicia / Batman v. Superman. Dawn of Justice	Zack Snyder	Warner Bros Int'l	EU/US	24/03	725	4677	B	13 259 960	630 763 242
La vida secreta de tus mascotas / The Secret Life of Pets	Chris Renaud Yarrow Cheney	Universal Int'l	EU/US	29/07	729	3596	AA	10 882 564	421 597 696
Buscando a Dory / Finding Dory	Andrew Stanton	Walt Disney Int'l	EU/US	15/07	739	3966	AA	10 167 369	460 011 839
Escuadrón suicida / Suicide Squad	David Ayer	Warner Bros Int'l	EU/US	5/08	436	3076	B	9 938 442	514 743 874
El libro de la selva / The Jungle Book	Jon Favreau	Walt Disney Int'l	EU/US	15/04	718	2952	A	9 514 036	428 366 014
La era de hielo, Choque de mundos / Ice Ages, Collision Course	Roberto Orci	Fox Int'l	EU/US	1/07	726	3529	AA	9 326 032	417 583 116
El conjuro 2 / The Conjuring 2	James Wan	Warner Bros Int'l	EU/US	9/06	718	4204	B-15	8 194 711	380 643 342
Deadpool	Timothy Miller	Fox Int'l	EU/US	12/02	685	3213	B-15	8 098 619	351 491 757
Zootopia	Byron Howard	Walt Disney Int'l	EU/US	19/02	715	2823	AA	7 719 766	306 008 586

2015. However, this picture of a beleaguered national industry does not match another picture presented in the 2015 *anuario* which embraces the successes of Mexican directors abroad including Iñárritu and Cuarón and their Oscars for Best Director in 2015 (for *Birdman*) and 2014 (for *Gravity*) and Michel Franco and his win at the Cannes Film Festival for *Chronic* (2015) (IMCINE 2016: 260, 269).

Although it did not make one of the top ten slots, 2016's *anuario* did report the awards (BAFTAS, Golden Globes and Oscars) success of Iñárritu's Twentieth Century Fox-produced *The Revenant*, which made $530 million worldwide and $89 million pesos at the Mexican box office (IMCINE 2017: 257; Anon. 2016a). Although, as the Epilogue will explore, *The Revenant* situates itself against many of the political and ethnic tenets of an Anglo Hollywood, financially and in exhibition terms it operates in Mexican markets in the same way any other big budgeted Hollywood film operates: released with more prints, in more cinemas and with more marketing than Mexican films, it dominates Mexican screen space. Although the film's financial and Oscar success has been welcomed by critics and commentators in Mexico (by all but esteemed film critic Jorge Ayala Blanco), it is worth noting that *The Revenant* effectively operates as competition to Mexican cinema. As director Gabriel Retes (*Bienvenido/Welcome* 1994, *El bulto/Excess Baggage* 1992) suggested at the 2016 IGFF, because of Hollywood cinema there is less screen time for Mexican films (Vertiz de La Fuente 2016).

Although this financial account of *The Revenant* and how it operates in the Mexican market might suggest otherwise, Iñárritu, and his equally success-ful compatriots also working in Hollywood, Cuarón and del Toro still have a significant relationship to the successes of contemporary Mexican cinema and indeed to Mexican cinema of the last twenty-five years. This introduc-tory section, which acts as a platform for the director-centred film analyses of Chapters 1, 2 and 3, describes that relationship. As well as looking at these directors' ongoing connections to Mexico's national film culture and 'industry' through their films and film-related activities, this section offers an account of their beginnings in filmmaking in Mexico in the 1990s and early 2000s, and the industrial, political, legislative, and production model changes that were instrumental in shaping their careers and the varied fortunes of Mexican cinema during this period. It suggests that these changes are vital to under-standing the films these directors made in Mexico, and to a certain extent their subsequent deterritorialised films made outside Mexico and also analysed in Chapters 1, 2 and 3.

Cuarón and del Toro both began their feature film directorial careers in the midst of the intense neoliberal transitions in the Mexican economy and society of the early 1990s. In a pre-North American Free Trade Agreement (NAFTA) move President Carlos Salinas de Gortari (1988–1994) drastically reduced government investments in the film industry by privatising the state film production system: selling off the national exhibition chain, Compañía de Teatros (COTSA) and the production facilities Estudios América. Conversely, at the same time, through IMCINE the government supported the debuts of del Toro, Cuarón and those of a select group of filmmakers (Carlos Carrera, María Novaro, Busi Cortés and Maryse Sistach) in a move that was also part of the pre-NAFTA agenda: promoting Mexico abroad as an equal business partner to the United States *and* assuaging Mexicans' fears of cultural imperialism (de la Mora 2006: 135; MacLaird 2013a: 22). Many of these state sponsored films were successful in Mexico and, as was intended, abroad. Cuarón's romantic comedy *Sólo con tu pareja* (*Love in a Time of Hysteria* 1991) did well at a number of international film festivals including Toronto. Del Toro's *Cronos* (1993) won the Mercedes Benz award at the Cannes Film Festival. *Como agua para chocolate/Like Water for Chocolate* (Alfonso Arau 1992) broke box office records in Mexico, and attracted huge audiences in Latin America and the US (de la Mora 2006: 145).[1]

As Chapters 2 and 3 explore, *Sólo con tu pareja* and *Cronos* fulfilled aspects of their pre-NAFTA brief rearticulating 'the *official* national discourse of mexi-canidad,' in a way that was simultaneously 'highly exportable', 'recognizable, modern' and in keeping with both the government's business and cultural concerns pre NAFTA (de La Mora 2006: 137). However, the films' thinly veiled critiques of NAFTA and its likely outcomes subsequently put Cuarón and del Toro in an awkward position with IMCINE and its then vision of a government circumscribed national(ist) film culture. Both directors report difficulties with the national film institute after the completion of their films and blame the culture of government favouritism and patronage that was the only way to get films made and exhibited in Mexico in the early 1990s for their subsequent departures for the United States film industry. Cuarón, for instance, suggests that his leaving for Hollywood where he was contracted as director for hire to make *A Little Princess* (1995) and *Great Expectations* (1998) was inevitable given that with *Sólo con tu pareja* he had effectively 'burned his bridges' and that if he was ever going to return to filmmaking in Mexico the way films were made would have to change (Wood 2006: 41). Del Toro similarly talks about how his hopes for a change in attitude from IMCINE towards the culturally disreputable genre of horror after the success of *Cronos* were dashed when he presented his subsequent project for funding, an early version of the screenplay of *El espinazo del diablo* (Wood 2006: 112). He also left for the US where he eventually made *Mimic* (1997). Of course, the economic crisis that ensued after the signing of the NAFTA agreement, which made it almost impossible for Ernesto Zedillo's (1994–2000) government to provide 'promised support for the cultural industries,' and the absence of the state's production and exhibition infrastructure also created an unfavourable climate for film production meaning fewer films could be made. After the government-funded production boom that del Toro and Cuarón participated in, numbers decreased instantly, with five films produced by the state in 1995 and seven in both 1996 and 1997 (MacLaird 2013a: 28; McIntosh 2008: 67–68). This initiated the period of filmmaking labelled Mexico's 'post-industrial cinema,' by critic Juan Carlos Vargas (2005). However, the seeds of change that would enable Cuarón and del Toro's 'return' to filmmaking in Mexico and the revival of the country's filmmaking fortunes had actually already been sown.

The 'key factor' to the 1999–2002 box office and critical renaissance in Mexican cinema to which Iñárritu's *Amores perros*, Cuarón's *Y tu mamá también* and del Toro's *El espinazo del diablo* all belong was the 1992 deregulation of box office prices (MacLaird 2013a: 45). The 1992 Federal Film Law's deregulation of movie ticket prices made investment in new multiplex theatres (to replace the outdated and decrepit formerly state-owned single theatres) attractive to investors (MacLaird 2013a: 45–47). The US-style and some US-owned multiplexes (CINEMARK, CINEMEX and Mexican-owned Cinépolis) that began appearing in the mid-1990s in large shopping malls in affluent areas tripled the size and, more significantly, changed the demographic of the local audience to a predominantly urban upper middle class audience with a large disposable income (Elena 2008: 2). The potential for profit from this new exhibition system and its wealthy audiences also generated interest from corporate media in film production. Altavista Films, who produced *Amores perros* and other films associated with the boom such as *Todo el poder* (*Gimmie Power* Fernando Sariñana 2000), 'was established in 1998 as part of Latin America's largest media and entertainment corporations, CIE' (MacLaird 2013a: 47), as were other private production companies such as Anhelo, which produced *Y tu mamá también* and *El espinazo del diablo*. As Misha MacLaird points out:

> The new wave of privately funded film production was most significant in establishing *a new approach to the market*, both in identifying the most lucrative target audience and in a drastically increased budget for reaching this audience with publicity and merchandising. (2013a: 47)

A significant precursor to *Amores perros* and *Y tu mamá también*, the part privately and part state-funded *Sexo, pudor y lágrimas* (*Sex, Shame and Tears* Antonio Serrano 1999) therefore targeted the 'new Cineplex-goers' with a screenplay about 'sexuality among urban middle-class couples' living in the same kinds of 'upscale' neighbourhood they lived in, such as Mexico City's Polanco where it was filmed (MacLaird 2013a: 48–49). *Sexo, pudor y lágrimas* also targeted its audience through genre, basing itself on the domestic success of Hollywood and Mexican romantic comedies, e.g. Cuarón's own *Sólo con tu pareja* and also *Cilantro y perejil* (*Recipes to Stay Together* Rafael Montero 1995) (MacLaird 2013a: 47–48).

Amores perros and *Y tu mamá también* also directed themselves at Mexico's youth, a second new audience, through music soundtracks and broad publicity campaigns – which for *Amores perros* included a lavish Mexican premiere and post-premiere party, teaser trailers played at Hard Rock Cafés throughout Mexico, a spot on MTV, postcards, stickers, T-shirts, baseball caps, watches and 'handsome press kits' (Smith 2003a: 16) – and, in the case of *Y tu mamá también* through the use of the teen movie genre itself (see Chapter 2 for more on this). It should be noted at this point that Iñárritu's previous career history, as a disc jockey at Mexico City radio station WFM throughout the 1980s and early 1990s – making playlists for his young audience and as an advertising executive and director of commercials in the 1990s was also not insignificant in *Amores perros*' success in this new consumer- and youth-led market (Smith 2016).

Sexo, pudor y lágrimas,[2] *Amores perros, Y tu mamá también,* and another film that was part privately and part government-financed (*El crimen del padre Amaro*)[3] broke box office records on their release in Mexico with the latter three also scoring broad critical and relative box office success internationally (Alvaray 2008: 51) (Table 5).[4] Beyond their production models, it is largely agreed that a mixture of aesthetic renewal, commercial genres, a certain timeliness (embodying aspects of Mexico's political transition at the end of the 71-year rule of the Partido Revolucionario Institucional, the PRI) and the *absence* of state funding all contributed to these films' success (de la Mora 2003: 14, 25; Smith 2003b: 398; MacLaird 2013a: 5).

However, it is important to highlight that the state was involved in two of these films of the so-called renaissance via the *Fondo para la Producción Cinematográfica de Calidad* (FOPROCINE Fund for Quality Film Production) established in 1997, and that this symbolised a reconfiguration of state involvement, as co-producer in a new model of often privately and transnationally financed filmmaking. *El crimen del padre Amaro* was also made with monies from Argentina, France and Spain. *El espinazo del diablo* was a privately produced Mexico/Spain co-production with monies from Deseo S. A., Almodóvar's production company. FOPROCINE, together with another fund set up in 2001 by the administration of the new president Vicente Fox (2000–2006), *Fondo de Inversión y Estímulos al Cine* (FIDECINE) specifically designed 'to foster primarily the production of good *commercial* cinema' transformed future government involvement in film and the model of filmmaking as it had previously existed (cited in MacLaird 2013a: 29, my emphasis).

But in 2002, even as Mexican cinema was experiencing its greatest success, it was also experiencing its greatest difficulties (MacLaird 2013a: 2). Production figures showed little sign of recovery at the beginning of 2003 (de la Mora, 2003: 14). Funding allocations for FIDECINE in 2001 and 2002 were either

Table 5 Top grossing Mexican films 2000–2015 (IMCINE 2016: 70)

Película Film	Director	Año Year	Asistentes (millones) Admissions (millions)	Ingresos (millones de pesos) Revenue (millions of pesos)
No se aceptan devoluciones / *Instructions not Included*	Eugenio Derbez	2013	15.2	600.3
Nosotros los Nobles	Gary Alazraki	2013	7.1	340.3
El crimen del padre Amaro	Carlos Carrera	2002	5.2	162.2
La dictadura perfecta	Luis Estrada	2014	4.2	189.2
Un gallo con muchos huevos	Gabriel Riva Palacio Alatriste, Rodolfo Riva Palacio Alatriste	2015	4.1	167.8
Cásase quien pueda	Marco Polo Constandse	2014	4	168.3
Una película de huevos	Gabriel Riva Palacio Alatriste, Rodolfo Riva Palacio Alatriste	2006	4	142.3
Y tu mamá también	Alfonso Cuarón	2001	3.5	101.7
El gran pequeño / Little boy	Alejandro Gómez Monteverde	2015	3.3	148.3
Amores perros	Alejandro González Iñárritu	2000	3.3	95.2

Fuente: Imcine con datos de Rentrak / Source: Imcine with data from Rentrak.

irregular or non-existent (MacLaird 2013a: 30). When FIDECINE 'recovered its funding in 2003' production figures rallied and by the second half of Fox's presidency annual production figures rose to '60 features a year, considered the minimum for stabilising the domestic market' (MacLaird 2013a: 31).

MacLaird points out how during this period of return to increased production and increased private and government monies for filmmaking 'several high-profile production houses sprang up' 'which followed recent private-production models' (2013a: 31). CANANA was founded with the 'celebrity status and financial backing' of two key actors of the cinematic renaissance, stars of *Y tu mamá también* Gael García Bernal and Diego Luna, and also producer Pablo Cruz. CANANA 'maintains a concern for social issues and regional diversity' and has produced recently *Las elejidas* (*The Chosen Ones* David Pablos 2015), an exposé of forced prostitution amongst teenage girls.[5] Lemon Films was set up by 'heirs to the Azcárraga/Televisa fortune' Billy and Fernando Rovzar. Lemon aims to 'revive popular genres that are considered unachievable under Mexican budget and technical restraints' (horror, science fiction) (MacLaird 2013a: 67–68). Lemon has produced some of the biggest box office successes – *KM 31* (*Kilometre 31* Rigoberto Castañeda 2006) – and critical successes – *Después de Lucía* (*After Lucia* Franco 2012).

These new production companies took their cue not just from the increased availability of monies but also the late 1990s and early 2000s era of predominantly privately financed production that followed as well as production models privileging artistic innovation and commercial genres and features. Cuarón, del Toro and Iñárritu were also involved in establishing new production companies to produce their own and each others' films and to foster filmmaking in Mexico. After suffering a lack of creative control making *Mimic*, his first feature in the US, del Toro founded Tequila Gang in 1998 with Rosa Bosch, Laura Esquivel (screenwriter for *Como agua para chocolate*), Bertha Navarro and Alejandra Moreno Toscano. Tequila Gang has subsequently produced all of del Toro's Spanish language films (*El espinazo del diablo*, *El laberinto del fauno*) as well as other Mexican productions (*Cosas insignificantes/ Insignificant Things* Andrea Martínez 2008; and *A Painting Lesson* [Pablo Perelman 2011]) and Mexican co-productions *El cobrador: In god we trust* (Paul Leduc 2006). Cuarón founded Esperanto Filmoj in 1991 and through it also co-produced del Toro's *El laberinto del fauno*, Mexican independent hit *Temporada de patos* (*Duck Season* Fernando Eimbcke 2004) and his own *Gravity* (2013). In 2008 Cuarón, del Toro and Iñárritu together founded Cha Cha Chá Producciones to ensure they could work together to foster Mexican film production. As part of a $100 million, five-picture agreement with Hollywood major Universal Pictures and its specialist division Focus Features (who also produced Iñárritu's *21 Grams*), Cha Cha Chá has produced *Rudo y Cursi* (Carlos Cuarón 2008) *Mother and Child* (Rodrigo García 2009) and Iñárritu's own *Biutiful* (Rohter 2009: n.p; Donoghue 2014a: 8).

Thanks to the successes of Iñárritu, Cuarón and del Toro outside of Mexico (Cuarón's *Harry Potter and the Prisoner of Azkaban*, [2004] and *Children of Men* [2006], del Toro's *Hellboy* [2004] and *El laberinto del fauno* [2006], Iñárritu's *21 Grams* [2003] and *Babel* [2006]), there was increased attention for Mexican cinema during the latter half of Fox's Presidency which also saw a rise of 'more than 120 per cent in the number of feature films produced,' compared to the previous administration (MacLaird 2013a: 23). The very strong showing of the three directors at the 2007 Academy Awards where they, their crews and their films *El laberinto*, *Children of Men* and *Babel* garnered a total of 13 nominations and four Oscars between them[6] also contributed to the standing of Mexican cinema in global industry terms, not least because *El laberinto* was officially presented as a Mexico/Spain co-production and put forward as Mexico's entry for the Best Oscar category. Measures of Mexican cinema's reputation are represented in the increased interest in working with Mexican local talent from independent specialty houses and in specific deals such as the Universal/Focus Features agreement (Alvaray 2011: 74). Alongside this industry success, the international success of art house directors working in Mexico – a win at Cannes for Reygadas' *Japón*, and nomination for his *Batalla en el cielo*, nominations and Independent Spirit award for Eimbcke's *Temporada de patos* – also contributed to the rising position of Mexican cinema in global film culture. Additionally, at home these twin successes 'helped to improve the image of Mexican cinema in the eyes of its national audiences, its cultural institutions, and the private business sector' (MacLaird 2013a: 23). For instance, it was only in the wake of his success on the festival circuit that the IMCINE began to support Reygadas' films. In 2007 a new income tax law (Article 226), put in place by Fox, but not approved until the following presidential term of Felipe Calderón (2006–2012) went into effect allowing the private business sector including companies or individuals to put money into film production via a tax credit system (MacLaird 2013a: 24).

This law or el EFICINE, the body that awards the funds it collects, was responsible for a surge in production in 2007 (Anon. 2007) and a 'stead[ying] of production figures around 70 features' throughout Calderón's term in office (MacLaird 2013a: 31). Although there have been criticisms of the fund; that it lowers production standards, 'favours films with a commercial bent' (Fiesco qtd in Smith 2014: 244), and skews ideological content towards the views of its investors, by 2012 el EFICINE, as noted by an IMCINE report, had supported 239 productions (MacLaird 2013a: 33). Significantly, 83 per cent of its funded films were made by first-time directors. Additionally, critically acclaimed art house directors such as Reygadas, Eimbcke (*Lake Tahoe*, *Club sándwich* 2013), and Escalante (*Los bastardos*) as well as commercially successful projects like *No eres tú, soy yo* (*It's Not You, It's Me* Alejandro Springall 2011) and *Nosotros los Nobles* (*The Noble Family* Gary Alazraki 2013) were also funded by el EFICINE.

Conclusion

El EFICINE 189 (renamed after a policy change) has been claimed as the answer to Mexico's production problems (Salgado 2014). However, despite the exception of several recent box office hits such as *No se aceptan devoluciones*, which received funds from FIDECINE and el EFICINE and has become the biggest box office film in Mexican history (attracting a viewing public of 15.2 million), the injection of capital provided by the stimulus has not increased the number of successful national films overall or solved the problems of distribution. With respect to the low market share of the domestic cinema, Alejandro Ramírez, CEO of Cinépolis the largest cineplex chain in Mexico and Latin America, has suggested that it is a question of Mexican films not positioning themselves 'better in relationship to public tastes' (qtd in Smith 2014: 228; Caballero 2011). For others in the industry, such as art director Jesús Mario Lozano (*Así* [*Like This* 2005] *Ventanas al mar* [*Windows to the Sea* 2012]) it is the market and how it dictates subject matter that is the biggest problem for Mexican cinema (qtd in Smith 2014: 232).

There is actually less of a confrontation between the mainstream represented by Ramírez and an art cinema represented by Lozano in the efforts to increase Mexican cinema's domestic market share than Ramírez' and Lozano's two statements may suggest. As Daniela Michel, head of the Morelia Film Festival (FICM) points out 'thanks to the initiatives by exhibitors [including Cinépolis], distributors and production companies it has been possible to build a circuit for independent and art cinema.' Michel is referring both to the 'Sala de Arte' in Cinépolis, which makes space for art cinema in 21 of the chain's theatres and the numerous festivals (Morelia, Ambulante) established and sponsored by Ramírez and through Cinépolis. Also significant according to Michel, in respect of broadening access to exhibition, are the efforts of small producers such as CANANA, Mantarraya and Ambulante (qtd in Smith 2014: 235). Extended distribution platforms online and via cable television have also increased the possibilities for the exhibition of Mexican films (as detailed in the *Statistical Yearbook*). Despite such initiatives the market share for Mexican cinema remains at 10 per cent, which is coincidentally the figure of an exhibition quota brought in several years ago but rarely enforced (Ugalde qtd in Falicov 2008: 265). Only in certain years with the success of exceptional films like *No se aceptan devoluciones* does the market share rise above this figure.

Although, for a time, the successes of del Toro, Iñárritu and Cuarón had a knock-on effect, attracting a number of independent US producers into the Mexican market to work with private production companies, such as Focus Features who co-produced *Sin nombre* (Cary Fukunaga 2009) with Bernal and Luna's CANANA and also distributed Bernal's directorial debut *Déficit* (2007), in the present moment many of the private production companies established in the wake of the withdrawal of the Mexican Government are having tough times (MacLaird 2016). Producers and distributors warn that the distribution market in Mexico is 'brutal' and getting worse. Local producers and distributors with strong names can't even make their money back (MacLaird 2016).

The system of government favouritism and patronage that Cuarón and del Toro railed against in the early 1990s changed over the course of the decade as a consequence of the re-organisation of the industry and the influx of private capital. Government involvement in, and decision making with respect to, the funding and promotion of Mexican cinema is now made with a greater level of transparency (of which the *Statistical Yearbooks* are a part), which suggests that accusations of favouritism and corruption associated with the PRI-ista state cinema have been addressed. Cuarón and del Toro were able to take advantage of those changes, 'returning' to Mexico (or in the case of del Toro to official co-productions part financed in Mexico) to make independent films *El espinazo del diablo, El laberinto del fauno* and *Y tu mamá también*. Iñárritu has also 'returned' making two co-productions part financed in Mexico *Babel* and *Biutiful* (2010). As a measure of how much it was embraced as a 'national' film, *Biutiful* was Mexico's entry to the Oscars for Best Foreign Film, and won a string of Arieles, Mexico's own industry awards.

In addition to benefiting from these changes, these directors have also been influential in bringing about certain shifts in the language of filmmaking in Mexico. Del Toro's success in horror has both rehabilitated the genre from the cultural disreputability it suffered in the early 1990s and also facilitated more horror production in Mexico (and indeed the rest of Latin America). Recent Mexican horror successes include *KM 31, KM 31-2* (Rigoberto Castañeda 2016) *Somos lo que hay* (*We Are What We Are* Jorge Michel Grau 2010) the recipient of state funding through FOPROCINE, and *Halley* (Sebastián Hofman 2012).

Despite benefitting from the changes in the production model where most films now involve some government and private monies, there is also an acknowledgement on the part of these directors that some element of government help is still required if Mexico is to have a viable national film industry. In 2003 when Fox announced the sale of the state's remaining film assets (IMCINE, Estudios Churubusco, and the state-run film school Centro de Capacitación Cinematográfica) Iñárritu, del Toro and Cuarón were part of the film community in Mexico who protested against the sale, which was never carried through (MacLaird 2013a: 31). Similarly, del Toro has called for measures that will protect and strengthen Mexican cinema including greater financial and government support and a rewriting of the culture clauses in the NAFTA agreement (MacLaird 2013a: 36), which have no effective measures to protect Mexican films in the domestic market.

But as much as Iñárritu, del Toro and Cuarón can, and have helped in production terms, that is concretely through their own production companies and through patronage of individual projects such as Iñárritu's and Cuarón's recent 'talking up' of *Tenemos la carne/We are the Flesh* (Emiliano Rocha Minter 2016) (Cantú 2016), as well as more indirectly by making Mexican filmmaking attractive to invest in, they cannot intervene in or effect change in what remain, according to commentators like Paul Julian Smith and MacLaird, the critical problems for Mexican cinema: distribution and exhibition.

NOTES

1. *Como agua para chocolate* made $6 million at the Mexican box office and $20 million in the United States (Sánchez Prado 2014: 15).
2. *Sexo, pudor y lágrimas* had two production companies; Titan Producciones led by Christian Valdelièvre and Argos Cinema, which is part of the larger Argos Comunicación. It also received some government funding, from the FOPROCINE fund.
3. *El crimen del padre Amaro* was supported in part by state funds channelled through FOPROCINE.
4. In the top ten grossing films of 2000–2015 in the 2015 *anuario*, *Amores perros* and *Y tu mamá también* appear at numbers 10 (95 million pesos) and 7 (101.7 million pesos) respectively. *Sexo, pudor y lágrimas*, which was released in 1999, is outside the frame of reference for this list but attracted 5.3 million spectators (MacLaird 2013a: 37) at the box office more than the current number 3, *El crimen del padre Amaro*, which attracted 5.2 million spectators and made 162.2 million (IMCINE 2016: 69).
5. Its production slate also includes *Revolución* (Reygadas et al. 2010) – an anthology film that commemorates Mexico's 1910–1920 Revolution and highlights ongoing instances of social exclusion and marginalisation, and *Miss Bala* (Gerardo Naranjo 2011), which is about political corruption at the heart of Mexico's drug wars, as well as co-productions with other counties *¡No!* (Pablo Larraín Chile 2012).
6. *El laberinto del fauno* had six nominations including nominations for Art Direction, Screenplay, Foreign Language Film, and Cinematography. It won three Oscars. *Children of Men* received three nominations including Cinematography and Adapted Screenplay. *Babel* received four nominations including Best Director and Best Picture. Gustavo Santaolalla won Best Score for *Babel*.

I. ALEJANDRO GONZÁLEZ IÑÁRRITU: MEXICAN DIRECTOR WITHOUT BORDERS

> I'm a very proud Mexican and I feel even more Mexican the further I go from my country. [...] It's a great thing for an artist to travel, because it gives an even greater perspective of oneself and of one's country. [...] Why is it that painters and writers can go and live and work in other countries but film-makers cannot?
>
> (Iñárritu qtd in Wood 2006: 142)

Alejandro González Iñárritu's role as a marketing executive in the 1990s, running his own advertising agency and making adverts for a number of clients including Mexican television company Televisa, has been cited as key to his ultimate success as a filmmaker and his ability to connect with Mexico's new middle class cinema audience (Sánchez Prado 2014: 70). The 1990s neoliberal changes to the film industry, the consequent shift away from an art cinema-dominated model of state patronised national cinema, and the emergence of new production companies and private funding, are also cited as significant factors in the advent of independent films that follow commercial formats and, like Iñárritu's debut feature *Amores perros*, consequently achieve a high level of box office success (de la Mora, 2003: 14). After *Amores perros* (2000), Iñárritu was courted by the US industry and has gone on to make his subsequent five features, *21 Grams* (2003), *Babel* (2006), *Biutiful* (2010), *Birdman* (2013) and most recently *The Revenant* (2015) within its expanding parameters: firstly, with the US independent speciality divisions and most recently with a major studio (Twentieth Century Fox).

Although insistently still called a 'Mexican' filmmaker in the press, – indeed, in the run up to the 88th Academy Awards he was held up as the only person of colour to be nominated for a major award behind *or* in front of the camera (Binelli 2016) – Iñárritu's *films* have been increasingly written about in English language criticism in ways that emphasise; their US pedigree (McGowan 2008: 405), their 'globalised art cinema' credentials (Kerr 2010), their 'global Hollywood gaze' (Shaw 2011) or their 'global cinema lens' (Begin 2015: 1) and de-emphasise their Mexican/Latin American features and stylistics. Most recently, *The Revenant* has been perceived as a straightforward 'white settler narrative' supporting and privileging the abilities of one white man to survive the harsh winter and a near death experience (Quayson, 2016). Some Mexican criticism has taken a similar position towards not just Iñárritu, but the collectivity of directors, writers, cinematographers and actors working in the US. Writing on the occasion of the 2007 Academy Awards for which Iñárritu, del Toro and Cuarón's films were all heavily nominated, in an article tellingly entitled 'Hay cine mexicano después del Oscar?'/'Is there a Mexican Cinema after the Oscars?' Mexican film critic Carlos Bonfíl, very firmly categorises the US-produced work of Iñárritu and other Mexican filmmakers as a 'foreign cinema' ('cine extranjero'), that is a cinema that is not Mexican (2007).[1] This is in direct contrast to Iñárritu's own impulse which, as illustrated by his comments in the epigraph to this chapter, has been to assert his Mexicanness, arguing implicitly that, rather than take him away from a national perspective, the travel across borders ultimately gives him 'a greater perspective of oneself and one's country' (Iñárritu qtd in Wood 2006: 142). Iñárritu's other comments quoted in the epigraph – that filmmakers 'cannot' travel – gestures towards the transnational practices that are increasingly common in Latin American filmmaking and the impact these have on the perceived nationality of film texts. The capital-intensive nature of film production and the large industrial infrastructure filmmaking requires means that when a director or any creative individual connected with film does travel, their nationality is not perceived to 'go' with them but is instead overwritten by the necessities and forces of global capital.

Paul Kerr's reading of *Babel* (2010) reflects one such capital-based interpretation of filmmaking. Kerr treats *Babel* and Iñárritu's previous films as products of the mainstreaming of the '(global) network narrative,' popular in the 1990s in 'mainstream' and 'art house' cinema (*Pulp Fiction* [Quentin Tarantino 1994], *Chungking Express* [Kar-Wai Wong 1994]) (2010: 40). Kerr argues that the globalised network narrative format – several stories, set in different parts of the world – facilitates not just star involvement (which requires less time for just one story and therefore less money) but also the wider contribution by 'globalised, casualised labour' brought together by international agencies (2010: 44). But focusing on *Babel* in these globalised terms – seeking European (Krzysztof Kieslowski's *Trois Couleurs/Three Colours* trilogy 1993–1994), North African, and US precedents for its style as Kerr does, belies the cultural specificity of form in Iñárritu's films and the labour of the predominantly Mexican, and collectively Latin American core creative team (Mexican cinematographer Rodrigo Prieto, Mexican sound engineer Martín Hernández, Mexican screenwriter Guillermo Arriaga; Mexican, but German by birth production designer Brigitte Broch, Mexican and Argentinean composer Gustavo Santaolalla) who worked with him on his initial trilogy (*Amores perros*, *21 Grams*, and *Babel*), and also (with the exception of Arriaga) on *Biutiful*, as well as the labour of the Mexicans and Latin Americans who worked with him on *Birdman* (Hernández, Mexican cinematographer Emmanuel Lubezki, Argentine scriptwriters Armando Bo and Nicolás Giacobone and Mexican soundtrack composer/jazz drummer Antonio Sánchez) and *The Revenant* (Hernández and Lubezki).

Laura Podalsky produces a more specific, local perspective on *Babel* through a different and compelling reading of the film's formal features. She stresses the importance of the film's 'Mexican film-makers' in infusing an English-language film with 'the traditions of the Mexican melodrama' (2011: 129). Podalsky highlights how Mexican cultural forms, like the melodramatic *canción ranchera*/ranchera song and the equally melodramatic *telenovela*/series drama, are characterised by an emotional excess (2011: 143). *Babel*, she argues, privileges this Mexican emotional excess in the face of a dominant (in terms of its production location, financing and stars) Anglo-Protestant Puritan register of (restrained) emotion. This use of the particularly Mexican emotional register of melodrama in *Babel*, Podalsky argues, is about 'tutor[ing] non-Mexican audiences in other ways of feeling' often contrasting 'emotionless' law enforcement with the 'traumatic suffering of everyday people'. (2011: 129–130)

This chapter mediates its analysis of Iñárritu's first four transnationalised film projects (*Birdman* and *The Revenant* are analysed in the Epilogue) through the perspectives of Kerr (2010), Podalsky (2011) Deborah Shaw (2011) and others arguing that whilst the mobility in Iñárritu's own career trajectory (between Mexico, the US and Spain) may point towards a borderless world, his films and their film style attest to the complete opposite; against a 'borderless,' globalised interpretation of these films. Without being romantically auteurist (i.e. showing no sense of the industrial 'systems' in which Iñárritu operates), the chapter takes a director-centred approach – acknowledging Iñárritu as the orchestrator of a creative team which functions, it suggests, to forward the concerns and ideas of a transnationalised Mexican national cinema and for a coherency between these geographically diverse films. This chapter will explore how the ideological and aesthetic consistencies between Iñárritu's films offer a model of transnational exchange. It will further suggest that rather than purely imitate Hollywood or US traditions his films embody a perspective aligned with Mexico, Latin America and more broadly (in the case of *Babel* and *Biutiful*) the peoples of the Global South.

This chapter examines these US-made and Spanish-made films alongside the Mexican-made films and the broader concerns and features of a Mexican national cinema. To this end, the chapter analyses the ways his films counter the formal precepts and ideological tenets of classical Hollywood style and how these may be predicated upon anti-neoliberal perspectives rooted in a Mexican/Latin American perspective. It begins by charting the counter cinematic similarities between *Amores perros* and *21 Grams* looking at how the existence of such similarities in the face of very different production, cultural and political contexts, subverts the geographical and developmental divisions which supposedly separate the two films. It then examines how *Babel* explicitly addresses the reality of cultural and political borders, and further develops the issues and concerns of Iñárritu's first two films. The chapter concludes with an analysis of how *Biutiful* extends and develops the themes established in the trilogy. Throughout, the chapter keeps in mind how Iñárritu explores the issues of borders themselves.

Similarities between *Amores perros* and *21 Grams*

Amores perros presents three stories of three different pairs of characters: Octavio (Gael García Bernal), who wants to run away with his brother's wife Susana (Vanessa Bauche) and gets involved in dog fighting in order to raise the money; Daniel (Álvaro Guerrero), a publicist who leaves his wife and children to set up home with Valeria (Goya Toledo), a supermodel; El Chivo (Emilio Echeverría), an ex-revolutionary guerrilla and now semi-homeless contract killer and Maru (Lourdes Echeverría) the daughter he abandoned and whom he now wishes to see again. These three disparate pairs of characters from different social classes are brought together through a car crash. In the crash, Octavio and Valeria are seriously injured. El Chivo rescues Octavio's injured fighting dog, Cofi, and takes him home. Octavio still tries to run away with Susana – whose husband Ramiro is now dead – but she refuses. Valeria loses her leg in complications from the accident. Her idyllic relationship with Daniel is similarly damaged. Seeing himself in Cofi (both have been trained to kill), El Chivo gives up contract killing and decides to try to find a way back to his daughter.

21 Grams is similarly organised around a car crash and around three characters; Jack (Benicio del Toro) is an ex-convict and born-again Christian, who runs down and kills a man and his two daughters and then leaves his own children and wife to endure a self-castigating exile in the New Mexico desert; Paul (Sean Penn) is a maths professor suffering from terminal heart disease who is given the heart of the dead man and begins a relationship with his widow and Cristina (Naomi Watts) is the wife and mother who turns to drugs (and Paul) after the death of her husband and daughters. When Cristina decides she wants to get revenge for the death of her family by killing Jack she gets

Paul to help her. However, Paul cannot bring himself to kill Jack. When Jack comes looking for Paul (to make Paul shoot him) Paul shoots himself instead. At the hospital, Jack tries to take the blame for Paul's injuries but Paul and Cristina contradict his false confession, meaning he is free to go. Jack returns 'redeemed' to his family. Paul hovers between life and death as his body rejects the new heart. Cristina discovers she is pregnant with Paul's child.

As these plot summaries suggest *Amores perros'* and *21 Grams'* narratives are non-classical, fragmentary and determined by multiple stories. Their openings immediately signal their difference to classical, mainstream film-making styles. The opening of *Amores perros* presents us with two characters involved in a car chase. However, it is some moments before we realise this. The first few moments of the film are a mass of out-of-focus, or tightly framed shots. We first see blurred white lines, which we later work out are those in the middle of the road, and then hands of an, as yet unknown person, reaching into the frame to touch a bleeding dog. By withholding the establishing shot, a shot which in a Hollywood film would orient the spectator as to where the players are situated in the scene, and by presenting the action almost totally through very close shots (only some long shots show the car going through intersections), we get a fragmented and impressionistic opening to the film and a sense of the characters' anxiety and claustrophobia. Like them, we are also unsure of where the threat/the other car is.

The opening of *21 Grams* presents us with all three of its major characters and sets up some of the ways they will come together. However again, like *Amores perros* it is some moments before we realise this. The first few moments of the film string together a sequence of short, seemingly unconnected scenes: a man sitting on a bed beside a naked woman, a blank screen on which is imposed the title '21 Grams', a father with his two young girls finishing up and leaving a café, a woman at group therapy, an older man trying to help a 'troubled' younger man, a sunset and a man lying in a hospital bed whose interior monologue comments 'So this is death's waiting room'. These opening scenes present Jack, Cristina and Paul but, as Geoff King points out, raise more questions than answers as to how they are connected (2004: 85, 86). For instance, through Cristina's monologue at therapy we learn she has a husband and two daughters – hence we link her to the father and two girls leaving the café. What then, we are led to ask ourselves, is she doing in bed with Paul? Furthermore, if Paul is dying then how can he also be simultaneously healthy and carrying on what we presume to be an affair? This confounding series of questions leads us to understand that this opening is not the beginning to the classical communicative narrative which tells the spectator all that he/she needs to know in order to be able to follow the story (Bordwell 1985: 158). It is only later, as we see more of the film, that these questions are answered as we deduce that some scenes are from the beginning of the story whilst another is from some point in the middle when Cristina's family are dead and Paul is temporarily healthy again after his heart transplant (King 2004: 85).

Hence, both *Amores perros* and *21 Grams* open with sequences that in different ways announce the films' departure from mainstream conventions. This departure is deepened by the narratives which follow. *Amores perros* returns three further times to the crash during the film. This strategy – returning to a scene, to show it from a different perspective, in the case of *Amores perros* to show it from the perspective of each character – ruptures the time-space continuum of classical narrative (Bordwell 1985: 160). It also suggests a problematisation of the unified, classical perspective on the action. *21 Grams* continues with its disjunctive, seemingly random organisation of initial scenes from its opening sequence onwards. After the first few scenes, rather than move chronologically onwards *21 Grams* jumps first to near the end of the story (Cristina taking drugs in a motel) then backwards to the beginning of the story (Paul and his wife Mary at the gynaecologist before the transplant). In *21 Grams*, this backwards and forwards narrative organisation, plus the withholding of the actual crash itself, which takes place off screen about halfway through the film, also fragments the idea of classical perspective. And this fragmentation of classical perspective is in turn emblematic of the film's pondering and confounding not merely of issues of classical causality (cause and effect, fate and guilt) but also of how things 'are connected to one another' (King 2004: 90; Bordwell 1985: 162).

That both films seek to produce unconventional narratives, undoing classical causality and its chain of events where one happening causes another, is indicated by the very randomness of the event around which both films are constructed – a car crash. In *Amores perros*, the crash itself brings together characters that otherwise would not interact with each other in contemporary Mexico City: underclass El Chivo, middle class Valeria and working class Octavio. However, rather than suggest the crash is a one-off event, *Amores perros* continues to connect its characters, sometimes just coincidentally but also sometimes meaningfully. El Chivo appears during the narratives of the other characters, for example outside Valeria's car window just before the crash. Other characters appear during his narrative. For example, Ramiro and Susana walk by the photo booth where El Chivo is about to get his photo taken. In *21 Grams*, connections between characters begin in a similarly coincidental manner – Jack kills Cristina's family in an accident; however, these connections become much more deliberate. For example, Paul benefits from the crash by getting Cristina's dead husband's heart and subsequently seeks her out. In turn they go looking for Jack in New Mexico.

Amores perros and *21 Grams* also share distinctive visual qualities which are similarly part of the films' counter-classical vision. Both films depart from the classical convention of using one film stock (i.e. in keeping with

Figure 3   *Amores perros* (Alejandro González Iñárritu 2000)

the classical unified perspective) to make use of two visibly different photographic stocks; one fast (Kodak Vision 800T 5289), and the other slow
(Vision 500T 5279). Initially the use of two different stocks produces images
that map social or emotional differences between characters. For example,
in *Amores perros* the faster stock used in the first and third stories that
focus on working class Octavio and underclass El Chivo produces a grainy
image (heightened by use of a bleach-bypass process) that gives the impression
of a realistic, visually authentic, close-up look at poverty and marginalisation
(Figure 3).[2] The slower stock used in the second story, which focuses on middle
class Valeria and Daniel, produces a much less contrasted, more muted, and
consequently, much less emotionally realistic representation of the frivolous
world of magazine modelling and adultery (Figure 4). *21 Grams'* use of different stock is equally invested in mapping differences between characters.[3]
However, in *21 Grams* these differences are immediately emotional rather
than social. For example, just after working class Jack has knocked down
and killed middle class Cristina's family, the image shifts mid-scene at his
birthday party from low-contrast images that reflect his relatively 'happy'
family life (even though he's yet to arrive), to a high-contrast, bleach-bypass
heightened, heavy-grained image of him telling his wife what he has done
(Figures 5 and 6). Interestingly enough, when it cuts back from high-contrast
Jack to the waiting party guests inside, these are shown in low-contrast image
that is bathed in a (filtered) yellow glow, ironically counter-pointing the
devastating scene that is going on outside where Jack is telling his wife what
he has just done.

Figure 4   *Amores perros* (Alejandro González Iñárritu 2000)

Figure 5   *21 Grams* (Alejandro González Iñárritu 2003)

Ultimately, the social and emotional differences between characters in both films, signalled by shifts between slower and faster stocks and corresponding low and high-contrast images, are levelled out by the narrative and visual style. At the end of *Amores perros*, use of the same stock brings Valeria, El Chivo and Octavio together in what Marvin D'Lugo calls 'a new moral and cultural landscape of spiritual desolation rooted in the modern megalopolis'

Figure 6   *21 Grams* (Alejandro González Iñárritu 2003)

Figure 7   *Amores perros* (Alejandro González Iñárritu 2000)

(2003b: 224). Valeria looks out of her apartment window at the newly availa-ble billboard where her once perfect body, as model for Enchant, had been dis-played. As she contemplates the loss of her leg and perhaps of her relationship with Daniel, she is briefly shot with the faster stock of stories one and three (Figure 7). As with Octavio and El Chivo, the resultant high-contrast image, which emphasises even the pores on her skin, communicates *her* feelings of desperation and marginalisation. Similarly, in *21 Grams* the high-contrast images of the New Mexico desert sequence that are actually interspersed throughout the film also bring the three central characters, college professor Paul, working class Jack and middle class Cristina, together in a 'landscape of spiritual desolation' (but not one rooted in the city).

Another remarkable counter-cinematic similarity between *Amores perros* and *21 Grams* is the use of a hand-held camera. Interestingly, in *Amores perros* use of the visibly hand-held camera is more evident on viewing in stories one (Octavio's) and three (El Chivo's), where there is a greater investment in realistically depicting social and economic marginalisation. For example, one of its most striking uses occurs when Octavio stabs Jarocho, who has just shot his dog Cofi. The camera follows Octavio as he and his friend carry the dog to the car, as he goes back inside to stab Jarocho *and* then as he runs outside whilst being chased by Jarocho's gang, jumps into the car and speeds off. The take finishes as the camera pans down to reveal the bloody knife left behind on the ground. Here, the hand-held camera, together with another technique, the long take (as opposed to a series of shots) serves a number of different purposes. By reproducing the bumps and jiggles of Octavio's struggle first with his dog and then to get away, the hand-held camera allies the movement of the spectator with that of the actor or character, creating an impression of immediacy and 'heightened emotional proximity' (King 2004: 88). In this case, use of the hand-held camera intensifies the visual authenticity of the high-contrast, grainy images.

21 Grams is also completely shot with a hand-held camera. In most instances, the camera tends to hover over the shoulders of the different characters, functioning as a participant observer. For example, when Jack intervenes in a fight outside the church the camera begins at a position just behind him, but then swings wildly between him, the young man and the Reverend. Here the hand-held camera replicates the explosiveness of the moment; Jack has to be dragged off the boy, and the camera gives us a sense of Jack's temporary loss of control. On another occasion, a very sick Paul is in the bathroom sneaking a cigarette when his wife arrives home. In one long extended take the camera stays close to Paul as he extinguishes the cigarette, and opens the bathroom door to go out and greet his wife. It follows him along the corridor and shows, in long shot, his wife kissing him and then coming into the bathroom to find the cigarettes he has been hiding. The hand-held camera communicates a sense of co-conspiracy, allying itself and the spectator with Paul against his very tense wife.

CROSSING ARTISTIC, AESTHETIC AND INDUSTRIAL BORDERS

How might we theorise *Amores perros*' and *21 Grams*' shared stylistics in relation to the concept of borders and what happens to discourses of national cinema when these stylistic strategies are *already* read as not necessarily nationally specific? In the case of *Amores perros*, most scholars of

Mexican national cinema avow the film's partial dependence on 'foreign [US] visual models' (D'Lugo 2003b: 222). Some, theorise the film's aesthetics as *Hollywood*-derived and reflective of a post-NAFTA sensibility – desirous of cultural 'alliance with United States culture' (Hind 2004: 98, 95).[4] It is possible, however, to suggest that the style of *Amores perros* and *21 Grams* evoke not the stylistics of hegemonic Hollywood but of a very different aesthetic regime which significantly positions itself stylistically and also ideologically if not always financially, *against* Hollywood and mainstream American culture; American Independent Cinema.

It is already a film criticism cliché to equate *Amores perros* with, a seminal text of American Independent Cinema, Quentin Tarantino's *Pulp Fiction* (1994) because both films have three interlocking stories (Lawrenson 2001: 28), although these criticisms rarely make an issue of the 'independent' rather than strictly Hollywood nature of the latter film. However, rather than dismiss this equation as superficial, as one might do if one wanted to defend the 'borders' of Mexican national cinema, this chapter suggests that there are many more significant connections between *Amores perros*, *Pulp Fiction* and the movement the latter represents and that these connections are not necessarily a 'threat' to the project of Mexican national cinema.

Amores perros' and *21 Grams*' interest in random fate or what Jeffrey Sconce likes to call protagonists 'fucked by fate' (2002: 363) is also very much a feature of American Independent Cinema. Like Iñárritu's first two films, 'indie' cinema also likes to deliberately counter the 'elaborately constructed causality' of classical Hollywood narratives by exploring the 'unrealistic coincidences or synchronicities of everyday life' (Sconce 2002: 363).[5] Another feature of American Independent Cinema that *Amores perros* and *21 Grams* share is the innovative use of capture mediums to produce different visual textures within the same film. For example, 'indie' director Steven Soderbergh makes use of video and celluloid in *sex, lies and videotape* (1989), using video to represent the emotional authenticity of characters' sexual secrets. Similarly, *Amores perros* and *21 Grams* use two different kinds of photographic stock to create different visual textures and different meanings; high contrast signals emotional pain and poverty, low contrast signals happy life and financial well-being. What is also notable is that in the case of *sex, lies and videotape*, as with *Amores perros* and *21 Grams*, video or faster stock is often used to create heightened realism or just a different aesthetic to the polished realism that is still dominant in Hollywood filmmaking. In fact the kind of realism *Amores perros* and *21 Grams* promote – the shaky image of the hand-held camera, together with the grainy image, mobile frame and long take – is one we associate less with fiction and more with a documentary or *vérité* style.[6] Given its multiple similarities with American Independent cinema, *Amores perros* could almost be read as a proto 'indie' film.

However, reading *21 Grams* as an unproblematically American 'indie' film and *Amores perros* as proto-'indie' is complicated by the fact that both films' alternative stylistics can *also* be linked to more Mexican influences – particularly to New Mexican Cinema of the 1970s, 1980s and early 1990s (Smith 2003b: 30). New Mexican Cinema is equally as invested in multiple narrative films as American Independent Cinema. See for instance Mexican multiple narrative films *La mujer del puerto* (*The Woman of the Port* Ripstein 1991) and *Callejón de los milagros* (*Midaq Alley* Jorge Fons 1995), which critics point to as antecedents for the multiple narratives in *Amores perros* (Leonardo García Tsao in Wood 2006: 90). New Mexican cinema is also interested, in the way *Amores perros* is, in exploring new specifically Mexican ways of depicting reality (Smith 2003b: 27–30). Hence, the formal innovation of *Amores perros* and *21 Grams* should also be framed as part of a tendency of New Mexican Cinema to differentiate itself from Hollywood. And it is perhaps because both American Independent Cinema and New Mexican Cinema seek to be different to Hollywood (as indeed do many cinemas of peripheral filmmaking communities) that *Amores perros appears* to aspire to an 'indie' aesthetic and that Iñárritu's *21 Grams*, although originally intended for production in Mexico (Deleyto and Mar Azcona 2010: 3) could be made within the stylistic and institutional position of American independent cinema without any changes to its intended textual features. *Amores perros* and *21 Grams* seemingly replicate so many aesthetic strategies of American Independent Cinema not out of deliberate imitation but because Iñárritu is similarly interested in producing a product that is very different from the mainstream product (Hollywood).

SOCIAL AND POLITICAL CONTEXT AND CRITIQUE

Both *21 Grams* and *Amores perros* situate themselves on the borders of institutionalised film production: *21 Grams* was funded independently by the US independent production company Focus Features. *Amores perros* was made by a newly formed independent production company Altavista funded with transnational capital by a rich entrepreneurial individual (Jorge Vergara). Although made and shot in two different political, social and cultural contexts (*Amores perros* shot and premiered in pre-2000-election Mexico City, *21 Grams* in George W. Bush's post-9/11 America) there is continuity in the position they take on cultural, social and political issues.

The focus on social problems in *Amores perros*, reflects a crucial moment of transition in Mexican society – from a Mexico governed by the largely corrupt Partido Revolucionario Institucional (PRI) to one governed by Vicente Fox's conservative Partido de Acción Nacional (PAN) (Smith 2003b: 16). Paul Julian Smith points out how *Amores perros* explores 'new issues' (teenage pregnancy, lack of access to/education about contraception and abortion, absent fathers, alcoholism and unemployment) (2003: 16).[7] One of the film's most explicit statements about social change lies in its representation of El Chivo. The ex-university professor, ex-guerrilla fighter and actual contract killer has been read as a 'composite' figure, representing a variety of pan Latin American historical revolutionary figures (including Mexican teacher turned guerrilla leader Lucio Cabañas) (Solomianski 2006: 32). The film's ending – El Chivo departing into a dusty wasteground, Octavio, dispirited, and alone at the bus station where Susana has failed to show up – foreshadows a social order that will continue to be determined by absent fathers, inequality and social stratification.

21 Grams was shot in a moment of profound cultural and psychologi-cal shift in a post-9/11 United States (Iñárritu in Wood 2006: 143). Whilst Iñárritu's contribution to the anthology film *11'09'01–September 11* (2002) and *Babel* treat the event or its effects more directly (*Babel* in its depiction of paranoia about illegal aliens and terrorist attacks, *11'09'01* by its showing of victims jumping from the towers) by choosing to shoot *21 Grams* in Memphis, one of the US's poorest major cities, Iñárritu calls attention to issues of social justice and welfare. Jack, a born-again Christian, is bowed down by his reli-gion to accept life as part of a white underclass in which he will suffer low-income jobs with no security.

Although made in different countries, *21 Grams* and *Amores perros* are tied together by a common critique of what has, in analyses of *Amores perros*, been called the 'inequalities of neo-liberalism' (Podalsky 2003: 293). Both films emphasise the results of neoliberalist policies: extreme wealth of the few versus the extreme poverty and lack of social mobility of others, rigid social stratifi-cation and disenfranchisement of the poor. Hence, in *Amores perros* there is an emphasis on the extreme wealth of the business partners/brothers who will pay any price to have the other executed. In both the films, it is suggested that working class characters can only hope to gain the trappings of wealth such as a truck or a car through luck (in Jack's case a raffle) or through illegal means (in Octavio's case the use of Cofi for dog fighting). In *21 Grams*, the camera highlights how Jack at the Golf Club will always be different to the privileged members shot insouciantly sipping beer who eventually have him fired because of his tattoos. In *21 Grams* and *Amores perros* the results of neoliberal policies are experienced equally in Mexico and in the United States.

What emerges from this analysis of these two films alongside each other is how *21 Grams*, made in the United States, is similarly thematically and stylisti-cally political, retaining the perspective of a filmmaker from a peripheral film-making nation. In the process of shifting the production site from the Mexican to the US independent sector rather than become absorbed into the larger ideo-logical mind-set of US filmmaking, the stylistic, narrative and even national spe-cificities of *Amores perros*, use of different stocks, narrative experimentation, interest in random fate, critique of the effects of neoliberalism, are retained and further radicalised in *21 Grams*. From reading *Amores perros* and *21 Grams* alongside one another it becomes clear that these texts are similarly political and similarly invested in a critical representation of the world.

Furthermore, *21 Grams* subverts the geographical and geocultural divides between the US and Mexico by presenting both countries through the same visual style (unlike Soderbergh's *Traffic* [2000] which uses coloured filters to map differences between a modern US/San Diego that is photographed with a blue filter and an underdeveloped Mexico/Tijuana which is shot with a sepia filter). In *Amores perros* and *21 Grams* we view a violent, chaotic, shabby Mexico City and Memphis mediated through the same representational strategies. By filming *21 Grams* in Memphis, and by focusing on Jack's shabby church, his shabbier house, the seedy bars Cristina frequents, the dusty wasteland and shabby motels of New Mexico, the film suggests that uneven development and the struggle to come to terms with modernity is not only the problem of the developing world. And by suggesting that underdevelopment is an issue on US soil as well, the film echoes a central text of American Independent Cinema, Jim Jarmusch's *Stranger Than Paradise* (1984). Shot in black-and-white, *Stranger Than Paradise* opens on a bleak wasteground that we later learn to be JFK Airport in New York. Like *Stranger Than Paradise*, *21 Grams* makes strange the representation of the United States to contest certainties of US ideology, such as its own modernity and development.

Babel

As the third film in the trilogy, *Babel* engages with many of the issues of fate, inequality and emotional pain raised in *Amores perros* and *21 Grams*, and shares many of the same counter-classical strategies; use of different stocks and shaky hand-held camera, temporal disruption and multiple narratives. Significantly, for the purposes of this book about the transnational styles and trajectories of Latin American film and filmmakers, the film (which has four stories, set in the United States, Mexico, Japan and Morocco) makes the question of borders and border crossings central to its aesthetic project. The film suggests that borders are in some cases permeable and in other cases impassable and in doing so recasts the biblical story of the tower of Babel within the context of a globalised post-9/11 twenty-first century, recounting different stories of miscommunication or misconnect both across and within cultures.[8]

Like *Amores perros* and *21 Grams*, *Babel* is organised around one cataclysmic event and multiple story lines. It situates these stories across four countries; Mexico, the US, Japan and Morocco. In Morocco, Abdullah (Mustapha Rachidi) buys a rifle and gives it to his rivalrous sons Yussef and Ahmed so that they can guard the family's goats. Also in Morocco, an American couple,

Richard (Brad Pitt) and Susan (Cate Blanchett) take a holiday following the death of their child from SIDS (Sudden Infant Death Syndrome). Susan is shot in an accident. In Japan, Chieko (Rinko Kikuchi) a deaf and mute teenager experiences problems in her emotional relationships with her father, friends and boys. In the US Mexican nanny Amelia (Adriana Barraza) takes the two American children in her charge, Mike (Nathan Gamble) and Debbie (Elle Fanning), to Mexico for her son's wedding.

Babel, like *Amores perros* and *21 Grams*, has an unconventional narrative structure, continually swapping between its four different narratives. It also disrupts the chronology of the four stories so that they run asynchronously to each other during the film. In the analysis of *Amores perros*, I suggested that this kind of temporal disjunction leads us to scrutinise the mechanics of causality, making us ponder what has brought all three characters to the moment of the crash. In *Babel*, one of the effects of temporal disjunction is again to bring the focus onto causality – but our scrutiny on causality is focused in a much more global and directly political sense.

For instance, near the beginning of the film, during Amelia's story, and before Susan and Richard have even been introduced as characters, Richard (who is father to the children Amelia looks after) calls to speak to her. We see the conversation from the perspective of Amelia who is shot in close up whilst Richard is reduced to a voice mediated through a telephone line. A later phone conversation, where he tells her she will have to continue to look after the children, is again presented from Amelia's perspective. By only showing Amelia in both these telephone conversations rather than cutting to Richard at the other end of the phone, the emphasis falls on the employee/employer relationship (she calls him 'sir') and, in the second call, the apparently unreasonable demands he makes of her, as well as on Richard and Susan's seeming lack of parental care (going to Morocco and leaving their children behind). Amelia's attempts to protest when Richard says she will have to cancel her son's wedding to stay and look after the children fall on deaf ears, he has put down the phone. Because of the temporal disjunction the viewer does not get to see the conversation from Richard's perspective until the end of the film when we see the circumstances in which it was made; from a Casablanca hospital. At this point, near the end of the film the earlier telephone call's representation of Richard as a demanding American employer and uncaring parent is mitigated by his obvious distress and concern for his wife and children. However, by shifting this other end of the phone call to a point near the end of the film, narrative organisation first stresses the class and economic differences which separate Amelia and Richard, and their corresponding roles of servant and master and only subsequently Richard's love and concern for the wellbeing of his children.[9]

Similarly, in another instance of disrupted chronology, as Chieko channel-surfs in her technology-laden, luxurious penthouse apartment, an image appears on the television news of Yussef (who has – in his story – so far escaped detection as the shooter), but who the news tells us is already in custody for shooting 'an American tourist'. As well as indicating fatalistically that Yussef's capture is inevitable, bringing him together with Chieko collapses the geographic space that separates them and emphasises the level of inequality that exists between them. Yussef already has to work since his labour is important to the family's survival. Chieko does not, and can spend her time at school and in leisure activities; we see her playing volleyball, eating with friends, playing arcade games and dancing in a discotheque. The disrupted chronology and swapping between different narratives makes the connection between them long before we learn that they are connected through the gun.

Babel's disrupted chronology, placing (what gradually emerge to be) linked stories out of time with each other, initially figures Susan's shooting as an accident. However, it emerges that the shooting although an *accident*, is not purely *accidental*. *Babel* constructs it as a direct consequence of a vastly unequal world order. Towards the beginning of the film Yussef and Ahmed are trying out the gun and increasingly convinced that it cannot shoot a great distance, when it hits the unlikely target of the moving tour bus on which Susan and Richard are travelling. When the shooting happens in Susan's story (rather than in Yussef and Ahmed's story, where the shot cuts from the stopping bus and the boys running away in fright to Mike running round the house in Amelia's story in San Diego), we immediately see its effect on her and we have already seen its (knock-on) effect on Amelia, who is forced to take Mike and Debbie to Mexico. Not until the near end of the film, in a visit from Japanese police officers to Chieko's apartment do we learn the actual 'cause' of the shooting. The gun originally belonged to Chieko's father who gave it to his guide on a hunting trip in Morocco. At this point, the shooting takes on a much less random nature unlike the car crashes in *21 Grams* and *Amores perros*. The film suggests that the shooting is largely caused by the careless giving away of a gun by a wealthy man for whom it is an object of leisure, to someone from a much less wealthy country, for whom a gun can make the difference between prosperity and poverty (Denby 2007). The shooting and all the events which it triggers (an international incident with the US government accusing Morocco of harbouring terrorists, the gun's initial recipient Mohammed is beaten by Moroccan police, Ahmed is fatally wounded whilst trying to run from the police, Amelia and the children end up close to death wandering in the desert, she is subsequently deported back to Mexico) are framed as a direct result of the inequalities of global capitalist practices. One such practice, the film suggests, is the freedom with which residents of certain countries may cross borders; Chieko's father's hunting trip to Morocco, Susan and Richard's trip to Morocco. The movie points out how the reverse is not possible. When those from less wealthy countries cross into the US, as Amelia and her nephew

Santiago try to do after the wedding, even though they happen to also live and work there, they are automatically viewed with suspicion. This is before the Border Patrol smell alcohol on Santiago's breath and, frightened his illegal status will be discovered, he takes off into the desert.

And this emphasis on the *differences* between countries and the status of their inhabitants is something that *Babel* underlines on a visual level through its approach to the film's visual texture(s). Unlike *21 Grams* and *Amores perros*, in which there was a conscious and indeed subversive attempt *not* to differentiate between the United States and Mexico, in *Babel* there is an attempt to emphasise different countries and different class groups within those countries (Susan and Richard, and Yussef and Ahmed) in Morocco through the use of different stocks, different formats and, in the case of Japan, even different lenses (Bosley 2006: 1). Morocco, in particular, looks noticeably different to San Diego because it was shot on Super 16mm, a format that is historically connected with a number of realist-oriented counter-cinema movements – British Free Cinema, American Direct Cinema, New Latin American Cinema – where it was used primarily for its cheapness and portability. In *Babel*, as Prieto affirms, 16mm together with a faster stock (similar to the faster stock used for *21 Grams* and *Amores perros*) were used for the 'grainy' picture they would produce, to make Morocco 'feel difficult, almost dirty, because of what transpires there' (Bosley 2006: 1). The use of bleach bypass, achieved digitally rather than photo chemically, to heighten the contrast of the images further adds to Morocco's 'difficulty' and also to the emotional register of the sequences set there between Susan and Richard.[10] High contrast maps Richard's emotional suffering by picking out the grey in the (usually youthful) Pitt's hair and beard. As in *21 Grams* and *Amores perros*, high contrast communicates emotional pain and suffering.

Use of hand-held camera is also most conspicuous and radical in the Morocco sequences. For example, immediately after Susan is shot, the hand-held camera jiggles as it tries to alternate between her, the guide (Anwar), her husband and the other passengers on the bus. At the same time, framing becomes decentred and unclassical as the bodies of panicking tourists obscure Susan and, floppy from the loss of blood, she drops out of frame. The effect of the hand-held camera at this point is that we as spectators become confused as to what is going on. Coupled with later jiggling shots from the tour bus as it pulls into the guide's village to find help for Susan, the hand-held camera communicates a Eurocentric orientalist panic (at the presumed danger of the 'East'). It is potentially a mistake however to equate this orientalist panic with the perspective of the film itself, or to therefore suggest that the film projects a neocolonialist 'tourist gaze' on the inhabitants of Morocco (Shaw 2011: 18). Through the sequencing of shots, (shots of tourists looking and then shots through the bus window of what they see, sometimes with the Tour Company lettering on the bus window visible for emphasis), Iñárritu places this 'hegemonic colonial' gaze on the village inhabitants within quotation marks. That the film is critiquing the colonialist gaze rather than uncritically reproducing it is later backed up when the very kind treatment and selfless help extended to Susan and Richard in the village is counterpointed by the harsh comments of one of the other tourists anxious to leave the village because 'In Egypt in a town like this, they slit 30 tourists' throats'.[11]

Babel's investment in a critique of the colonialist gaze is made evident particularly in its treatment of the question of border crossing. Whilst the ability of Iñárritu and other creative personnel involved in the trilogy to cross borders has been widely commented upon (Jafaar 2006: 15)[12] the final film in the trilogy bears witness to the borders that many are economically compelled to, and yet cannot, cross. Amelia's crossing into Mexico to go to her son's wedding is emphasised as quick and easy but her journey back into the United States is physically and politically impossible. In this sense, *Babel* also bears witness to the post-9/11 'paranoia' of the Bush administration, manifesting itself both in US foreign policy (the inaccurate assumption that Susan's shooting is a terrorist act) and also in the tightening of US/Mexico border controls (Gilchrist 2006: 2).

From the textual analysis of *Babel* we can see that like *Amores perros* and *21 Grams* it is invested in an idea of heightened realism, with an added sensitivity towards the contingencies that structure life in the Global North and South. Like *21 Grams* and *Amores perros*, *Babel's* shaky image and use of the hand-held camera, together with the mobile frame and long take achieves, particularly in the Morocco sequences, a documentary style. However, how we interpret the use of these counter-mainstream stylistics in terms of national and industrial borders is further complicated by a shifting mainstream and by progressively more porous boundaries between mainstream and non-mainstream cinemas.

Industrially and also textually, Hollywood is increasingly less defined by a hegemonic classicism against which a non-US, (Mexican) or American Independent Cinema may define itself. In 2012 for instance, a production like *The Artist* (Michael Hazanavicius 2011) by a French creative team starring French actors (Jean Dujardin and Bérénice Bejo), offering a French perspective on the US, and with only two spoken words of English, could, because of financial involvement from Warner Bros., qualify as a straightforward Hollywood (rather than foreign language) film for the purposes of the Oscars (Hoad 2012a). In addition to the fact that Hollywood has always sought to recruit commercial and/or critically successful directors from overseas, since the 1990s Hollywood studios have increasingly moved into independent production in the US.[13] Beginning with Disney's purchase of pioneering independent distributor and producer Miramax in 1993, different Hollywood studios bought up existing indie/speciality-oriented distributors and/or producers or opened their own indie subsidiaries in order to corner a very profitable niche of the market (King 2009: 4). Both *21 Grams* and *Babel* are products of these speciality divisions, sometimes called 'The Hollywood Independents' because of their hybrid institutional position. *21 Grams* was made with Focus Features, a subsidiary of Universal Pictures and *Babel* was made with Paramount Vantage, a subsidiary of Paramount (King 2009: 4). And like Hollywood in the 1930s and 1960s, these subsidiaries have sought to harness the talent of prestigious and commercially successful 'world' filmmakers like Iñárritu (King 2009: 248). Focus Features in particular has, in addition to Iñárritu, financed and produced features of other Latin American directors, such as Salles' *Diarios de motocicleta* (*Motorcycle Diaries* 2004) and Mereilles' *The Constant Gardener* (2005).

These industrial shifts have made the stylistics of independent cinema more common and desirable in mainstream cinema. The techniques of counter cinema in *Amores perros*, *21 Grams* and *Babel* are increasingly evident in Hollywood studio *and* independent projects. For instance, the multi-strand narrative became commonplace in other issue-centred 'Indiewood' features of the 2000s like *Crash* (Lionsgate, Paul Haggis 2004), *Traffic* (USA Films) and *Syriana* (Warner Bros., Stephen Gaghan 2005). Also, the shaky, hand-held camera that defines Iñárritu's films has become so much a part of mainstream film vocabulary that it can appear in films such as *The Bourne Ultimatum* (Universal Pictures, Paul Greengrass 2007) and *Cloverfield* (Matt Reeves, 2008) which have no aspirations towards independence from the studios, even though, similar to Iñárritu's films, it is used to add pseudo-documentary weight to the films' psychological realism.

In the analysis of *Amores perros* and *21 Grams*, I suggested that the counter-cinema techniques of both films allied the concerns of Mexican national cinema with the vision and ideology of American Independent Cinema. With *Babel* I suggest that its counter-cinema techniques anchor the concerns of Mexican national cinema simultaneously within a peripheral, radical perspective and within a Hollywood-sponsored World Cinema/Independent aesthetic which is actually different from the North Americanist centred Hollywood World Cinema that Shaw suggests characterises the film (2011: 14). In *Babel*, we see the people of the Global South badly treated by their employers in the Global North (Amelia in the phone conversation with Richard), and by the authorities (Mohammed by the police investigating the shooting, Amelia and Santiago by US Border Control) whilst for the residents of the Global North (like Susan and Richard, even if they find themselves in the South) there is the assurance of a helicopter out of pre-modern living conditions to the safety of sanitised hospital care.

Babel's use of counter-cinema strategies evokes previous radical (not only Latin American) filmmaking movements but also represents a diversification of

Hollywood classicism or the latter's co-opting (but not subsuming) of marginal aesthetics. *Babel* broadens out the political critiques of *Amores perros* and *21 Grams* to address the reality of cultural and political borders in a global sense. Between *Amores perros* and *Babel* Iñárritu's films shift slightly from attempting to differentiate the Mexican product from Hollywood to a position where they are simultaneously co-existing with the Hollywood film (or some contemporary manifestation of it) *and* yet also different to it. Stylistically Iñárritu's films might reflect the non-classical aspects of some contemporary Hollywood films but this represents more a shift in the Hollywood mainstream to incorporate not just marginal aesthetics but also their critical and 'strange-making' representation of the United States (e.g. *Crash*'s criticism of racism, *Syriana*'s criticism of the United States' secret oil-fuelled interventions in international politics).

And yet, at the same time, it is important to acknowledge that for all its radical politics *Babel* still ends on a politically and racially conservative note: the privileged (white) family is saved/rescued and instead it is the (dark-skinned) inhabitants of the Global South who suffer (Amelia) or die (Ahmed). A more radical ending would have been for Richard's children to have died (and thus the United States to get a taste of its own repressive border controls) or for his wife to have died whilst waiting for a helicopter to safety (and thus the United States to get a taste of its own aggressive foreign policy). However, the conservatism of its ending does not necessarily imply that *Babel* conforms to Hollywood paradigms and ideology, nor that it necessarily abandons its concern for the peoples of the Global South or the themes of Mexican national cinema. The fatalism of *Babel*'s ending, confirming a stratified social and racial world order recalls the similarly pessimistic ending of *Amores perros* and other Mexican films from this era. Take, for instance, Gerardo Tort's *De la calle* (*Streeters*, 2001) about homeless youth in Mexico City which Misha MacLaird argues is one of a series of films that like *Amores perros* fatalistically depicts the crisis in Mexico's social sphere in the late 1990s (2013a: 99).

Ultimately, then it is possible to read *Babel* as a successful critique (on a more global scale) of the issues critiqued in *Amores perros* and *21 Grams* and take from this reading the idea that rather than be subsumed into a global Hollywood gaze as Shaw suggests, the ideological independence and specificity of Iñárritu's authorial style is retained and even developed. That *Babel* was ultimately followed by a Spanish-language, Spanish-made production – albeit with involvement from the US indie sector – rather than a wholly Hollywood production seemingly confirms this idea of authorial specificity trumping institutional conformity even though with *The Revenant* the ultimate destination of Iñárritu's filmmaking trajectory is eventually the US mainstream industry (see the Epilogue for how this institutional position squares with his authorial style in *The Revenant*).

BIUTIFUL

Biutiful engages with many of the issues explored in *Amores perros*, *21 Grams*, *and Babel*: poverty, emotional and also physical pain. *Biutiful* also shares some of the different counter-classical strategies of the first three films. Like them, it makes use of a gamut of realist techniques – grainy image, hand-held camera and long mobile takes – but unlike these films it does not make use of intertwined multiple narratives or chronological disruption, nor does it use stocks of noticeably different speeds (Benjamin 2011: 1) Thematically, *Biutiful* picks up some plot strands from Iñárritu's previous films; the (fractured) relationships between parents and children (*Amores perros* and *Babel*) and the perilous and tenuous situation of illegal immigrants (*Babel*). Ultimately, the film's aesthetic project maintains a commitment to the post-colonialist and socially progressive realism of Iñárritu's death trilogy, marshalling its techniques to draw attention to the inequities of global capitalism, as manifested in a visibly impoverished European city.

Biutiful focuses on Uxbal (Javier Bardem) who makes a living on Barcelona's streets by supplying Senegalese street sellers with fake designer goods, brokering the wages of the Chinese sweatshop workers who make the goods, and paying the police to turn a blind eye. He also picks up money on the side by helping the spirits of the dead pass over. He has two children, Mateo (Guillermo Estrella) and Ana (Hanaa Bouchaib) who live with him. When Uxbal learns he has terminal cancer he begins trying to settle his affairs in terms of the future of his children and the wellbeing of the immigrant workers. This includes an unsuccessful attempt to reconcile with his Argentinean ex-wife Marambra (Maricel Álvarez) and to improve the living conditions of the Chinese workers. He also has to deal with the embalmed body of the father he never knew – who left Spain fleeing Francoist persecution and died soon after arriving in Mexico – which has been disinterred to make way for a shopping mall. Disaster strikes when the Chinese workers die in a locked warehouse cellar after Uxbal buys them faulty gas heaters and the Senegalese street sellers are captured and deported by the authorities. Uxbal invites Ige (Diaryatou Daff), the wife of Ekweme (Cheikh Ndiaye) one of the deported street sellers, to stay in his flat with her small baby Samuel. As Uxbal grows weaker Ige takes over the care of his children and nurses him through the last days of his life. Uxbal dies leaving Ige to look after his children.

This chapter's analysis of Iñárritu's first three films has revealed the ways in which counter-cinematic techniques (the texture of the image as established by fast and slow film stocks and bleach bypassing treatments of the negative) differentiate between geographical locations (*Babel*) or between social class and corresponding levels of power (*Amores perros*). The chapter's analysis also points out how *21 Grams*' (set in the US) use of the same fast stock and bleach bypass process used to depict poverty in *Amores perros* (set in Mexico) subversively points to the uneven modernity of both the Global North and the Global South. In *Biutiful*, set in Barcelona, explicit differences of social class and corresponding levels of power are not presented in as cinematographically divisive terms as the other films because, the film suggests, they do not exist between the characters. A common cinematic language signalling poverty and emotional pain is used to depict Uxbal, the Senegalese street sellers, and the Chinese workers as well as the homes they inhabit. Through shots of peeling paint and broken bathroom tiles and the cluttered rooms in Uxbal's apartment as well as claustrophobically close hand-held camera work, the film suggests that he experiences a poverty and powerlessness analogous to that of the immigrants he both helps and exploits. Admittedly, unlike the Senegalese and Chinese workers, Uxbal is a legal citizen and is therefore not threatened by deportation, he also does not live in *as* squalid and overcrowded conditions and he has been able to get together a wad of cash, (largely on the backs of their labour), which he secretes in socks, bedside tables and holdalls. Although this money represents a significant amount for Uxbal and the other characters (at one point he hands his stash of money to Ige saying 'this will pay rent for one or two years' and she contemplates using it to follow her deported husband back to Senegal), the sheer quantity (of notes) and the fact Uxbal still lives in slum-like conditions, actually points towards the very low 'real value' of this money. Like the small case of money Octavio is able to collect from the dog fighting winnings in *Amores perros*, it cannot buy the characters very much or a way out of the lives they are living.[14] The uniform shabby interiors of the film suggest that Uxbal is not wealthy, nor is his wife, his brother (who also seems be a wheeling/dealing hustler), the other medium he visits, nor the variety of people to whom he offers his services as a medium.

As with *Amores perros*, it is *Biutiful*'s grainy image that adds to this sense of a close up look at poverty and marginalisation and at the same time gives a sense of aesthetic differentiation from a more 'plastic' mainstream. Prieto refers to the film's use of the grainy image '[as Iñárritu's] reaction to all the digital developments [making] movies [...] look too clean and plastic' (Benjamin 2011: 1). Additional signs of the film's commitment to counter mainstream realism are emphasised in the director's 'Film Notes' that accompany the DVD. In this short film Iñárritu talks about a range of realist techniques *Biutiful* draws upon including use of non-professional actors who have experienced life as street sellers and illegal workers to play the Senegalese characters, location shooting in the same poor working class neighbourhoods (Badalona, and Santa Coloma) in which the film is set and improvisation (Iñárritu 2011).[15] *Biutiful* continues the progressive realism of the earlier films and also extends it through self-reflexive techniques to gesture towards inexplicable and metaphysical aspects

Figure 8   *Biutiful* (Alejandro González Iñárritu 2010)

Figure 9   *Biutiful* (Alejandro González Iñárritu 2010)

of the narrative. At one point Uxbal walks past a television shop in which all the screens show whales stranded on a beach (pre-figuring the washed up bodies of the dead Chinese people) (Figure 8). Once Uxbal is aware of his impending death, his reflection (in a window or a mirror) acts like his spirit self, detaching from him to comment metatextually on his behaviour: with his head down counting money, his reflection/spirit looks back at him with a knowing smile (Figure 9).

In its close up, realist exploration of poverty and marginality, *Biutiful* deliberately represents Barcelona against the Catalan, chic modernist city of architect Antonio Gaudi presented in *Vicky Cristina Barcelona* (Woody Allen, 2008) which also stars Javier Bardem.[16] As with Mexico City in *Amores perros* and Memphis in *21 Grams*, the representation of the city is deliberately unfamiliar and alienating. Barcelona's iconic spaces are refigured to act either as battlegrounds – baton-wielding police chase street sellers through Plaça de Catalunya and Las Rambla – or dumping grounds – the shoreline is littered with the bodies of asphyxiated Chinese workers thrown overboard at sea. *Biutiful*'s Barcelona is mostly constituted by an industrial landscape of grimy factories, run-down apartments and bars populated by a mix of nationalities: Chinese, Spanish, Catalans, and Senegalese. *Biutiful* distils the global scope of *Babel* into one city. Early on, we glimpse a telenovela in which a young (seemingly) European girl and a (seemingly) Chinese boy speak Spanish. The television is watched by Lili, a Chinese worker taking care of Ana and Mateo in the backroom of a Chinese-owned hardware store whose multilingual sign features Chinese characters and Spanish words. The city is so much a multi-cultural and multilingual space that Catalan, Barcelona's official language, is almost completely marginalised in the film. Apart from the two phrases of Catalan that Uxbal utters to his children (who, growing up in Catalunya would almost certainly be native speakers), it is not spoken at all.[17] Uxbal and his brother are not from Barcelona either but are internal migrants from the South. The absence of Catalan and the presence of Mandarin and Wolof in the film points towards the diasporic nature of contemporary cities in the Global North, where everyone is from somewhere else.

Although *Biutiful*'s single strand narrative and lack of chronological fragmentation has been attributed to the very public break-up of Arriaga and Iñárritu's partnership over the writing credit for *Babel*[18] (Hoad 2012b; Chang 2010), the linearity of the narrative may also be rationalised in terms of the film's diasporic figuring of the European city, where a multiplicity of languages and peoples co-exist, rather than accidentally collide as in *Amores perros*, *21 Grams* and *Babel*. Into this refiguring of Barcelona, Iñárritu inserts an important moment in Spain's history, opening and closing the narrative with Uxbal's dreamed or post-death encounter with his father as a young man.[19] Earlier in the chapter I suggested that the disrupted chronologies of *Amores perros*, *21 Grams* and *Babel* emphasise causality, and also economic differences of class, race and, additionally in *Babel*, of geography. *Biutiful*'s cyclical structure opening and beginning with the exiled father makes a much more political statement that is both local (Spanish) and transatlantic in scope, signalling the unspoken trauma of Francoist repression in Spain's past (which deprived Uxbal and his brother of a father) and the hand of solidarity that was extended to Spain's Republican exiles by Mexico in the 1940s. On a personal level, the re-encounter not just with the father, but the son in the father (he utters the same lines about a dying owl that Mateo speaks in the film) also posits a 'happy ending' for Uxbal and his children (in as much as it gestures towards a future meeting in an unspecified 'afterlife').

With respect to *Babel* and in particular the sequences set in Morocco, I suggested that the grainy image and hand-held camera reproduce and criticise the 'orientalist panic' of the Western tourists in the immediate aftermath of Susan's shooting. *Biutiful*, however, despite its attempt to portray the 'exploitation of human capital' in its depiction of the sweatshop trade, problematically presents both the Chinese bosses and Chinese undocumented immigrant workers in ways which reify 'stereotypes' as well as 'neoliberal fears of immigration' and unlike *Babel* does so without critical distance (Begin 2015: 2). The undocumented workers work long hours, live in pityingly basic conditions (in a locked room), are paid very little for their work and are treated poorly by their bosses Liwei (Luo Jin) and Hai (Taisheng Cheng) 'who are shown to be morally bankrupt' (Begin 2015: 9). Paul Begin suggests that, despite its liberal intentions – showing the poor treatment and effective slavery of undocumented migrants – *Biutiful* reflects the 'contemporary issue of resentment towards the Chinese' particularly in the context of the ongoing Spanish economic crisis, near 30 per cent unemployment and the Chinese encroachment into the Spanish economy (2015: 5). Even more problematic, is the way the film connects the unethical behaviour of the Chinese business owners Liwei and Hai 'towards their fellow compatriots' (which, in addition to inhuman working conditions includes covering up their deaths in order to avoid prison) to what is portrayed as 'sexual deviance': Hai and Liwei are shown to be having an affair. The film's homophobic depiction of Liwei (it is more sympathetic to the married Hai), as an effeminate and cruel gang master (who is happy to overwork and exploit his compatriots) has all the marks of classical Hollywood prejudice where, under the constraints of the Production Code, 'oriental' décor and venality were synonymous with homosexuality, as in the interior of the home of Geiger (the pornographer) in *The Big Sleep* (Howard Hawks 1946).

As Ayala Blanco has pointed out, the Chinese sweatshop workers themselves are also presented as less than human (2014: 155). Shown awaking in the locked cellar each morning and shuffling like zombies towards their breakfast and work, after death some appear as malign spirits clinging to the ceiling glimpsed over Uxbal's shoulder. This threatening representation is in direct contradistinction to the very normal way the (ethnically European) spirits Uxbal communes with in his sideline as a medium are represented. They are usually shown seated or standing and with very neutral facial expressions. As a result of the way the Chinese workers are depicted in life and death, the effect is less one of sympathy but instead an evocation of codes of horror cinema. So, although Uxbal and the Senegalese immigrants, like Ekweme and Ige are humanised through their interactions with their families (Deveny 2012: 127), with the exception of Lili – who looks after Uxbal's children and notably has her own baby, Hai and the other Chinese characters are treated visually in such a way that they remain disconnected from the emotional core of the film.

Despite these problems in its representation of the Chinese gang masters and workers noted by Begin (2015) and also Deleyto and Lopez (2012), *Biutiful* extends the critique of neoliberalist practices from *Amores perros, 21 Grams* and *Babel* to the hidden sweatshop industries exploiting immigrants from the Global South. The deaths by gas inhalation of the Chinese workers, including Lili and her baby Li recall recent real-world incidents of industrial negligence where undocumented migrant workers have died.[20] A connected strand of this critique is the film's portrayal of the counterfeiting that goes on in these sweatshops. If the circulation of copyrighted goods is like knowledge 'organised in the major centres of [colonial] power' (Aléman, 2009: 263), the production of counterfeit copies of these goods (which may include films) we see taking place in *Biutiful* acts as a potential challenge to these power structures and the colonialist currents which regulate them. *Biutiful*, as partly the financial product of the Global North (and aware of the likelihood of its own probable future of being pirated), is perhaps doubly ironic in its depiction of this commerce (selling inferior copies of Western culture back to the West). How we read *Biutiful*'s ideological critique is dependent in part on its complex institutional position. Internationally financed (rather than just financed by US monies as has been suggested) and produced by a variety of corporations including US independent distributors (Focus Features International, Lionsgate and Roadside Attractions), European government bodies (the UK Film Council), a Mexican production company (Ménage Atroz), two Spanish production companies (Ikiru Films and Mod Producciones), Spanish and Catalan television companies (Televisión Española [TVE] and Televisió de Catalunya) and officially a Spain-Mexico co-production, *Biutiful* is considered Mexican enough to be put forward by Mexico's official film body IMCINE as its entry to the 2010 Academy Awards and nominated for Best Foreign Film.[21] At the same time it is considered American enough to be nominated for non-foreign language awards such as Best Actor (Bardem) even though it is a Spanish-language film. *Biutiful* also sits between the newer wave of independent (from state funding) Mexican cinema, contemporary Spanish filmmaking (in which Spanish television companies are the largest investors) and US independent production houses (Focus Features, Lionsgate and Roadside Attractions), some of which have shown particular interest in working with other Mexican filmmakers – see CANANA's deal with Focus Features detailed in the Introduction to the Mexican industry. Although the US continues to be a part of the equation of Iñárritu's deterritorialised filmmaking, the position and text of *Biutiful* triangulated between Mexico, Spain and the US counters any notion of a simple 'progression' in his career trajectory from Mexico to an institutionalised Hollywood, and similarly counters the neocolonialist sympathies that some have argued inevitably results from such an institutionalised position (Shaw 2011: 11).

Biutiful, like Iñárritu's first three film projects, both participates in and criticises the processes of globalisation. A product of the stimulation provided by the 'free flow of films, talent and funding between the film industries in the United States, Europe and Latin America' (Alvaray 2011: 70), it also criticises the nefarious practices that result from the free trade and deregulated economies globalisation facilitates in a way that connects with Iñárritu's previous films. For instance, on a narrative level, *Biutiful* and *Babel* invest emotionally in characters marginalised by the global currents of capitalism and all its discontents; tourism and illegal immigration. Inequalities themselves are not viewed from a 'we are all the same' globalised perspective as some have argued (Shaw, others) but very firmly from a position of sympathy and identification with the residents of the Global South, who may be badly treated, deported and/or die at the hands of the authorities (*Biutiful* depicts the particularly brutal arrest of Ekweme and the other Senegalese street sellers). The stance Iñárritu takes against the results of neoliberal, free flowing commerce appears to be quite firmly rooted in the South – although this sometimes results in readings that are, as Ayala Blanco suggests, from the victimising perspectives of 'misery porn' (2014: 155).

This chapter has explored the coherencies between *Amores perros*, *21 Grams*, *Babel* and *Biutiful* and suggested that, despite the differing institutional 'systems' in which Iñárritu and his creative team function there is the idea of a transnationalised Mexican national cinema. This chapter has explored how the ideological and aesthetic consistencies between Iñárritu's films offer a model of transnational exchange seemingly approximating the stylistic traditions of US filmmaking but always from a peripheral position. Ultimately, reading *Biutiful* as a successful critique of the issues critiqued in *Amores perros*, *21 Grams* and *Babel* suggests that Iñárritu defies the belief of the peripheral filmmaker 'effaced' when they work in the US (Naficy 1996: 120). In the shift from the southern periphery to the north, there is no loss of the originary style or culture, but instead, in keeping with contemporary theories of transnational exchange, an actual invasion of (or flowing into) First World culture (Appadurai 1996).

Notes

1. In the article he laments how the 'increasing presence of Mexican filmmakers, scriptwriters, cinematographers and actors in the US and Europe' was 'symptomatic of the unmistakeable crisis in film production in Mexico' (2007). However, the critical position of Bonfíl and others is not shared by other commentators or by Mexico's official film body IMCINE, which put forward Iñárritu's *Biutiful* (2010), an internationally financed, Spanish-Mexican co-production, as Mexico's entry to the 2010 Academy Awards, where it was nominated for Best Foreign Film.

2. Iñárritu and Prieto discuss the use of different stocks on the DVD commentary of *Amores perros*. Prieto talks about the use of these same two stocks in *21 Grams* in an interview in *American Cinematographer* (Calhoun 2003).

3. Initially, the use of different stocks is the only way by which we can orient ourselves in the film's fragmented narrative. For example, a high-contrast scene of Cristina and Paul seeking out Jack and her saying 'I want to kill him,' is a scene we learn to read (even before players and dialogue gives us definite clues) as post-crash because high-contrast images predominate in these scenes. Similarly, the low-contrast shot of Cristina making cookies with her daughters, is a scene we learn to read as pre-crash because low-contrast images predominate in these sequences and for a short while in Paul's post-transplant life.

4. Emily Hind suggests that *Amores perros'* Hollywood style can be traced through its 'rapid pacing, stylish clothing, contemporary settings, naturalistic gore, [and] pop scoring.' She further suggests that *Amores perros* offers a positive treatment of North America and that its use of English language in dialogue (bizness, bróder), sound track ('Long Cool Woman' The Hollies), and décor reaffirm 'Mexicans' status as participatory members of the Americas in a cultural block' and also a '[d]esire to work on the other side of the border' (2004: 98, 95, 100n).

5. Hence in a film like *Election* (Alexander Payne, 1999) a seemingly insignificant action can have huge repercussions (Sconce 2002: 363). Mathew Broderick's character misses the bin when he insouciantly tosses a piece of trash. This evokes the ire of the caretaker. Later on in the film, the caretaker takes his revenge.

6. This kind of camera work became common in the late 1950s and early 1960s with the growth of *cinéma vérité* documentary (Jean Rouche, Maysle brothers, D. A. Pennebaker) when hand-held cameras first became widely available. Although these are techniques that originate in documentary filmmaking, in fiction film they can add an air of authenticity to mockumentaries like *The Blair Witch Project* (Daniel Myrick and Eduardo Sánchez 1999).

7. Although it is also worth pointing out how in the early 1990s, years before *Amores perros*, a series of female-directed films *Danzón* (María Novaro 1991), *Lola* (Novaro 1989) *Angel de fuego* (*Angel of Fire* Dana Rotberg 1992) and *Novia que te vea* (*Like a Bride* Guita Schyfter 1994) broke new ground in their focus on and identification with society's others including single mothers, prostitutes and transvestites (Haddu 2007: iv).

8. The biblical story explains how different languages came to be spoken on the earth. Man decided to build a tower so tall it would reach to heaven. On seeing this God decided to thwart the project by making man speak different languages and be thus unable to communicate or consequently work together on the project of building the tower (Genesis 11: 1–9).

9. Interestingly, and perhaps symptomatically of the Eurocentric position from which he writes, Kerr suggests that the reordered temporality of the narrative, 'functions to conceal the irresponsibility of Amelia in opting to take the two children in her charge to Mexico for her son's wedding' and similarly to conceal the irresponsibility of the boys for firing the gun (2010: 42).

10. Although at the same time this 'difficulty' and 'dirtiness' is something we as spectators experience as reflective of Susan and Richard's 'First World' perspective. That this is how they see Morocco is communicated particularly in their first scene in the film where they sit down to have lunch and Susan suspiciously throws away the ice in her and Richard's glasses and compulsively rubs sanitiser into her hands.

11. When, as the helicopter is about to take off, Richard offers his guide Anwar money as a thank you for his help, Anwar refuses to take it.

12. After the initial success of *Amores perros* the film's mostly Mexican creative team went on to work separately as individuals, rather than together, on Hollywood studio (and only occasionally Mexican) projects. In between *Amores perros* and *21 Grams* Prieto worked on *8 Mile* (Curtis Hanson 2002) *25th Hour* (Spike Lee 2002) and *Frida* (Julie Taymor 2002). Since *Amores perros* he has worked on numerous US projects including *Brokeback Mountain* (Ang Lee 2005), *Wall Street: Money Never Sleeps* (Oliver Stone 2010) and *We bought a Zoo* (Cameron Crowe 2011). Arriaga has also worked on US projects writing *The Three Burials of Melquiades Estrada* (Tommy Lee Jones 2006) and directing his first film *The Burning Plain* (2008).

13. This incorporation of successful directors has often taken place in waves, take for instance, the Austrian and German expressionist directors, Fritz Lang, Billy Wilder and others in the 1930s/40s, European new wave directors John Boorman, Miloš Forman, Michelangelo Antonioni and others in the 1960s, independent directors like Soderbergh and Robert Rodriguez in the 1990s. See Tierney (2011) for an analysis of Hollywood's co-opting of Emilio Fernández, Mexico's most famous classical director.

14. Vanessa and Ramiro depart with all the money Octavio has won. Evidently it is quickly spent when several days later Ramiro, in apparent need of more money, attempts to rob a bank and is shot dead by a policeman.

15. Diaryou Deff (Ige) was working 'illegally' in Spain as a hairdresser when she was cast in the film, and the production itself sought legal status for her. Similarly, Chiekh N (Ekweme) had worked as a street seller.

16. Gaudi's famous unfinished cathedral La sagrada familia is glimpsed above the rooftops by Uxbal as he undergoes chemotherapy.

17. At one point Uxbal says 'mol ben' ('muy bien' 'very good') to Ana and on another he says to them 'anem' ('vamos', 'let's go').

18. Arriaga went on to write another film with disrupted chronology *The Three Burials of Melquiades Estrada*.

19. At the opening of the film, the shot cuts from Uxbal and Ana lying in bed talking, to Uxbal in a snowy wood. A young man walks through the snow, lights a cigarette, offers one to Uxbal and looking at a dead owl on the ground begins talking. 'Did you know, that when they die owls spit out a ball of feathers?' When the scene is replayed at the end we realise this is Uxbal's last conversation with Ana before he dies, and that the encounter with the father is a reworking of both of the personal effects of his father he has with him in the film (his lighter, a photograph of him in a snowy wood) and lines spoken by Mateo (about the owl). As such this conversation becomes a reminder of the son in the father and also, the suggestion that, just as Uxbal dreams of/can enjoy a reunion with his own father so will his own son share such a reunion with him.

20. In 2004, 21 Chinese migrant workers were drowned in Morecambe Bay, United Kingdom, when they were cut off by the incoming tide.

21. Phil Hoad points out how co-productions may be discounted by the American Academy who (rather than the nominating nation) decides whether a film is national 'enough' to merit carrying the flag for a particular country. This was the case with *Diarios de motocicleta* which was not perceived to have enough of a single nationality to receive a nomination. However, another Spain–Mexico co-production *El laberinto del fauno* (del Toro) was submitted to the Academy as a Mexican film and subsequently nominated as Best Foreign Film in 2007.

2. 'FROM HOLLYWOOD AND BACK': ALFONSO CUARÓN'S ADVENTURES IN GENRE

Alfonso Cuarón's first feature, the state funded *Sólo con tu pareja* (1991), has been cited as an early manifestation of a key genre of the neoliberal era of 1990s and the subsequent box office boom of 1999–2001 – the romantic comedy (MacLaird 2013a: 48; Sánchez Prado 2014: 63). Genre has continued to be a feature in all of Cuarón's post *Sólo con tu pareja* features, both in terms of his Mexican made and deterritorialised productions including; the studio/industry projects made as 'director for hire' in the United States and the United Kingdom – novel adaptations *A Little Princess* (1995), *Great Expectations* (1998) and *Harry Potter and the Prisoner of Azkaban* (2004) – and the auteurist projects made in Mexico and the United Kingdom – the privately funded *Y tu mamá también* (co-written with his brother Carlos 2001), the studio funded *Children of Men* (2006) and *Gravity* (co-written with his son Jonás 2013).

It is perhaps the association with genre in his English language films that led the New York film critic J. Hoberman, in a blog post about *Gravity*, to call Cuarón 'nobody's idea of an auteur' (Hoberman 2013). Hoberman's comment is less a value judgement on Cuarón (who did after all go on to win the Oscar for Best Director for *Gravity* in 2014) and more a reflection on how traditional auteurist studies, as André Bazin's critique points out, tended not to consider genre directors true 'auteurs' because the 'standardisation' genre implies was considered inhibiting to 'the creation and development of film' as an art form (Ryall 1998: 327).

Subsequently, of course, in film studies, ideas changed so that genre and auteurism could usefully coexist in a system in which the former provided a useful 'framework' within which directors could express themselves (McArthur cited in Ryall 1998: 327). However, a residual mistrust of genre remains the norm in some film criticism and is evident in the way Cuarón's films are approached: certain discipline-related imperatives encourage scholars to ignore genre and mainstream filmmaking. For instance, in Latin American film studies, in which the theoretical perspectives of the 1960s and 1970s considered genres as culturally derivative of the Hollywood industry and complicit with its bourgeois ideologies (Colina and Díaz Torres 1972: 16), genre and mainstream filmmaking are incompatible with the idea of a Latin American or Mexican auteur as an autonomous artist. Latin American film scholarship has shifted away from this mistrust towards studying popular genres, with important work on melodrama in the 1990s (López 1991; 1993; Tierney 1997) and more recently, the romantic comedy and its rise to hegemonic status in post-political-transition Mexico (Misha MacLaird 2013a: 10; Sánchez Prado 2014: 69). Despite these shifts, some otherwise compelling accounts of *Y tu mamá también* and *Children of Men* from within Latin American film studies, or Romance Languages sideline or completely ignore the films' genre borrowings, malign (in the case of *Children of Men*) their origins in 'the multinational capitalist entertainment machine' (Amago 2010: 219) and privilege instead the realist and self-conscious aspects which more comfortably fit within traditional notions of the auteur: long takes, hand-held cameras, (Middents and Fernández 2013; Acevedo-Muñoz 2004; Baer and Long 2004) and thematic comparisons with T. S. Eliot's *The Waste Land* (1922) (Amago 2010: 217–218). There's a similar sidelining of genre in approaches to Cuarón rooted in English literature and Art History, where the focus is again on realist camera work (in *Children of Men*), the film's anti-neoconservative politics (Boyle 2009) and its metacinematic qualities (Ogrodnik 2014). Although these essays and one video essay speak very relevantly on significant aspects of these two films' style and connect them to their politics, they miss out on how genre perspective and a sense of the industrial contexts in which the films were made adds considerably to the understanding of the critiques these theorists identify.

It is the contention of this chapter that it is through the manipulation of genre that Cuarón expresses his political concerns both in terms of his Mexican made and deterritorialised projects. The chapter takes a cue from other studies of the use of Hollywood genres in Mexican cinema, which suggest that engaging with Hollywood genres doesn't necessarily imply complicity with any perceived ideological conservatism (Berg 2000: 4; López 2000a: 43).[1] It also takes a cue from studies of other significant players in Mexican cinema (Dolores Del Rio) who, like Cuarón, have gone to 'Hollywood', come 'back' to Mexico and subsequently departed for Hollywood again, forming a part of a transnationalised, yet still national Mexican cinema (López 1998: 7). It also departs from the understanding that Hollywood genre films themselves can equally be the sponsor of ideological dissonance and indeed have been so at key moments in its history (Wood 2003: xxxv).[2] Furthermore, this chapter emphasises how genre-based analysis of Mexican cinema that takes into account the Hollywood vector in Cuarón's career produces readings that emphasise (trans) national cultural invention and innovation rather than simple homogenisation and imitation (Tierney 2007: 139–140, 112–118; López 1998).

Rather than consider the entirety of Cuarón's oeuvre (as a straightforward aueurist analysis might do) this chapter looks at Cuarón's avowedly personal productions (*Sólo con tu pareja, Y tu mamá también* and *Children of Men*) as well as the differing commercial imperatives and textual implications of the filmmaking venues in which these films were made. This chapter takes into consideration the 1990s state-patronised industrial filmmaking in *Sólo con tu pareja*, the post-industrial, privately financed and market-oriented filmmaking of the late 1990s in *Y tu mamá también* and the Hollywood studio-sponsored auteurist filmmaking of *Children of Men. Gravity* is analysed in the Epilogue.

The chapter begins by analysing Cuarón's first feature *Sólo con tu pareja* with respect to how it defines the sexy *comedia/comedia light/*romantic comedy genre. It goes on to look at *Y tu mamá también* (2001) exploring how the film adopts and adapts two Hollywood genres – the road movie and the teen or youth movie – to the moment of Mexico's political and social transition. Finally, it explores *Children of Men* analysing how it subverts the narrative and textual conventions of the Hollywood disaster film and critiques the ideologies which underpin the genre's presentation of disaster and destruction. In the chapter's genre-oriented analysis of *Y tu mamá también* and *Children of Men*, the focus will be on Cuarón's contestatory use of genre as a marker of both auteurist practice and as a key commercial strategy.

SÓLO CON TU PAREJA

Cuarón's first feature, *Sólo con tu pareja* was financed by IMCINE along with several other projects by other mainly young directors which were designed to sell a certain image of Mexico to the world in the lead up to the signing of the North American Free Trade Agreement. As Sergio de la Mora points out, *Sólo con tu pareja,* together with *Como agua para chocolate* (Alfonso Arau 1992) *Cronos,* (del Toro 1993), *Danzón* (María Novaro 1991) and other films were 'an integral component of government diplomacy' and '[were] particularly important to both the Salinas de Gortari administration and his beleaguered party, the PRI' (2006: 136). Breaking from the 'official discourses on [Mexico's] Revolution' in which both the PRI and state-funded cultural nationalism had been heavily invested, these films presented Mexico 'as a young, modern, changing, affluent and attractive place to invest' (de la Mora 2006: 144). As one of these films, characterised as a break with the past, *Sólo con tu pareja* becomes a transition film broaching both the 'new thematic territory' of 'sexuality among upper middle-class couples' whilst at the same time targeting this same demographic as an audience (MacLaird 2013a: 48). *Sólo con tu pareja* is an early example of a new genre key to the emergence of Mexican cinema's new audience of the mid-1990s; identified by Francisco Sánchez as the '*comedia light*' (2002: 227) and by others as the sexy *comedia*. Like the later, and, according to Sánchez, most emblematic film of the genre *Sexo, pudor y lágrimas*, *Sólo con tu pareja*'s urban setting (Mexico City), its thirty something middle class characters – protagonist Tomás Tomás (Daniel Giménez Cacho) and his neighbours Mateo Mateos (Luis de Icaza) and Clarisa (Claudia Ramírez) – dramatic premise (the romantic and/or sexual proclivities of its characters) and its 'light tone' 'superficiality', and 'quick pace' are key features of the genre (Sánchez 2002: 229).

Tomás is an advertising executive who seduces women wherever and whenever he can (at a wedding, at the supermarket, whilst out jogging). He is halted in his philandering tracks by Silvia (Dobrina Liubomirova) an unsatisfied sexual conquest who falsifies some test results, wrongly convincing him he is HIV positive. Falling in love with his air-stewardess neighbour Clarisa, who is also despairing because she has been cheated on by her pilot partner, they decide to commit suicide together by jumping from the Torre Latinoamericana. The pair are eventually saved by the arrival of Silvia, Mateo and the pilot who, after a comedic race through Mexico City and up the stairs of the Torre inform Tomás that the HIV diagnosis was nothing but a cruel joke.

As the location of Tomás and Clarisa's planned suicide suggests, *Sólo con tu pareja* embodies the sexy *comedia's* simultaneous showcasing of, and ironic distancing from, the symbols of Mexican nationalism and modernity (Sánchez 2002: 229; Sánchez Prado 2014: 72). The Torre Latinoamericana (which is significantly viewed in other government films of the pre-NAFTA cycle such as *Danzón*) is both showcased through spectacular aerial photography and debased through equally comedic visual treatment. Before Tomás and Clarisa make love on it her underwear flutters down from its heights to the floor below. Other symbols of modernity are also made fun of throughout the film. A newspaper story of a French poodle mistakenly cooked to death in a microwave oven by its 'gringa' owner, is repeated several times and a comic paging service relays Tomás' increasingly absurd suicide messages to his doctor friend Mateo. In keeping with the strategic aims of its pre-NAFTA government funding, (to break with the cultural nationalism of the past) *Sólo con tu pareja* as MacLaird argues, makes visible economic progress amongst the middle class, but also maintains a 'certain level of nationalism' (2013a: 49).

Like later examples of the *comedia* light/romantic comedy genre, *Sólo con tu pareja*'s limits its nationalism, bracketing folkloric Mexico and various national icons away from the narrative and featuring them instead in several parodic interludes. In *Sólo con tu pareja* these interludes are as much about the representation and framing of the nation as they are straightforward markers of nationalism. The first of these interludes take place five minutes into the film in the form of a television advertisement for 'Chiles Jalapeños Caseros Gómez' (Gómez Home-Style Jalapeños) the slogan for which Tomás is desperately working on. The advert is initially presented without an establishing shot so that the sudden change from Tomás' apartment to a beach scene immediately appears as 'strange' rather than naturalised within the *mise-en-scène*. Indigenous characters catch a big fish and present it to Aztec Emperor Moctezuma. Spanish Conquistador Hernán Cortés presents him with a tin of jalapeños which are the product of the non-Mexican sounding Hamson-Trausmussen (Haddu, 2007: 200). The scenario and the heightened advertising discourse (Tomás, reading from advertising copy calls the jalapeños 'our national pride') parodies both the colonial exploitation of Mexico in the past, and the potential future neocolonial exploitation envisaged by the implementation of NAFTA, and undercuts the epic portrayal of Mexico's history.

Subsequent incidences of Mexican folklore, patrimony or history, are similarly debased or made strange. In one, Tomás tries to discreetly sneak along a window ledge between two apartments and two women. His towel falls leaving him naked just as a mariachi band strikes up on the street below and a young serenader sings 'Despierta' a bolero made famous by the 1940s and 1950s star Pedro Infante. Tomás is able to duck into a window without being spotted by one of his conquests, and a neighbouring couple (Clarisa and her pilot boyfriend) who also lean out the window to listen. In other sequences, Mexico is presented through a tourist's perspective. An early visit to the Torre Latinoamericana is presented as something to be endured (by Tomás) for the purposes of entertaining Japanese doctors in the city for a conference. Similarly, Plaza Garibaldi the famous meeting ground for Mexico City's mariachis is another site for the Japanese doctors, presented in a distanced fashion through the use of classical music and a gaudy mural which features on a wall behind the action. National patrimony is thus most commonly presented throughout *Sólo con tu pareja* as a commodity to be packaged and sold, either back to Mexico via Europe as with the German produced jalapeños, or to the Japanese doctors.

In addition to its bracketing of national patrimony and national figures, *Sólo con tu pareja* gives few initial visual clues that the action is even taking place in Mexico (Long 2006: 8). The film opens on a high-ceilinged, wooden-floored apartment in a nineteenth-century French building and any street views or geographical landmarks are delayed until half an hour into the film. This rarefied presentation of a stylised Mexico City (and the absence of a 'realist' sense of city space) points to the influence of the Europeanised art-house sex comedy, recalling similarly stylised representations of Madrid in the early films of

Spanish director Pedro Almodóvar (*Mujeres al borde de un ataque de nervios/ Women on the verge of a nervous breakdown* 1988) (Haddu 2007: 195).[3] *Sólo con tu pareja* also casts outwards in narrative nods towards transnationality (Sánchez Prado 2014: 72). Clarisa is significantly an air stewardess who although flying with national airline AeroMexico and within national airspace at one point practices her safety drill accompanied by an English language safety announcement.

Fittingly, for a film designed to highlight Mexican film talent abroad *Sólo con tu pareja*'s premiere took place at the Toronto Film Festival in 1992. It was only shown in Mexico two years later where it was a box office success. According to Cuarón, the Mexican Government had initially shelved the film after its completion (Durbin 2002: 4). That *Sólo con tu pareja* was initially shelved by the Government after its production suggests that like del Toro's *Cronos*, funded in the same cycle of pre-NAFTAism, it 'ran counter to the preferred, nationalist, realist, auteurist mould' usually favoured with Government patronage (Tierney, Davies, Shaw 2014: 1). Cuarón figures his subsequent transition, after *Sólo con tu pareja*'s debut at Toronto, to work in Hollywood as inevitable:

> I ended up in Hollywood not because I wanted to; I ended up in Hollywood because I didn't have any choice. When I did [*Sólo con tu pareja*] I burned my bridges with the government, and I knew that if I were going to go back, the way of doing films in Mexico or the ways *I* knew of doing films in Mexico would have to change. Most films had a big percentage in terms of input from the government; my first film had 40 per cent. (Wood 2006: 41)

Cuarón's account reveals the extent of Government control and patronage within Mexico's film industry in the early 1990s (Wood 2006: 41–42). By talking about a necessary 'change' in how films were made in Mexico, Cuarón's account describes the subsequent dismantling of the Government-owned or supported filmmaking infrastructure and shift to private, commercially-oriented, arty and innovative filmmaking that coincided with Mexico's political transition, which arguably provided the preconditions for his return (Sánchez Prado 2014: 185)

Y tu mamá también: Genre and Gender Bending

Almost ten years later and after an extended sojourn in Hollywood, making *A Little Princess* and *Great Expectations*, Cuarón returned to Mexico and made *Y tu mamá también*. *Y tu mamá también* premiered at Cannes in 2001. But in difference to *Sólo con tu pareja* this festival exposure was not as a result of a government programme designed to showcase Mexican culture, but a deliberate commercial strategy on the part of its private production company Anhelo (backed by Mexican billionaire Carlos Slim), to harness the cultural prestige of the film festival circuit to commercially launch the film globally. Cuarón's return to Mexico was a return to a changed cinematic landscape where thanks to now common-place commercial strategies like sending the film to Cannes, the deliberate targeting of a majority, young and middle class audience and the inclusion of a marketed soundtrack, the film was extraordinarily successful breaking box office records in Mexico and the US for a foreign language film.[4] Another of Cuarón's commercial strategies was the (re)use of the successful romantic comedy genre – a genre which he was partly responsible for engendering with *Sólo con tu pareja* (MacLaird 2013a: 153). In the intervening period from the mid- to late 1990s the genre had been highly successful including films like *Cilantro y perejil/Recipes to Stay Together* (Rafael Montero 1998) and *Sexo, pudor y lágrimas*. In *Y tu mamá también*, Cuarón heightens the genre's conventions, exaggerating its critical elements and its seeming bracketing/engagement with topics of nationalism. Most significantly, *Y tu mamá también*'s engagement with Mexico and Mexico City is tellingly less stylised and abstracted and more socio-politically informed in genre and gender terms than *Sólo con tu pareja* and the other highly successful manifestations of the genre.

Y tu mamá también, together with *Amores perros* and *Sexo, pudor y lágrimas* was produced in a period of political change. Made and set in the run up to the 2000 elections where Vicente Fox's rightist PAN party, which campaigned on a message of change, triumphed, *Y tu mamá también* marked the end of the PRI's seventy-one-year rule of Mexico, and can be interpreted as a self-conscious reflection on the legacies of PRI ideology. Ignacio Sánchez Prado also suggests it represents the left-oriented view of the Mexican intelligentsia with close ties to the Partido de la Revolución Democrática (PRD) which took power in Mexico City in 2000 when Manuel López Obrador was elected mayor (Sánchez Prado 2014: 186).

Alternatively referred to as a *comedia light* and a romantic comedy, *Y tu mamá también* is firmly rooted in the prevailing (post) industrial trends in Mexican filmmaking (MacLaird 2010: 48; Sánchez 2002: 230) but it also extends beyond Mexican traditions with an investment in other genres and modes which to date have received scant critical attention. *Y tu mamá también* has generated an extraordinary amount of sometimes contradictory scholarship focusing on its myriad aspects including; national identity and its 'tourist vision' (Finnegan 2007), the 'tourist vision' as an inability to represent the national (Sánchez Prado 2014: 188); its connection with global trends (Baer and Long 2004); discussions of Mexican sovereignty (Saldaña-Portillo 2005); a focus on Mexico's 'other' and the provinces (Noble 2005: 123, 140–141);

'economic and cultural exchange between Latin American and Europe' (Smith 2003a) and alternately progressive and traditional representations of sexuality, gender and class (Amaya and Blair 2008 Acevedo-Muñoz 2004). This work is almost always concerned in some way with Y *tu mamá también*'s (differently conceived) globalisation of style (Acevedo-Muñoz 2004: 39, 40, 42; Baer and Long 2004: 150). But there has been little exploration of what globalisation actually means in the film in relation to genre. Whilst some scholarship offers (limited) exploration of the film's engagement with the Hollywood genre of the road movie (de la Garza 2009; Noble 2005; Smith 2002; Acevedo-Muñoz 2004: 43, 44), what's missing in the very excellent work on Y *tu mamá también* is a sustained analysis of the road movie and the other Hollywood genre with which the film most directly engages – the teen movie or youth film – which, this chapter suggests, is also key to understanding its exploration of Mexico's social and political reality.

Despite Y *tu mamá también*'s showcasing of 'fart jokes, poolside masturbation, and drug-enhanced summer escapades' and the basic narrative premise 'of two playful yet self-absorbed best friends [...] as they wrap up their blissful high school life' (MacLaird 2010: 47), the 'teen' or 'youth film', the genre in which these kinds of (or similar) features predominate, has not yet received significant scholarly attention.[5] This absence of the teen movie in Y *tu mamá*'s critical bibliography is despite Cuarón's own description of the film in these precise terms (qtd in Wood 2006: 95), and Mexican critic Leonardo García Tsao's (disparaging) likening of it to two contemporaneous Hollywood teen movies; a 'south of the border *Beavis & Butthead* [Mike Judge 1996]' (García Tsao 2001) and a 'Latin *Dude, Where's my Car?* [Danny Leiner 2000]' (García Tsao qtd in Brooks 2002). It is the contention of this chapter that analysis of Y *tu mamá también* from the perspective of the genres – the road movie and the teen movie or youth film – from which it takes its lead significantly enriches the understanding of its political and critical project.

On a purely national economic level, Cuarón's espousal of the teen movie genre in Y *tu mamá también* is a market driven decision simply designed to make the film appeal to Mexico's predominantly young and affluent new multiplex audience[6] (MacLaird 2013a: 28, 45–49). The resurgence of the Hollywood teen movie in the 1980s represented a similar response to the new multiplex audience in the United States (Shary 2005: 54).[7] Recourse to the teen movie genre also further explains Y *tu mamá también*'s 'cross-over appeal with US and other overseas audiences' – teen movie *American Pie* (Paul Weitz 1999) was one of the top twenty grossing films of the previous year[8] and Cuarón cites the Hollywood film as a reference in a 2002 interview. On a more political and textual level, the espousal of the teen movie also appears driven by national political conditions. The choice of the teen movie genre makes sense in the context of what might have appeared then to be Mexico's incipient democratic era. Cuarón even refers to *Y tu mamá también* as being 'about [...] a teenage country trying to find its identity as a grown up nation' (Lawrenson 2002).

Y tu mamá también borrows from the conventions of the teen movie and road movie to narrate the story of two 'stoner' friends Julio (Gael García Bernal) and Tenoch (Diego Luna) and their road trip to the Pacific coast during which they hope to impress and seduce the Spanish wife of Tenoch's cousin, Luisa (Maribel Verdú). In its visual style, the film most noticeably borrows from the road movie with a predominance of wide shots, sweeping crane shots, and driving sequences which are designed to privilege the terrain through which the boys and Luisa journey, and at the same time to emphasise the boys' sense of insouciant mastery over the land. Simultaneously, however, these genre conventions are evoked in order that their racial and gender associations (white male territorial mastery as in the road movie's key antecedent the Western) are questioned and undermined (Roberts 1997: 45). During Julio, Tenoch and Luisa's journey, from Mexico City through the underdeveloped states of Oaxaca and Puebla, out the window of their car we see *indígenas* and *campesinos* unfairly treated by the authorities. On at least three occasions we see 'darker Mexicans' pulled over at the side of the road being searched at gunpoint for drugs while Julio, Tenoch and Luisa, who are carrying and consuming drugs, drive past. The rough passage of these subaltern figures in *Y tu mamá también* contrasts with the relative ease with which Julio, Tenoch and Luisa pass through Mexico. These and other glimpses of (the unfair treatment of) Mexico's indigenous and mestizo population invite a critical conclusion regarding the persistence of social abuses and poverty despite the populist and neoliberal ideology of the post-Revolutionary PRI in the 1990s.

Relatedly, *Y tu mamá también* nationalises the masculinist associations of the road movie (and the Western) through implicit reference to one of the males of Mexico's institutionalised revolutionary discourse; Julio's surname (Zapata) is significantly the same as that of one of Mexico's revolutionary heroes (Emiliano Zapata), a figure who actualises the figuration of the Mexican male as virile macho (O'Malley 1986: 3).[9] But Cuarón's evocation of these simultaneously national and transnational genre and gender associations is set up only to be undercut by the narrative. First, Julio has no interest in the movement derived from the historical individual with whom he shares a name, though his sister, the omniscient narrator (Giménez Cacho who played Tomás Tomás in *Sólo con tu pareja*) suggests, does, and will depart once the boys have returned with the car to bring supplies (we presume) to the Zapatistas in Chiapas:

> His sister, Manuela, was a Political Science major, at the National University of Mexico, and a left-wing activist. After a difficult negotiation, Julio managed to borrow the car for five days. Then she would get it for

the following three weeks so she and her friends could go to Chiapas to deliver food, clothing, and medicine.

Through the narrator's gesture towards the EZLN (Ejército Zapatista de Liberación Nacional/Zapatista Army of National Liberation), the revolutionary leftist group whose 1994 uprising challenged the legitimacy of the government and its neoliberal capitalist practices in the wake of the signing of NAFTA, the film thematises both Mexico's Revolution and the notion of indigenous self-determination. Zapata's notion of 'Tierra y Libertad' ('Land and Freedom') resonates throughout *Y tu mamá también*'s road trip through Mexico's neglected provinces, despite and, indeed, because of its city-dwelling characters' apoliticism. Connectedly, the film undermines the ideological absolutes of the road movie in its classic phase (though, as Ina Rae Hark points out, by the 1980s and 1990s even Hollywood was questioning the road movie and its assumption of hegemonic masculinity) and also the nationalist associations of virility and masculinity when Luisa's comments that rather than sleep with each other's girlfriends, what the boys really want to do is 'f**k each other' (Hark 1997: 206).

Y tu mamá también, in addition to masturbation, fart jokes and drug taking, also borrows from teen movie conventions and particularly the set pieces of *American Pie*. These include: awkward sexual interludes (the opening copulations of both Julio and Tenoch with their girlfriends, both boys' premature ejaculation during sex with Luisa), a locker room sequence (at Tenoch's father's country club), and (an attempt at) spying on undressing women (Luisa). In *American Pie* these set pieces are, in keeping with the film and the genre's ideological thrust, designed to emphasise the boys' late adolescent (hetero)sexuality and at the same time to posit a carefree world with a lack of 'real' problems. But in *Y tu mamá también*, as with the road movie, these teen movie conventions are evoked in order that their class and gender associations (white, affluent middle class families, heterosexual 'coming of age' stories) may be questioned and undermined in the context of Mexico's revolutionary philosophy.

In accordance with the US ideology of its own 'classless' society, class is usually invisible and rarely an issue in Hollywood teen movies, particularly those of the late 1990s (*American Pie*) with which *Y tu mamá también* directly engages. If any class conflict exists, as it does between Andie (Molly Ringwald) and Blane (Andrew Macarthy) in *Pretty in Pink* (Howard Deutch 1986), it is neatly resolved by the film's conclusion (Shary 2005: 71). In *Y tu mamá también* Cuarón counters this teen movie convention by making visible the workings of class in contemporary Mexico, not just between a subaltern rural class and a metropolitan elite but also within the country's (relatively) privileged classes. From early on in the film, and before the protagonists are even introduced, class (and consequently class difference) is made visible. The omniscient narrator's first intervention in the film relates the professions of the protagonists' girlfriends' parents, and therefore establishes their class identity. In the transition between Tenoch and his girlfriend having sex in her home to Julio sitting on the sofa in his girlfriend's house we hear:

> *Ana's mother, a French divorcee, taught at the Learning Institute for Foreigners. She did not object to Tenoch sleeping with her daughter. For Julio it was different. He could stay with Cecilia only until dinner and had to come back in the morning for the trip to the airport. Cecilia's father, a paediatrician specialising in allergies, thought his daughter's relationship with Julio had gone too far. Her mother, a Lacanian psychologist, saw it differently. She believed their relationship was innocent.*

Tenoch and Julio's class status (upper class/political elite and lower middle class respectively) are similarly established in later narrator interventions about the professions of their parents. We learn that Tenoch is the child of 'a Harvard-trained economist and Secretary of State' and a 'housewife who spends her time at various spiritual workshops', and that Julio is the son of a 'secretary who has worked all her life in a large corporation' and a father 'he has not seen since he was five.' These narrator interventions are spoken over shots of their (hugely different in size and capital base) respective homes. Later, and significantly at the end of their pronouncement of the 'charolastra' manifesto which supposedly brings them together, the narrator speaks about the awkwardness class difference creates for the boys when at each other's homes (Acevedo-Muñoz 2004: 9–10). The narrator tells us that Tenoch lifts the lid of Julio's toilet with his foot (to avoid touching it) and Julio lights a match after using Tenoch's bathroom (to avoid leaving a smell). After this initial investment in the boys' class difference, and their unspoken awareness of it, the fight between them (when it emerges they have both slept with each other's girlfriends) takes place around class- (and in the case of Tenoch race-) based insults. While Julio calls Tenoch 'Pirrurri de mierda' ('a fucking petit bourgeois'), Tenoch calls Julio 'pinche nacote.' The word *nacote* (or big '*naco*'), is in fact a racial slur against anyone who is *indígena* or *mestizo*, although the English subtitles miss out on this meaning by translating Tenoch's insult as 'white trash.' For Tenoch, Julio is symbolically darkened by his lower economic class.

At the end of *American Pie*, after the climactic prom night, normative values of heterosexuality and male friendship are reaffirmed. The boys have all achieved the goal of losing their virginities established at the beginning of the film and in further keeping with conservative ideology, have achieved it within heterosexual and sometimes monogamous relationships.[10] The last scene of the film places the four protagonists together appropriately over a hamburger. Raising a toast to their future, Finch (Eddie Kaye Thomas) says 'After this everything is going to be different' and then they all say 'To the next step.' *American Pie*'s ending projects forward into the boys' college lives (and the sequel *American Pie 2* [J. B. Rodgers 2001]), the infinite possibilities of American society and on-going friendship between the boys.

In contrast, at the end of *Y tu mamá también* and after a similarly climactic night there is no such affirmative and normative closure. After having had sex with each other, confirming Luisa's earlier comment, the boys are awkward and embarrassed and get ready to leave the coast to go back to the city. The shot cuts to what is their subsequent and final meeting. In a static, long take of a busy traffic intersection in Mexico City, cars and mounted police pass by. Two figures, not instantly recognisable as Julio and Tenoch, cross from opposite sides of the intersection and bump into each other (Figure 10).

Over the scene the film's omniscient narrator informs us of the following:

> *After returning from Europe, Cecilia and Ana broke up with Tenoch and Julio. Two months later, Tenoch started dating his neighbour. Nine months later, Julio started dating a girl from his French class. Julio and Tenoch stopped seeing each other. The following summer, the ruling party lost the presidential election for the first time in 71 years. Julio ran into Tenoch on the way to the dentist. Going for a cup of coffee was easier than making excuses to avoid it.*

The commentary ties together the personal and the political; the simultaneous endings of the boys' friendship and their relationships with their girlfriends and their chance encounter on the street are embedded with and appended to the end of the PRI's extended regime. Unlike the friendly burger restaurant

Figure 10   *Y tu mamá también* (Alfonso Cuarón 2001)

Figure 11   *Y tu mamá también* (Alfonso Cuarón 2001)

in *American Pie* Tenoch and Julio meet in a sterile chain restaurant, a static two-shot emphasising the awkwardness of the reunion as they sit across from each other (Figure 11).

And rather than cast forward into an optimistic future, in the way *American Pie* does, the last moments of the film predict a situation of continued class stratification in which Tenoch and Julio will go to colleges that reflect their socio-economic statuses (Tenoch to the elite university and Julio to the public metropolitan university) and, as the voice-over states, will 'never meet again':

> *Luisa spent her last four days in the hospital in Santa Maria Colotepec. At her request, Chuy and Mabel never mentioned her adventure with Julio and Tenoch. She gave Lucero the little stuffed mouse named Luisa. ... Tenoch excused himself. His girlfriend was waiting for him at the movies. Julio insisted on paying the check. They will never meet again.*

The voice-over's ending of *Y tu mamá también* obtains its political charge from the simultaneous evocation and inversion of teen movie conventions: *American Pie*'s casting into a hopeful future becomes in *Y tu mamá también* a projection into a dismal present of Luisa's death from cancer and Tenoch and Julio's permanent estrangement. The voice-over and its revelation of events the narrative has not revealed (the giving of the stuffed mouse to Lucero) is a part of this inversion.

Like a lot of other world cinema criticism, analyses of *Y tu mamá también* focus on the film's 'smart' and 'politically correct' elements and ignore its 'popular genre' elements (Andrew 2006: 23; Sánchez Prado 2014: 188–190).

In these analyses the 'Godardian' voice-over and long take cinematography are separated out as the explicitly political strategies of the film while its genre features, the teen and road movie, are deemed 'apolitical' (Saldaña-Portillo 2005: 752; Lawrenson 2002). Admittedly, the voice-over is responsible for voicing the realities of Mexico's unjust political and social system including the inequities of global capitalism (which, we learn, will permanently dislocate Chuy Carranza from the beach he and his family have fished from for generations), the structural inadequacies of Mexico City's planning and its fatal consequences for the city's economically disadvantaged (which we learn are responsible for the death of Marcelino Escutía who dies crossing a busy street because of a footbridge '2km out of his way'), and the exploitation of its indigenous population (which, we learn means child workers like Tenoch's nanny Leodegaria leaving their villages to mind the children of the wealthy). The voice-over is also, by Cuarón's own admission, a Godardian device, with his use of it deliberately evoking the avant-garde French director's *Masculin Féminin* (1966) and *Bande à part/Band of Outsiders* (1964) (Lawrenson 2002). Similarly, long take cinematography and often hand-held camera work, or what Ernesto Acevedo-Muñoz calls the film's 'wandering eye' (2004: 43) is responsible for drawing out the political critique in the film; emphasising the gap between the perspectives of its metropolitan characters and that of the film itself. For example, after Julio and Tenoch drive by the body of Escutía, the camera pans through the side windows of their car, continuing to focus on the migrant worker's body even though the boys are no longer looking. The camera's focus is on the 'other' Mexico, which is poor, mestizo and indigenous and, unlike Julio and Tenoch, not protected by class and racial privilege. There are numerous other occasions where the camera tracks away from the protagonists to follow in a single take the subaltern characters as they move across the frame; a waitress carrying trays of food to the bodyguards and drivers at Tenoch's cousin's upper-class wedding, an indigenous neighbour calling on her friends living and cooking in the backroom of a restaurant where Tenoch, Julio and Luisa are eating. The long take, like the voice-over interventions, ruptures the film's (bourgeois) classical narrative bubble by tracking away from the central story to focus on this 'other' Mexico. And by calling attention to the 'other' Mexico ignored in 'the materialistic consumer world of other romantic comedies' (MacLaird 2013a: 58), like *Sexo, pudor y lágrimas*,[11] the long take and voice-over interventions also rupture the façade of neoliberal ideology of post-Revolutionary PRI in the 1990s which advocated social justice and equal rights.

Although the critical voice-over, long take and hand-held cinematography undoubtedly contribute to the political project of *Y tu mamá también*, separating them out from the supposedly apolitical teen and road movie genre elements actually does considerable disservice to the political potential and critical features of the genre film as used and subverted by Cuarón. Teen films like *Ferris Bueller's Day Off* (John Hughes 1986) show a similarity of plot and sensibility to *Y tu mamá también*. *Ferris Bueller* also involves two guys and a girl taking time off for a (day) trip and shows a modernist self-awareness with respect to issues of class and gender; although it's an apolitical Ferris (Matthew Broderick) himself (rather than a non-diegetic narrator) who is turning to camera to give the dispassionate voice-over about class, the importance of getting into a good college, and the uselessness of a test on European socialism. Additionally, contemporaneously with *Y tu mamá también* the teen movie was experiencing a particularly self-conscious turn with a multiplicity of self-reflexive films that voice knowledge of and play with the genre's and subgenre's conventions (the *Scream* trilogy [Wes Craven 1996, 1997, 2000], *Not Another Teen Movie* [Joel Gallen 2001] (Dixon 2000: 126). In addition, the use of teen movie conventions in *Y tu mamá también* (particularly the 'care-free' nature of teenagers' lives) elucidates socio-political conditions in contemporary Mexico; the worrying apoliticism of Mexico's privileged youth in the face of social inequality and police brutality is itself a political element.[12] In this respect, the use of the teen movie is not just a commercial strategy but also a textual element used to highlight political aspects of the narrative.

The strategy throughout *Y tu mamá también* is not a separating out of (teen and road movie) narrative from (long take- and voice-over-led) class and racial politics but a scrambling of the personal (including the road and teen movie narratives) with the political. Realist camera work, in the form of long takes and hand-held mobility, plays a large part in both the revelation of political meaning but also in forwarding teen movie conventions. For example, in one long take the camera pans and tracks away from Julio and Tenoch dancing at a party, to Saba in another room experiencing (as the voice-over informs us) 'group sex for the first time.' In *Y tu mamá también* we see the road movie and the teen movie used both commercially and politically, adapted and adopted to the needs and contemporary social concerns of Mexico in cultural and political transition.

CHILDREN OF MEN: COUNTERING THE AESTHETICS AND IDEOLOGIES OF DISASTER MOVIES

After *Y tu mamá también* and in the context of mainstream genre filmmaking, Cuarón's subsequent project, as 'director for hire' of an already successful children/teen franchise appears to be a very rational progression. Cuarón's *Harry Potter and the Prisoner of Azkaban* (2004) was another successful instalment of the Harry Potter series, grossing $796 million for Warner Bros.[13] Cuarón's next film *Children of Men* was a hybrid project, funded by one of the major studios (Universal) but produced independently in the UK (by Hit and Run and Strike). Co-written by Cuarón with Tim Sexton, the film was adapted from the 1992 novel of the same name by P. D. James.

Children of Men is set in 2027. It presents a dystopic future United Kingdom which, like the rest of the world, is suffering from a nineteen-year-long crisis of infertility and the social, economic and political chaos which has resulted from this crisis. In the face of environmental degradation and dwindling resources, the UK has become a fascist state, violently guarding its borders against the illegal immigrants (Fugees) who flock there and aiming to suppress the rebel group (the Fishes) who fight for Fugee rights. Adverts on buses, televisions and other ubiquitous screens, encourage inhabitants to report illegal immigrants and also advertise the Government-provided suicide kits (Quietus) which encourage the aging population to self-euthanise. The pavements are lined with uncollected rubbish and cages which serve as temporary prisons for captured Fugees menaced by fascistic police and snarling dogs. Theo (Clive Owen), a disillusioned former activist is given the mission of helping the Fugee Kee (Claire-Hope Ashitey) on a treacherous journey through a hostile UK to its coastal border by Julian (Julianne Moore) his former partner who is now the leader of the Fishes.

Children of Men has generated a smaller bibliography than *Y tu mamá también*. Criticism tends to approach the film in ways that emphasise its art cinema poetics and politics including: its self-conscious realist camera work/narration (Ogrodnik 2014), its use of the long take (Udden 2009), its contestation of neoliberal ideologies (Boyle 2009), and how its realist camera work enacts this political critique (Amago 2010). But there has been little engagement of how the film's politics relate to the question of its genre. Some of this scholarship at least acknowledges *Children of Men* in genre terms calling it a 'dystopian science fiction film' (Amago 2010: 213; Boyle 2009: 1), or a 'science fiction blockbuster' (Ogrodnik 2014). However, in the rush to posit this film as a '[non] traditional action [or science fiction] picture' (Udden 2009: 30) and locate its contestatory aesthetics and politics elsewhere than genre and in a number of high art, philosophical and theoretical texts (Jameson 1986, *The Waste Land*[14]), scholarship on *Children of Men* tends to disavow the film's status as a product of (niche-marketed) Hollywood and the extent to which it engages with the norms and conventions of the Hollywood disaster film. What is missing therefore is an analysis of how the film's politics are related to its status as a genre film.

Like *Y tu mamá también*, *Children of Men* both conforms to and frustrates a number of expectations of the Hollywood genre it most resembles. In its narrative premise, it borrows from the contemporary disaster film in which natural or man-made disasters including epidemics, (*Blindness* [Meirelles 2008], *Contagion* [Steven Soderbergh 2011]), aliens (*Independence Day*

[Roland Emmerich 1996], *War of the Worlds* [Stephen Spielberg 2005], *Mars Attacks* [Tim Burton 1996]) and climate change (*The Day After Tomorrow* [Emmerich 2004], *2012* [Emmerich 2009]) threaten the future of the human race. Additionally, it uses the disaster genre's mixture of action adventure sequences (chases) and the science-fiction genre's end-of-time disaster scenarios to shape its plot. Like many disaster movie heroes, *Children of Men*'s Theo is dishevelled, heavy drinking and cynical about the mission he has been given. He appears, like Tom Cruise's Ray in *War of the Worlds* or John Cusack's Jackson in *2012* ripe for the possibilities of rebirth offered by the disaster plot's 'ritualised legitimation of strong male leadership' (Keane 2001: 27). Similarly, and also following the conventions of the disaster movie, the film anticipates a final reunion between Theo and Julian where Theo's 'successful completion of the calamitous task [will be] responsible for actively bringing them back together' (Keane 2001: 57). Yet, *Children of Men* thwarts the reaffirmation of heterosexual coupledom when Julian is killed in a surprise attack (which later turns out to be a counter plot from within her own organisation). The film redoubles the assertion of strong male leadership and additionally the genre's 'traditional moral values' when Theo's mission becomes to deliver the miraculously pregnant Kee and her baby to safety from multiple dangers (the now threatening Fishes, one of the prison guards, an uprising in the refugee camp) (Keane 2001: 35). But any ultimate sense of 'strong male leadership' is undermined by Theo's continued dishevelled appearance (no bulging biceps or sweaty white vest as with mainstream disaster film heroes) and by the fact that he dies at the end of the movie once he has successfully delivered Kee and her baby to the Human Project.

Unlike the vast majority of 1990s and early 2000s disaster movies which privilege the East Coast of the United States, *Children of Men* is set in London. Without the US as its main locale, a significant element of the iconography of the disaster movie as established in its mainstream studio and 1990s and early 2000s iterations (*Day After Tomorrow*, *Deep Impact* [Mimi Leder 1998], *Armageddon* [Michael Bay 1998] *Independence Day* [Emmerich 1996]) is missing from the film as well as the ideology that is reinforced by these visual elements. In a 2011 video essay, 'American Un-Frontiers: Universality and Apocalypse Blockbusters', Richard Langley suggests that the contemporary Hollywood subgenre of apocalypse blockbuster (disaster film) where an imminent danger threatens the human race, uses the destruction of the US, its famous cities and its landmarks (New York, the Chrysler Building, the World Trade Center) to posit 'the American story [...] writ large on a global campus [...].' In these films the destruction of the US and its iconic locations is not just about the pleasures of spectacular imagery, Langley argues but also about 'endors[ing] American global leadership and its hegemonic position' (2011). In *Independence Day* and *Day After Tomorrow*, speeches at the ends of the films present the world as a new frontier and assert a future based on a US-led world order (even if, as in *Day After Tomorrow*, the ex-imperial powers of the North find themselves residing in the 'former Third World' due to the effects of a global storm). The idea of (the US's) global leadership is reinforced by another key convention in the contemporary disaster film, the global montage – 'featuring identifiable postcard locations' from around the world similarly affected/menaced by annihilation (Keane 2001: 102) but brought symbolically under the protective wing of the US. Although *Children of Men* contains this particular disaster genre convention (showing glimpses of various global cities, identified, in classical narrative fashion, by famous landmarks, Paris – the Eiffel Tower (Figure 12), Kuala Lumpur – Petronas Towers) it does not present the UK (and the US of which it is a displaced representation) as a global leader as Langley argues mainstream films do. *Children* makes explicit the UK's (and a displaced US) separatism by embedding its global montage in the quasi-fascist ideology of a television news broadcast which proclaims 'Britain' (a term with imperialist connotations) as the 'only' country 'soldier[ing] on.'[15, 16]

Children of Men is different to the contemporary disaster film not only in its location and the ideological significance of that location but also in its visual organisation of disaster. Historically, disaster films are visually organised around spectacular events of destruction (Sontag 1966: 213–214). In the contemporary era, disaster films abound in images of buildings, cities, and cars exploding or being destroyed by; meteorites (*Deep Impact, Armageddon*), giant tidal waves (*The Day After Tomorrow, Deep Impact*) extra-terrestrials (*Independence Day, War of the Worlds*) and molten rock (*Volcano* [Ben

Figure 12   *Children of Men* (Alfonso Cuarón 2006)

Fogg 2007]). Scenes of destruction in these films are usually predicated on the spectacular use of colour, computer generated imagery and fast-paced editing, with disaster movies in particular featuring some of the shortest average shot lengths in contemporary ('intensified continuity') filmmaking. *Armageddon*, which has an average shot length of 2.3 seconds, exemplifies this tendency (Bordwell 2002b: 17).

In terms of both the length of take and the manner in which it renders disaster and destruction, *Children of Men* presents itself as almost completely opposed to these mainstream 'aesthetics of destruction' (Sontag 1966: 213). For instance, a single take in the opening scene follows Theo out of a café (where the rest of the customers watch a television report about the death of the world's youngest person 'Baby Diego') and onto the street where, after he stops to add whisky to his coffee, a bomb explodes from inside the cafe. The same shot tracks in to catch a woman staggering out of the café holding her own severed arm (Figure 13). The entire shot lasts for almost a minute. In addition to the dullness of the colour palette and the relatively realistic explosion (which appears from the 'making of' feature to reflect a pro-filmic event and not one created digitally in post-production), the long take makes the moment of destruction less spectacular but consequently much more shocking. The length of the take and the consequent eschewal of genre-based editing patterns has in no way signalled (as more conventional disaster films might do) that an explosion is about to happen. Furthermore, unlike contemporary and older Hollywood films which 'invite a dispassionate, aesthetic view of destruction and disaster' (Sontag 1966: 216), by minimising effects on real human flesh, *Children of Men* repeatedly relays the effects of the explosions (the woman

Figure 13   *Children of Men* (Alfonso Cuarón 2006)

holding her severed arm) and, in later segments gunfire, with an emphasis on the death and bloody injuries that result from them.

A key element of *Children of Men*'s difference from the mainstream disaster film is a reliance on the effects of violent destruction rendered through long takes, particularly in many of its chase and destruction scenes. In one of these long takes, Julian, Theo, Kee, Miriam (the midwife travelling with them) and Luke, (another one of the Fishes) are attacked as they drive through a forest. Julian is shot and dies whilst they try to escape. The take lasts almost 11 minutes. In it we see Julian bleed to death in 'real time.' The use of the long take is a touchstone of realist filmmaking as conceived by Bazin, facilitating the sense of an uninterrupted recording of an actual event. The use of the long take here heightens the impact of Julian's death. Another use of the long take occurs in *Children* towards the end of the film, and similarly highlights a 'real-world' referent (of actual human suffering) as well as the deviation from the genre conventions of a disaster film. In a climactic chase sequence Kee is captured by the Fishes and Theo has to run through the streets of the Bexhill refugee camp trying to find her. Much of the sequence is presented in a single, 'unbroken' seven-minute take that follows Theo as he tries to dodge not just the crossfire between the Army and the Fishes but also the Army's indiscriminate shooting (at one point the Army opens fire on a group of unarmed refugees who are waving white flags). The bumps and jiggles of the frame indicate that this is shot using a hand-held camera. And as in *Amores perros*, the evident movement of the camera gives us a greater alignment with the feelings and subjectivity of the characters (Theo's panic and fear as he tries to find Kee). But in the context of the ongoing battle between the Army and the Fishes, the bumps and jiggles also create a quality of news-style reportage and attendant associations of authenticity, which are redoubled when imperfections appear in the image. These imperfections include a blood splatter that appears and remains on the lens for some of the shot. When representational norms would dictate a reshoot of what is in classical language a 'mistake,' leaving the splatter on screen (and not editing it out in post-production) gives a greater sense of action captured in real time (Figure 14). The combined realist effect of these numerous features (long take, hand-held camera, blood splatter) correlates with Cuarón's expressed interest in recreating the look of contemporary conflicts zones 'the Middle East, Baghdad, Iraq, Sri Lanka, the Balkans, Palestine' (Anon. 2006).

Children of Men's use of long takes and realist camera work, as well as its investment in creating images from present day conflicts encourages us to read the film as a more than usually transparent (for the disaster film) reflection of its social-political context.[17] This transparency between film and context is also encouraged by the language and imagery used to depict the UK of 2027. Firstly, the future London it portrays is not, except for the ubiquitous screens and the differently shaped cars, that different to London in

Figure 14   *Children of Men* (Alfonso Cuarón 2006)

2006. Contemporary Fleet Street, including the current Goldman Sachs (but former Daily Express) building (used as the location for where Theo works) is recognisable beside the café that explodes. Secondly, the opening clip from TV news includes the ratification of a 'Homeland Security Bill' including the continued closure (after eight years) of the UK's borders, 'the deportation of illegal immigrants' and we presume the existence of the street detention/cages and the prison at the film's end at the entrance of which is written Homeland Security. The use of the term 'Homeland Security' suggests *Children of Men*'s future UK is also a displaced representation of the United States where a government department of the same name was created to cover border security in the wake of the 9/11 terrorist attacks. Further indications of *Children of Men*'s allegorical rendering of the US include the Bexhill prison where illegal immigrants are sent and into which Theo, Kee and Miriam 'break' towards the end of the film. When Miriam is taken off the bus inside the prison Theo and Kee can only watch helplessly out the window as she is hooded. As the bus moves away we see other blindfolded prisoners standing in rows and another hooded prisoner standing with arms outstretched on a box (Figure 15).

These images of Miriam and other prisoners as well as the *mise-en- scène* of the prison point to the real world abuses of the US-run Guantanamo detention camp and the Abu Ghraib torture scandal in which US soldiers were found to have physically and sexually abused Iraqi prisoners.[18] *Children of Men* encourages us to read these very specific references to Guantanamo and Abu Ghraib and other more general references (at one point we see a Hamas-style funeral complete with signs in Arabic and mourners with machine guns) in terms of

Figure 15   *Children of Men* (Alfonso Cuarón 2006)

the contemporary political moment. The cages, prison camps and repressive practices resonate with the post-9/11 US and anticipate the post-7/7 UK where in addition to the abuses at Guantanamo and Abu Ghraib, border security has been tightened, powers of arrest and detention have been extended, and treatment of asylum seekers has become more draconian and adversarial.[19] The film also encourages us (via its displaced representation of the United States) to read its representation of transnational migration and the brutal treatment of migrants in relation to the situation of the US/Mexico border.[20] By setting the action in the United Kingdom, the film realistically sets up its illegal immigrants as mostly European and African. But had *Children of Men* been set in the US, these immigrants would have been mostly Mexican and Central American. That the asymmetries and inequalities of globalisation and transnational migration (particularly between Latin America and the US) are a key concern of the film is signalled in the displaced representation of the US and by the fact that it makes the miraculously pregnant woman a refugee or 'Fugee' (in the novel it is Julian who is pregnant). *Children of Men* both highlights the circumstances of migrants in a post-9/11 world and anticipates conservative attitudes towards immigration in a post-7/7 UK, making it a disaster film that is political and critical of the status quo. As a realist film that openly eschews the 'action, spectacle and [...] escap[ist]' elements of the disaster genre *Children of Men* fails to function as mainstream disaster films do as 'an antidote to the end of the world' (Keane 2001: 95). If London 2027 looks so real and so much like our lived present, including news footage of war and destruction, then the other disasters it presents (the infertility crisis, the resulting social breakdown) also seem threateningly possible.

These multiple differences in ideology, genre features and aesthetics seemingly set *Children of Men* apart from its mainstream origins (Universal Pictures), and its studio-sized budget ($74–$90 million) and place it more firmly within art cinema and auteurist norms. However, this apparent contradiction is as much a deliberate strategy of a diversifying mainstream as it is a function of Cuarón's politicised filmmaking. Universal's involvement with *Children of Men* and Cuarón is actually a means of diversification and product differentiation that has become a common strategy amongst the studios in the last fifteen years. It is primarily the prestige of the critically and commercially successful *Y tu mamá también* which made $33 million for its US distributor and was similarly widely nominated for awards and not the 'director for hire' of *Harry Potter and the Prisoner of Azkaban* that is mobilised by the studios in the packaging and marketing (posters, trailers) of *Children of Men*. For example the multiple 'ancillary texts' that accompany its DVD release (Grant 2008: 102) include; a making of documentary 'Under Attack' that emphasises the film's realist camera work, a video essay by noted philosopher Slavoj Žižek who argues that *Children of Men* 'is [...] a remake of *Y tu mamá también*' and 'not' a 'Hollywood story' (Hinojosa 2006; Žižek 2006a) and a documentary *The Possibility of Hope* (Alfonso Cuarón 2006), which features prominent writers and academics (Naomi Klein, James Lovelock, Žižek, Saskia Sassen, John Gray) speaking about the themes (globalisation, climate change, overpopulation, fear) that *Children of Men* explores. Although these ancillary texts appear to function in opposition to a commercial mainstream, they in fact function in its interests as marketing strategies that emphasise the film's and its director's art cinema credentials with all the associated cultural capital and counter mainstream politics that go with them (Grant 2008: 105). The institutional position of *Children of Men* might read 'mainstream commercial' but this is a mainstream that has (as explored in Chapter 1) shifted in position in order to make cultural and commercial capital out of the niche indie/speciality market (King, 2009: 4). *Children of Men* only partially delivered in one of these areas. It was critically acclaimed receiving multiple award nominations including three for Oscars (Cinematography, Adapted Screenplay, Editing). Commercially however, the film did not deliver, only recouping its production costs.[21]

Cuarón's realist and auteurist credentials are flamboyantly displayed in the *mise-en- scène* of *Children of Men* and in its ancillary materials. These establish the 'quality' of the film as 'art' (ideologically differentiated from the mainstream) rather than a studio produced genre film (formulaic conservative product) although, as this analysis has shown, it is actually as much a part of the mainstream as it is not. The film's realist credentials are based in part on a misrepresentation of aspects of the film's realism and the way in which it is achieved. The 'authenticating' blood splatter that appears on the lens during the long take/chase through the Bexhill prison disappears from the image (after Theo has entered a building and an explosion victim has reached out to him) without an evident break or cut. This signals that this is not (as marketing, interviews and the 'making of' documentary suggest) a single take, but instead multiple shots digitally spliced together in post-production. Referring to an account in a specialist industry (rather than critical) magazine (Fordham 2007), James Udden points to the different (masked) digital edits in this and other long takes in *Children of Men* as evidence of the film's constructed auteurist sensibility (Udden 2009: 29). Although not the first auteur to use masked cuts (Hitchcock famously used them in *Rope* [1949], Iñárritu uses them in *Birdman*), Cuarón's use of them here to facilitate long take photography enables the practice of genre contestation (against the editing conventions of the disaster movie) and simultaneously the (studio's) mobilisation of Cuarón's auteurist signature (through association with *Y tu mamá también* and its much talked about long takes) as commodity. However, even though it may be achieved digitally, rather than in a profilmic manner, and co-opted in part by commercial interests, the long take realism of *Children of Men* together with its transparent rendering of contemporary repressive geopolitical practices (border controls, harsh treatment of immigrants etc.) enables and facilitates the film's social and political critique.

Although some critical perspectives would disavow the relevance of genre to the analysis of Cuarón's oeuvre, this chapter's analysis has shown how his use of commercial genres – the romantic comedy, the teen movie, the road movie and the disaster movie – position him both as an industrial filmmaker responding to the commercial imperatives of the industry but also points towards his auteurist (contestatory) practice; a difference from the mainstream and the embodiment of national and continental political concerns. In *Sólo con tu pareja* Cuarón's use and establishment of genre establishes the model for future commercial filmmaking practice in Mexico and at the same time presents a thinly veiled critique of Mexico's future in the NAFTA era. In *Y tu mamá también*, Cuarón presents a 'stoner' teen/road movie that targets its youth audience through music and the familiar scenarios of *American Pie* but at the same time enables a critique of the legacies of the PRI state and contemporary apolitical culture. In *Children of Men* genre provides us with end-of-world scenarios, dramatic destruction and the promise of strong male leadership, but also highlights the fate of immigrants from the Global South in a newly militarised and fascistic North.

Notes

1. Berg points out how the case of *El automóvil gris* (*The Grey Car* Enrique Rosas 1919), aptly illustrates the synthesis of Mexico's documentary style (in terms of a

fidelity to chronology of events and accuracy of facts), Italian tradition (in terms of period detail and mobile camera), French crime serials and the emerging Hollywood paradigm (in terms of goal-driven protagonist(s), causal narrative, editing and shooting) (2000: 4).

2. Work by Thomas Elsaesser ([1972] 1991) on the melodramas of Douglas Sirk explores how this genre's norms are used to counter the conservative ideologies of 1950s America.

3. The opening of *Mujeres* is a seeming establishing shot of a very unreal looking apartment complex and sky which turn out to be an architect's model in a property company office that features later in the film.

4. MacLaird says '[i]ts ample gestation time for marketing resulted in one of the biggest box-office openings in the history of Mexican cinema: coming home from premiering in Cannes, the film took in $2.2 million in its first week (2010: 48). *Y tu mamá también* made $33 million for Twentieth Century Fox, its US distributor (Alvaray 2008: 53).

5. It is mentioned by many critics but none go beyond these mentions or two- or three-line descriptions or engage with the structure of the genre. Armida de la Garza identifies it a 'teen movie' (2009: 109). Sergio de la Mora and Nuala Finnegan go a little further and mention the genre and the specific teen film from which it takes its lead, *American Pie* (de la Mora 2006: 177; Finnegan 2007: 31).

6. And indeed was not the only attempt at the genre. See *Por la libre* (Juan Carlos de Llaca 2000).

7. The relocation of cinemas within shopping malls during the 1980s created a consequent 'need to cater to the young audience who frequented those malls' (Shary 2005: 54).

8. Source <http://www.boxofficemojo.com/movies/?page=main&id=americanpie.htm> (last accessed 11 July 2012).

9. The other protagonists are also significantly named after national figures. Tenoch Iturbide recalls Mexico's first post-Independence leader. Luisa Cortés refers to the Spanish conquistador Hernán Cortés. These naming devices have been interpreted as significant in both allegorising the nation (Saldana-Portillo 2005) and also as an ironic 'voiding' of national signifiers by denaturalising them (Sánchez Prado 2014: 192).

10. Oz (Chris Klein) has slept with the jazz choir girl Heather (Mena Suvari). Jim (Jason Biggs) has slept with the 'band' girl (Alyson Hannigan). Finch (Eddie Kaye Thomas) has slept with Stifler's mom (Jennifer Coolidge) and Kevin (Thomas Ian Nicholas) has slept with Vicky (Tara Reid) his girlfriend.

11. I refer particularly to the multiplicity of servants who wait on the middle class protagonists without attention from within or outside the diegesis.

12. The YoSoy132/I am the 132nd movement, actually contests this notion of an apolitical youth. YoSoy132 is a student protest movement which began in opposition to the 2012 PRI candidate, and now president, Enrique Peña Nieto, and the supposedly positively biased media coverage he received during the 2012 electoral campaign. The movement began as a protest of 131 students who were accused by the then candidate of not being legitimate protesters but agents of other parties. In response the students put out a YouTube video showing their student IDs. Other supporters showing solidarity with the movement began tweeting and chanting the slogan 'YoSoy132'. The movement is connected to social media and has since organised many protests.

13. Figures from boxofficemojo.com

14. Samuel Amago bases his analysis of the film in relation to *The Waste Land* on the fact that they are both dystopian texts.

15. Emmerich, the director of many contemporary Hollywood disaster films is, as a German director, and like many of the transnational directors focused on in this book, also part of the 'global flow' of talent towards Hollywood and this has always been how Hollywood has recruited its workforce (Behlil 2016: 12). But unlike Cuarón and his *Children of Men*, which situates itself differently with respect to the ideological discourses of the genre, Emmerich's films are (read by Langley and others as) fully part of the representational poetics and ideological discourse of mainstream contemporary Hollywood.

16. Although distancing itself from US disaster films, *Children of Men* still allies itself with other contemporary science-fiction films based in the United Kingdom such as *V for Vendetta* (James McTeigue 2005), *28 Days Later* (Danny Boyle 2002) by showcasing London's landmarks and significant buildings (St Paul's Cathedral, Trafalgar Square, the Mall, St James's Park, Battersea Power Station, Fleet Street). It doesn't destroy them in the way Hollywood disaster films do. But it does join with a series of post-9/11, Iraq War era films that critique the institutions which have legitimised this and other US-led wars (including Afghanistan).

17. Although, disaster movies 'can be said to address issues pertinent to the times in which they are made' (Keane 2001: 73), Nick Roddick points out that it is problematic to make 'automatic associations between film cycles and socio-political context' or between 'cause and effect' (qtd in Keane 2001: 14).

18. Abu Ghraib was a prison in Bagdad run by US forces. In 2004 evidence of human rights violations emerged in photographs of Iraqi prisoners being abused by US soldiers.

19. For instance, and a measure of the film's prescient realism, in 2013 the then Home Secretary and later Prime Minister, Theresa May piloted a scheme of 'Go home' vans in several boroughs in London carrying the message 'In the UK illegally? Go home or face arrest' with a textbox '106 arrests last week.' It is unclear at the time of writing (2017) what the further implications of the United Kingdom's Brexit vote will be for asylum seekers and migrants.

20. Cuarón's assertions support this interpretation of the film: 'I have to question the ethics of borders when there is humanity in need. When we start segregating ourselves from what humanity needs we lose more and more of the sense of humanity as a whole [...] I'm a Mexican. There's been a constant migration between Mexico and the United States. And the anti-immigration laws are getting tougher. The United States is clinging to archaic solutions, instead of trying to find new structures. The same country that praises the tearing apart of the Berlin Wall is building a single wall between Mexico and the States (Von Busack 2007).

21. boxofficemojo.com put its worldwide box office at $69 million.

3. GUILLERMO DEL TORO'S TRANSNATIONAL POLITICAL HORROR: *CRONOS* (1993), *EL ESPINAZO DEL DIABLO* (*THE DEVIL'S BACKBONE 2001*) AND *EL LABERINTO DEL FAUNO* (*PAN'S LABYRINTH 2006*)

Like Cuarón, Guillermo del Toro began his directorial career as part of the state funded revival of the early 1990s with the contemporary vampire film *Cronos* (1993), and subsequently also departed to work in Hollywood. Since then he has enjoyed arguably the most 'deterritorialised' of the careers of the transnational Mexican auteurs, not returning to Mexico to direct a film, but continuing to travel between directing projects in the US (*Mimic* 1997, *Blade II: Blood Hunt* 2002, *Hellboy* 2004 and *Hellboy II: The Golden Army* 2008, *Pacific Rim* 2014, *Crimson Peak* 2015, *The Shape of Water* 2017) and Spain (*El espinazo del diablo/The Devil's Backbone* 2001, *El laberinto del fauno/Pan's Labyrinth* 2006) whilst also producing, writing and developing projects in Mexico, Spain, the US and New Zealand.[1] In Chapters 1 and 2 we analysed the cinematic transnationality of del Toro's compatriots Iñárritu and Cuarón through differently focused auteurist methods (the former's in terms of style and aesthetic continuities, the latter's in terms of genre manipulations and institutional locations). With Iñárritu, it was possible to argue that the non hegemonic funding structures and (almost) consistent core creative team of all four of his productions facilitated the function of a coherent political and aesthetic critique. With Cuarón, who has worked as both an independent and an industry director, it was possible to separate out the avowedly more auteurist productions from those made 'for hire' (*Harry Potter and The Prisoner of Azkaban, A Little Princess, Great Expectations*) to explore how genre contestation and manipulation forward aesthetic (and commercially oriented product) differentiation whilst at the same time addressing socio-political issues. With del Toro however, the task of locating a sense of authorial, national or continental specificity and any political charge that may go with it, is made difficult by the fact that his work straddles so many different categories and locales of filmmaking and because, as his own and others' affirmations suggest, in his work the industry/auteurist divide between English language and Spanish language co-productions is not consistently drawn (del Toro 2008: 38; Kermode 2006: 20; Davies 2006: 135). His Spanish language films are considerably informed by industry trends – *El laberinto del fauno*'s fantasy elements tap into the renewed popularity of the genre post the success of several different franchises (Peter Jackson's *The Lord of the Rings* trilogy, the *Harry Potter* films, and the *Chronicles of Narnia*) and *El espinazo del diablo and Hellboy* mine the increasing popularity of comic book adaptations (Beaty 2011) – while (some of) his industry films (the *Hellboy* films in particular) have substantial crossovers with his Spanish language films.

Del Toro operates within the context of global Hollywood and more specifically within its niche market of the horror/fantasy and comic book film in which he works as director, writer and producer of his own and others' (*Don't be Afraid of the Dark* [Troy Nixey 2010], *Mama* [Andrés Muschietti 2013], *The Book of Life* [Jorge R. Gutiérrez 2014]) projects. His US fantasy/horror work is best emblematised by some of his most recent Hollywood projects *Crimson Peak*, the Marvel comic book adaptations (*Hellboy* and *Hellboy II, Pacific Rim*), his continued popularity at the annual Comic Con International and *The Strain Trilogy* of vampire novels he has co-authored with Chuck Hogan (*The Strain* 2009, *The Fall* 2010, and *The Night Eternal* 2011).[2] Del Toro's success in the US-centred horror/fantasy arena impacts on and facilitates his work within the industrial and political context of contemporary Spanish horror cinema in which he has directed two films (*El espinazo del diablo*, and *El laberinto del fauno*) and used the leverage of his Hollywood commercial success to produce and facilitate the production of several others (*Los ojos de Julia/Julia's Eyes* [Guillem Morales 2010] *El orfanato/The Orphanage* [Juan Antonio Bayona 2007]). This success has also legitimated and facilitated more horror production in Mexico (and indeed the rest of Latin America). Recent Mexican horror successes include *KM 31/ Kilometre 31* (Rigoberto Castañeda 2006), *KM 31-2* (Castañeda 2016) *Somos lo que hay/We Are What We Are* (Jorge Michel Grau 2010) and *Halley* (Sebastián Hofman 2012). Recent Latin American horror successes include Uruguayan Gustavo Hernández's *La casa muda/The Silent House* (2010), and Argentinians Adrián García Bogliano's *Sudor frío/Cold Sweat*, (2010) and Nicolás Goldbart's *Fase 7/Phase 7* (2011). Del Toro's success in both global Hollywood and world/art cinema further facilitates his role as a Mexican filmmaker championing, producing and collaborating on projects of other Mexican directors (Iñárritu's *Biutiful*, Carlos Cuarón's *Rudo y cursi* [2008], Andrea Martínez's *Cosas insignificantes* [2008]), facilitating the restoration of 'lost' films from Mexico's film past (*El vampiro y el sexo* [Rene Cardona 1969])[3] and calling for measures that will protect and strengthen Mexican cinema (greater financial and government support, a rewriting of the culture clauses in the NAFTA agreement) (MacLaird 2013a: 36).

Despite the disparity of the different fields and geographical locations in which del Toro works (in the Mexican and Spanish film industries and in an increasingly globally dispersed Hollywood), the constancy of the horror genre has characterised the majority of his work as director, producer, writer, curator, and film advocate to date. But although he has consistently worked in the horror genre, critical readings of del Toro's films have rarely focused on the (political) workings of the horror genre itself, preferring instead to displace their studies onto other topics. Critical readings of *Cronos*, for example, 'treat vampirism as a metaphor or cover story for something else,' letting the film's 'vampiric surface' virtually disappear (Davies 2008: 395). The neglect of horror in *Cronos* can be explained in part by the critical disreputability of the horror genre both in Mexican official culture and in Latin American cultural discourse, which has meant that the genre has had little or no presence in its national film canons (and that del Toro struggled to find institutional funding for both *Cronos* and *El espinazo del diablo* in Mexico). In Spain, by contrast, the horror film (and its tropes of violence, monsters, and ghosts) has been *the* favoured genre – both for Franco-era explorations of life under repression (*Furtivos/Poachers* [José Luis Borau 1975], *Cría cuervos/Raise Ravens* [Carlos Saura 1975], and *El espíritu de la colmena/The Spirit of the Beehive* [Víctor Erice 1973]) – as well as for more recent explorations of the country's traumatic past (*Tesis/Thesis, The Others* [Alejandro Amenábar 1996, 2001] and *El orfanato*) and has received commensurate critical attention (Acevedo-Muñoz 2008; Davies 2006; 2008; Labanyi 2007; Lázaro-Reboll 2007, 2012; Smith 2001). What is missing in some of the very useful writing on del Toro and Spanish horror in both Latin American and Spanish contexts is more attention to the political function of horror itself and the way it is used to address particular issues: the impact of NAFTA on Mexico and the question of (the recovery of) historical memory in Spain.

Anglo-American film studies in the 1980s and 1990s rehabilitated the horror genre from critical disreputability with a string of key studies based on Freudian, feminist, and Marxist frameworks by Robin Wood (1985), Tania Modleski (1999), Linda Williams (1989), Carol Clover (1992), and others. These studies were groundbreaking in that they defended the horror film against those who would dismiss its significance and explored its hitherto unacknowledged political potential. Wood notes that in the modern horror film of the late 1960s and 1970s (*Night of the Living Dead*, [George A. Romero 1968] *The Texas Chainsaw Massacre* [Tobe Hooper 1974, *Carrie* [Brian De Palma 1976], *Halloween* [John Carpenter 1978]) all that bourgeois, patriarchal capitalism tries to repress (homosexuality, alternative ideologies, and all that can be considered 'the other') returns often in monstrous form (1985: 195–156). Citing many of the same films (and adding into the analysis later films *Videodrome* [David Cronenberg 1983], *The Brood* [Cronenberg 1979], and others), Modleski suggests that the political progressiveness of the modern horror film lies in its ability to show the 'other' side of mainstream culture and society (1999, 694). No Latin American/Spanish film critics have disputed the existence of politics in del Toro's Spanish-language trilogy: *Cronos*'s NAFTA-era exploration of Mexican identity threatened by US trade (Kraniauskas 1998; Stock 1999), *El espinazo del diablo*'s microcosmic exploration of the struggle between Republican and Fascist forces in the Spanish Civil War (Davies 2006; Lázaro-Reboll 2007: 42), and *El laberinto del fauno*'s exploration of Fascist repression in post-civil war Spain (Lázaro-Reboll 2007: 43). Some have also made very useful analyses of the trilogy's horrific aspects (the vampire in *Cronos* [Davies 2008]; the abject, the uncanny, and historical allegory in *El espinazo* [Acevedo-Muñoz 2008; Davies 2006; Smith 2001]). Nonetheless, there has been little exploration of how horror itself functions politically in these three films (with respect to Mexico and Spain) and how this political function of horror in turn figures the films' complex relationship to American horror cinema.

Following Wood, Modleski, and other horror theorists, this chapter addresses the political function of horror and horrific tropes (including aspects of horror's *mise-en-scène*) in *Cronos*, *El espinazo*, and *El laberinto*. It takes into consideration the significant transnationality of the horror genre itself both in terms of its classical Hollywood origins that effectively absorbed a range of stylistic, cultural, and industrial practices of nations outside the United States, as well as what critics have argued is its potential as a genre for 'travel[ing] ... across different national cultures and contexts [and] also across media forms and fan culture' (Lázaro-Reboll 2007: 46).[4] This includes *Cronos*'s acknowledgment of Mexico's own horror/fantasy film tradition, which is heavily hybridised, drawing in particular on the style, iconography, and even narratives of the 1930s Universal horror films *Frankenstein* (James Whale 1931), *Dracula* (Tod Browning 1931), and *Mystery of the Wax Museum* (Michael Curtiz 1933) (Syder and Tierney 2005: 38). The chapter positions del Toro as a part of this hybridised and transnational film history with institutional roots on both sides of the US/Mexico border. It also contends that these films take advantage of a shared Hispanic imaginary and explore cultural, local, and political material specific to Mexico, Latin America and Spain.

CRONOS

Del Toro's first feature film, *Cronos*, was partially financed by Mexico's National Film Institute IMCINE as one of a group of early 1990s films (*Danzón* [María Novaro 1992], *Como agua para chocolate/Like Water for Chocolate* [Alfonso Arau 1992], *Sólo con tu pareja/Love in a Time of Hysteria* [Alfonso Cuarón 1991]) that were designed to sell Mexico to the world, in the lead-up to the signing of the NAFTA agreement. Due to the critical disreputability of horror in Mexican cultural discourse, in contradistinction to the other pre-NAFTA films it funded, IMCINE had to be persuaded that a horror movie like *Cronos* was a suitable project to showcase Mexico. IMCINE initially rejected it for funding, concerned that, as a non-art film, it would not 'go to any festivals [or] win any prizes' (Wood 2006: 38). *Cronos* was eventually produced as a co-production with additional financing from Los Angeles-based Ventana Films. Against IMCINE's expectations, the film did triumph on the global festival circuit and won many prizes, including the Mercedes Benz award at the Cannes Film Festival. *Cronos* may not *sell* Mexico abroad in the same way *Como agua para chocolate* or *Sólo con tu pareja* do, but it does engage, via its overtly transnationalised text and the appropriate genre of the vampire movie, with the impact of selling (free trade) on Mexico and its national patrimony.

Cronos is set in 1997, three years after the signing of the NAFTA agreement. Traffic signs in Russian, English, Chinese, Arabic, and Spanish in the credit sequence figure the fanciful future transformations of NAFTA, portraying Mexico City as a multilingual city. The film continues this multilingual thrust with a mixture of English and Spanish-language dialogue. When Angel (US actor Ron Perlman) comes into the antique shop of Jesús Gris (Federico Luppi) looking for the Cronos device his uncle Dieter de la Guardia (Mexican horror actor Claudio Brook) wants because of its life extending capabilities, Angel speaks in English, and Jesús responds in Spanish.[5] On his visits to the factory, de la Guardia similarly speaks to Jesús in a mixture of Spanish and English.

The film is similarly comfortably fluent in its use of the familiar tropes of Hollywood vampirism: sexual potency, blood lust, immortality, and a nocturnal existence. When Jesús examines the Cronos device (which he has found hidden in an archangel statue) and is accidentally 'bitten' by it, he begins a process of physical change commensurate with these tropes. That night he is overcome by a terrible thirst, then by a desire for blood (he eyes some raw meat in the fridge), and subsequently by a furious itching that he desperately (and dangerously) scratches with scissors. After using the device a second time, he experiences an aversion to sunlight, feels younger and fitter, and makes his surprised wife, Mercedes (Margarita Isabel), giggle like a teenager. As a vampire, he becomes immortal, ultimately able to survive Angel's several attempts to kill him. After his first 'death', Jesús becomes the living dead, sleeping by day in a 'coffin' that loudly creaks open when he awakens at night.

Although it is Jesús who is transformed, it is the cane-wielding business-man, de la Guardia, who is presented as the film's real vampire, trying to get his hands on the device so that he can 'suck the lifeblood' out of Mexico. De la Guardia is one in a genealogy of capitalist characters in Western literature and culture who, like capital itself, are represented in vampiric terms: 'Capital is dead labour which, vampire-like; lives only by sucking living labour, and lives the more, the more labour it sucks' (Marx, quoted in Kraniauskas 1998: 144–145). Cinematically, with his combed-back hair, pale countenance, and nocturnal habits (he tells Jesús he is around 'all night'), de la Guardia evokes the sinister, gentlemanly appearance of various film Count Draculas (Bela Lugosi in Browning's *Dracula* or Christopher Lee in various Hammer film productions). De la Guardia's implied vampirism also connects to the film's critique of NAFTA, imagining the facilitation of free trade between the United States and Mexico as a monstrous draining of Mexico's (human) resources.

Although there is an evident transnationalism in the use of Hollywood norms to represent vampirism, *Cronos*'s use of the vampire trope (with respect to de la Guardia in particular) is also a 'reterritorialization' (García Canclini 1995) of a constellation of continental myths and popular fantasies about blood-sucking beings who visit in the night. These include Perú's rural *kharisi* (or *nehaq* or *pishtakos*), which has both a pre-Hispanic and subsequent colonial manifestation (with 'gringo' features), and the more modern twentieth-century *sacaojos*, who are usually white, government-appointed doctors (Kraniauskas 1998: 150–152). These figures function, John Kraniauskas argues, as 'postco-lonial and transcultural signs of contemporary social processes evoking as they do the cultural memory of changes in the social experiences of the body and its perceived invasion and colonisation by new institutions (medical) and regimes (technological)' (1998: 152).

If de la Guardia is the vampire with 'gringo' features in *Cronos*, Jesús's vam-pirism can also be rationalised within the NAFTA-era discourse of the film. *Cronos* actually recalls another 'local' vampire myth, specific to Mesoamerica/Mexico (the only place in the world where the vampire bat is indigenous). The chronicles of sixteenth-century conquistadors recount tales of soldiers awak-ening weakened and drained after nocturnal visits from bats in human form.[6] If the film portrays de la Guardia as a malevolent vampire, Jesús is a kind of postcolonial vampire, resistant to the colonisation of the (national) body. It is therefore in keeping with the film's political critique (of free trade) that Jesús is an atypical vampire and that *Cronos* counters some of the similarly colonis-ing conventions of Eurocentric (Hollywood) vampire mythology. Jesús does not behave like a stereotypical cinematic vampire. When he is transfixed by the sight of a man with a bleeding nose, rather than lunge at his neck, he waits politely for a chance to lick up his spilled blood. The 'coffin' Jesús sleeps in during the day is Aurora's cleared-out toy chest. And most significantly, he is never a threat to his granddaughter, wife, or any human (except Angel and de la Guardia when they threaten his family). After his wake when he comes back to life, he is a pathetic figure shuffling around outside the funeral parlour wearing the aristocratic Count Dracula-like tuxedo he was 'dressed' in back to front. He goes back to his house and struggles to write a letter to his wife. That he retains his human impulses (love for his granddaughter and wife) to the point of being able to resist his vampiric urges (to suck Aurora's blood) makes Jesús a sympathetic monster. After he smashes the machine – releasing himself and the insect from their slavery to bloodlust, but also ensuring that they both will die – he significantly says, 'Soy Jesús Gris' ('I am Jesús Gris'), and this expression of his subjectivity redeems him.

The insect trapped inside the Cronos device is also given a kind of subjectivity. The film achieves this in a number of ways. Jesús speaks to it, asking it to 'take care of' his 'soul' when he goes to use the device for the first time deliberately. On another occasion, just after using the device, he asks it, 'Who are you little one? A god?' On both occasions, subsequent shots show the interior of the device, including the turning cogs and wheels of its mechanism and the insect encased inside, suggesting the insect and Jesús are interacting with each other. Jesús and the insect are shown to both be victims of the device and what it symbolises. In the context of NAFTA, shots that show the insect's heaving thorax elicit comparisons between the trapped insect and the Mexican workforce, as well as the blood the insect consumes and the Latin American raw materials extracted from the continent and made into consumer goods for the US economy. The US-Mexican De la Guardia Corporation is presented as a malevolent presence in Mexico City. Its interiors (particularly de la Guardia's sanitised inner chamber) are dimly lit and dressed in dark grey and black colours, in contrast to Jesús's relatively light and airy antique shop.

The sympathetic representation of Jesús (and of the insect) makes explicit what Wood contends is a key element of the monster in American horror films. Combining Marxist and Freudian paradigms, Wood argues that, just like in our dreams, the figure of the monster represents the actual re-emergence 'of all that our [capitalist] civilization represses or oppresses' in the interests of patriarchal, heterosexual, bourgeois monogamy, including 'women,' 'the proletariat,' 'other cultures,' 'ethnic groups,' 'alternative ideologies,' 'homosexuality and bisexuality' (1985: 200–201). In Wood's theory of the American horror film, classic screen monsters like Frankenstein's monster (*Frankenstein*) or more contemporary monsters like the chainsaw-wielding Leatherface (*Texas Chainsaw Massacre*) are 'the dramatization of the dual concept of the repressed/other' (1985: 201). Wood argues that 'pervasive class references' in both these films (Boris Karloff's costume of labourers' clothes, the 'slaughterhouse' trade of the family in *Chainsaw*) cast their monsters as proletariats, wreaking havoc on a normality (heterosexual monogamy, the family, social institutions) that has oppressed and excluded them or, in Leatherface and his family's case, made them redundant (1985: 201, 204). Wood also suggests that these monsters are ambiguously threatening and sympathetic (1985: 205). He argues that in films like *Frankenstein*, the monster is 'clearly the emotional centre and much more human than the cardboard representatives of normality' (1985: 205). In *Cronos*, Jesús is never really a 'monster' in the way Leatherface or Frankenstein's monster are, and only momentarily threatening (when he is transfixed by the stranger with the nosebleed or licks his lips at Aurora's bleeding hands). But it is significant with respect to the film's broader postcolonial and NAFTA-era political critique that it makes him a sympathetic monster by allowing him to retain an emotional humanity once he becomes a vampire, despite his peeling skin, his disintegrating body and, after he drinks from an injured de la Guardia's neck, his bloodied mouth. Jesús's sympathetic nature means that spectators want to see him drink the blood of the predatory US capitalist de la Guardia and pull the violent (though not unsympathetic) Angel to his death.

If the monster is created by the psychic repressions or (in political terms) oppressions of bourgeois (and neocolonial) culture and its related ideologies, the progressive impulse in these horror films can be identified as the desire to 'overthrow' these repressions (Wood 1985: 196). Modleski points out how many contemporary horror films are engaged in an assault on the institutions of bourgeois culture (the school, the family) and, in the case of *Cronos*, we could also add imperialistic free trade (1999: 694). Hinting at its progressivity, *Cronos* significantly cites a key scene from another contemporary horror film, *Videodrome*, which also probes the insidious nature of contemporary (bourgeois consumer) culture (Modleski 1999: 695). After Jesús has fallen from the De la Guardia building, he puts his hand into a gash in his stomach, rooting around before lifting away dead flesh to reveal new, white skin beneath. His actions recall those of Max (James Woods) in *Videodrome*. Max is the victim of a massive dose of a video signal being developed by unscrupulous businessmen capitalising on society's urge to consume video images. As a result, Max develops a massive gaping wound in his stomach, in which he roots around and which subsequently becomes the video player through which the businessmen program him to kill their enemies (and himself). The visual reference in *Cronos* to *Videodrome* connects it to a culture of political horror filmmaking and the broader (postcolonial) critique of the victimisation of the masses. With respect to this broader critique, it is noteworthy that *Cronos*'s vampire, Jesús, is not Mexican but (like Luppi) Argentinean. The film stresses his Argentinean nationality through the tango music that plays over the credits and at several points during the film. This gives the film a broader resonance beyond Mexico, to embrace the continental reality of US penetration into Latin America's economies.

EL ESPINAZO DEL DIABLO

After the success of *Cronos*, del Toro hoped IMCINE's 'attitude [to him and the horror genre] would change' (Wood 2006: 112). In the meantime, he was courted by Universal Pictures, who invited him to write a script (*Spanky*, based on a novel by Christopher Fowler), and he eventually made *Mimic*. He blames his departure for the United States and subsequently for Spain on difficulties with IMCINE and its approach to funding: 'I would have been perfectly happy to make movies in Mexico for the rest of my life but there was never an open door, you were always, every time, having to kick it open' (Wood 2006: 112).

The lack of creative control he experienced making *Mimic*, his first English-language feature in the United States, for independent producer Miramax's Dimension led del Toro to set up his own production company, Tequila Gang, with Bertha Navarro, Laura Esquivel (screenwriter for *Like Water for Chocolate*), Rosa Bosch, and Alejandra Moreno Toscano, and to revisit *El espinazo*, a project that he had already developed prior to *Mimic* but had had to put aside because he could not find funding in Mexico (Wood 2006: 43, 45). *El espinazo* was made as a transatlantic co-production between the Mexican Anhelo Producciones, del Toro's Tequila Gang, and El Deseo S. A., which is owned by the Almodóvar brothers. *El espinazo* was the first Latin American project produced by Pedro Almodóvar and his brother Agustín as part of the expansion of their production company into Latin America. *El espinazo* was Anhelo's second production after *Y tu mamá también* (Cuarón 2001) and is hence also part of the same boom of film production motivated by artistic innovation and experimentation coupled with commercial interests of Mexico's so-called filmmaking renaissance (Smith 2003a: 396). *El espinazo* is a transatlantic hybrid project. Successful at the box office in Spain and Mexico and also in art cinemas and multiplexes in the United States, *El espinazo* illustrates the benefits of commercially oriented co-production to its co-producing nations (Lázaro-Reboll 2007: 39). It also demonstrates the significant possibilities that a transnationalised horror cinema may offer to its producing cultures.

Isabel Santaolalla interprets *El espinazo*, which is set in an orphanage toward the end of the Spanish Civil War, as part of a subversive and postcolonial process of 'writing back' to the hegemonic culture of empire, in which Latin American filmmakers 'reread and rewrite [works from Spain's] literary [cinematic] and historical archives' (2005: 220). *El espinazo*, Santaolalla suggests, rereads and rewrites the civil war (1936–1939), as the most significant event of Spain's twentieth-century history. Through the figure of the orphanage director, Argentinian doctor Casares (and particularly Luppi who plays him), who listens to tangos by Argentinian singer Carlos Gardel and recites poetry by Mexican poet Sor Juana Inés de la Cruz to the headmistress Carmen (Marisa Paredes), the film presents a foreign, (Latin) Americanist perspective on Spain's history. It also emphasises the participation of non-Spaniards in the war. The execution of members of the International Brigade – including six Canadians, a Chinese man, and the two Republicans, Ayala and Domínguez, who drop off the orphan protagonist, Carlos (Fernando Tielve) at the orphanage – is one of the few war events directly depicted in the film.[7] As each *brigadista* is shot, Casares shudders, emphasising 'how he recognises himself in these foreigners' (Santaolalla 2005: 223).

On another level, however, *El espinazo* draws on a tradition of 'rewriting' or 'reinscription' that is already part of Spanish cinema's own history of cinematic subversion. Oppositional filmmaking of the New Spanish Cinema from the Franco era (*Muerte de un ciclista/Death of a Cyclist* [Juan Antonio Bardem 1955], *Bienvenido Mr Marshall/Welcome Mr. Marshall* [Luis García Berlanga 1953], *Calle Mayor/Main Street* [Juan Antonio Bardem 1956], *El espíritu de la colmena*) used Hollywood (and Italian neorealist) models to circumscribe the conservative, Catholic version of Spanish culture imposed by the Franco regime (1939–1975) and its strict censorship laws (Kinder 1993: 19). *El espíritu de la colmena*, for instance, famously re-inscribes the Hollywood conventions (and what Wood would call the 'political subtext') of *Frankenstein* and the classical horror genre to offer a veiled criticism of the regime's post-civil war repression of remnants of the country's Republican past.

Although not compelled by the dictates of political censorship as New Spanish Cinema was, but motivated by similar oppositional concerns, del Toro also rewrites and re-inscribes Hollywood horror conventions in *El espinazo* in the way the film visualises the monster threat. Initially *El espinazo* follows classical Hollywood and its gothic (literature-derived) principles of horror, which depend on a tension between what can and cannot be seen and on the equation between what is knowable and unknowable, safe and dangerous (Kawin: 1999). These are determined via textual elements that obscure the sight of the camera/spectator/character, such as fog and darkness (Tierney 2002: 357; Tudor 1974: 203), and typified in such Hollywood films as *Cat People* (Jacques Tourneur 1942). In the early part of *El espinazo*, when the ghost of Santi (a young boy murdered at the orphanage) is presented as an unknowable threat, an encounter between it and Carlos employs these gothic 'mysteries of light and shade' (Tudor 1974: 207). When Carlos goes down to the basement at night, the space is broken up into pools of light (safety) and darkness (danger). As he moves around, fleeting shadows suggest that someone (not visible and therefore unknowable) is with him in the basement. But *El espinazo* also re-inscribes many of these gothic principles in a manner that is ultimately relevant to the context of the civil war and the process of the re-inscription of Hollywood key to New Spanish Cinema. During the basement encounter, for instance, the camera pans into the shadowy corner. But rather than stop to suggest the presence of an unknown threat, it unexpectedly continues panning to reveal to the spectator (but not to Carlos) Santi's (frightened) face. Similarly, during a pursuit through the orphanage, the camera exposes the ghost with its shattered skull, visible skeleton, and surrounding water bubbles to the spectator *and* to Carlos in all its physicality. Rather than withhold the image of the monster (as Hollywood's classical horror cinema's gothic principles dictate), the ghost is exposed and made known to the audience and to Carlos early on in the film. This revelation of the ghost is, as Paul Julian Smith points out, 'too prosaic' for the horror genre, (2001: 39). It considerably 'defuse[s]' any threat the ghost might represent (del Toro 2002). Santi's emergence from the shadows is actually part of a deliberate strategy of revelation in *El espinazo* that actually goes against the principles of gothic horror as established in classical Hollywood. As in *El espíritu de la colmena* – which also features a child protagonist, Ana (Ana Torrent), and her relationship with a 'monster'– it is not the ghost/spirit (the fugitive Republican fighter) but the broader political context that is the threat. Santi's prophecy, 'Many of you will die,' is not meant as a menace but as a warning/revelation to the boys at the orphanage about the proto-Fascist Jacinto (Eduardo Noriega), who murdered him, and the danger Jacinto represents to them. Santi, it emerges, just wants revenge for his murder.

With this idea of Santi in mind, Wood's theory about the American horror film as a challenge to psychic and political repression inflicted on society's 'others' is of particular relevance both to the text and to the 'monsters' in *El espinazo*. Wood's theory is also relevant to the film *El espinazo* most consciously emulates, *El espíritu de la colmena*, and to the different periods in which both films were produced, as well as to the sense in which we can read the films in transnational terms. It is worth noting some of the similarities and differences between these two texts, largely because these further illuminate del Toro's aesthetic strategies. *El espíritu* was made in a period of harsh cinematic restriction, with tightened censorship (after the relative *apertura* of the 1960s) from a regime that felt threatened by increased calls for democracy (Triana-Toribio 2003: 95–97). The gaps and silences of its art-cinema text (elliptical style, lack of dialogue and exposition) imagine the effects of a history of political repression (of the political left) and also hint at a broader reality beneath this repressed surface. In *El espíritu* Ana, her family, and the injured Republican fighter hiding out in the barn near the town (Labanyi 2007: 93) represent Wood's repressed other. After he is shot by the authorities, the fighter 'returns' in Ana's imagination (in the likeness of Boris Karloff's monster from the Whale film and, as in the original, as a sympathetic rather than frightening figure). The film further underlines the association between the Republican fighter and Frankenstein's monster when the former's body is laid out in the village hall in front of the screen on which Whale's film was earlier projected. It is significant that Erice chose *Frankenstein* in particular for the village to watch and for its monster to become Ana's identificatory figure rather than any of the other monsters from Universal's early 1930s Dracula or the Mummy films. Frankenstein's monster highlights the class dimension specific to the repression of the Spanish Civil War and the ideological repression of the post-civil war era. Wood argues that the Frankenstein monster with his 'labourer's clothes' represents the proletariat, which capitalism represses in order to make them productive subjects in its system (1985: 201). Wood's interpretation of Whale's monster correlates with the film's critique of the ideology of the Nationalist alliance that repressed Spain's working classes (through the use of slave labour and state-controlled unions) for the maximum benefit of the dominant classes (Labanyi 2007: 91).

As Jo Labanyi points out, *El espinazo* needs to be read in the context of Spain's 1990s and early-2000s 'memory boom' of novels and films representing the civil war, as well the contemporaneous and more literal 'digging up the past': 'the excavation of mass graves containing the bodies of victims of Francoist repression during and after the civil war' (2007: 95). Emerging as he does from the shadows, with his broken skull and skeletal form, Santi functions not just as 'the haunting presence of the violent past in the present' (Labanyi 2007: 102), but also as the monstrous 'return of [Spain's Republican] repressed' (Wood 1985: 202). It is important to see Santi not just as a ghost but as the return of the repressed because in Wood's evaluation of the horror film, psychic repression carries with it the notion of political oppression, and Santi is to be read as a political victim and his murder as a political murder. The climactic killing of Jacinto (by Santi but aided by the children of 'Reds') consequently takes on the symbolic value of 'reparation' rather than straight revenge, and reparation was, as Labanyi points out, a concern in the years before the film was made. Although Jacinto's murder, in one sense, 'lay[s]' Santi 'to rest' (Labanyi 2007: 102), it does not provide ultimate closure either within the film or implicitly for the victims of Nationalist violence. *El espinazo* ends with another ghost, Casares, killed as a result of Jacinto's sabotage. Casares's monologue that opens and closes the film points to this lack of closure in its description of 'a ghost' as '[a] tragedy condemned to repeat itself time and time again'. *El espinazo*'s open-endedness points to the unresolved tensions/historical memory of the repressed past and their ongoing political repercussions in Spain's present, which the director attempts to resolve in his subsequent Spanish-language film dealing with the civil war, *El laberinto del fauno*.

EL LABERINTO DEL FAUNO

In June 2010, Almodóvar released a controversial nine-minute video in which he and a cast of famous Spanish and Latin American actors (Maribel Verdú, Javier Bardem, Pilar Bardem, Juan Diego Botto, and others) recited first-person testimonies of fifteen individual victims of summary execution during the civil war and its aftermath. Each account finished with the same words: 'I had no trial, no lawyer, no sentence. My family is still looking for me. How much longer?' (Almodóvar 2010). Paul Preston points out that, while there were atrocities and summary executions committed by both sides during the civil war, the Nationalist right murdered a far greater number of people in a campaign of systematic annihilation of Republicans and anyone associated with them (2012: xvii–xviii). While the victims of Republican violence were lionised and celebrated (and their numbers often inflated) throughout the thirty-five years of the Franco regime, these other victims, on whose behalf Almodóvar and the others speak, were forgotten, their numbers hidden, and attempts to discover their resting places blocked (Preston 2012: xix). *El laberinto del fauno* – made and released in 2006 as the Spanish Congress was discussing the controversial 'Ley de Memoria Histórica' (Law of Historical Memory), which was passed in 2007 – can be seen as part of a 'collective project of recovery of the Spanish past' (Andrés del Pozo 2010: 2–3) and an attempt to redress both the imbalances of official histories of the civil war and the erasures of the 1977 'Pacto del olvido' (Pact of Forgetting). Through its fantasy/horror narrative, *El laberinto* self-consciously takes on the political work of restoring Spain's historical memory and the equally political task of historical representation.

A Spanish/Mexican co-production, *El laberinto* involved monies from del Toro's Tequila Gang, Spanish Estudios Picasso (a film unit of the Spanish television company Telecinco), and Cuarón's Esperanto Filmoj. A French company, Wild Bunch, distributed the film internationally, and Picturehouse distributed the film in the United States (Lázaro-Reboll, 2008). At Spain's annual Goya Awards, *El laberinto* was accepted 'without controversy' as a Spanish film (Smith 2007: 4). In Mexico, it was similarly accepted as a national film and put forward to the Academy Awards as the country's nomination for Best Foreign Film. In the United States, *El laberinto* was received by English-language audiences as an adult fairy tale about good and evil, following broad generic trends popular in contemporary filmmaking (Lázaro-Reboll 2008: 72). *El laberinto* eventually won several Oscars (for Makeup, Cinematography, and Art Direction) but tellingly missed out on Best Foreign Film. All these facts point to *El laberinto* as a transnational product, simultaneously within and without national borders. Further evidence to this fact includes its finances. It had an average Spanish film budget ($18 million) but grossed a more Hollywood-sized $80 million worldwide, making it one of the most successful Spanish-language films in terms of box office returns.[8] At the same time, despite this evidence of its apparent transnationality, *El laberinto* is also engaging with a very specific, local reality directed not just at Spanish audiences but also Latin American audiences – who have also experienced totalitarian governments carrying out systematic plans of annihilation with impunity and have processed these traumas through cinematic representation (Patricio Guzmán's *Nostalgia de la luz/Nostalgia for the Light* [2011] and Pablo Larraín's *Post Mortem* [2010], among many other possible examples). *El laberinto* is therefore a mixture of American horror and other transnational generic references, as well as very local, specific references.

For instance, like *El espinazo*, *El laberinto* recalls and reworks elements of Spain's cinematic past through the use of some of the same features as *El espíritu de la colmena*. It is set similarly in the post war era; it has a child protagonist, Ofelia (Ivana Baquero), and is based loosely around the conventions of horror and also fantasy. There is a scary house/mill (the military outpost), where Ofelia and her mother go to live (with her army captain stepfather). There is also a 'monster' she meets (a faun in a labyrinth who sends her on a quest). And, like *El espinazo* and *El espíritu*, *El laberinto* uses the fantasy and horror aspects of its diegesis to explore the political task of historical representation and memory.

The film opens with an on-screen legend situating the action within historical reality. It is 'Spain 1944,' 'the war is over,' and 'armed men are still fighting the new fascist regime'. The subsequent image shifts from this historical reality into a fairy tale world. A close-up on a bleeding (and dying) Ofelia moves closer into her eye as the film 're-starts' this time with a standard fairy tale beginning: 'A long time ago in … '. The shot fades from Ofelia's pupil into 'the Underground Realm,' a dark, cave-like city, and follows a young 'princess' (Ofelia) escaping to the 'human world' up a long spiral staircase. The voice-over continues: 'Once outside, the brightness blinded her and erased her memory. She forgot who she was.' As if mimicking this erasure (but also signalling the importance of cinematography in the task of both disavowing and reclaiming historical memory), the upward camera movement transitions via a blinding flash to show the ruined town of Belchite, site of a key civil war battle and famously preserved in the present moment in its ruinous state. Cars with Fascist symbols sweep through the ruins carrying Ofelia and her mother to join the captain at his military outpost (the mill).

The camera's movement into Ofelia's eye and the voice-over description of the underground world as one where 'there are no lies or pain' have perhaps led some critics to interpret the fairy tale/fantasy elements of *El laberinto* as an 'escape' or 'retreat' from the 'real life horror' of the Spanish Civil War (Miles 2011: 197; Smith 2007: 5). But as del Toro himself points out, the fairy tales *El laberinto* borrows from represent an already 'brutal' world (Kermode

2006: 23) that is akin rather than separate to horror. Indeed, like many fairy tale characters (Cinderella, Snow White, Hansel and Gretel), Ofelia undergoes deprivation and hardship: losing her mother and having to submit to and eventually outwit an evil stepparent (Capitán Vidal).[9] The tasks the faun gives her are dirty and dangerous and bear an (ultimately realised) real risk of her own death. The faun himself is menacing and untrustworthy and offers her little reassurance from the fears and troubles she faces in the real world or assurances that the promises he makes to her are even reliable.

Rather than an escape, therefore, the film's fairy tale/fantasy elements are more of an alternative and sometimes horrific form of representing the (historical) reality around Ofelia. At key moments in Ofelia's narrative, such as her first encounter in the woods with the mantis/fairy and her entry into the fig tree root, pollen floating visibly in the air signals the presence of the fantasy realm. Pollen is equally visible in the world of the Republican fighters, shining around them in the morning sun as they descend through the woods. This association between the fighters (the *maquis*) and the fairy tale/fantasy elements is part of a larger process in the film that equates Ofelia's struggle in the fantasy world with the anti-Fascist struggle of Mercedes (Verdú) (the housekeeper at the mill) and the *maquis*. Like Ofelia, who has to get hold of a key and then a dagger, Mercedes's support for the *maquis* also involves a key (to the storeroom) and a knife, which she eventually uses to 'gut' Vidal. Editing patterns also suggest the contiguity of the world of fantasy/political resistance alongside or sometimes underneath the 'real' world of Fascism and that the latter is unable to see or experience the former, despite its proximity. The film often moves between these contiguous realms in long continuous takes, moving from Ofelia's brother listening in the womb to the (imaginary) story of the rose at the top of the mountain of thorns. Sometimes these continuous takes are created through the use of masked cuts. When Vidal and his soldiers retreat down the mountain having failed to find the *maquis*, a 'continuous' pan (that uses the movement behind the trees to mask the edit) reveals the *maquis* standing in plain sight watching the soldiers ride away. The fairy tale logic also substitutes for historical reality in part by figuring the film's ending in (historically inaccurate) happy terms: Vidal is killed, and the army is defeated. The *maquis* have won this small battle and are hopeful of future help in the fight against Franco from the Allies.[10]

Emphasising the horrific elements of fantasy, as less like our 'dreams' and more like what Wood would call 'collective nightmares' (1985: 203), *El laberinto* draws on the abject to make the distinction between Fascist Spain and the fantasy (or resistant/alternative) world of historical representation/of Ofelia and the *maquis*. Indeed, as Barbara Creed points out, 'in the way that it does not "respect borders, positions, rules," and is that which "disturbs identity, system, order" abjection is the ideal vehicle to oppose fascism' (Creed 1999: 252). The formation of the self and the entry into the symbolic order (or 'law of the father') necessarily entails a separation from the mother and the rejection or repression of all forms of behaviour that are regarded as unacceptable, improper, or unclean. This includes in particular the proper control of all bodily fluids (shit, mucus, spittle, vomit, blood, urine), which become the abject. As Creed has noted, horror films that abound in images of abjection, such as *The Exorcist* (William Friedkin 1973), pose a challenge to patriarchal authority (1999: 253). In *El laberinto* Ofelia's first task sends her into the roots of a dying fig tree to retrieve a key from a gigantic toad that lives there. The womblike shape of the opening to the tree root itself and the dark, sticky mud Ofelia has to crawl through characterise it as the locus of the abject. When she successfully retrieves the key, she is left covered in mud and the toad's mucus. Underlining Ofelia's dirtiness as a form of (political) opposition, as she emerges filthy from the tree, Vidal holds a dinner party for his cronies (the priest, the local mayor, and others) at which he states that one of his reasons for fighting the *maquis* is so his son can be born in a 'new and clean Spain.' Further underlining her dirtiness as opposition is Ofelia's mother's pronouncement that in dirtying her dress she has hurt 'her father' (Vidal) much more than her mother. In line with theories of abjection, Vidal and the film equate the patriarchal and Fascist order with cleanliness. On several occasions Vidal is shown shining his boots and shaving. Through her dirtiness, Ofelia is like the possessed Reagan in *The Exorcist*. She refuses to take up her proper place in the symbolic order. Her protest (against her 'father's' law) is represented as a return to the pre-Oedipal order. In Ofelia we get a return of the untrained, unsymbolised body. Abjection is constructed as a rebellion of filthy, female flesh.

Unlike other more 'saccharine' treatments of the Spanish Civil War or its aftermath (*La lengua de las mariposas/Butterfly's Tongue* [José Luis Cuerda 1999]), the brutality of the post-war fighting is fully present in *El laberinto* (Smith 2007: 6); it is rendered visible in the various skirmishes between the army and the *maquis* and in particular in the graphically depicted actions of Capitán Vidal, who beats a young hunter to death in the face with a bottle and tortures a captured resistance fighter (El Tarta). In part the directness with which these events are depicted in *El laberinto* relates to the historical moment of the film's production (post-censorship and a moment of recovery of historical past). But *El laberinto* also circumvents what have been classed as the problems of directly representing the Spanish Civil War in part through recourse to a horror-inflected fantasy world. David Archibald has suggested that in addition to the 'legacy of fear' caused by post-war repression and the 'pacto del olvido', another reason why the Spanish Civil War has been less represented in Spanish cinema and in Spanish culture in general is because as a 'holocaustal' event it 'may be un-representable by conventional artistic modes' (2004: 78). Archibald's comments find a point of contact with the film's fantasy elements and in particular their Freudian-inflected horror scenarios.

For instance, Ofelia's second task is readable through the dream-work (condensation, displacement) Freud identifies in his *Interpretations of Dreams*: dream-work that, he argues, permits the representation of taboo, forbidden and traumatic elements of our conscious life that would otherwise be 'unrepresentable' (1991: 383–413, 414–419).[11] In the task, she encounters a monstrous Pale Man in an underground realm she has entered via a door drawn with a piece of magic chalk. The Pale Man appears as a *displaced* version of Vidal with a number of textual parallels suggesting this connection where physical resemblance does not. Both sit at the end of long tables laden with food, in front of roaring fires (Figure 16 and Figure 17).

Both chase after Ofelia with stumbling, halting steps when she disturbs their order (eating some grapes from the Pale Man's table, taking the 'son' who will carry on his line). The Pale Man is also a *condensed* version of the broader brutalities of Fascist and holocaustal violence. This is suggested by the Goyaesque images of him eating or killing children (recalling 'Saturno devorando a su hijo'), as well as by the pile of children's shoes on the floor in the underground chamber (Figure 18).

These shoes both recall the historical reality of the holocaust (specifically the death camp at Auschwitz, where piles of belongings, including the shoes, of its victims are displayed as a testament to the murder of millions of Jewish people) and *stand in* for those missing children. The use of holocaustal imagery in this scene correlates with the growing use of the term in accounts of the numerous deaths in Spain's Civil War and its aftermath. Preston argues that his choice of the word for his book *The Spanish Holocaust* is to reflect the Nationalists'

Figure 16   *El laberinto del fauno* (Guillermo del Toro 2006)

Figure 17   *El laberinto del fauno* (Guillermo del Toro 2006)

Figure 18   *El laberinto del fauno* (Guillermo del Toro 2006)

'prior plan of systematic mass murder and their subsequent regime of state terror' (2012: xii).

In addition to the Freudian-inflected horror scenarios that draw together Francoist Fascism and the holocaust (suggesting the realm of the Pale Man as a condensed and displaced version of Fascism), the critique of a patriarchal order associated with Fascism (and embodied in Vidal, who uses the masculine 'bienvenidos' [welcome] to greet Ofelia, her mother, and the unborn child to the mill) is also supported by the female imagery in the film, which further establishes some aspects of the fantasy world in opposition to the Fascist world. The branches of the dead tree twist and curve in the shape of fallopian tubes; the faun's horns are similarly fallopian (and not phallically) shaped (Smith 2007: 6).

Ultimately, the film ends with a reference to its broader social project. The final shot of a single flower blooming on the now living fig tree and the voice-over commentary that accompanies it – 'And like most of us, she left behind small traces of her time on earth. Visible only to those who know where to look' – point to Ofelia's existence and represent the reclamation of historical memory for the erased Republican victims. This contrasts with Mercedes's assertion to Vidal just before he is shot dead by the *maquis* that his child (which he hands over to them) will not even learn his father's name.

This chapter has explored how horror and horrific tropes in *Cronos*, *El laberinto del fauno*, and *El espinazo del diablo* function on a political level. It has suggested that the monsters, although sometimes terrifying and ambiguous (particularly Santi and the Faun), are either the sympathetic victims of neocolonialist expansion (Jesús), civil war, or Nationalist impunity (Santi), or, in the case of the Faun, the agents by which those victims (Ofelia) are memorialised. It has also noted how some monsters are unambiguously evil and stand in for Fascism (the Pale Man). It has traced how these films respond to and reproduce a shared Hispanic imaginary, history, and politics of Mesoamerican vampires, ghosts, and systematic violence, against all forms of political opposition but also adapt and adopt Hollywood horror conventions as these have been read in political terms (Wood's idea of the sympathetic monster as a product of social and psychic, and – in this case – political repression, the gothic mysteries of light and shade, and Creed's idea of the filthy, female child as a resistance to patriarchal oppression). Ultimately, the films speak not only to local/national issues but also to transatlantic political concerns (repression, regimes of systematic violence) that horror cinema, with its progressive impulse, is ideally suited to address.

NOTES

1. Del Toro spent two years in development for *The Hobbit* in New Zealand before pulling out of the project (receiving a production credit) and then a further year in Los Angeles and Canada in development for the adaptation of H. P. Lovecraft's *At the Mountains of Madness* (Hewitt 2010; Vlessing 2011). See Rebecca Janicker for more on the perceived sympathies between Lovecraft and del Toro's 'creative outputs' (2014: 45).
2. For more on del Toro's co-authored trilogy see Simon Bacon (2014).
3. Thanks to del Toro's financial backing a print of the only extant copy of about six 'adult' versions of popular wrestling films that Santo and other masked wrestlers

including Blue Demon appeared in, in the late 1960s and the early 1970s was restored.

4. I refer here to the stylistic borrowings from German expressionism and the role of German, Austrian, and other émigré directors (Jacques Tourneur, Alfred Hitchcock) in the development of horror and lighting conventions and its subsequent influences on the development of other national horror styles.

5. Brook played the evil Dr Karol in the wrestling/horror hybrid *Santo en el museo de cera* (*Santo in the Wax Museum* Alfonso Corona Blake 1963) and starred in several other wrestling/horror hybrid films, including *Neutrón contra el Dr. Caronte* (*Neutrón vs. Dr. Caronte* Federico Curiel 1963).

6. My thanks to Alberto Moreiras for pointing this out.

7. The film makes us aware of the war raging at a distance from the orphanage through conversations about its likely outcome, information gleaned from Ayala and Domínguez, and the boys' talk of 'lights in the sky.'

8. Source: boxofficemojo.com

9. Objects also point to fairy tales or works of children's literature: Vidal's pocket watch, the 'tree root' (rabbit hole) into which Ofelia descends to kill the toad, and the green, white apron-covered dress she wears all recall Lewis Carroll's *Alice in Wonderland* (1865), though Alice's apron-covered dress is blue. The *maquis* act a little like the Lost Boys from Barrie's *Peter Pan* (1904), with Mercedes (who looks after them) as their Wendy.

10. See Shaw for more on the relationship between the fantasy and the historical and the political significance of the happy ending (2013a: 80–90).

11. In Chapter 6, 'The Dream-Work', Freud talks about dream's use of symbolism for the disguised representation of latent thoughts and the ways in which the unconscious mind would do this through processes of condensation (putting several objects together in strange ways – the face of one person, the dress of another, the name of a third, and the voice of a fourth), reversals (something meaning the opposite to what we would expect it to mean), and displacement (the representation of one thing by another or transfer of psychic energy from an unacceptable element to an acceptable one).

BRAZIL: INTRODUCTION

Figures over the last few years for the film industry in Brazil, including those published by Brazil's National Film Agency (ANCINE, *Agência Nacional do Cinema*) in its *Anuário Estatístico do Cinema Brasileira* (*Statistical Yearbook of Brazilian Cinema*) and those on the website of the film magazine *Revista Filme B*, point towards its continued expansion. Domestic production is increasing: with 130 national films produced in 2015 up on the 114 films produced in 2014 (Filme B 2016a; ANCINE 2015: 19). Current production numbers are now higher than the 100 films released annually between 1978 and 1980, previously the height of production in Brazilian filmmaking (Johnson 2005: 18). There is also significant growth in the number of screens – 3,000 screens in 2015, compared with 2,465 in 2012 – and consequently in audiences, with ticket sales that are up to 170 million (ANCINE 2015: 10, 12; 2016: 9). Growth in audience numbers overall 'translates' to larger audiences for local films (Donoghue 2014b: 539). The two highest grossing national films of 2016 *Os Dez Mandamentos – O Filme* (Alexandre Avancini) and *Minha Mãe é uma Peça 2* (*My Mother is a Character 2* César Rodrigues) brought in audiences of over 11 and 9 million respectively (Table 6). Unlike Mexico's annual film industry reports, figures published by both ANCINE and Filme B do not specify the number of films supported by the Government because all films produced in Brazil receive some kind of state support (Butcher 2016), although as this section will explore actual funding comes from a variety of sources and not necessarily directly from the state.

Table 6 Top twenty Brazilian box office films 2000–2016 (Filme B: 2017)

1	Os dez Mandamentos-O Filme	DTF/Paris	2016	**11.261.270**	116.418.000
2	Tropa de Elite 2	Zazen/Riof	2010	**11.204.815**	103.812.200
3	Minha Mãe É uma Peça 2	DTF/Paris	2016	**9.311.431**	124.208.504
4	Se eu Fosse Você 2	Fox	2009	**6.137.345**	50.543.885
5	Dois Filhos de Francisco	Sony	2005	**5.319.677**	36.728.278
6	De Pernas pro Ar 2	DTF/Paris	2012	**4.794.658**	50.292.566
7	Carandiru	Sony	2003	**4.693.853**	29.623.481
8	Minha Mãe É uma Peça-O Filme	DTF/Paris	2013	**4.604.505**	49.534.000
9	Nosso Lar	Fox	2010	**4.060.000**	36.126.000
10	Até Que a Sorte nos Separe 2	DTF/Paris	2013	**3.988.386**	45.355.454
11	Se Eu Fosse Você	Fox	2006	**3.780.941**	28.916.137
12	Loucas pra Casar	DTF/Paris	2015	**3.779.702**	45.905.145
13	De Pernas pro AR	DTF/Paris	2011	**3.563.723**	31.521.072
14	Até Que a Sorte nos Separe	DTF/Paris	2012	**3.435.824**	34.802.906
15	Chico Xavier	DTF/Sony	2010	**3.414.900**	30.300.000
16	Cidade de Deus	Lumiêre	2002	**3.370.871**	19.066.087
17	Até Que a Sorte nos Separe 3	DTF/Paris	2015	**3.329.770**	42.251.460
18	Vai Que Cola	H2O	2015	**3.317.275**	41.910.200
19	Lisbela E O Prisioneiro	Fox	2003	**3.174.643**	19.915.933
20	Meu Passado me Condena	DTF/Paris	2013	**3.171.446**	34.977.047

Other figures circulated in the *anuários* and by Filme B are less positive in terms of how Brazil's national cinema is performing in its own market. As in Mexico, the Brazilian market is dominated by US films and US distributors (ANCINE 2015: 48–49). In 2014, US titles and Motion Picture Association (MPA) member companies, Twentieth Century Fox, Disney, Warner, Paramount and Sony were responsible for all but one of Brazil's box office top twenty films, including Brazilian director José Padilha's (*Ônibus 174/Bus 174* [2002], *Tropa de Elite/Elite Squad* [2007], *Tropa de Elite 2: O Inimigo Agora é Outro/Elite Squad: The Enemy Within* [2010]) remake of *RoboCop*, which occupies the twentieth slot. In 2015, things were a little better with MPA member companies responsible for seventeen of the top twenty films and local films *Loucas pra Casar*, *Vai que Cola* (*What if Something Happens* César Rodrigues 2015) at numbers 10 and 12 respectively and *Meu Passado Me Condena 2* (*Condemned by my Past* Julia Rezende 2015) just in at number 20 (Table 7). Some commentators point out that at the moment mostly comedies like *Loucas pra Casar* (*Mad to Marry* Roberto Santucci) and *Vai que Cola*, and in particular comedy franchises like *Até que a sorte nos separe* (*Til Luck Us do Part* Roberto Santucci 2012, 2013 and 2016) and *Se Eu Fosse Vôce* (*If I were you* Daniel Filho 2006 and 2009) do well in the Brazilian market (Butcher 2016). While other commentators suggest that local successes (like the *Tropa de Elite* films) are dependent on the appropriation of 'Hollywood style action [and other genre] film[s]' (Bentes 2013: 104). What is true is that since the beginnings of the recovery (*retomada*) of the Brazilian film industry in 1995 after its near demise in 1990, Brazil's share of its own market has always fluctuated. Although it has not returned to the near 30 per cent of the late 1970s (Johnson 2005: 18), certain extremely successful films like *Os Dez Mandamentos – O Filme* and *Tropa de Elite 2*, which are not just the top grossing national films of the last fifteen years but have also broken the previous record of ten million spectators held by *Dona Flor e seus Dois Maridos* (*Dona Flor and Her Two Husbands* Bruno Barreto 1976), have pushed the domestic industry's share above 15 per cent and even higher in some years (see Tables 6 and 8).[1] In 2016 the *anuário* recounts a drop in the domestic cinema's share of the annual box office which was 18.6 per cent in 2013 to 13 per cent in 2015 (ANCINE 2015: 16 ; 2016: 9). Filme B offers some slight variation with 2015's audience share lower at 12.7 per cent (Filme B 2016b). Although, in comparative terms, these figures look much better for Brazil than for Mexico (Mexico's market share in 2015 was 6.1 per cent, Argentina's was 14.49 per cent), the picture of Hollywood domination of the local industry where the top ten US films represent 35 per cent to 45 per cent of the market, is still very much the same (Butcher 2016).

However, the current state of Brazilian cinema is also much more complicated than straightforward Hollywood hegemony (Alvaray 2008: 54–55). As media studies scholar Courtney Brannon Donoghue points out, Brazilian films that perform outstandingly well in the national market, the '*blockbuster*[s] *brasileiro*[s]' (Brazilian blockbusters), including the body swap comedy *Se Eu Fosse Vôce 2*, which achieved the fourth largest audience in fifteen years (6.1 million) and the prison drama *Carandiru* (Hector Babenco 2003) which had the seventh largest audience (4.6 million) in the same period, are also predominantly distributed by MPA member companies. She also points out that their box office success is largely dependent on the advantages of scale – in terms of budgets, numbers of prints/screens and marketing campaigns – that the MPA companies can provide (often through local partnerships) (2014b: 543) (see Table 6).[2] *Se Eu Fosse Vôce 2* was distributed by Fox and *Carandiru* was distributed by Sony. Brazilian blockbusters also do well in the local market, Donoghue suggests, not simply because they emulate Hollywood style or genre, but because of their 'exceptionality on a local level' and also convergence (sharing stars and formats between television and film such as Globo's recent *Vai que Cola*), which itself is part of that local exceptionality (Donoghue 2014b: 538).

Table 7 Top twenty box office films Brazil 2015 (ANCINE 2016: 12)

No	Título	Gênero	País	Distribuidora	Data de lançamento	Salas no lançamento	Público 2015	Renda (r$) 2015
1	Vingadores: A Era de Ultron	Ficção	Estados Unidos	Disney	23/04/2015	1.356	10.129.071	146.184.931,00
2	Velozes e Furiosos 7	Ficção	Estados Unidos	Universal	02/04/2015	1.046	9.857.946	142.465.883,37
3	Minions	Animação	Estados Unidos	Universal	25/06/2015	1.084	8.912.094	119.998.320,79
4	Cinquenta Tons de Cinza	Ficção	Estados Unidos	Universal	12/02/2015	1.087	6.685.086	87.741.026,57
5	Jurassic World: O mundo Dos dinossauros	Ficção	Estados Unidos	Universal	11/06/2015	1.001	6.356.559	90.707.161,19
6	Star Wars: Episódio VII - O despertar da Força	Ficção	Estados Unidos	Disney	17/12/2015	1.505	5.558.321	90.448.267,00
7	Jogos Vorazes: A esperança - O final	Ficção	Estados Unidos	Paris	19/11/2015	1.718	4.392.977	63.524.902,67
8	Cinderela	Ficção	Estados Unidos	Disney	26/03/2015	931	4.199.697	50.079.019,00
9	Divertida Mente	Animação	Estados Unidos	Disney	18/06/2015	879	3.780.325	45.644.493,00
10	**Loucas pra Casar**	**Ficção**	**Brasil**	**Downtown/ Paris**	**08/01/2015**	**604**	**3.726.547**	**45.688.069,53**
11	Bob Esponja: Um Herói Fora d'água	Animação	Estados Unidos	Paramount	05/02/2015	818	3.719.487	48.261.491,00
12	**Vai que Cola - O Filme**	**Ficção**	**Brasil**	**H2o Films**	**01/10/2015**	**636**	**3.307.837**	**41.803.908,21**
13	Hotel Transilvânia 2	Animação	Estados Unidos	Sony	24/09/2015	577	3.272.742	42.073.475,85
14	Os Pinguins de Madagascar	Animação	Estados Unidos	Fox	15/01/2015	911	3.133.452	40.478.965,00

	Título	Gênero	País	Distribuidora	Data	Salas	Público	Renda
15	Homem-Formiga	Ficção	Estados Unidos	Disney	16/07/2015	860	2.927.606	41.539.259,00
16	A Série Divergente - Insurgente	Ficção	Estados Unidos	Paris	19/03/2015	1.101	2.819.817	39.037.020,04
17	Missão impossível - nação secreta	Ficção	Estados Unidos	Paramount	13/08/20150	947	2.711.422	37.270.687,00
18	Uma Noite no Museu 3: O Segredo da Tumba	Ficção	Estados Unidos, Reino Unido	Fox	01/01/2015	610	2.707.296	30.904.464,00
19	O Último Caçador de Bruxas	Ficção	Estados Unidos	Paris	29/10/2015	1.050	2.658.580	34.438.709,33
20	**Meu Passado Me Condena 2**	**Ficção**	**Brasil**	**Downtown/Paris**	**20/07/015**	**618**	**2.639.935**	**32.941.689,75**

Table 8 Evolution of market share (Brazil) (Filme B: 2016b)

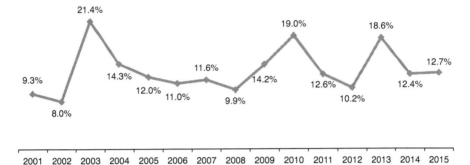

| 2001 | 2002 | 2003 | 2004 | 2005 | 2006 | 2007 | 2008 | 2009 | 2010 | 2011 | 2012 | 2013 | 2014 | 2015 |

Donoghue's argument about the cycle of local blockbusters which have done well in Brazil since the 2000s and their connections to global and local trends in media industries *and* local culture is a significant reframing of 'conversations' about Brazilian cinema. These conversations, she points out, have tended to revolve around the *retomada* and its base in state-supported cultural policies (Donoghue 2014b: 537). Although the state has undoubtedly been significant in the recovery of Brazilian cinema, Donoghue's approach also emphasises the importance of the interplay between 'cultural industries and globalization' extending beyond Brazil and its role in the resurgence of the national cinema (2014b: 537).

Donoghue's framing of the current situation and recent history of Brazilian cinema which emphasises the complicated intermingling of strategies and relationships between the Brazilian and Hollywood industries (2014b: 541) rather than the narratives of imperialism and domination emphasised by others (Rêgo 2011: 39) is a fitting starting point to this introduction to Brazilian Cinema. Particularly because, in addition to establishing how Fernando Meirelles and Walter Salles are key figures in Brazilian film culture and its resurgence, this section acts as a platform to director-centred Chapters 4 and 5 which explore Meirelles' and Salles' directorial interactions with and borrowings from Hollywood and its independent environs. Meirelles' and Salles' initial transnational successes and subsequent career trajectories can also be related to the shifts in global media strategies – increased transnational partnerships, commercialisation, franchises and convergence – outlined by Donoghue and also by Luisela Alvaray (Donoghue 2014b: 537; Alvaray 2008, 2011). Meirelles' *Cidade de Deus*, which was developed through the Sundance Screenwriters Lab, consciously borrows genre and commercialised formats (as explored in Chapter 4), received global advertising and distribution through Miramax and attracted audiences of 3.3 million in Brazil, was one of the first in the '*blockbuster brasileiro*' cycle that Donoghue identifies.

Its television spin-off series *Cidade dos Homens* (*City of Men* 2002–2005), partly directed by Meirelles, produced through his company O2Filmes and aired on Rede Globo make it part of a 'cross-media franchise' (Donoghue 2011: 62).[3] Similarly, Salles' *Central do Brasil*, which was developed and financed internationally also through the Sundance Screenwriters Lab and through pre-sales in several international territories by several companies including Disney subsidiary Buena Vista and Miramax on the strength of its script, is also in many ways the first '*blockbuster brasileiro*' although it was produced two years before the cycle Donohue identifies and attracted a more modest domestic audience (in comparison with the *blockbusters brasileiros*) of 1.5 million (Nagib 2006: 95–96; Rodríguez Isaza 2012: 65–66; Shaw 2013b: 27).

This section's account of the resurgence of Brazilian cinema in the last twenty years centres itself around Salles and Meirelles as exemplary products of, as well as primary participants in, the *retomada* and the global shifts in media strategies as they have occurred in Brazil and includes their producing as well as directorial activities. It focuses both on the state's fiscal measures and (re-configured) involvement in the industry and the strategies on the part of transnational media conglomerates and local media which have reinvigorated and renewed filmmaking in Brazil.

The closure of the state-run film enterprise Embrafilme in 1990, together with the withdrawal of funding and the elimination of screen quotas by Brazil's first democratically elected president in twenty years, Fernando Collor de Mello (1990–1992) reduced production from seventy-four features in 1989 to single figures (Alvaray 2008: 50). Whilst Salles, who had up to this point been making documentaries for television, made the 'for hire' English language co-production *Exposure* (*A Grande Arte* 1991), many other directors found it 'difficult' if not 'impossible' to make films without Government investment (Rêgo 2005: 85; Marzon 2009: 37; Matheou 2010: 32).

Two new laws implemented in 1992 and 1993 facilitated the re-emergence of Brazilian cinema. The first was the Rouanet Law, which encouraged corporate investment in local productions through a tax incentive system. The second was the *Lei do Audiovisual* (Audiovisual Law), which allowed producers to 'float individual projects on the Brazilian stock market,' and 'foreign distributors with local subsidiaries to invest up to seventy per cent of their income tax on profits in Brazil in local film projects' (Rêgo 2011: 38). In keeping with a range of other neoliberal measures, the idea behind these laws was to re-establish public support for Brazilian films until they could compete 'on a more equal footing with foreign products' (Rêgo 2005: 88) and to create 'a self-sustainable industry by attracting foreign financial resources and expanding the market' (Alvaray 2008: 60). The Audiovisual Law's tax incentive provisions had an 'almost immediate impact'. MPA member studios grabbed the opportunity to invest and make money from local features (Alvaray 2008: 60). Since 1993, the Rouanet Law and the Audiovisual Law have partially financed 'almost all' Brazilian films (Alvaray 2008: 60).

Walter Salles' *Terra estrangeira* (*Foreign Land* co-directed with Daniela Thomas, 1995) was part of the first wave of films benefitting from the new incentive laws that signalled the industry's box office and critical 'rebirth'. As the new incentive laws as well as another Government initiative, the *Prêmio Resgate do Cinema Brasileiro* (Brazilian Cinema Rescue Award) began to show their first positive results it was one of several successful films released in 1995. Others included *Carlota Joaquina, princesa do Brazil* (*Carlota Joaquina* Carla Camurati), which attracted over a million spectators, *Cinema de Lágrimas* (*Cinema of Tears* Nelson Pereira dos Santos) and *O Quatrilho* (Fábio Barreto) (Rêgo 2011: 36; Marzon 2009: 69).[4]

Also driving the Brazilian film industry's 'growth and expansion', was Sony Pictures International, the first of several MPA companies attracted by the new incentive laws to enter into co-productions in Brazil. Through its 'Local Language Unit' (designed to co-produce and distribute films and television programmes specifically for regional and local audiences), Sony do Brasil, it co-produced ten productions including *Tieta do Agreste* (*Tieta* Carlos Diegues 1998) and *O Que é isso, Companheiro?* (*Four Days in September* Bruno Barreto 1997) (Donoghue 2014a: 5, 17–18). Further enabling the *retomada*, the growth in theatrical infrastructure and consequently the number of screens allowed audiences for Brazilian cinema to rise throughout the period, with the number of people watching Brazilian cinema 'climb[ing] to 7.2 million' in 2000 from a low of 36,000 in 1992 (Shaw and Dennison 2007: 36–37; Donoghue 2014b: 539). In addition to starting to bring Brazilian audiences back to its national cinema, the other great achievement of the *retomada* period was the 'widespread recognition' both in Brazil and globally directors like Salles brought to Brazilian filmmaking (Moisés 2003: 3). Sony Picture Classics distributed Salles' *Central do Brasil* (1998) which, in addition to making $21 million in worldwide box office was one of three Brazilian films, together with *O Quatrilho* and *O Que é Isso, Companheiro?* that was nominated for the Oscar for Best Foreign Film in a three-year period (Moisés 2003: 3; Alvaray 2008: 51). Salles' film also became a critical success in Europe, winning the Golden Bear at the Berlin Film Festival in 1998 as well as Best Actress for Fernanda Montenegro, who also won the US Golden Globe and the British BAFTA (Nagib 2003: xviii).

The entry of the Brazilian media conglomerate, and largest television producer Rede Globo into filmmaking in 1998, the beginning of the period of growth after the *retomada* known as the *pós-retomada*, was another significant factor in the expansion of the Brazilian film industry and the increase in the audience share for national films (Rêgo 2011: 41; Shaw and Dennison 2007: 38).[5] Globo's creation of producing and distribution partnerships with Motion Picture Association companies including Sony (and its film division Columbia), Fox and Warner Bros. was one of its most successful 'strategies' (Donoghue 2011: 56). Whilst Globo (as a non-independent producer) has been unable to take advantage of the tax incentive laws, 'foreign-owned' member companies have been able to raise funds under the law, allowing them to make 'low-risk investments' through co-producing and distributing local films (Donoghue 2011: 56). These partnerships give MPA member companies access to local knowledge and Globo access to the distribution resources the MPA member companies (through their long term domination of distribution and exhibition in Brazil) have at their disposal. It also, however, gives Globo and its MPA partners, who have co-produced seventeen of Brazil's top twenty box office films in the period 2000–2016 including four of the top five, *Tropa de Elite 2*, *Minha Mãe é uma Peça 2*, *Se Eu Fosse Vôce 2*, and *Dois Filhos de Francisco* (*Two Sons of Francisco* Breno Silveira 2005), an effective box office monopoly in a 'supposedly openly-commercial market' (Donoghue 2011: 56–57; Table 6).[6] This leaves independent filmmakers with no automatic access to distribution and exhibition and, it has been suggested, with 'few chances of success' (Donoghue 2011: 57).

However, Meirelles and Salles are two independent filmmakers and producers who have benefited from relationships with MPA member companies and Globo Filmes. They both secured MPA distribution deals for their initial international directorial successes and MPA co-production and/or distribution deals for subsequent domestic and transnational projects. Salles' *Central do Brasil* secured a distribution deal with Sony Picture Classics. His *Motorcycle Diaries* was a Brazil, Argentina, Perú, France, UK and US co-production that involved monies from Universal's specialist division, Focus Features. His *Abril Despedaçado* (*Behind the Sun* 2001), although a Brazil, France, Switzerland co-production, was distributed through Disney Subsidiary Buena Vista, and Miramax. *Linha de passe* (co-directed with Daniela Thomas, 2008) was another Brazil, France co-production distributed through Universal.[7] Meirelles' *Cidade de Deus* (which was co-produced by Salles through his VideoFilmes) was wholly funded by Meirelles, but distributed and advertised globally through Miramax. *The Constant Gardener* was co-produced with Focus Features. Through his (São Paulo-based) production company O2Filmes and like del Toro, Cuarón and Iñárritu's Mexico/US production company Cha Cha Chá, Meirelles established a multipicture deal with Focus Features that has produced *Blindness* (2010) (Donoghue 2014a: 8). Meirelles has also entered into film and cross-media collaborations; with Globo for the *Cidade de Deus*-spin off television series *Cidade dos Homens*, which stars some of the same non-professional actors (Darlan Cunha and Douglas Silva) and again with Globo and Twentieth Century Fox for the follow up film to the television series *Cidade dos Homens* (*City of Men* Paulo Morelli 2007).

In addition to Salles' and Meirelles' own films, their partnerships with MPA member companies and, in the case of Meirelles, partnerships with Globo Filmes have facilitated their fostering of young independent filmmakers (Andrucha Waddington, Tata Amaral, Cao Hamburger, Sérgio Machado, Karim Aïnouz, Marcelo Gomes), often through their production companies: Salles' Rio-based Videofilmes and Meirelles' O2Filmes. Waddington, who gained work experience on set with Salles has had *Eu Tu Eles* (*Me You Them* 2000) and *Casa de Areia* (*House of Sand* 2005) co-produced and, in the case of *Casa de Areia*, developed with MPA local language unit Columbia Filmes do Brasil, Globo Filmes and his own production company Conspiração (Matheou 2010: 26–27).[8] Meirelles' O2Filmes and Globo Filmes have also co-produced Amaral's *Antônia* (2006).[9] Cao Hamburger's *O Ano em que Meus Pais Saíram de Férias* (*The Year My Parents Went on Vacation* 2006) was co-produced with Globo and his epic *Xingu* (2012) was co-produced with Globo and O2Filmes. As independent producers running major production companies (that also produce commercials as well as films and, in Meirelles' case, television series) Meirelles and Salles have also been able to take advantage of the Globo Filmes financial and technological services, as well as the access to advertising on its network and the MPA's access to distribution and tax incentive monies (Rêgo 2011: 43). What these production narratives show is that, although Globo Filmes and MPA member companies may dominate the majority of the market with both Hollywood films and local blockbusters, they are also helping to diversify film production by co-producing independent productions like *Eu Tu Eles, Casa de Areia* and *Aquarius* (Kleber Mendonça Filho 2015) as well as enabling these smaller films to circulate outside of Brazil.

However, despite helping to foster Brazil's independent sector and the support of industry veterans like producer and screenwriter Luiz Carlos Barreto and director Carlos Diegues and film scholars like Randal Johnson, Globo's involvement in film production in Brazil remains a point of contention (Johnson 2007: 99; Donoghue 2011: 58).[10] Salles himself and others have been critical of Globo Filmes' 'perceived dumbing down of national films' (Matheou 2010: 25; Shaw and Dennison 2007: 39), suggesting that films based on its own successful television series (*A Grande Família – O Filme/The Big Family – The Film* Maurício Farias 2007) effectively televisualise cinema. Equally in line for criticism is the way Globo's film success normalises the high production values the network's huge resources can provide including its contract television stars (who represent the star system in Brazil). Consequently, critics suggest, lower budgeted productions find the audience's taste skewed against them (Rêgo 2011: 43; Donoghue 2011: 62). However, what these criticisms perhaps don't take into account is that Globo is also involved in lower budgeted productions like *Eu Tu Eles* and that these productions are considerably helped by the presence of Rede Globo stars such as soap opera actors Lima Duerte and Stênio Garcia who appear in *Eu Tu Eles*. Additionally, and as Donohue would likely argue, the presence of television stars in Globo films, is part of what ensures Globo films' local 'exceptionality' (2014b).

For Salles, who has not partnered with Globo for his own films, a more attractive means of fostering younger filmmakers who have worked with him as writers and assistants on his films (Aïnouz, Machado and Gomes) has been a similar route to the one he has taken in his own directorial projects: traditional co-productions within Latin America and Europe, with help from the US independent sector.[11] In 2010 through VideoFilmes, and not unlike Meirelles' agreement with Focus Features, Salles established a development, production and distribution agreement with French production company Studio Canal, whose first production was Machado's *Quincas Berro D'Agua/ The Two Deaths of Quincas Wateryell* (2010) (Hopewell 2010). The film was ultimately also co-produced through Globo Filmes.

International co-productions with various European and Latin American producers or states has also been facilitated by the Brazillian Government. Brazil holds multiple bilateral and multilateral co-production agreements with countries across Latin America, North America and Europe, including Germany, Chile, Canada, Argentina, Venezuela, Portugal, Italy and France. As Alessandra Meleiro points out, as well as the Latin-American Film Co-production Agreement (1989) and the Ibermedia Programme (explored in the Introduction), 'the creation of the "Mercosul Audiovisual" programme, in partnership with the European Union (EU), has strengthened audiovisual co-production ties between Brazil and Europe through the injection of some €1.8 million' (2010: 13). A festival favourite in 2016 was *Boi Neon* (*Neon Bull* Gabriel Mascaro 2015), which was funded through the Ibermedia programme. In addition to access to public funding sources in the co-producing country, what these co-production partnerships offer is greater access to distribution.[12] Meireilles' *Blindness* was the first feature film to be produced from the Brazil-Canada Agreement (1995). A co-production between O2Filmes, Rhombus Media (Canada) and Bee Vine Pictures (Japan), *Blindness* had a budget of $25 million, funded exclusively from Brazilian tax incentive laws (Meleiro 2010: 15). In addition to the film's distribution in Brazil through Twentieth Century Fox (largely secured through Meirelles' previous box office success) the partnership also ensured the film's release abroad, in the US, Canada and Japan (Meleiro 2010: 15) and globally by Miramax.

In 2016 Brazil set up a new co-production fund – Fundo Setorial do Audiovisual (FSA Fund) – of $1.6 million to invest in minority Brazilian co-productions with nineteen Latin American countries. The fund was designed to increase the number of Latin American films shown in Brazil and expand 'the presence of Brazilian cinema in the international market' (De Pablos 2015). One of the first productions to be produced by the fund was *Zoom* (Pedro Morelli 2015) a Brazil/Canada co-production which stars Gael García Bernal and was co-produced with Meirelles' O2Filmes (Cajueiro 2016).

As the figures offered at the beginning of this section show, since the introduction of the tax incentive laws and subsequent measures which have added to and ensured the effectiveness of these laws (such as Brazil's FSA fund and a tax on foreign distributors) and the expansion of the theatrical sector, Brazilian cinema has maintained a significant share of its own market and a rise in its production numbers. However, although production has become easier, exhibition remains an obstacle to filmmakers in Brazil (as indeed it does in all Latin American countries). As Melina Marzon points out, in 1990, with the closure of Embrafilme, Brazilian cinema lost not just its principle financer and nationwide distributor but also any legislated protection against foreign, principally Hollywood films (2009: 23–24). The new laws of 1990s did not make financial provision for the distribution and exhibition of the films they have helped to produce (Rêgo 2011: 38, 42) and consequently, many Brazilian films struggle to receive theatrical runs that 'realise their income potential' (Donoghue 2011: 53; Diegues qtd in Donoghue 2011: 53).

Whilst ANCINE was created (in 2002) to precisely address these issues of exhibition, distribution and protection (a task previously performed by Embrafilme), it has not been able to 'offset' the 'chronic structural conditions [foreign domination of the exhibition and distribution sector, difficulty of amortising costs in the domestic market] that make Brazilian cinema vulnerable' (Rêgo 2011: 39). Although it has been successful in clawing back some of the profit foreign distributors make in Brazilian markets through a tax on all foreign films as a way of 'subsidizing national film production' (Rêgo 2011: 41), it has been unsuccessful in controlling the flow of foreign film via a quota system (Rêgo 2011: 41).

CONCLUSION

Since the early 1990s the terrain for filmmaking in Brazil has improved considerably. Overall figures for cinema attendance have risen, production levels have also recovered from the single figures of the early 1990s. The attempted 'marketisation' of the Brazilian cinema has achieved great successes producing more films that are popular with audiences, but the foreign domination of the national market remains unchanged. Salles and Meirelles have been a part of the former and have tried to remedy the latter. They have translated the cultural capital (or 'leverage') their transnational successes have provided them with to foster independent filmmaking in Brazil (Matheou 2010: 191). They are able to point out that continued domination of screen space by Hollywood blockbusters is a key reason for the failure of Brazilian cinema (Meirelles qtd in Carneiro: 2012) whilst at the same time embracing the necessity of MPA involvement through co-productions and formal alliances.

For all that Salles and Meirelles can do, Brazilian filmmaking remains dependent on financial support from the state and is still some way away from achieving the official objective of self sufficiency. The state may no longer have a direct role in film production but it maintains its now more indirect role through government sponsored production financing pro-grammes which outweigh any other financial investment in the industry. In 2008 for instance, $182 million was invested in filmmaking through local, regional and national incentives, subsidies and support programmes including that of the Brazilian National Development Bank (BNDES), and the giant state owned oil enterprise (Petrobrás), whereas the total invested through international agreements (Ibermedia, Brazil-Portugal Co-production, Brazilian-Galicia Co-production Agreement) was a relatively small $2 million (Meleiro 2010: 18).

Brazil's cinematic recovery from the single figures of the early 1990s to the 130 films produced in 2015, is often considered both a hard won victory by Brazilian filmmakers and something that is intrinsically connected to the country's post-1990 democracy. Hence the protest at the 2016 Cannes Film Festival where the cast and crew of Filho's *Aquarius*, including its star Sônia Braga, staged a red carpet demonstration. They were protesting the impeach-ment of president Dilma Rousseff who was forced from office, and interim president Michel Temer's controversial decision to close Brazil's culture min-istry (Smith 2016). At the time of writing [2017], the consequences of Brazil's current political turmoil for film legislation that will foster and protect the national industry are unclear. The announced closure of the Cinemateca Brasileira, which restores and preserves Brazilian films, amongst other activities, in July 2016 however, does not bode well even though, after much protest from filmmakers the closure was reversed. Similarly predictive of dif-ficult times to come is the effective blacklisting of *Aquarius* in the wake of the Cannes protest with respect to the 2017 Oscars. Having previously been the favourite for nomination, a government-appointed Oscar committee did not put it forward as Brazil's entry to the Best Foreign Picture category (Romero 2016). The wider scandal of the 'lava jato' (car wash), which has uncovered a network of bribery and kickbacks between major corporations, executives and politicians – including former president Luiz Inácio Lula da Silva who is now facing a ten-year jail sentence for corruption and four further trials – also threatens future film production (Phillips 2017) given that two of the biggest state companies and financial backers for Brazilian cinema (BNDES and Petrobrás) are caught up in it.

NOTES

1. *Cidade de Deus*, *Carandiru* and *Dois Filhos de Francisco* all boosted audience figures for Brazilian cinema (2002, 2003 and 2005) to record levels in the years of their release. In 2010, *Tropa de Elite 2* outsold its rival Hollywood blockbuster *Shrek Forever After* (Mike Mitchell) by over 3 million spectators helping the national cinema to achieve an audience share of 19 per cent (ANCINE 2010: 2; Filme B 2016b).

2. With respect to the scale of openings that the majors can provide, journalist and contributor to website Filme B Pedro Butcher notes: 'With the exception of *Tropa de Elite 2*, that was released in a number of screens similar to the biggest blockbusters (900 screens), most Brazilian films with market ambitions get a 400–500 screens release. *Captain America – Civil War* (Joe and Anthony Russo 2016) and *Batman vs. Superman* (Zack Snyder 2016) were released in around 1,400 screens (that's half the circuit of Brazil)' (Butcher 2016).

3. The new season of *Cidade dos Homens* produced by O2Filmes aired in January 2017 (O2Filmes 2017).

4. The *Prêmio Resgate do Cinema Brasileiro* was established at the same time as the Lei Audiovisual. Using the funds of the old Embrafilme it funded a series of feature films selected from a competition. At the time it was considered a return to the old practices of Embrafilme as films were chosen on similar political criteria (Marzon 2009: 59). *Carlota Joaquina* was funded through the *Resgate*.

5. Globo Filmes does not finance films directly but instead provides its co-productions with valuable media exposure including publicity spots, interviews and cross-media advertising (including product placement in its television programmes) through their production companies: Salles' Rio-based VideoFilmes (Butcher 2006).

6. Donoghue had made the observation of an earlier period (1995–2007).

7. *On the Road* was, unusually, not distributed through a major but through a number of different countries internationally. IFC/Sundance in the US, Wanda Vision in Spain and MK2 Difusion in France.

8. It was also developed at the Sundance Screenwriters Lab.

9. Through O2Filmes, Meirelles also co-produced the eponymous television spin-off of Amaral's film (imdb.com).

10. Johnson notes '[T]here is little doubt that in purely aesthetic terms the best that Brazilian Cinema has to offer is not necessarily co-produced by Globo Filmes, but it is just as certain that Brazilian cinema would not have made the strides it has in reoccupying at least a portion of its own market without Globo Filmes and its association with U.S. major distributors' (2007: 99).

11. Salles co-produced through VideoFilmes Machado's *Cidade Baixa* (*Lower City* 2005). VideoFilmes also co-produced Aïnouz' *Madam Satã* (2002) and *O Céu de Suely* (*Love for Sale* 2006).

12. Cláudia da Natividade, producer of the Brazil-Italy co-production *Estômago* (*Estomago: A Gastronomic Story* Marcos Jorge 2007), points out that 'co-production ensures that a Brazilian film will be released in at least one other country', adding 'in the case of European partnerships, European certification helps a lot in terms of access to the international market' (Meleiro 2010: 16).

4. FERNANDO MEIRELLES AS TRANSNATIONAL AUTEUR

In 2016 Fernando Meirelles was one of the co-directors (along with Daniela Thomas [*Linha de Passe* 2008, *Terra estrangeira/Foreign Land* 1996, *O Primeiro Dia/Midnight* 1998 all co-directed with Salles] and Andrucha Waddington [*Eu Tu Eles/Me You them* 2000, *Casa de Areia/House of Sand* 2005]) of the opening ceremony of the Olympic Games in Rio's Maracaña Stadium. This is the third time in the recent history of the Olympics that a film director (or in the case of Brazil a team of filmmakers) has been charged with producing a positive image of the nation for global consumption (an estimated audience of three billion). In Beijing in 2008 it was Yimou Zhang (*House of the Flying Daggers* 2004, *Hero* 2002, *Raise the Red Lantern* 1991). In London in 2012 it was Danny Boyle (*Trainspotting 2* 2017, *Trance* 2013, *127 Hours* 2010, *Slumdog Millionaire* 2008, *Trainspotting* 1996). Some commentators have suggested that Meirelles was an 'unexpected choice' to (co)direct the Games' opening ceremony given his 'grim depiction of Rio's crime riddled favelas' in *Cidade de Deus* (2002) (Locke 2016) while others have problematically suggested his suitability for the job given his 'proven track record [in *Cidade de Deus*] of looking at ugly subject matter and rendering it elegantly' (Acevedo-Muñoz cited in Locke 2016).[1]

That Meirelles' representation of Brazil in his first international success *Cidade de Deus* (co-directed with Kátia Lund) should still figure in contemporary Olympics-related references to him, almost fifteen years after the film's release, suggests the 'heated public debates' the film's 'alleged stereotyping of poverty and violence' ignited about how to represent Brazil to the world are still ongoing (Andermann and Bravo 2013: 6). In recent years these debates have expanded to incorporate films which deal with similar subject matter: José Padilha's exploration of the drug war in Rio's *favelas* told from the perspective of a special police unit *Tropa de Elite* (2007) and *Tropa de Elite 2: O Enimigo Agora e Outro* (2011) (Bentes 2013). Brazilian critic Ivana Bentes has directed this criticism in particular at Meirelles and Padilha's use of the heightened aesthetics of the 'Hollywood style action [and other genre] film[s]' and the ideological complicity with a conservative worldview that supposedly goes with these Hollywood borrowings: reducing, this criticism suggests, the lives of Brazil's *comunidades* (the term residents prefer over *favelas*) to 'easily accessible [Hollywood] action codes' (Bentes 2013: 104, 111). Seemingly confirming Bentes' thesis, Padilha has gone from *Tropa de Elite 2* straight to the US to direct the *RoboCop* (2014) reboot and episodes of the Netflix/Telemundo series *Narcos* about Colombian drug kingpin Pablo Escobar (2015, 2016), which he also produced. Meirelles, on the other hand, has been propelled by the success of *Cidade de Deus* (making $27 million worldwide for its US distributors Miramax and winning four Oscar nominations for Cinematography, Editing, Screenplay, and Director) into a series of transnational, deterritorialised film projects none of which sit classically or institutionally completely within Hollywood parametres; a noir thriller *The Constant Gardener* set in Africa, London and Germany (2005), a dystopic science-fiction film *Blindness* (2008) set in a 'global city' and a multi-strand narrative *360* (2011) set in London, Paris, Vienna, Phoenix, Denver and Berlin.

However, despite what this chapter will argue is the non institutional and non classical position of *Cidade de Deus*, *The Constant Gardener* and *Blindness* they have, like the films of some of the other deterritorialised transnational auteurs, been the focus of criticism that situates their aesthetic strategies and ideologies almost totally within hegemonic codes of representation (an undifferentiated Hollywood dominant) and neglects consideration of the political and sometimes relatively peripheral position from which these films speak. For instance, as with *Amores perros* which has been classed as a 'Mexican *Pulp Fiction*', *Cidade de Deus* has been likened (and sometimes derided for its similarity) to a 'Brazilian *Goodfellas*' (Martin Scorsese 1990) as well as a host of other Hollywood films and genres (Shaw 2005: 58; Sampaio 2011: 5; Bentes 2013: 111). Meirelles' English language *The Constant Gardener* has been similarly folded into Western colonialist regimes of representation because of its reliance on 'some of the most basic formulas in Western fiction films about Africa' (Mafe 2011: 74) or simply for being a financially transnational but still 'culturally English' film (Higson 2011: 67). *Blindness* has been equally evaluated as 'bound' by 'Hollywood-derived' 'cinematic codes' and the rules of dominant cinema (Sampaio 2011: 1; Overhoff Ferreira 2013: 13). As a continuation of this book's project of contesting the notion that directors from the Global South are 'effaced' when they work in Hollywood or its related systems (Naficy 1996: 120), and that the use of Hollywood genres necessarily precludes any political commitment this chapter wishes to explore the links between *Cidade de Deus* and two of Meirelles' deterritorialised films *The Constant Gardener* and *Blindness* in ways that account for their cultural specificity and the position of their director in a global economy of representation. Drawing on the work of those who have sought to emphasise the 'rooted[ness] in Brazilian reality' of *Cidade de Deus* (Nagib 2004) as well as others who have commented on its 'distinctive[ness]' in international spaces (Vieira 2007: 51) this chapter seeks to unpick the complex aesthetic and industrial position of Meirelles' local and deterritorialised films. At the same time, the chapter mounts a robust defence of the political potential of the genre film and the ways in which Meirelles uses it in *Cidade de Deus*, *The Constant Gardener* and *Blindness*.

In making these arguments the aim however, is not to 'save' these films from what is often seen as an always hegemonic Hollywood only to redeem them as part of an arguably homogenised world cinema system of representation as other critics have attempted to do with other transnational Latin American films (see for instance Paul Kerr's approach to *Amores perros* in Chapter 1). Eleftheria Thanouli, for instance, groups *Cidade de Deus* together with *Pulp Fiction* (Quentin Tarantino 1994), *Amelie* (Jean Pierre Jeunet 2001) and, *Chungking Express* (Kar-wai Wong 1994) as films which share a vocabulary that is mainstream but not rooted in any cinematic tradition, including Hollywood (Thanouli 2008: 8). Whilst it is problematic to view the totality of *Cidade de Deus* within Hollywood, it is equally difficult to situate the film solely within a 'world cinema' tradition that is not Hollywood. Both approaches do not pay enough attention to the locality and specificity of the film in the moment of its production and how its aesthetics can be related to the history of Brazil's militant filmmaking movement of the 1960s (Cinema Novo) or to its significant borrowings and subversions of a Hollywood genre and subgenre. At the same time, however, it is also important to acknowledge that Brazilian cinema, Hollywood and 'world cinema' are not necessarily completely discrete fields of production either as illustrated by the institutional position of Meirelles' films' US distributors. Miramax (*Cidade de Deus*, *Blindness*) and Focus Features (*The Constant Gardener*) are (or in Miramax's case have become) both specialist divisions of the major studios (Disney and Universal respectively) that seek to financially benefit from films that 'are somewhere between Hollywood and the farthest reaches of independence', which can include the work of 'noted international filmmakers' like Meirelles (King 2009: 241, 240). It is also important to note the productivity of exploring the very useful links between *Cidade de Deus*, *The Constant Gardener* and *Blindness* and the US genres they engage with and translate this into an approach which acknowledges the myriad ways Meirelles' local and deterritorialised films have challenged the aesthetic and industrial norms of Hollywood classicism.

In wanting to theorise the aesthetics of Meirelles' films as the products of an individual Brazilian director, this chapter acknowledges the problematic nature of its seemingly auteurist approach given that Meirelles, having worked in advertising, children's films, television and collaboratively, with Lund, in *Cidade de Deus* (Nagib 2006: 96), has not always conformed to or indeed been considered an 'auteur' in the sense of an individual artist producing non mainstream films. Indeed, the chapter acknowledges how it is only from the international marketing of *Cidade de Deus* onwards that a certain construction of Meirelles emerges which is dependant both on norms of transnational auteurism (resistance to commercial imperatives) and a selective account of his oeuvre (that more often than not excises his first feature *Menino Maluquinho 2* [*The Nutty Boy 2* 1998] and children's television series *Castelo Rá-Tim-Bum* [Ra Tim Bum Castle 1989) – as well as the collaborative processes behind the making of *Cidade de Deus*), and on basic premises underlying the understanding of him as a Brazilian director. It investigates the limits of this construction arguing that although it may emphasise the political nature of Meirelles' filmmaking (particularly with respect to the country's history of political filmmaking) in some cases it also is governed by neocolonialist paradigms.

This chapter looks at Meirelles' English language films alongside *Cidade de Deus* and connects them to a sensibility that it not solely Hollywood or 'world cinema' but transnational and rooted in a Brazilian, postcolonial perspective. As with the English language films of other Latin American transnational auteurs, *21 Grams*, *Babel* and *Children of Men*, the aim is to align *The Constant Gardener* and *Blindness* with identity politics that are both continental and also associated with the former Third World. The chapter begins by analysing *Cidade de Deus* including its connections to mainstream and non-mainstream traditions. The chapter rehearses the terms of the critical arguments ignited by the film's commerciality, 'foreignness' and mainstream depictions of violence, reconciling them with the critical realism and political engagement which it suggests the film also displays. The chapter continues with a look at the key features of Meirelles' deterritorialised films exploring how these fit within normative concepts of the transnational and global, previously 'Third World' auteur and goes on to argue that aspects of the Cinema Novo-inspired ideological critique of *Cidade de Deus* are carried into these films – the UK/US co-produced *The Constant Gardener* and the international co-production *Blindness* (Brazil/Canada/Japan).

Cidade de Deus

Cidade de Deus, based on the eponymous novel by Paulo Lins (1997), deals with the violent deterioration of life in a poor community outside Rio de Janeiro over three decades: the 1960s, 1970s, and 1980s. In addition to its global success, the film attracted audiences of over three million in Brazil. When *Cidade de Deus* was released in 2002 it became the immediate focus of an already on-going controversy over aesthetics in Brazilian cinema centred around recent films *Guerra de Canudos* (*The Battle of Canudos* Sérgio Rezende 1997), *Central do Brasil* (Walter Salles 1998), *Baile perfumado* (*Perfumed Ball* Lírio Ferreira and Paulo Caldas 1999), *Orfeu* (*Orpheus* Carlos Diegues 1999) and the way they represented Brazil's 'territories of poverty' (Bentes 2003: 112). Although Bentes recognised *Cidade de Deus* as a 'landmark film' she suggested that it spectacularises the violence of Brazil's *favelas* for the viewing pleasure of its spectators and ignores the causes of this violence (2003: 108, 110). She also argued that *Cidade de Deus* and films like it reproduce an exoticised, tourist (colonialist) view of Brazil and thus betray the anti-imperialist, radical and anti-capitalist politics of Cinema Novo. Citing, Glauber Rocha's manifesto essay 'A estética da fome' ('An Esthetic of Hunger') (Rocha 1994 [1965]), and its commitment to showing the violence and hunger of Brazil's impoverished *sertão* and *favelas*. She argued that Meirelles' commercialised depiction of the favelas was more a ' "cosmetics" of hunger' (Bentes 2003: 117). Some European scholarship reproduced Bentes' criticisms of the 'cosmetics of hunger' in Brazilian film, condemning *Cidade de Deus* for its seemingly 'sensationalist' treatment of the 'sub-human conditions of Rio de Janeiro's *favelas*' (Chan and Vitali 2010: 16).

Indeed, the *in media res* opening of *Cidade de Deus,* which intercuts black screen with a knife being sharpened, other party preparations (gyrating hips, music and *capirinhas*) and an increasingly worried chicken destined for the pot, is often cited as a clear example of the film's sensationalist and kinetic style (Chan and Vitali 2010: 19–20). The later rotating 360° shots of the film's narrator Buscapé/Rocket (Alexandre Rodrigues), stuck in the middle of a stand-off between the gangster Zé Pequeno/L'il Zé (Leandro Firmino de Hora), his gang and the police, is another (Smith 2003c) (Figure 19, Figure 20, Figure 21). The frenetic opening does (seemingly) mix (the threat of) violence (the knife being sharpened), together with an exoticised and pleasurable image of life in Brazil (alcohol and dancing) to confirm Bentes', Vitali and Chan's thesis that politics and context are absent. Indeed, up to when the chicken escapes followed by gun-toting children and Zé Pequeno and the shot widens to show the squalid and cramped *favela* in which the 'party' preparations are taking place, the sequence is entirely made up of very close shots that give no sense of the party's location. However, we could equally argue (as Lúcia Nagib and Rosalind Galt

Figure 19 *Cidade de Deus* (Fernando Meirelles and Kátia Lund 2002)

Figure 20 *Cidade de Deus* (Fernando Meirelles and Kátia Lund 2002)

have done) that the film's frenetic form is key to its social commitment and that music plays a key part in displaying that social commitment. In contradistinction to what has been argued are the effects of its hyper-kinetic, effects-based style of contemporary Hollywood cinema, often called 'MTV style aesthetics' or even 'the language of television, advertising and video clips' (Johnson 2006: 121), social context is not obscured or 'pushed to the background' (Nagib 2004: 239–250; Galt 2011: 18–19). Indeed, as David Treece has argued,

Figure 21   *Cidade de Deus* (Fernando Meirelles and Kátia Lund 2002)

the use of music in particular is less part of an exoticising background, and more a recreation of the environment and the different epochs through which the film moves (1960s, 1970s and 1980s) as well as a reflection of a changed perspective on national culture (qtd in Shaw and Dennison 2007: 104–105). As Treece points out, the soundtrack's shift from samba to soul and funk reflects the challenging of 'an optimistic, one nation, populist consensus rooted in [...] an integrated *mestiço* culture [symbolised by samba]' by a 'self-conscious and militant identification with non-local, diasporic black musical idioms.' And the repeated shots of a 'traumatized chicken' attempting to escape its fate, are not necessarily a depoliticised stylistic flourish as some have suggested but as Walter Salles has noted, a symbolic stand in 'for so many Brazilians trapped in an unjust country' (qtd in Vieira 2010: 33).

Cidade de Deus's commitment to the socially progressive ideals of Cinema Novo is evident in the opening's musical and symbolic representation of one aspect of Brazil's unjust society the under-examined violent lives of *favela*-dwelling Brazilians (Vieira 2010: 29). It is also evident in the 'laborious' and 'costly' casting process undertaken in order to most accurately shape this representation, which reportedly took over a year and involved non-professional actors from the same *favelas* or communities in which *Cidade de Deus* was set and filmed (Nagib 2004: 244; Shaw and Dennison 2007: 103). All the major parts in the film: were played by residents of different communities including: Buscapé, Zé Pequeno, Bené (Phellipe Haagensen), Cabeleira (Jonatan Haagensen), Dadinho (Douglas Silva) except for rival drug chief Cenoura who was played by experienced actor Matheus Nachtergaele, Angela who was played by novice actress Alice Braga, and Mané Galinha who was played by singer and songwriter Seu Jorge. Professional and non-professional actors participated in extensive workshops and 'improvisational exercises' around set pieces which were subsequently incorporated into revised versions of Bráulio Montavani's script, which also attests to an Italian neorealist way of making films. Cinema Novo was highly influenced by neorealist practices (Shaw and Dennison 2007: 103). These European new cinema-like production methods contribute to the film's authenticity, to its naturalistic portrayal of life in the *favelas*, and above all to its realism (Shaw and Dennison 2007: 103).

Whilst scholarship has noted these politics in *Cidade de Deus*' realist production methods, what has not really been acknowledged is how the quoting from the gangster film and the self-conscious realism of several of its iterations also politicises the film's discourse about crime and social context. When critics cast *Cidade de Deus* as a 'Brazilian *Goodfellas*' (Shaw 2005: 58; Flory 2008: 296–297) or as a US 'gangster movie' (Bentes 2003: 110), they often do it as an easy means of categorising its mainstream qualities and the presumption of conservative ideology that goes with them. But calling *Cidade de Deus* a 'Brazilian *Goodfellas*' is not the 'simplistic' categorisation that Miranda Shaw has suggested (2005: 58) but actually a very accurate description of the similarities it shares with Scorsese's film in terms of its narrative, its focus on poverty and exclusion and most significantly its self-conscious formal features.

In *Goodfellas,* after an opening sequence in which Henry (Ray Liotta), Jimmy (Robert De Niro) and Tommy (Joe Pesci) stop to kill a victim in the boot of their car, a freeze frame on Henry's face is followed by the line 'As far back as I remember, I'd always wanted to be a gangster.' The film then flashes back to the 1950s (via an intertitle) where we see a young Henry running errands for the gangsters. In the same way, in *Cidade de Deus*'s opening scene, the film flashes back (via the dizzying rotating 360° shot around a trapped Buscapé) to an intertitled previous era when he was a child playing football ('the 1960s'), and also does it as the protagonist's narration begins; 'A photo might have changed my life, but in the Cidade de Deus, if you run you're dead [...] if you stay you're dead again. It had always been like that since I was a kid.' (Figure 22). Once in the 1960s Cidade de Deus, we see the young Zé Pequeno bully his way into a football match and ask the goalie his name. At which point Buscapé interjects: 'Sorry, I forgot to introduce myself' whilst his young face is caught (like Henry's) in freeze frame (but this time accompanied by the sound of a camera shutter opening and closing). The formal self-consciousness of these and other scenes from *Cidade de Deus*, with Buscapé manipulating and sometimes backtracking on his own narration (as when he stops the narration to introduce himself), connects it to the similarly self-aware narration of *Goodfellas*.

Figure 22   *Cidade de Deus* (Fernando Meirelles and Kátia Lund 2002)

Bentes' biggest criticism of *Cidade de Deus* is that it shows the drug trafficking and violence of the *favelas* without showing that these have 'a base outside the favela' (2013: 110). Consequently, she suggests, there's no criticism of the social conditions and the corruption that gives rise to this violence, and no criticism of the violence itself which is instead presented, she suggests, as 'spectacular and thrilling' (2013: 110).

> *Cidade de Deus* links the most auto-destructive impulses to easily accessible action-movie codes, in an efficient combination of realism and naturalism. In this way, the film holds the viewers hostage to its narrative and solicits their complicity with its universe, whose vital energy and youthful virility come together in a kind of celebratory self-destruction. (2013: 111)

Other than the fact that the film does actually show a base for the drug trafficking and violence outside the *favela*, in scenes that trace the guns used by the different gangs to the police and show the same police receiving kick backs from the gangs,[2] and indeed in the presence of addicts like Tiago who represents middle class demand from outside the *favela*, *Cidade de Deus*' formal self-consciousness, also performs the critical perspective Bentes suggests the film lacks. Most significantly, as with *Goodfellas*, and in contrast to what Bentes suggests above, *Cidade de Deus* questions spectator complicity in the violence it portrays 'bring[ing] under investigation the generic gaze of the gangster movie as well as a large question of why audiences are so eager to look at gangsters on the screen' (Kolker 2011: 218–219). As with *Goodfellas, Cidade de Deus'* use of matching formal self-conscious strategies, including Buscapé's voice-over narration, returning to its opening scenes (the police/Zé Pequeno standoff) and other editing-based manipulations of time and space (split-screen to show Filé com Fritas being brought back to Cenoura's hideout, and Cenoura and Mané Galinha waiting for his return, overlapping editing to represent Buscapé and the female journalist smoking a joint and a montage condensing 'The Story of the Apartment') encourage the spectator to identify with Buscapé, and not Zé Pequeno or the other gangsters and also reflect on the violence (s)he is being shown.

Cidade de Deus's citation of *Goodfellas* represents one kind of political representation of a film in which others – Italians, and liminally the Irish, find support, protection and self assertion[3] in groups defined along ethnic lines away from the white, Anglo Saxon dominant. *Cidade de Deus* is also overtly political, in its citation of another kind of racialised gangster (or gangsta) film – the new black cinema of the 1980s/1990s and the formal self-consciousness that defines it. Films like *Do the Right Thing* (Spike Lee 1989) and *Menace II Society*, (Hughes Brothers 1993) seek to represent the reality of young, black and often inner city youths and the tensions which give rise to violence. Dan Flory usefully suggests the trace of this new black cinema is most evident in the gangsta poses adopted by Zé Pequeno and his young cohorts when Buscapé takes their picture in the street (Figure 23) (2008: 299). The experimental editing of *Cidade de Deus* also makes a nod towards the innovative formalist features of new black films like *Do the Right Thing* which, like *Goodfellas*

Figure 23   *Cidade de Deus* (Fernando Meirelles and Kátia Lund 2002)

(and indeed like *Reservoir Dogs* [Tarantino 1992] and *Pulp Fiction* [Tarantino 1994] which are frequently cited in relation to *Cidade de Deus*) are invested in a modernist, French New Wave-influenced cinema that questions the representational and ideological norms of the mainstream (Matheou 2010: 113). And it is perhaps in these more political terms, rather than the sometimes disparagingly used 'MTV style aesthetics' or even 'the language of television, advertising and video clips' (Johnson 2006: 121) that the editing of *Cidade de Deus* makes its most significant intervention.

The commercial and critical global success of *Cidade de Deus* can in part be attributed to this engagement with a frenetic hyper-realist style and gangster genre that are non-Brazilian traditions but, as this analysis has shown, these traditions can work to forward nationally specific ideological aims. In the wake of its depictions of *favela* life, the new President, Luiz Inácio Lula da Silva, announced a programme of social assistance in the *coumunidades*. Additionally, its (Brazilian tax-incentive law-benefiting) distribution deal with Miramax (who also paid for its Oscar campaign in 2003) and the script support it received from the Sundance Screenwriters Lab (like other important films of the *retomada*, such as *Central Station* and *Madame Satâ* [Karim Aïnouz 2002]) were also key to its success (Vieira 2007: 51; Nagib 2006: 96). In Nagib's opinion, this script support makes *Cidade de Deus* the beneficiary of a 'new transnational cinema aesthetics' that encapsulates both New Brazilian cinema as well as other recent new cinema movements in Latin America (Argentina and Mexico) and around the world (Bosnia and Palestine) (2006: 95–96). Equally, however, there is a 'continuity' between the subject matter of films like *Cidade de Deus*, and other post-*retomada* films that deal with marginal identities; *Madame Satâ*, *O Invasor* (*The Trespasser* Beto Brant 2002) and *Ônibus 174* (*Bus 174* José Padilha 2002) which, director Kleber Mendonça Filho (*O Som ao Redor/Neighbouring Sounds* 2012, *Aquarius* 2015) suggests 'rediscovered' the social tensions of Cinema Novo masterpieces such as *Terra em Transe* (Glauber Rocha 1967) (Johnson 2006: 118). In particular, as Pedro Butcher points out, *Cidade de Deus* like other Brazilian 'fiction films of great impact of the last few years [*Carandiru* Hector Babenco 2003 and *Central Do Brasil*] was very much influenced by' a previously made documentary *Noticia de uma Guerra privada* (*News from a private war* Kátia Lund and João Salles 1999) (Butcher 2006).[4]

It is ultimately important to stress the social and political form and aesthetics of *Cidade de Deus* as these are filtered through non Brazilian genres and sources for this chapter which takes issues of continental identity and locality as its main focus. Not least because, in the vast bibliography that the film has generated, these have been used to emphasise the film's commitment to social criticism, which in turn has been a significant element in elevating Meirelles to the status of auteur. The narrative of the film's production as circulated in the film's paratexts (interviews with the director) and criticism has similarly emphasised Meirelles as a committed artist. This narrative recounts Meirelles' self financing of most of the film when Miramax failed to come through with funding (Matheou 2010: 165–166), his consequent control over the project, the link to a social and political agenda, the challenging of hegemonic (Hollywood) models – the transformation of the gangster and western genre as theorised by Else Vieira (2007: 53), and individualistic work practices – workshopping with the actors (Vieira 2007: 61). This is both how *Cidade de Deus* was made and a consciously shaped narrative, designed to appeal to consumers of world/art cinema at whom the film was directed. It makes little of or excises altogether the collaborative processes of production with Kátia Lund or Guti Fraga, founder of the 'Nós do Morro group, an acclaimed amateur theatre group composed of *favela* inhabitants' who ran the improvisational exercises (Nagib 2004: 244), and Meirelles' work in advertising and children's television.[5]

THE CONSTANT GARDENER

This auteurist narrative and some of the tensions involved in such a narrative, feed into Meirelles' subsequent project *The Constant Gardener*. When *Cidade de Deus* was such a relative financial success, making $27 million for its distributors Miramax and Disney's Buena Vista International (Alvaray 2008: 53), Meirelles was offered numerous projects 'in Hollywood' all of which he turned down to take up instead the late British producer Simon Channing's offer of a project directing an adaptation of the John Le Carré novel *The Constant Gardener* (2001) (Matheou 2010: 126). This fact alone, repeated in multiple press accounts, increases Meirelles' auteurist credentials in as much as it points to his desire to work outside of the Hollywood system albeit in a way that is still tangentially involved with that system through (the Universal Pictures subsidiary) Focus Features. The nature of *The Constant Gardener* – a thriller about the greed of global pharmaceutical companies in their ruthless exploitation of poor Kenyan test subjects – also heightens the sense of the director as auteur because of its focus on a 'political'/humanitarian subject, the nefarious practices of capitalism and the complicity of the Kenyan and British Government in these practices.

However, despite the seemingly progressive and anti-colonialist politics of its plot (and those of its director's previous films *Cidade de Deus*, and also *Domésticas/Maids* 2001), *The Constant Gardener* has, like *Cidade de Deus* become part of a controversy centred around the coloniality of its representational politics. In March 2012, in a series of tweets responding to the film *Kony 2012* (Jason Russell 2012) and in a subsequent article in *The Atlantic*, Nigerian-American writer Teju Cole identified *The Constant Gardener* as part of what he called 'The White Savior Industrial Complex'. In this complex, he argued that:

> Africa serves as a backdrop for white fantasies of conquest and heroism. From the colonial project of *Out of Africa* to *The Constant Gardener* and *Kony 2012*, Africa has *provided a space onto which white egos can conveniently be projected*. It is a liberated space in which the usual rules do not apply: a *nobody from America or Europe* can go to Africa and become a *godlike savior* or, at the very least, have his or her emotional needs satisfied. (Cole 2012, my emphasis)

Cole's criticisms of *The Constant Gardener* as part of a 'colonial project' find a point of contact with Diana Adesola Mafe's criticisms of the film, most prominently in the way she argues it is 'less about black social problems than [...] about white male solutions' (2011: 72). Cole and Mafe's observations about the coloniality of *The Constant Gardener* are accurate in terms of the film's funding, plot and character types. The UK Film Council, Scion Features, a British company, and Focus Features provided the funds for its production. It *is* a white story about one white hero Justin Quayle (Ralph Fiennes). Quayle is a member of the British Diplomatic Corps working at the British High Commission in Nairobi who seeks to discover first why his activist wife (Tessa) was killed and then expose the conspiracy to illegally test TB drugs on HIV sufferers in Kenya (and to cover up any resulting deaths). Furthermore, it is *also* a project begun by his white wife Tessa (Rachel Weisz) who is killed for her efforts at the beginning of the film. This plot summary and the fact that the only significant black character in the film is Tessa's colleague and co-investigator Arnold Bluhm (Hubert Koundé), a Belgian doctor (working with the fictional 'Médicins dans l'Univers') rather than a Kenyan, *does* support Mafe's point about the seeming coloniality of the film; black Kenyans are effectively robbed of any agency in determining their own fate (2011: 76–77).

However, how Mafe arrives at these conclusions about *The Constant Gardener* misses out on significant anti-colonialist elements of the film. A large part of her argument resides in plot summary and identifying white archetypes. Thus in Mafe's critique, Tessa (who is seen frequently in flashbacks working in Kibera, a slum district in Nairobi) is the 'White Goddess' '[b]eautiful [...] magical, powerful [...] ruler of hordes of black people by virtue of her whiteness' (2010: 75) whilst Justin 'as an upper class civil servant' is 'a new millennium incarnation of the Imperial man' (2011: 74). As Robert Stam and Louise Spence point out in their seminal methodology for anti-colonialist film analysis, looking merely at the plot and racial types as Mafe does, misses out on the exploration of 'questions concerning the apparatus, the position of the spectator, and the specifically cinematic codes' (1983: 3). Looking just at plot and racial types can also, they suggest, re-ify the racist representation anti-colonialist film analysis is supposed to challenge. They go on to argue:

> The exclusive preoccupation with images, however, whether positive or negative, can lead to both the privileging of characterlogical concerns (to the detriment of other important considerations) and also to a kind of essentialism, as the critic reduces a complex diversity of portrayals to a limited set of reified stereotypes. Behind every black child performer [...] the critic discerns a 'pickaninny', behind every attractive black actor a 'buck'. (Stam and Spence 1983: 10)

In the rush to find problematic types and evidence to support the argument that this is a colonialist 'misimagining' of Africa, Mafe misreads various aspects of the film, passes over issues of style and point of view, and sometimes makes mistakes about what happens in the plot. She argues for instance that the horrific death of Arnold and Tessa is focused on in order to 'endorse the myth of African savagery' (2011: 79) when the film actually suggests (through briefly seen glimpses of the assassins buying beer and cigarettes later found at the scene) that Arnold and Tessa were killed by white men who (it later reveals) were employed by a white corporation. Or she argues that, at the mortuary Tessa's naked body is respectfully covered by a white sheet, whilst black dead bodies lie uncovered beside her and Arnold's body when it is discovered is portrayed graphically (2011: 78), when actually Tessa's covering with a sheet appears (from its cleanliness) to be a protocol of the identification process for grieving relatives and Arnold's body is only briefly shown in long shot (though the description of his torture and dismemberment is very graphic). Indeed, interpreting *The Constant Gardener* as a wholly colonialist (British and US) text that conforms to some perceived notion of Hollywood logic in its racial politics and additionally in its representation of race effectively erases the agency, perspective and indeed representational politics of its Brazilian director and Uruguayan cinematographer Cesar Charlone neither of whom are from 'America or Europe' (Cole 2012). It also misreads the institutional position of the film and paints Hollywood as monolithically Eurocentric in its perspective. Meirelles' representational politics in *The Constant Gardener* may feature the 'white egos' of which Cole is so critical, but these egos are viewed from a different perspective and representational position than that of the film's Western institutional base.

The Constant Gardener is critical of colonialist practices and, in as much as the film does this, it concurs with the perspective of Le Carré's novel, particularly in its representation of 'white privilege' which, the British author emphasises, makes Tessa's death much more important (to the press covering the case) than that of Noah, the black driver of the jeep Tessa and Arnold were travelling in when they were attacked: 'Noah only made it to the first editions, then died a second death. Black blood, as every Fleet Street schoolboy knows, is not news' (Le Carré 2006: 62). In comments like these and others which include descriptions of the incongruously lavish houses of the British diplomatic workers in Nairobi: 'mock Tudor windows, electric fences and intruder alarms' (2006: 37), Le Carré emphasises 'white privilege' and its presence in the postcolonial world of British diplomacy in Kenya. In the film, Meirelles' similarly undermines the practices of white privilege but does so not just through the homes the various diplomatic staff live in, but also cinematically, subverting classical film language as the ultimate product of Renaissance codes of perspective and the mastery of the colonial 'I'/eye implicit within these codes (Stam and Spence 1983: 4). Rather than seeing the world from a perspective that privileges white culture, power and superiority, *The Constant Gardener* sees the world from an 'other' perspective. Like radical movements that use film language as a form of anticolonialist critique (the New Latin American Cinema, the Black LA Film School) Meirelles uses counter cinematic techniques to throw off classical film style and the colonial perspective of its implied spectator (Massood 1999: 25).

From the opening moments of the film, where Justin says goodbye to Tessa and Arnold at the airport *The Constant Gardener* sets up an aesthetic sensibility of partiality and incompleteness. We first hear Justin and Tessa's farewell conversation over the black screen of the credit sequence. The image gradually fades in from black to show Tessa kissing Justin tenderly and then going with Arnold to the plane. As they walk away, the image keeps Justin who is looking after them in focus as Tessa and Arnold disappear into a whitened-out blur. From this opening scene, the shot cuts to a canted angle of a jeep falling onto its side and a flock of birds taking off from the lake beside it. Soldiers arrive to examine the jeep and carry a body bag away. Only later do we learn that this is the jeep Tessa and Arnold were travelling in when they were attacked. In both instances – the goodbye at the airport and the jeep – there is no establishing shot to give information and clearly demarcate spatial and causal relations. In these opening moments *The Constant Gardener* is characterised by a multiplicity of cinematic practices that destabilise and decentre the norms of classical film style and which together can be interpreted as part of a resistant, counter cinematic strategy.

Most recognisable of these counter cinematic strategies is the nonlinear development of the plot, which *The Constant Gardener* shares with the films of another deterritorialised Latin American director Alejandro González Iñárritu (*Amores perros, 21 Grams, Babel*). For instance, we move from Justin being informed of Tessa's death by his boss Sandy Woodrow (Danny Huston) to him giving a speech in London at the end of which Tessa asks a question. Once

Tessa is identified in the audience this scene is defined as their first meeting and hence a flashback. In part, these flashbacks (usually of Tessa involved in her activist work in Kibera or Tessa, Justin and sometimes Arnold at home or at parties at the High Commission) can be explained generically. The incompleteness of the information they offer Justin and the spectator conform in some part to the thriller genre, which is built on the piecing together of a mystery or puzzle that the hero must solve. And indeed Justin is piecing together both a personal mystery (Was his wife having an affair with Arnold?) and a political one (Why and by whom was she murdered?). To a certain extent, as the late Roger Ebert has also pointed out, the partial nature of what we are told is also a feature of Le Carré's narratives (Ebert 2005). Meirelles intensifies the process of partiality, to make it much more radical and decentring. The incompleteness of the film and its perspectives become not just a feature of the film's genre but also act to deconstruct a colonialist perspective on Africa – showing us a world that is out of kilter not just in genre terms but also socially and politically. Indeed, even Mafe acknowledges that *The Constant Gardener* does not 'resort [...] to predictable and essential representations of Africa' and 'resists the visual eroticization of Africa so common in British and US cinema' (2011: 73) through its focus on the urban setting of Nairobi and Kibera, rather than on a colonised image of Africa 'of safaris and sunsets' (2010: 73). Although the introductory shots of Kibera are a mass of colours and people and thus appear part of this 'visual eroticization,' these are soon replaced by shots of dirty streams and piles of rubbish and waste – which forestall any exotic associations.

The style of the film is about more than just resisting exoticising images of Africa. It is also about challenging rather than reproducing the prejudices of the colonial perspective. For instance, when Sandy enters the hospital to see Tessa the shot first cuts to show a black baby suckling at a white breast. Then the shot opens out to show it is Tessa who is feeding a black baby and Arnold and Justin are sitting on either side of her bed. For a moment, the composition suggests she has been feeding her and Arnold's baby (at this point in the diegesis it is still unclear whether or not they were having an affair). Sandy (Head of the High Commission and hence the representative of colonial power in the film) is initially confused at being confronted by the 'product' of an interracial affair – and Justin's seeming acceptance of it ... 'I don't quite see how ...' he stutters. Then it emerges that Tessa and Justin's baby has died and the baby Tessa has been feeding belongs to Wanza, a patient dying in a nearby bed, who (as Tessa tells Sandy) is a victim of the experimental TB drug tests.

It is in moments like these, which foreground and challenge the colonialist gaze and its assumptions, that Meirelles' position as a director from the Global South is most clearly defined. This directorial position is similarly defined in moments which emphasise the persistence of the colonial structures of power. In one scene for instance at a High Commission reception, we cut not to the High Commission guests, but first to Jomo the husband of one of Arnold's HIV positive patients from Kibera (who Tessa also visits) and other Kenyans working feverishly in the kitchens to prepare the food and drinks the guests will consume. We are thus made aware of the mechanics of (and the black labour that facilitates) white privilege rather than that white privilege being transparently reproduced.

There are several scenes like those at the reception, which are organised to criticise white privilege and, relatedly, to point out how it depends upon continued political and financial interference in former colonies. In this respect, Meirelles' *The Constant Gardener* recalls a seminal anti-colonialist text, Senegalese filmmaker Ousmane Sembene's *Xala* (1976) which also shows the continuity of colonial power/and interests in Senegal's supposedly post-colonial independent new government. In *Xala*'s opening scene a new post-Independence Government is handed briefcases of money by the departing French officials, one of whom significantly remains behind as an 'advisor'. In a scene in *The Constant Gardener* with similar critical connotations, the Kenyan Minister of Health is seen arriving to the High Commission Reception in a limousine – which (as Tessa 'embarrassingly' points out) was likely bought with Western aid money intended for the purchase of sterilising equipment for a new clinic. Indeed, the film's central narrative revolves around Justin's uncovering of the covert forwarding of British financial interests (the British medical supply company 3 Bees, the Canadian pharmaceutical company KVH providing jobs in South Wales) and the resulting deaths of 'poor and desperate Kenyans as guinea pigs for experimental drugs' (Flory 2008: 304) and also the collusion of his colleagues in the British diplomatic corps in his wife's murder. It turns out that Tessa was killed after a tip-off from Sandy because she was about to hand over her evidence of the drug trials' mortality rates to an activist who would make it public.

Stylistically integral to the development of its 'post-imperial' perspective on Kenya, and its challenge to the perception of the English upper classes and 'their institutions as bastions of uprightness and probity' (Higson 2011: 84–85) is the documentary mode *The Constant Gardener* adopts. This is in part a reflection of the source material studied by Meirelles: the Channel 4 documentary *Dying for Drugs* (Michael Simkins and Brian Woods 2003) (Caine 2006: 144–145), which documents the nefarious practices of some pharmaceutical companies carrying out questionable trials in the 'poorer countries of the world' (Simkins and Wood 2003). It is also wholly commensurate with the shooting practices followed in *Cidade de Deus*. As Else Vieira points out in '*Cidade de Deus* Challenges to Hollywood, Steps to *The Constant Gardener*' Meirelles' 'spontaneous way of directing is carried over from *Cidade de Deus* to [*The Constant Gardener*] through improvisation, workshops and the incorporat[ion] of ideas from both into the script as well as "de-performing" and non-photography' (Vieira 2007: 62–63). The notion of de-performing and non-photography correlates with the description of the shoot by Huston who suggests 'It was as if we were a small documentary crew filming on location and it allowed for things to be very organic and spontaneous, it felt like reportage, or guerrilla filmmaking' (Caine 2006 153). De-performing and non-photography are also present throughout the film in the oblique or decentred framing of shots (Tessa's hand knocking on a door, Justin's fingers pruning a plant), which tends to give us an incomplete view. Sequences in Kibera and another slum some distance from Nairobi are the most overtly documentary-like; both camera work and performance styles suggest it is the actors themselves interacting with the children who gather around them (saying 'How do you do' or asking for money to enter the slum), rather than the characters they are playing. This is further supported by the fact that all the Kibera inhabitants in the film are played by real people from the community (Caine 2006: 154).[6]

Whilst fulfilling the generic conventions of the international thriller (chases, fights, flashbacks, multiple locations including London and Germany in addition to Kenya), stylistically and thematically *The Constant Gardener* also explores the situation of capitalist exploitation in a postcolonial nation. To a certain extent, that it can fulfil both a mainstream generic and a committed political function is a result of its interstitial institutional position. Made with Hollywood and UK money, it has 'Hollywood' actors (Fiennes and Weisz) and mainstream genre conventions. Directed by a Brazilian director, it is stylistically invested in a non-mainstream (non-Eurocentric) representation of the world. It is, like other English language films from other deterritorialised Latin American directors (Iñárritu's *21 Grams, Babel* and *Biutiful*, and Cuarón's *Children of Men*) 'somewhere between Hollywood and the farthest reaches of independence' (King 2009: 241). And like these other films *The Constant Gardener* is designed to make cultural and commercial capital out of the niche indie/speciality market (King, 2009: 4) *The Constant Gardener* delivered in both of these areas. It was critically acclaimed, winning an Oscar for Best Supporting Actress for Weisz as well as other award nominations (Academy award for Screenplay, Editing and Music). It also delivered commercially making $82 million.[7]

BLINDNESS

The Constant Gardener meets all the criteria of both prestige and financial success for the Hollywood/Independent production. Meirelles' subsequent project was not, however, another straightforward financial Hollywood/European/independent hybrid but *Blindness* (2008) an international co-production between Brazil, Canada and Japan funded exclusively through Brazilian tax incentive laws (Meleiro 2010: 15) albeit with production input and distribution from Focus Features. As an adaptation of Portuguese author and Nobel prize-winner José Saramago's novel *Ensaio sobre a cegueira/ Essay on Blindness* (1995), *Blindness* continues to carry the associations of an auteurist project – like Meirelles' previous films. However, despite the evident auteurist nature of the project and its interstitial institutional position, *Blindness* has attracted criticism for betraying the universalism and political content of the novel through its recourse to 'Hollywood-derived' 'cinematic codes' (Sampaio 2011: 2), namely those of the Hollywood disaster movie.

The narrative premise of *Blindness* – of a global epidemic of sightlessness – is certainly one of the conventional Hollywood disaster film in which movies about contagion form an important subgenre (*Contagion* [Steven Sodebergh 2011], *Outbreak* [Wolfgang Petersen 1995]). A man goes blind behind the wheel of his car (the First Blind Man – Yusuke Iseya), as do all those who have contact with him over the next few hours (the Good Samaritan who brings him home but then steals his car (Don McKellar), the Doctor who sees him (Mark Ruffalo), other patients from the Doctor's office). This initial group of blind people (including the Doctor's Wife (Julianne Moore), who is not blind) and subsequently other groups (some of whom we see coming into contact with members of the first group) are quarantined in a disused mental hospital. But as with Meirelles' two other films *The Constant Gardener* and *Cidade de Deus*, genre and its conventions become a vehicle and not an obstacle for the exploration of political concerns.

Because of the allegorical features of Saramago's novel which the film largely retains – characters identified by their role (the Doctor, the Doctor's Wife, the First Blind Man) rather than their proper name and the seeming non-specificity of its megalopolis setting – and also what Frederick Jameson calls the 'necessarily allegorical' nature of 'Third World texts,' one might be tempted to read *Blindness*'s politics through allegory (1986: 69). It may be more productive however, particularly given that the nomenclature has shifted, not to use Jameson's Eurocentric and homogenising paradigm to think about *Blindness*. Afterall, the label 'Third World' is no longer used and Brazil is now more commonly referred to as an 'emerging economy'. Additionally, two of the film's co-producing countries (Canada and Japan) are part of the Global North. It makes more sense in these terms to read *Blindness*'s politics through the mainstream genre with which it engages: the big budget post-apocalyptic science fiction film. From alien or giant insect invasion films of the 1950s (*Them!* [Gordon Douglas 1954] *Invasion of the Body Snatchers* [Donald Siegel 1956], *The Day the Earth Stood Still* [Robert Wise 1951]) to contemporary off-planet fantasies (*Avatar* [James Cameron] 2009, *Elysium* [Neil Blomkamp 2013), Hollywood disaster/science fiction films have also been interpreted as allegorical and, more importantly, as political in the way they deploy allegory (Biskind 2000: 123–145)

Blindness's recourse to the Hollywood disaster film makes an interesting parallel with Cuarón's *Children of Men*. Like Cuarón's film, *Blindness* negotiates the terms of its engagement with the genre: following some disaster film conventions and twisting others. *Blindness* works within the norms of commercial filmmaking in terms of its main leads (it features Hollywood players Moore, Ruffalo and Danny Glover), its budget (it has a small-scale Hollywood-sized budget of $25 million) and its use of disaster films' 'model scenarios' as described by Susan Sontag (1966: 209). These 'model scenarios' in *Blindness* include spectacular shots of destruction (buses and planes crashing as their drivers/pilots also lose their sight), and 'conferences [often] between the military and sciences' (Sontag 1966: 209). In *Blindness*'s case the latter takes the form of a global seminar of 'ophthalmologists and neurologists' at which one man goes dramatically blind.

However, *Blindness* also situates itself outside these commercial norms and the ideologies that underpin them. Like *Children of Men* it displaces the location of its drama away from the generic location of the continental United States, (Langley 2011) to an anonymous global mega city realistically inhabited by an international group of people (Japanese, Brazilian, Mexican, North American) who nevertheless all speak English. As if to help this anonymous representation of globality, three locations are used for three distinct parts of the film. São Paulo is the ultra modern mega city of the opening including the smart doctor's offices, skyscraper glass hotels, wide highways and luxurious shops. Toronto is the location where the psychiatric hospital is situated. Montevideo is the post-apocalyptic city into which the blind 'prisoners' emerge towards the end of the film.

Although many critics have suggested the sum of these locations is a space that is unrecognisable, some aspects of the setting point towards a more localist, though not unproblematically Latin American-based reading and this has important connotations for the politics of the film's allegory. The AM radio station through which the Man with the Black Eye Patch (Glover) has been listening to the outside world plays Brazilian music. Two Latin American stars, Brazilian Braga and Mexican Gael García Bernal, both feature in prominent roles in the film. Braga, a sex worker (the Woman in Dark Glasses), is one of the first group to be infected from the Doctor's office. Bernal, the Bartender, comes to the asylum later.

Paul Julian Smith's criticism of *Blindness* is that its 'politics [are] stubbornly obscure' (2008b). Indeed, aspects of the film's locality are confused by the fact that Braga and Bernal both play characters with subordinate occupations in society (bartender and sex worker) whilst all the characters further up the social hierarchy – doctors (Ruffalo), scientists and government ministers – are played by North American actors (the Minister of Health is played by Canadian actress Sandra Oh). However, the politics of *Blindness* appear clearer in terms of the resonances of its representation of the various practices used for containing the epidemic. Initially the response to the epidemic (the very next morning) is commensurate with the *mise-en-scène* of mainstream epidemic films such as *Contagion*. Men in protective white suits and ambulances come to collect those infected and the Doctor and his wife submit willingly. However, other responses to the epidemic which take place later in the film are much more extreme. That same morning, other men (identified as Government agents) appear at the doctor's office to forcibly seize his patient files and the Receptionist (although she has not yet gone blind). As the epidemic progresses (we learn from the Man with the Black Eye Patch's subsequent narration of events) the blind are dragged away often by soldiers dressed in fatigues and in army trucks. On the arrival of the first group at the asylum a message replays on a video screen; 'We are in a state of crisis: the decision to quarantine all those affected is not taken without careful consideration.' Parts of the message are replayed over and over again throughout the film, and as conditions deteriorate within the asylum, the video's broken message becomes increasingly authoritarian and chilling. The film's shift from a worried democracy to a totalitarian, repressive state is most clearly communicated when one of the patients arriving at the asylum is 'shot' by one of the guards without hesitation or warning because his proximity brings with it the fear of infection.

It is on the terms of the increasing totalitarianism of the state in handling the epidemic and the hysteria with which the 'infection' is met, that *Blindness* resonates politically with the historical facts of Latin America's repressive regimes of the 1960s, 1970s and 1980s (Brazil 1966–1985, Argentina, 1976–1983, Chile 1973–1990, Uruguay 1973–1985, Paraguay 1954–1989). As Naomi Klein points out, the danger of (Marxist) 'infection' became the justification for the mass incarceration, torture and murder of anyone who campaigned for social justice (2007: 107).[8] *Blindness*'s setting also resonates with the (in Freudian terms) displaced representations of those regimes. In the post-dictatorship period in Argentina the psychiatric hospital acts as a metaphor for the repressive military regime of the late 1970s (Kantaris 2000: 158). In a key film of this period *Hombre mirando al sudeste* (*Man Facing Southeast*, Eliseo Subiela 1986) political prisoners are represented as psychiatric patients who wander (as some of the blind do in *Blindness*) naked and are given treatment methods (electroshock therapy) that reflect the torture methods of Argentina's secret police.

Equally pointing towards a more localist reading is the city the 'patients' encounter when, realising the guards are long gone, they flee the asylum. The original group (the Doctor, the Man with the Black Eye Patch, the Woman in Dark Glasses, the First Blind Man and his Wife) emerge into a city in which, as in the asylum, all order has broken down. Groups of blind people forage for food and look for shelter. Dogs feast on scattered dead bodies. Groups of street children overpower the old and frail to take their possessions. That Montevideo, the capital of Uruguay, which suffered its own dictatorship (1973–1985) during which leftists were kidnapped and killed, is used as a location for this post-apocalyptic city is therefore significant.

Although it has been argued that, like many of Uruguayan art films of the 2000s (*Whiskey* [Juan Pablo Rebella and Pablo Stoll 2004]), *Blindness* erases recognisable features of the city of Montevideo making it disappear (Martin-Jones and Martínez 2013: 49–50), the city into which the first group emerges is still recognisably Montevideo. Martin-Jones and Martínez cite as evidence of this erasure the digital alteration of the city skyline as revealed in the 'Making of' documentary ('A Vision of Blindness'). However, the digital alteration of the image that they refer to (adding a skyscraper or two to the skyline) actually helps with the film's continuity (linking the post-apocalyptic city with the ultra modern city from before the epidemic) whilst original aspects of Montevideo (the Ciudad Vieja, where the escapees huddle in a shop and the Banco de la República Oriental de Uruguay, which acts as the church) remain as a recognisable part of the city. Like many Latin American nations, the cityscape we see in the film includes the old (Ciudad Vieja) the modern (tall glass buildings, wide highways, contemporary cars), the antiquated (grandiose parliament buildings, rusted railway carriages) and the derelict (some institutions, the children, the old and frail). At the same time, it may help the allegorical reading that some aspects are changed or universalised (a C&A logo is visible suggesting that this city could equally be anywhere in the world).

It is perhaps because we can draw these lines of connection to the locatedness and specificity of *Blindness* in a Latin American context that the film was so well received in Brazil, doing spectacular box office (making over $4 million and out grossing the Hollywood competition[9]) but less so in the US (where it made just over $3 million). In connecting the response to the epidemic to past repressive practices in Latin American contemporary history Meirelles transposes the parable of Saramago's novel which highlights 'the perpetual possibility of the return of Fascism [to Portugal]' (Bloom 2005: xvii–xviii) from a Portuguese to a Latin American context.[10]

It's worth noting that the connection between Meirelles as a Latin American director and *Blindness* has been made at the level of international criticism – mainly via Meirelles' *Cidade de Deus*. On the one hand some critics have stressed Meirelles' production methods (workshops and improvisation were a key part of the preparation and used to 'submerge [the actors] all in the experience of being suddenly and inexplicably blind') in *Blindness* as continuous with those of *Cidade de Deus* (Gelb, Meirelles and Morreli 2008; McClennen 2011: 96 n1). On the other, *Guardian* reviewer Peter Bradshaw has made the connection between what he calls *Cidade de Deus*' 'shanty town jungle law' and the dissolution of society in *Blindness* (2008).[11] What is disquieting about Bradshaw's comments are the problematic neocolonialist assumptions which underpin his auteurist analysis of *Blindness* as revealed by the use of phrases like 'shanty town' and 'jungle law'. Even though, as this analysis has established, the film is set in an English speaking, modern city (where North Americans rule) Bradshaw makes assumptions that it (and indeed *Cidade de Deus*) represent an underdeveloped and savage Latin America. This may lead us to question the terms under which Bradshaw and others have read and understood *Blindness* and *Cidade de Deus* and perhaps acknowledge how the latter film's success lies partially in the way the film supports these assumptions about Latin America and Latin American directors. Jason Solomons' interview with Meirelles on the release of *Blindness* similarly draws all the director's films together as 'exotic journeys' equally fetishising a perceived 'third-worldness' (Solomons 2008). In *Blindness* Meirelles' work as an auteur retains original aspects of style and subject matter but there's a problematic neocolonialist assumption that he is better at depicting the breakdown of society (into 'jungle law') because he comes from a country previously considered to be 'third world.' The challenge to cultural hegemony is much less effective when its results are judged by Eurocentric paradigms.

This chapter has argued for the cultural specificity of *Cidade de Deus, The Constant Gardener* and *Blindness*, suggesting that this specificity is rooted in the films' textual reproduction of their director's peripheral perspective and position in a global economy of representation. The chapter has also outlined and navigated the contradictions of this peripheral auteurist identity that is nevertheless also ready for mainstream appropriation.

NOTES

1. For the record, the opening ceremony was reviewed as both a positive and political representation: showing that Brazil can still 'throw a good party' whilst also offering a 'meaningful political commentary [on environmental sustainability]' (Dennison 2016).
2. Additionally, it is suggested that the police are happy to let the violence between gangs continue and even escalate in the Cidade de Deus. They only chose to enter the *favela* (and make arrests) when pushed to by media comment or when Zé refuses to pay for the guns they have provided.
3. The theme of self-assertion through violence and the media is central to the film. It is not enough that Zé Pequeno choses violence – this has to be asserted through notoriety, i.e. his photograph (taken by Buscapé) appearing in the newspaper. At the same time, Buscapé choses culture over violence, i.e. for him becoming a photographer is his means of self-assertion and possible escape from the cycle of violence.
4. As Butcher points out: '*Central Station* was born out of [the Sundance-funded documentary] *Life Somewhere Else* (Walter Salles 1995)', whilst '*City of God* and *Carandiru* had the very interesting counterpoint of [Paulo Sacramento] *The Prisoner of the Iron Bars* (*O Prisioneiro da Grade de Ferro* 2004)' (2006).

5. 'We of the Hill'; *morro* (hill) is another term those living in marginal communities like City of God use to refer to their homes. Nós do cinema, the new group set up by Meirelles, provides filmmaking facilities to young people in these communities (Matheou 2010: 128)
6. The UK, on the other hand, is portrayed in bleak photography. Train stations, airports, and institutional buildings are all rendered in a colour palette characterised by greys and blues. The UK is also represented as being dominated by a culture of surveillance. From Justin's arrival in the UK (where he goes to find out more about Tessa's investigation into 3 Bees and its drug trials) we see him framed in numerous CCTV screens.
7. Box office mojo website <www.boxofficemojo.com/movies/?ide=constantgardener. htm>. (last accessed 10 August 2013).
8. Throughout the 1960s, 1970s, and 1980s different Latin American countries (Paraguay, Uruguay, Chile, Argentina, Brazil, Mexico) were governed by authoritarian (often military) regimes some of which came to power through violent coups. The regimes maintained their power through the severe repression, incarceration torture and murder of any opponents.
9. $4,051,714, source: boxofficemojo.com
10. Portugal was ruled by two Fascist dictators: Antonio de Oliveira Salazar (1932–1968) and Marcello Caetano (1968–1974).
11. '*Blindness* is an apocalyptic nightmare adapted from the 1995 novel by the Nobel laureate José Saramago and directed by Fernando Meirelles, who finds in it the brutal exposition of *shanty town jungle law* we saw in his 2002 *City of God*' (Bradshaw 2008).

5. REVOLUTIONARY ROAD MOVIES: WALTER SALLES' *DIARIOS DE MOTOCICLETA* *(MOTORCYCLE DIARIES 2004)* AND *ON THE ROAD* (2012)

> I believe that there is not just one Latin American Cinema [...] There are *cinemas*; made up of sometimes contradictory currents that often collide, yet come together in a desire to portray our *realities* in an *urgent* and *visceral* manner. We make films that are, like the melting pot that characterises our cultures, impure, *imperfect* and plural.
>
> (Salles 2003: xiv, emphasis added)

Walter Salles is known internationally as a significant figure of Brazil's post 1995 filmmaking revival (*retomada*) and more broadly of the Latin American cinematic renaissance (Shaw 2013b: 27; Williams 2007: 12). He is also known, like the other directors explored so far in this book, for an enormous critical and commercial success – his fourth feature *Central do Brasil* (*Central Station* 1998), which grossed $57.6 million worldwide and was nominated for the Oscar for Best Foreign Film – and for a series of high profile deterritorialised projects: *Diarios de motocicleta* (*Motorcycle Diaries* 2004), *Dark Water* (2005), *On the Road* (2012), and *Jia Zhanke: A Guy From Fenyang* (2014). At the same time, Salles has continued to make and produce films in Brazil: *Abril Despedaçado* (*Behind the Sun* 2001), *Linha de Passe* (with Daniela Thomas 2008), *Cidade de Deus, Cidade Baixa* (*Lower City* Sérgio Machado 2005), *Madam Satâ* (Karim Aïnouz 2002) *O Céu de Suely* (*Love for Sale* Aïnouz 2006), and across Latin America, *Leonera* (*Lion's Den* Pablo Trapero 2008) through his production company VideoFilmes. Salles is also defined by statements like those in the epigraph to this chapter in which, through his choice of words ('realities', 'urgent', 'visceral' and 'impure') and use of 'we', he connects contemporary and previous filmmaking in Latin America, including his own films, with the militantly political filmmaking of the New Latin American Cinema of the 1960s and 1970s. And yet, despite the new cinema-like sentiments of such statements, Salles' films, and in particular his deterritorialised productions, have sometimes attracted criticism for betraying the sentiments of the New Latin American cinema, for the way they engage with popular genres and mainstream filmmaking styles.

From Salles' second feature *Terra estrangeira (Foreign Land, 1995)*, a film noir set in Brazil, Portugal and on the borderland with Spain, many of his subsequent projects (*Central do Brasil, Diarios de motocicleta, On the Road,*) also 'leave home' (Sadlier 2007: 126) in as much as they are thematically concerned with journeys away from and sometimes to the home(land), and/or are made outside of Brazil with international funding and as co-productions with other countries. *Central do Brasil*, which is a Brazil/France co-production developed at the Sundance Screenwriters Lab and with support from Japanese television station NHK, tells the story of an older woman Dora (Fernanda Montenegro) and a young boy Josué (Vinícius de Oliveira) and their journey from Rio's Central Station to the remote *nordeste* (Northeast) region of Brazil where Josué hopes to find the father he has never met. *Diarios de motocicleta*, a co-production between the United States, United Kingdom, Germany, Argentina, Chile, Perú, and France, recounts the 'transcontinental trek' across Latin America by a young Ernesto Guevara de la Serna (Gael García Bernal) and his friend Alberto Granado (Rodrigo de la Serna).[1] *On the Road* is a France/Brazil co-production based on the beat novel of the same name (1957) by Jack Kerouac, about the coast-to-coast travels of Sal Paradise (Sam Riley) and Dean Moriarty (Garret Hedlund) across the United States in the late 1940s and early 1950s.

Whilst Latin American film criticism recognises that 'the road film is Salles' defining characteristic' (Podalsky 2011: 191, n2), it has not, to date, wholly embraced *On the Road* as part of Salles' auteurist trajectory with the film receiving scant attention by the group of Latin American film scholars who have examined his previous Portuguese and Spanish language works. Several recent, (excellent) monographs and anthologies by scholars in the field focus, in addition to road movies in the continent's history, on the growing corpus of road films made across Latin America over the last 30 years: *El viaje (The Voyage* Fernando Solanas 1992), *Profundo carmesí (Deep Crimson* Arturo Ripstein 1996), *Historias mínimas (Intimate Stories* Carlos Sorín 2002), *Bombón, el perro* (Sorín 2004), *Viva Cuba* (Juan Carlos Cremata 2005) *Guantanamera* (Tomás Gutiérrez Alea and Juan Carlos Tabio 1995), *Bajo California* (Carlos Bolado 1998), *Sin dejar huella (Without a Trace* María Novaro, 2000), *Y tu mamá también* (Cuarón 2001) *El Clown* (Pedro Adorno and Emilio Rodríguez 2006), *Bye, Bye Brasil* (Carlos Diegues 1979), *O Céu de Suely* and *Dois filhos de Francisco* among others (Pinazza 2014; Brandellero 2013; Gariboto and Pérez 2016) but do not include *On the Road* within this body of films.

This book has already explored the reasons why English language films of Latin American directors like *On the Road* are not routinely incorporated into Latin American film studies. Quite simply, in addition to the geographical and linguistic limitations circumscribing the field, English language films supposedly challenge standards of cultural autonomy as they are currently defined and understood within the parametres of Latin American film studies to necessarily reflect the monolithically conservative ideology of an industry (Hollywood) most commonly perceived as a 'bad' object. Relatedly, the auteurist (nationalist) sensibilities and styles of the directors working in these industries are seemingly 'inevitably' subsumed into and commodified by the ideologies of that industry. To a certain extent, these same critical positions are enacted in some of the scholarship on *Diarios do motocicleta*, despite the fact that it is an 'independent' Spanish-language film shot in, and co-produced by various Latin American countries, because its status as a genre film – a road movie – make it equally problematic for these same political and postcolonial paradigms of Latin American film scholarship. As explored in Chapter 2 in relation to Cuarón, a residual mistrust of the genre film (left over from critical perspectives of the 1960s and 1970s), again make it incompatible with the idea of Latin American cultural autonomy, or ill-suited to the complexities of Latin American history and reality. These positions result in analyses which sideline the use of genre (in Cuarón's *Y tu mamá también*) or, as in the case of *Diarios de motocicleta*, make negative criticism about genre features themselves.

Broader critiques of Latin America's commercially successful genre films have pitted *Diarios de motocicleta*'s 'formulaic' road movie narrative against the more 'innovative' format of the New Latin American Cinema suggesting that as a genre film which must follow particular conventions, *Diarios de motocicleta* cannot sufficiently account for Guevara's ideological conversion during his road trip around South America. David William Foster's analysis of *Diarios de motocicleta* for instance, criticises the road movie implicitly by suggesting the film is 'so filled with Hollywood clichés [...] as to lead one to wonder whether it was not planned as a grotesque burlesque of Guevara's and Granado's motorcycle trip from Buenos Aires to Caracas in 1954 [sic]' (2004: 192). What underpins these perspectives is the sense that the road movie, as a Hollywood genre, is unsuited not just to the exploration of Latin American politics but also to the task of depicting the figure of Guevara as a proto-Che. The critical disdain of 'Hollywood' and commerciality that some Latin American film criticism displays in relation to the genre film, and which Foster portrays in particular in relation to *Diarios de motocicleta*, is to be understood as part of a continental history of anti-imperialist political and cultural struggle for which Guevara is a symbol. It is this same history which has led some critics (like Bentes) to criticise one of Salles' domestic, Portuguese language films, *Central do Brazil*, for betraying this cultural struggle (and specifically Cinema Novo/Rocha's 'estética da fome'/'aesthetics of hunger') through its overtly 'cosmeticized' aesthetics (Bentes 2003: 121–137). But, as this book and other work has emphasised, these sentiments are out of place within the changed cultural and aesthetic imperatives of Latin America's increasingly globalised and transnationalised mediascapes and within the shift in the discipline itself towards a more cultural studies perspective on the political potential of the products of mass culture such as the group of blockbusters of the late 1990s to the early 2000s to which *Diarios de motocicleta* belongs (Blasini 2016: 97; Alvaray 2008: 48; Tierney 2004: 63).

Conversely, other less negative criticisms have usefully explored the suitability of a 're-signif[ied]', 're-inscri[bed]' and 're-configured' road movie, in the task of articulating aspects of Latin American reality and in depicting the young Guevara's journey in *Diarios de motocicleta* (Thornton 2007: 32; Blasini 2016: 98). Niamh Thornton, suggests Salles 'transpose[s]' the US genre 'onto the "other" America, to discover an authentic Latin America, one that is often set in opposition to their Northern neighbour' (2007: 32). Jeffrey Middents similarly suggests that the genre 'naturally lends itself to multiple, changing locations, [and] characters' and to the film's project of 'establishing "place" through the series of diverse locations it presents' (2013: 151). Natália Pinazza proposes that the film uses the genre's convention of 'geographical and cultural displacement as [a] means of self-discovery' but that this shifts in the course of the film so that the journey becomes 'increasingly motivated by the notion of collective identity' (2014: 105, 107).

Thornton, Gilberto Blasini, Pinazza and Middents' analyses of *Diarios do motocicleta* make very relevant observations about how the film uses the road movie. What could further expand perspectives on *Diarios de motocicleta*, is the consideration of an additional characteristic of the road movie that also underlines its suitability to the portrayal of Guevara's ideological conversion and which also tie it together with *On the Road*. While many critics analysing versions of the road movie across Latin American cinemas, including myself elsewhere in this book, have focused on the road movie's conservative antecedent, the Western (Thornton 2007), to date there's been no focus on the counter cultural politics and aesthetics of the genre in its late 1960s/early 1970s manifestation (*Easy Rider* Dennis Hopper 1969; *Two-Lane Blacktop* Monte Hellman 1971) and how these might be relevant to the exploration of Salles' two films. The road movie inflected analysis in Latin American film scholarship is often political – in terms of the exploration of the subversion of gender and sexual norms in *Y tu mamá también* (Amaya and Blair 2008

Acevedo-Muñoz 2004), or in terms of the false utopia of the post dictatorship moment in Latin America in *El viaje* (Ruétalo 2001: 414). However, these analyses rarely acknowledge the precisely political and ideological potential of rebellion (and revolution) in the road movie genre itself that Anglo scholarship identifies (Corrigan 1991: 148; Cohan and Hark 1997: 3; Laderman 2002: 4).[2] What this chapter wants to add to some of the very valuable writing on Salles' *Diarios de motocicleta* is the analysis of its companion piece *On the Road* and more attention to the politics of road movies themselves and the ways they are used in both films to address rather than 'gloss over' the political history of the continent.

Taking a cue from Shari Roberts and others who write about rebellion in the road movie genre, this chapter explores how *Diarios de motocicleta* and *On the Road* use road movie conventions to forward their different, but not unrelated political agendas. It begins by establishing the interconnectedness of both the journeys recounted in *Diarios de motocicleta* and *On the Road* and how these in turn can be linked to the genesis of the road movie genre. It goes on to analyse how both films use the political strategies of the road movie to (re)explore and update the beginnings of social, cultural and political revolutions that are linked in Salles' common vision of 'las Americas'. In keeping with the broader aims of this book, this chapter is about defending the political potential of the genre film and showing how the stylistic shift in Latin American cinemas that both films embody is not necessarily a shift away from dealing with regional politics.

Diarios de motocicleta and *On the Road* are tied together by more than the common genre of the road movie. The journeys which they recount and fictionalise reflect a shared sense of the possibilities of travel on the part of their young protagonists. Argentine novelist Ricardo Piglia, who notes that Guevara originally wanted to be a writer, observes:

> In 1950, Guevara, [...] sets off on his travels and takes to the road – on that voyage that consists in constructing experience so as to then write it. In that combination of both going on the road and registering the *immediacy* of facts we can see the relation between the young Guevara and the North American beat generation. Writers like Jack Kerouac, whose *On the Road* is the manifesto of a new avant-garde, are his contemporaries, and they are doing the same as he is. It is a matter of uniting art and life, writing what is lived: lived experience and immediate writing, almost automatic writing. Like him, the young North American writers – far from thinking of Europe as the model of the place to travel to, and where generations of intellectuals had wanted to go – take to the road to look for experience in America. (2008: 266, my emphasis)

Piglia draws a line of connection between these almost contemporaneous journeys and travellers – Kerouac's 1947–1951 trips between the East and West coasts of North America including a sojourn in Mexico, which form the basis of his book and Guevara's journeys around Latin American including the 1952 journey from Buenos Aires to Caracas. Tellingly, Piglia does not differentiate between the Northern and Southern hemispheres of the same continent, calling the locus of their travels simply 'America'. As films of the early twenty-first century, *Diarios de motocicleta* and *On the Road* are also linked in the way they cast forward portentously beyond the time frames of their own diegeses into broader political (and cinematic) trajectories that are historically intertwined. Through various experiences the young Ernesto (or 'Fúser' as Alberto calls him) has during his travels, *Diarios de motocicleta* prefigures Guevara's known future as 'El Che': the anti-imperialist, communist and revolutionary who fought in the Cuban Revolution, formed part of its revolutionary Government, subsequently sought to spread revolution globally fighting in the Congo (against the French) and Bolivia and was captured and killed there in 1967. Equally, through the behaviours, conversations and practices of Cassady, (Dean Moriarty), Kerouac (Sal Paradise) and other fictionalised members of the group (Allen Ginsberg/Carlo Marx, William S. Burrows/Bull Lee, Luanne Henderson/Marylou, Carolyn Cassady/Camille and Joan Vollmer/Jane), *On the Road* presents the moment before the beat generation, anticipating a movement that would itself form a prelude to late 1960s radicalism and the counter culture which considered both Kerouac and Guevara (in the wake of his 1967 death) as spokesmen/figures.[3]

The road movie has its origins in this culture of late 1960s radicalism. Even though it has antecedents in other film genres that involve travel (the Western), and several noteworthy films (*It Happened One Night* Frank Capra 1934), the road movie does not coalesce as a genre until the late 1960s with the release of the film *Easy Rider* (Roberts 1997: 5). *Easy Rider*, about the motorcycle journey of Billy (Dennis Hopper) and Wyatt (Peter Fonda) across the continental United States from Los Angeles to New Orleans, is the product of an America defined by 'social upheavals': women's liberation, civil rights and youth movements and 'the gradual increase in [and opposition to] American involvement in the Vietnam war' (Roberts 1997: 51). When *Easy Rider* came out it was 'embraced by a generation as a statement of youth, rebellion and counter-culture' (Roberts 1997: 51). Also, far from being a 'Hollywood' film (Sadlier 2007: 136), *Easy Rider* was an independent project, produced by Burt Schneider and Bob Raffleson – the creators of The Monkees. Additionally, *Easy Rider* was one of the films that heralded the beginnings of new low budget, independent production methods and a non classical/modernist film-making style that defined a 'new' Hollywood.

In part *Easy Rider* may embody the 'speed' and 'modernity' that according to Cohan and Hark and theorists of Latin American road movies, define the road movie in its US iteration (Cohan and Hark 1997: 3; Blasini 2016: 103; Pinazza 2014: 106; Williams 2007: 19) particularly in driving to music sequences that feature wide tarmacked roads ('Born to be wild') or in loving close ups which fetishise the shiny chopper motorcycles that Wyatt and Billy ride. However, *Easy Rider* also focuses on views of the United States' infrastructure, landscape and society that go against an irrefutable sense of the United States's own modernity or development. The film largely stays out of any major cities (Los Angeles is briefly viewed at the beginning), to focus instead on the poverty, inequality, small town prejudice, racism and provincialism all of which Wyatt and Billy encounter as they ride through the American South and Southwest.[4] Wyatt and Billy and their respective alter-egos, – Captain America, the cowboy and the historical figures their names evoke, Wyatt Earp and Billy the Kid – function as ironic counterpoints both to the Western (whose iconic locations they drive through including Monument Valley) and the myth of the West as it exists in mainstream American ideology. It is these contestatory aspects of the road movie's originary text that critics ignore when they suggest the genre necessarily embodies hegemonic and conservative ideologies, and that *Diarios de motocicleta* follows in these footsteps.[5] It is important to remember that *Easy Rider*'s very famous tag line – 'A man went looking for America and couldn't find it anywhere' – indicates its critique of mainstream American ideology as it was conceived in the late 1960s.

In addition to its characters and what they encounter on the road, a key way in which *Easy Rider* opposes itself to the classical conventions and attendant conservative ideologies of 'old' Hollywood, like other texts of the 'new' Hollywood (*Bonnie and Clyde* Arthur Penn 1967; *The Conversation* Francis Ford Coppola 1974) is through its use of various counter cinematic techniques. From the opening when Wyatt throws away his watch, an act which is shown from multiple camera angles and with overlapping editing, the film presents itself as a symbolic rejection both of classical conceptions of time and space and the ideological tenets of classical Hollywood. In addition to further counter cinematic editing and cinematographic techniques (cutting back and forth between scenes as a means of scene transition, lens flare, fish eye lenses and water on the lens) *Easy Rider* also relies on improvisation, non-professional actors, and use of hand-held cameras to present its counterculture view of America. For instance, the men who throw racist, homophobic and other insults at Wyatt, Billy and George (Jack Nicholson), a southern lawyer who has joined them on their trip, in a small town café in Louisiana, are all local, non-professional actors and the scene is one of several in the film that is entirely improvised. The characters played by these non-professional actors later attack the three 'outsiders' killing George. The outside Mardi

Gras sequences were shot entirely on location by a documentary crew using hand-held 16mm cameras and available light. The resulting sequences in New Orleans are a grainy, chaotic and euphoric representation of a city depicted as decidedly unmodern and decadent and very distant, as with many of the images of the film, from any mainstream notion of a modern United States. Wyatt and Billy's subsequent murder, by characters again played by local, non-professional actors, after leaving New Orleans, confirms the curtailment of the ideological freedoms of the 1960s, that Wyatt and Billy represent.

DIARIOS DE MOTOCICLETA

After the critical and commercial success of *Central do Brasil* which like *La ciénaga, Madeinusa, Lake Tahoe, Whiskey, Cidade de Deus* and other films of the Latin American resurgence, was supported practically and financially by the Sundance Institute (and the Sundance/NHK scheme) and had its premiere at the Sundance Festival,[6] Salles was invited by Robert Redford, the founder of the Institute, to direct *Diarios do motocicleta*. In addition to its Latin American (Chile, Perú, Argentina) and European funding (United Kingdom, France and Germany), the sources most commonly emphasised in critical accounts of the film, it was also co-produced by Universal speciality division Focus Features. The involvement of Redford and Focus Features in *Diarios de motocicleta*, highlights the role independent cinema or 'Indiewood' (the speciality divisions of Hollywood's major studios) has played in several of the deterritorialised projects explored in this book and the Latin American cinematic renaissance overall. Central to the support Focus Features and other speciality divisions have offered Latin American film, has been an understanding on the part of these agencies that these films are textually the 'non-US equivalent of indiewood films' (Tzioumakis 2012: 193) and can operate as such in the US market. However, this 'Indiewood' link is rarely highlighted in scholarship on *Diarios de motocicleta* which prefers the Latin America/Europe co-production vector, because the latter is more fitting to narratives which emphasise regional cultural autonomy against an imperialist US cultural sector (even if some analyses subsequently stress a textually North American genre heritage in the film). Nevertheless, as argued in Chapter 1, recognising American independent cinema as a source of support/oppositional aesthetics can still highlight how these films differentiate themselves from a North American mainstream whilst simultaneously also forming a diversified part of that mainstream.

Diarios de motocicleta presents a twenty-three-year-old Guevara, still in medical school and prior to his transformation into continental revolutionary. In January of 1952, together with his friend Alberto, a biochemist, he leaves from Buenos Aires with the plan to travel 8000km through Argentina, Chile, Perú and Colombia to the Guajira Penninsula in Venezuela on Alberto's

Norton 500 cc motorcycle, *La Poderosa* (The Powerful One). In that it shows much of this journey and the different typographies of Latin American geography that Guevara and Granado travel through, *Diarios de motocicleta* is at its most basic level a 'road movie.' But it also subscribes to many other cinematic features of the road movie genre albeit in ways that bend them to the specifics of the Latin American context. An early sequence of Guevara and Granado heading out of Buenos Aires into the Argentine *Pampa* for instance, uses the genre convention of a shot of the road unfolding and stretching into the horizon in front of them. Guevara and Granado then swing into frame on the back of *La Poderosa* as *charango* (a small Andean guitar) music (by Argentinian composer Gustavo Santaolalla) swells on the soundtrack. With voice-over commentary from Guevara about leaving behind 'Buenos Aires, [...] the uninspiring lectures, the papers and the exams', this first driving to music sequence performs the key road movie function of rebellion 'set[ing] the liberation of the road against the oppression of hegemonic norms' (Cohan and Hark 1997: 1). It also embodies a sense of the 'speed' and 'modernity' that define the road movie in its US iteration. However, these latter qualities are rapidly curtailed when *La Poderosa* cannot keep up with two *gauchos* (Argentine cowboys) on horseback and then skids into a nearby ditch. Juxtaposing the motorcycle (and the modern Buenos Aires including its Metro system, which is briefly glimpsed) with the *gauchos*, as well as the gradual deterioration in the modes of transport the two men have to use when the motorcycle breaks down definitively, actively engages with the specifics of the 'decentred, fragmentary and uneven process' which, Ana M. López points out, is peculiar to modernisation in Latin America (2000b: 49). In the very first few minutes of the film, Salles has both signalled that his film is within the tradition of the road movie, and also how the genre functions in a Latin American context by highlighting the 'temporal warp in which the pre-modern coexists and interacts with the modern' (López 2000b: 49; Blasini 2016: 103). Although, as illustrated by the focus on rural and small town America in *Easy Rider* even (new) 'Hollywood' road movies can also explore this tension between the modern and pre-modern.[7]

Guevara's road trip is often credited with 'politicising the future revolutionary' (Gilbey 2009: 10). The way *Diarios de motocicleta* depicts this awakening however, has been the source of some criticism with suggestions that the politics of it are largely ignored in both the 'narrative and the aesthetics' (Pinazza 2014: 105) and that Guevara is 'idealized,' 'romantic[ised]'and 'simplified' (Williams 2007: 15, 21; Sadlier 2007, 138; Gilbey 2009: 10).[8] And yet, a basic noting of some of the moments of the journey as recounted in *Diarios do motocicleta* suggests that, far from ignoring politics, the film is labouring to prefigure Guevara's radicalisation and future continental and global struggle on behalf of the dispossessed through the variety of encounters he has on the road and in the way it organises itself cinematically. For instance, in a

Peruvian hospital visiting the famous leprosy specialist, Dr. Pesce, Ernesto lies in bed reading a borrowed copy of Marxist thinker José Carlos Mariátegui's *7 Ensayos de Interpretación de la Realidad Peruana* (*Seven Interpretive Essays on Peruvian Reality*, 2007, [1928]). Travelling through Chile and Perú, he hears stories of forced expropriation and persecution from a Communist couple and a peasant farmer and ponders how the indigenous people he sees walking in a funeral procession are 'dispossessed in their own land'. At a visit to the American owned Chilean copper mine at Chuquicamata, having been ordered away by the foreman, he protests at how badly the workers are treated (shipped in an open truck and not given food or water). Writing in his journal in Machu Picchu, site of one of the last Inca strongholds to hold out against the Spanish, he ponders the vastness of the Inca's knowledge and how it could not protect them against the invaders who had gunpowder wondering: 'What would America look like today if things had been different?' In Cuzco, capital of the ancient Inca Empire, he meets Quechua women who tell him about the contemporary lack of access to education and opportunities. At the Leprosarium in the Amazon jungle he makes an arduous and risky night-time swim across the river so that he can celebrate his birthday with the patients on the other side.

The film also recounts particular moments from the published version of the diary *Motorcycle Diaries: Notes on a Latin American Journey* (2003 [1993]), that attest to Guevara's politics just/almost as they appear in the diary. Against the common practice at the hospital in the Amazon (and another hospital in the Peruvian Andes which does not appear in the film), he and Alberto choose not to wear protective gloves when they meet with leprosy patients (2003: 145). At the farewell/birthday party at the Leprosarium he gives a speech expressing a newfound sense of Pan-Americanism and ends with a call for a 'united America' (2003: 149). Additionally, Salles and José Rivera (the screenwriter) add moments that evidence Guevara's growing political commitment which do not appear in the diary, or retell them to better accommodate a narrative logic of his gradual political awakening.[9] These moments serve to externalise Guevara's emerging politics (the ostentatious reading of Mariátegui) or growing understanding of the privations and difficulties of the lives of the working classes and indigenous people in Latin America (meeting and talking to the Quechua women and, later, to a Quechua man who has been thrown off his land).

In the opening 'Entendámonos' ('So we understand each other'), and elsewhere in the published diaries, Guevara openly avows having recrafted and rewritten the notes made during his journey on his return to Buenos Aires, according to the newfound perspectives he has gained from his travels (2003: 31–32, 114). However, Salles and Rivera also necessarily update rather than 'idealise' many of Guevara's politics in accordance with a postcolonial, and class awareness that is lacking from the original diaries and, notably, dependent on the 'other' revolutions that took place after Guevara's death.[10] For instance, in the published diaries, although there are long praiseworthy paragraphs on the Incas inspired by visits to other Inca sites but not Machu Picchu (2003: 107, 111) and other praise for Latin America's pre-Columbian civilisations, there are also more problematic observations about the contemporary descendants of these civilisations, which betray prejudices common in Latin America's *criollo* (white, of European descent) middle-classes to which Guevara belonged. These include a tendency to idealise the 'dead Indian' of previous generations (who is unable to contest disenfranchisement by this same elite) whilst writing about contemporary indigenous people in dehumanising terms.[11] For instance, Guevara comments on the way back from Machu Picchu to Cuzco on the train (in which he travels in a different class carriage) on indigenous people's 'animal-like' 'concept' of 'modesty and hygiene' (2003: 116). When the truck they are all travelling in makes everyone walk while it makes a steep climb, he talks about a group of Aymara people 'trott[ing] along like llamas in single file' (2003: 95), a group he had previously referred to as 'human livestock' (2003: 94). Of the Communist couple he meets in the Atacama Desert, he condescendingly suggests they could 'never grasp' the essence of the doctrine to which they subscribe (2003: 78).

The film attributes Guevara with a keener consciousness about class and race than the historical Guevara exhibits in the diary and, more significantly, an ability to engage with contemporary working class and indigenous individuals – something that is not represented in the diaries. The film achieves this by excising anything that might contradict a (more post 1960s) sense of a progressive revolutionary including; problematic ideas about indigenous people and the black population in Caracas (2003: 161), praise for the conquistadors and their endurance in covering large swathes of territory in Latin America on foot (2003: 85), the extent of his and Granado's willingness to wangle free food and lodging and some of the bad behaviour they engage in (2003: 63, 56, 46), the comfortable relationship they have with the Civil Guard and other authority figures who often put them up for free (2003: 56, 130–131), and stowing away (unsuccessfully) on a cargo ship so as to *avoid* having to travel through the Atacama Desert (2003: 74).[12] It also shifts conversations from one context to another to highlight Guevara's growing awareness of his privileged position. For instance, in the diaries the question about *why* Guevara and Granado are travelling is made in a much less politically charged context. In the film, it is the Communist couple who have been forced off their land and are travelling both to escape the police and to look for work who ask them this question. Guevara's slightly embarrassed response, 'viajamos para viajar' ('we travel for the sake of it') and the couple's uncomprehending glance towards each other, underlines not just the class and racial privilege Guevara and Granado enjoy by having the freedom to travel just because they want to but also the fact that, meeting the couple, has made them aware of that privilege perhaps for the first time.

In addition to excising some parts of the diaries and transposing others, Salles also makes use of formal strategies, which are both part of his own filmmaking practice (particularly in *Central do Brasil*) and particular to the road movie, to update *Diarios de motocicleta* and its representation of Guevara as proto-revolutionary and to connect him with the subaltern subjects on whose behalf he would eventually take up arms. These strategies include a series of invented, improvised encounters between Ernesto and Alberto and characters played by local non-professional actors (who, met by the film crew during the filmmaking process, were spontaneously incorporated into the shoot).[13] One of these encounters takes place at the market in Temuco, Chile. The young Guevara greets and talks to various stall holders. He asks one lady who has just handed him a cup of *mate* her name and introduces himself as Ernesto, shaking her hand. He soon afterward asks a male stall holder to hold up a fish and eagerly takes a photograph, and responds to the stall holder's question, 'Are you travelling?' with a casual, 'Yes, we are. We're the ones with that beat-up bike over there', as he gestures out of frame. (Figure 24). Bernal's low-level acting here (in opposition to more ostentatious acting at other points) and the naturalistic acting of some of the stall owners who appear slightly stiff but interested (the man) and giggly (the woman) as they speak to Ernesto, underline the sense that Guevara is one of the people. Bernal simultaneously enacts Guevara's personal charm while underlining that this is a largely improvised encounter (albeit based around a dramatic premise).

We're the ones
with that beat-up bike out there.

Figure 24   *Diarios de motocicleta* (Walter Salles 2004)

Location and camera work also re-enforce the sense that this is a spontaneous interaction: the scene is filmed mostly in a master shot with occasional whip pans between Ernesto and the stall holders as they exchange conversation rather than following a more classical organisation of the scene via a shot/ reverse shot sequence.

More of these improvised encounters involving non-professional actors take place in Cuzco, Peru, the former capital of the Incan Empire. Whereas in the diaries, it is from Guevara or Guevara paraphrasing Howard Bingham, an American anthropologist, that we learn the history of Cuzco, in *Diarios de motocicleta* this history is told by an indigenous boy. Guevara and Granado have met 'Don' Néstor, who acts as their guide. Néstor gives Guevara and Granado a tour around the ancient city pointing out the walls made by the Incas and those made by 'los incapazes' ('the in-capables', that is, the Spaniards). In another improvised encounter in Cuzco, Ernesto and Alberto listen to two Quechua women talk about their lives (the younger woman has to translate for the older woman who we learn, not being able to speak Spanish, was unable to get an education) and then engage in ritual sharing and consumption of coca leaves. The position and movement of the 16mm hand-held camera rein-forces the sense that this is an improvised encounter (hovering alternately over the shoulders of one speaker and then the other). A sense of improvisation is further supported by the awkwardness of the non-professional actors, the fact that Bernal and Granado's lines sometimes accidentally overlap with those of the non-professional actors, the boredom of a child who lolls at his mother's side whilst she talks, and the intrusion of ambient sound (a child crying or a dog yawning) (Figure 25).[14]

Figure 25   *Diarios de motocicleta* (Walter Salles 2004)

Although, in addition to these realist features, the period detail of costume, hairstyle and artefacts also contribute to a sense that these encounters are a realistic and 'authentic' representation of the 1950s (Williams 2007: 13). The camera work and performance styles of both the professional and non-professional actors also give the encounters an immediacy and a sense that they are casting forward into the present and examining the past in the context of contemporary (ongoing) struggles. What *Diarios de motocicleta*'s improvised encounters do is highlight how the places that Ernesto and Alberto (or Bernal and de la Serna) are visiting, the lives of the people they meet and speak with, and 'the structural problems of poor distribution of land and wealth' have not changed significantly since the 1950s (Andrew 2004; Williams 2007: 16).[15]

This realism and, concomitantly, the immediacy of these problems is heightened by an innovative formal strategy that disrupts the narrative flow and classical form of *Diarios de motocicleta*, a point which many critics overlook in their argument that this is a wholly formulaic film that 'breaks no rules of classical film style' (Sadlier 2007: 138). After his trip to Cuzco, Guevara is shown reading Mariátegui in Lima. As he reads the following words are heard on the soundtrack:

> *Mariategui speaks of the revolutionary potential of the natives and farm workers of Latin America. He says the problem of the Indian [sic] is the problem of the land, and the revolution should not be an imitation, it should be original and indigenous. We are too few to be divided, everything unites us, nothing separates us.*

Meanwhile, black-and-white images of the people he has met so far on his journey appear on the screen: the Mapuche father and son with whom Guevara and Granado travelled in the back of a truck, the miners waiting on the rocks to be called by the foreman in Chuquicamata, a mestizo woman sitting destitute in the doorway of a grand colonial house in Cuzco, and a group of indigenous people standing in the ruins of an Inca edifice. The technique is used again, later in the film after Guevara notices the passengers travelling in a cramped third class boat pulled behind the comfortable first class boat he and Granado travel on in the Amazon, and a further time at the end of the film. These images show all the working class, indigenous and mestizo individuals they have met on their travels. The subjects of these images remain stock still and stare straight into the camera. Their presence in the text is to signal the impact meeting these people has made on Guevara. At the end of the journey (and film) after he has taken leave of Alberto in Caracas to fly home to Argentina, the sense that he has been changed by the realities encountered in their trip through South America is heightened by

Guevara's words from the opening of the published diaries which we hear in voice-over:

> *This isn't a tale of heroic feats. [...] It's about two lives running parallel for a while with common aspirations and similar dreams. Wandering around our America has changed me more than I thought. I am not me anymore at least not the same me I was.*

It is also heightened by a final montage of black-and-white images of people staring to camera, which prefaces these words. The montage includes: patients from the Leprosarium, 'Don' Néstor by an Inca wall, stall holders from the market in Temuco, and finally the Communist miner they met in the Atacama Desert (Figure 26). The images of these individuals represent a call to consciousness addressed not just to the diegetic Guevara, but also to the audience of *Diarios de motocicleta*. By staring into the camera, and consequently directly addressing the spectator, the images are reminiscent of the strategies of New Latin American Cinema, particularly of the dead stare of the real Guevara (from a photograph published after his death in Bolivia) which is included at the end of *La hora de los hornos* (*The Hour of the Furnaces* Solanas and Getino 1968), which is a seminal film of the movement (Figure 27). However, in difference to the still photo of Guevara, these are live footage images which significantly underline the fact that they show contemporary individuals, the non-professional actors who made up 90 per cent of the film's cast and are looking at us, the audience, and challenging us (as indeed the dead stare of Guevara was meant to challenge) with their gazes and their reality (Andrew 2004).

Figure 26   *Diarios de motocicleta* (Walter Salles 2004)

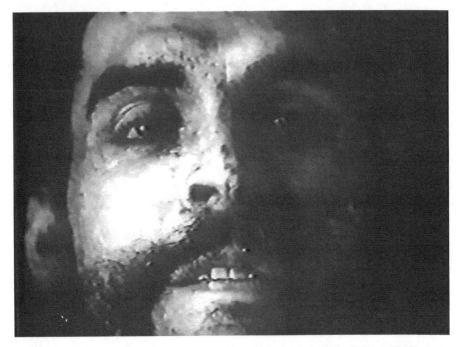

Figure 27   *La hora de los hornos* (Fernando Solanas and Octavio Getino 1968)

Diarios de motocicleta is often perceived as part of the late twentieth, and early twenty-first century's 'commodification of Che' (de la Mora 2006: 165) in which, bearded and wearing a beret as in Alberto Korda's March 1960 portrait of him, Che is detached from the political contexts of Cuba, Marxism and guerrilla warfare, and becomes a more general-ised icon for youthful rebellion, idealism, anti-imperialism and radicalism. Through its road-movie-focused analysis however, this chapter has argued that although rebellion is a central theme, *Diarios de motocicleta* does not depoliticise or simply commodify Guevara, but in fact stresses the processes of and encounters that bring about gradual political awakening. The inter-titles that end the film are very clear on Guevara's history after the Buenos Aires to Caracas journey, in Cuba and as a guerrilla. They refer to him as 'one of the most prominent and inspiring leaders of the Cuban revolu-tion' and recount that 'Che went on to fight for his ideals in the Congo and Bolivia where he was captured and with the support of the CIA murdered in October, 1967.' Additionally, rather than neglect politics, what the film does is present a congruent set of postcolonial and class politics that are arguably no less important to the contemporary imperatives of an engaged Latin American cinema and connected to (as the black-and-white montages suggest) rather than betraying the ideals of Latin America's New Cinema movements of the 1960s. For instance, New Latin America Cinema revived Pan-Americanism – a nineteenth-century discourse about continental unity. The film shows Guevara embracing, as a result of his trip, Pan-Americanism as the only solution to Latin America's deep problems of social injustice and economic inequality. At the goodbye/birthday party given by the staff at the Leprosarium in San Pablo he says:

> We believe, and after this journey more firmly than ever, that the division of America into unstable and illusory nations is a complete fiction. We are one mestizo race from Mexico to the Magellan Straits. And so in an attempt to free ourselves from narrowminded provincialism. I propose a toast to Perú and to a united America.

In his speech (which is taken verbatim from the diary) about America being a single mestizo race, the 'illusory' national boundaries that divide the continent into nation states, and the toast to a united America, Guevara evokes the central tenets of Pan-Americanism, emblematised by Cuban José Martí's *Nuestra américa* (*Our America* 1977 [1891]). Martí's text posits the indigenous person as the true Latin American and the existence of a Latin American identity that could be celebrated for its differences from Europe and the United States. That Salles' road movie proposes Pan-Americanism as a contemporary political agenda, and does so in part through the political strategies of the road movie (location shooting, improvisation, use of non-professionals and use of 16mm cameras), use of black-and-white, and new cinema-like montages, emphasises how, rather than 'gloss over' the political history of the continent, it self-consciously evokes and posits as relevant the aesthetics and politics of New Latin American Cinema to the contemporary moment.

ON THE ROAD

After the success of *Diarios de motocicleta*, Salles was invited to film *On the Road* by American producer and director Francis Ford Coppola through his company Zoetrope. Coppola has owned the rights to the novel since 1979 and tried unsuccessfully a number of times over the years to get a film version made. *Diarios de motocicleta* was finally produced with Salles, and funded by a French production company (MK2) and UK production house Film Four with support from French television companies Canal +, France 2, Salles' own VideoFilmes, and distribution from Lionsgate, Sundance and the Independent Film Channel (IFC) and produced by Coppola's son Roman. Institutionally therefore, like *Diarios de motocicleta*, *On the Road* is both a 'traditional' European/Latin American co-production and also a film with American independent cinema credentials. Salles jokingly refers to the participation of Steve Buscemi (who appears in cameo as the Tall Thin Salesman) as proof of the latter, saying 'I have a rule: it is not an indie film without Steve Buscemi' (Zakarin 2012).

In Salles' *On the Road* we are introduced to Sal Paradise, an aspiring writer living in New York in 1947 surrounded by a group of friends who also aspire to be writers. Sal meets Dean Moriarty, visiting New York from Denver, who has spent 'a third of his life in the pool hall, a third in jail and a third in the public library.' Sal is drawn to Dean who becomes the reason for his numerous journeys, driving, hitchhiking and riding Greyhound buses back and forth across North America, staying for short periods of time in California, Denver, San Francisco and Mexico. These journeys and his experiences with Dean inspire Sal, enabling him, at the end of the film, to write a novel which we recognise as *On the Road*.

On the Road, the novel, is a fictionalised account of Kerouac's adventures travelling across the United States with his friend Neil Cassady. When it was published in 1957, it was heralded as the novel of the 'beat generation', a so-called movement that defined itself against the conformism of post-war America, embracing drugs, sex, African American culture and jazz and life outside the constraints of work, marriage and convention. The published version of the novel is a reworked version of the 'original scroll' typed, famously, over a three-week period in April 1951, on a continuous roll of paper and with no paragraphs. The published version changes the names of the real artists, writers and intellectuals including Kerouac, Cassady, Ginsberg, Hal Chase, Burroughs, Hendersen, Carolyn Cassady, and Vollmer. Additionally, the published version changes the names of places and omits the original scroll's homosexual content and some of its explicit sexual content, to avoid potential libel cases as well as censorship (Charters 1991: xxiii–xxiv; Cunnel 2007: 28).

Salles' *On the Road* uses elements of Kerouac's original scroll (2007), putting back in much of the excised sexual content (including the relationship between Ginsberg and Cassady, the story of the monkey in the Los Angeles 'whorehouse' and a sex sequence in which Sal, Dean and Marylou (Kristen Stewart) are all naked in the front seat of a Hudson) and also the circumstances of how Kerouac really first met Cassady (as well as the way it was recounted in the original scroll) after the death of his father. The first words of the film, with the exception of the name Dean, are the first words of the scroll manuscript:

> *I first met Dean not long after my father died. I had just gotten over a serious illness that I won't bother to talk about except that it really had something to do with my father's death and my awful feeling that everything was dead.*

Although, unlike the scroll, the film does not use the names of the real individuals, its use of elements of the original scroll and Kerouac's biography, in addition to bringing the film closer to the early days of beat culture, further increases the connection between the protagonist of Kerouac's novel, Sal Paradise and Kerouac himself.[16]

On the Road is considered one of the great American novels, and has been relatedly interpreted as an Anglo 'colonial fantasy' in which its protagonist Sal 'fetishizes impoverished racial subjects as the conditions of possibility' for 'his white (Anglo) freedom' (Saldaña-Portillo 2002: 99). Other perspectives however, have stressed a different interpretation of the novel, based on the notion that Kerouac contested many of the interpretations of the term 'beat' (that it was about 'white male bohemia'), identified primarily as a French-speaking Canadian, and wrote an early version of *On the Road* in French (Cunnel 2007: 15; Morales 2012).[17] These perspectives suggest that, as one of the group of young writers who would form the beat generation, Kerouac felt that he had to suppress his Franco-Canadian identity 'in order to pass as American' (Stursberg 2016). Salles' and screenwriter Rivera's choice to make Sal Paradise of Québécois rather than Italian origin stresses Kerouac's felt outsider status in (Anglo) American culture.

Salles and Rivera also stress elements from the original scroll that support Kerouac's minority ethnic background. Hence in Salles' film, Sal speaks French, or more precisely *joual*, the form of popular Canadian French spoken by the French-speaking working class, as Kerouac did at home. He lives in Ozone Park, Queens with *Mémère* (his mother), as Kerouac did in between marriages and trips (Cunnel 2007: 8; Charters 1991: xxi). And when Sal takes to the road in the film to find Dean in Denver, although it is figured within the framework of the West (Sal calls him 'cowboy' when they first meet in New York), it is not presented as a straightforward colonial or Anglo west. On the road from New York we hear Sal in voice-over say:

> *With the coming of Dean Moriarty began the part of my life you could call my life on the road. Before that I'd often dreamed of going West. Always vaguely planning, but never cutting out. I was a young writer trying to take off.* (my emphasis)

Reading Sal as the outsider, the 'West' that he takes off into, is not necessarily the West of 'western expansionism' (Saldaña-Portillo 2002: 95) of which he can take ownership. Instead it is a West peopled with a community of marginal characters who are ethnically or economically at the edge of society, who are, in being 'others', both like Sal or to whom Sal (in the beat idea of living on no money – one of the meanings of beat that Kerouac did embrace) feels connected. Salles depicts Sal's 'taking off' scene through a number of road movie conventions. Firstly, as with *Diarios de motocicleta*, 'the liberation of the road [is set] against the oppression of hegemonic norms' (Cohan and Hark 1997: 1)

Figure 28   *On the Road* (Walter Salles 2012)

in phrases like 'cutting out' and 'tak[ing] off.' Salles also underlines the sense of freedom that the road embodies through a musical soundtrack (again by Santaolalla) that swells as Sal's voice-over finishes and the protagonist moves along the road. This first 'road' sequence shows Sal walking and hitch-hiking through predominantly rural areas. Some roads are tarmacked while others are dirt covered. Salles emphasises the latter through shots of Sal's feet crunching over earthy ground (Figure 28).

In these initial scenes and their focus on Sal's feet walking through rural America, before he begins driving with Dean, Salles, like Kerouac's novel, characterises road travel as 'outside of and opposed to mainstream urban culture' (Laderman 2002: 90). In this sense, Salles manifests how the novel *On the Road* is a 'rethinking of the road myth' (not necessarily tied to vehicular travel) as it was emerging in mid-twentieth-century America. *On the Road* also emphasises its protagonists' 'cultural marginality' emulating how the novel was in a way an anticipation of later road movie protagonists such as Wyatt and Billy in *Easy Rider* (Cohan and Hark 1997: 6). Sal is tied to the idea of the cowboy through Dean (as Wyatt and Billy are through their names) but he is not presented as a cowboy. Shots of his feet emphasise that he is wearing huarache sandals (the footwear of a Mexican *campesino*), not cowboy boots.

Salles' representation of Sal's romance with Terry (Alice Braga) the 'sweet Mexican girl' is also represented in a way that more forcefully articulates what Ann Charters calls Kerouac's own feelings about himself 'on the margins of society' and with a concomitant ability to 'sympathise' with society's others that he meets on the road (1991: xxi–xxii). For a while picking cotton with Terry in Selma, California, he becomes one of 'the itinerant labourers, the Mexicans, [and] the African-Americans' (Charters 1991: xxi–xxii). The film presents the interlude with Terry in idyllic terms. The golden hues of the cinematography – which shows sun-lit cotton fields, where Terry and Sal work together, and the tent to which they retire – are presented as a space outside the conservative social landscape that Sal is escaping from, although the film is still clear that the casual terms of their labour are exploitative (they live frugally in a tent city). Sal – who is still a city boy, is presented as less good at manual labour than Terry (she can pick more cotton than him), but their relationship is presented as one of equals both in terms of race – he attempts to live the life of a person of 'color' (Morales 2012) and in gender terms. Unlike the novel, she is not sexually objectified but presented as a sexual being – for whom the relationship with Sal offers physical satisfaction. Furthermore, in Sal's interactions with Terry and other others, the film does not reproduce parts of the novel which might emphasise elements which have been seen as part of its 'colonial fantasy' (Saldaña-Portillo 2002: 99); moments where Kerouac characterises Terry's brother as a 'wild-buck Mexican hotcat with a hunger for booze' (1991: 82) or talks about 'Indians who watched everything with their stony eyes' (1991: 32); or where, he notes of African Americans working the soil 'they picked cotton with the same God-Blessed patience their grandfathers had practised in anti-bellum Alabama' (1991: 87), or 'articulates Sal's white middle class frustration' (Laderman 2002: 22) 'wishing I were a Negro, feeling that the best the white world offered was not enough ecstasy for me, not enough life' (1991: 163).

The film's excising of passages which have been understood as emphasising the novel's colonial gaze and stress on Sal's/Kerouac's outsider status results in a more progressive and post-colonially aware representation of the beat's attitude to America of the post-war era. An additionally significant element of this updating is how the film portrays women and sexuality. In the novel, although sexual freedom is an important theme, it seems to centre more on the sexual freedom of men. Little is known about Marylou and Camille, Dean's two wives and the two women who figure most prominently in the novel, other than that they wait for Dean to come into and leave their lives. In the film, Salles returns to Camille (Kirsten Dunst) significant elements of the biography of Carolyn Cassady, the real individual her character is based upon. When Sal meets Camille in Denver she isn't just 'a brunette on the bed' that Dean is 'bang[ing] (1991: 38–39) but, like Cassady, taking a degree in set design having recently designed the set for a Eugene O Neill play *Desire Under the Elms*.[18] Returning biographical details to the character of Cassady, and also (in another scene) giving greater subjectivity to Marylou, who is shown to be aware of Dean's unfair treatment of her, makes it clearer that for all the sexual liberation their relationships with him may represent (there are several sequences where Marylou's enjoyment of sex is underlined), his treatment of them as women is still 'exploitative' (French 2012).[19] Similarly, not only is the relationship between Dean and Carlo Marx (Ginsberg, played by Tom Sturridge) reinserted into the story, the film focuses considerably on Carlo's love for Dean and Sal's sympathetic understanding of how Carlo is suffering in the relationship. Sal's use of homophobic terms to describe gay men from the novel do not appear in the film (1991: 182, 187).

The film also emphasises the claustrophobic, puritanical, conservative and repressive society that Sal and Dean (and the beat individuals surrounding them) are rebelling against through brief glimpses of the socio-political climate and dominant culture of the late 1940s and early 1950s. At his sister's house in North Carolina over Christmas 1948, Sal comments derisively in front of an audience of seemingly uptight and very Anglo (and, it is signalled, non-French speaking) in-laws about General McArthur banning kissing on the streets of Tokyo 'the puritanical old fart'. On the road to New Orleans we hear on the radio a snippet of President Harry Truman's inaugural address from January 1949: 'Communism subjects the individual to arrest without lawful cause. It decrees what information he shall receive what art he shall produce. Democracy is based on the conviction that has the moral [...].' The film also shows how Sal, Dean, Marylou and others are treated by this society for their bohemian lifestyle. Just after hearing Truman's words a police siren is heard and, Dean, Marylou, Ed and Sal are subjected to 'arrest without lawful cause' by a policeman who pulls them over and, not happy about the fact that Marylou (still a minor) is travelling with her 'ex husband,' threatens 'to slap a special California-boy charge on [Dean's] ass' unless they give him $25.

In addition to emphasising how the socio-political climate represses Sal, Dean and the others of the group, Salles emphasises its effects on the creative process – and the consequent need to go 'on the road' in order to both escape societal and political repression and find a space of creative permissiveness. As Sal sits down to write at his typewriter in Ozone Park, the image of an empty open road stretching into the horizon ahead (and, it is suggested, the limitless creative possibilities that the road represents) flashes into his mind (Figure 29). But hearing the hectoring tones of Senator Joseph McCarthy on the radio, which, like Truman's address, is also a reference to the cold war between the United States and Russia, 'The fight to expose the Communists and the dukes ... in the Kremlin have been and still are [...]' Sal is unable to write. Leaving the house, he crosses the street to a department store where, in the window a television set plays a public service announcement: 'the town in which you live has laws to control you, there are state laws ...' (Figure 30).

Jazz, and bebop are presented as an antidote to this stifling (Anglo) American culture. The film highlights how Sal, Dean and others are (like those of the beat generation) drawn to the bebop scene and the 'freedom' it represents by transposing a sequence in a nightclub that comes later in the novel and takes place in San Francisco to New York and the beginning of the film. In the Harlem nightclub we see Sal and Dean listening to a tenor sax soloist (Terence Howard). They are the only white people in the African-American club. As

Figure 29　*On the Road* (Walter Salles 2012)

Figure 30　*On the Road* (Walter Salles 2012)

with the cotton picking scenes in Selma, the club and jazz session is portrayed in rich, vibrant colours in direct contrast to the greyer New York world outside the club. Sal and Dean dance together and with everyone. In addition to this and other live jazz sequences (there's another with Slim Gaillard (Coati Mundi) in San Francisco), to further establish the alternative that jazz and bebop represent as the soundtrack of 'other' America with which the beat generation align themselves, the film counterpoints a playlist of African American jazz and blues artists (Billie Holiday, Slim Gaillard, Charlie Parker, Ella Fitzgerald, Son House, Dizzy Gillespie) often on record players, juke boxes and car radios with the music of the (white) mainstream, including crooning, country and popular music, e.g. Bing Crosby's 'Buttons and Bows'.

This sense of the freedom and creativity of jazz, is also reproduced famously, in the novel's attempt to emulate jazz's improvisatory nature, a fact to which the marathon three-week duration of its original production famously attests.

The film replicates some of the passages of the novel which align jazz and the impulsive and liberating journeying of Sal, Dean and Marylou 'on the road'. For instance, after leaving Bull Lee (Viggo Mortensen) in Algiers, Louisiana, Sal muses in voice-over: 'The purity of the road, the white line in the middle of the highway unrolled and hugged our left front tire as if glued to our groove.'[20] Beyond sequences like these, which use moments from Kerouac's book that seek to reproduce the free flow style of jazz, Salles also translates the improvisatory nature of the novel's jazz prose by encouraging the actors to improvise based on their knowledge of the characters, something which they did frequently and in particular in the scenes in Algiers, with Old Bull Lee (O'Connor 2012; Matheou 2012: 47).[21] One notable improvisation comes in an invented hallucination sequence in Mexico City, when Sal, suffering from dysentery, sees all his friends appear over him as he lies in bed: Dean, Camille, Marylou, Lee, Terry. He is admonished by Lee 'You can't deny the blood guilt. You're white.' This line, for instance, was wholly Mortensen's idea (Morales 2012).

In this improvised line, which comes near the end of the film, Salles most forcefully articulates that, despite an affinity for jazz, African American and other minority cultures, his own ethnic marginality as working class Québécois, and a desire to live in poverty, there are limits to Sal's otherness. The film also makes a note of the limitations to Sal's otherness by adding in gestures to segregation in the South which are not in the original novel, a form of repression to which Sal, Marylou and Dean, by dint of being white are not subjected. When, short of cash, Marylou sneaks into a shop in Flomaton, Alabama, to take food, a sign reading 'We serve whites only' hangs prominently on the wall. Outside meanwhile, Sal, Dean and Ed Dunkle (Danny Morgan) jokingly quote President Truman's exhortation 'We have to cut down on the cost of living.' When, unable to write, Sal suggests to Dean they take a trip to Mexico, it is similarly presented as an extension of the freedoms of the road but on this occasion these freedoms are presented as specifically white freedoms through the variety of activities Dean and Sal engage in. The music that plays as we see Dean's Hudson driving along a cactus lined dusty road, is notably the same 'striking out' music from Sal's initial 'tak[ing] off.' However, once in Mexico their sole activities are to smoke marijuana, visit a brothel, get drunk and get high. In these scenes, there is little sense of Sal seeking to live a life 'of color' (Morales 2012). Instead, Sal and Dean are seen enjoying the privileges of white colonial tourism.

With perhaps the exception of this excursion to Mexico, Salles' *On the Road* presents a slightly different perspective on the beat movement that foregrounds Kerouac's felt outsider status in the United States and rapprochement to others and 'other cultures' than that of a mainstream, Anglo America. In this respect, it concurs with what Podalsky has identified as a positive common feature (aside from commercial formats) amongst the deterritorialised films of certain

Latin American directors: an ambition 'to speak of/for "other" cultures' (2011: 127). Similarly, in *Diarios de motocicleta,* Salles makes Ernesto a post-colonially aware champion of injustice already aware that his political views would take him outside the norms of his middle class upbringing.

On the Road, the novel, has been identified as a kind of 'master narrative' for the road movie (Laderman 2002: 10). What Salles does with Kerouac's master narrative is try to reconcile some of the tenets of beat with the counter cultural politics and aesthetics of the road movie as it developed later. Ultimately, this chapter concludes, *On the Road* and *Diarios de motocicleta* productively mine the politics of road movies to adress the political history of the continent.

NOTES

1. The actor is indeed related to Guevara; they are distant cousins.
2. Adriana Rouanet does quote Laderman's understanding of taking to the road as 'an act of rebellion' (2013: 124) in her analysis of *Deus e Brasileiro* (*God is Brazilian* Carlos Diegues 2003).
3. Ann Charters point out that Kerouac largely rejected this role (1991).
4. Unable to find a motel that will let them stay, because their long haired look makes them dangerous and suspicious in the eyes of untrusting locals, Billy and Wyatt often have to camp out. One night they stay in a deserted barn beside a rusted out car. They see two kids going past on a mule and we later see other horse drawn vehicles. They go up a dirt road to a farm looking for somewhere to fix their bikes.
5. Podalsky suggests that *Diarios de motocicleta*, along with the other films of the Latin American renaissance 'mim[ick] the formal conventions of hegemonic cinemas (principally Hollywood)' and for this reason have been able to 'travel so far' (2011: 127).
6. The Sundance Institute awarded the script an initial $10,000, facilitated rewrites at its Screenwriters Lab (as with *La ciénaga, Madeinusa, Cidade de Deus*) and awarded it an additional $300,000 which enabled further development of the project (Rodríguez Isaza 2012: 57–71).
7. It's to be noted however, that the film over emphasises the temporal lag, and also the difficulties of their travels, by excising more modern forms of travel detailed in the original diaries such as the cargo ship they stowed away on from Valparaiso and the train they took from Cuzco to near Machu Picchu.
8. As Eva Bueno points out, critics who argue that Salles' *Diarios de motocicleta* is a mythfication of Ernesto Che Guevara that misses out on what he was really like, fail to understand that 'the "Real Che" is as unrecoverable as all legendary myths' (2007: 108).
9. For instance, in the published diary his visit to the Chuquicamata copper mine is a relevantly uneventful one that includes a guided tour (2003: 78–79). He doesn't confront a foreman or stand up for the workers as he does in the film, an act which politicises the moment. In the published diary, his visit to Machu Picchu involves a football game where he later recounts without modesty his prowess on the field (2003: 116). There's no musing about the greatness of the Inca civilisation and what might have become of it without colonisation by the Spanish but a lot of transcribing of the findings of American anthropologist Howard Bingham who 'discovered' the ruins in 1928. He does swim the Amazon, but recounts it in one line in the diary as a purely physical goal 'I determined to swim across the Amazon' (2003: 150). The feat has none of the symbolic meaning the film invests in it. He is

not met by anyone because it took two hours and 'Dr. Montoya ... had no desire to wait so long' (2003: 150). Also, in Lima, he records in his diary that he is reading not Mariátegui, but Tello (Dr Julio C. Tello, father of Peruvian archaeology) (2003: 136).

10. The film is also based on Alberto Granado's book about his travels *Con el Che por sudamérica* (2008) and several biographies of Guevara including the one by Pablo Ignacio Taibo II, *Ernesto Guevara: También conocido como el Che* (2009), as well as on Granado's own memories. Granado also acted as a consultant on the script.

11. After describing the wonders of a mountain plateau where there are Inca irrigation ditches Guevara continues 'But the people are not the same proud race that time after time rose up against Inca rule ... these people who watch us walk through the town streets are a defeated race. They look at us meekly, almost fearfully, completely indifferent to the outside world' (2003: 97).

12. Guevara and Granado successfully stow away on a boat from Valparaiso to Antofagasta but are unsuccessful in their attempt to stow away again on another boat leaving from Antofagasta and so have to travel through the Atacama Desert.

13. *Central do Brasil* makes use of non-professional actors throughout, but most notably the protagonist who was discovered at the station shining shoes. The actors in the opening sequence who dictate letters to Dora are all non-professional actors (Sadlier 2007: 132).

14. That Gael is also a transnational activist, committed to political causes and action gives his role as Guevara an even greater resonance, and in moments like these a sense that he too is invested in what ordinary people are telling him about their lives. By 2004 when the film came out he was already known for his outspoken comments at the 2003 Oscars where, introducing *Frida* (Julie Taymor 2002), he suggested Frida Kahlo would have been against the Iraq War.

15. In a 2004 interview Salles recounts: 'I didn't go ahead on *Motorcycle Diaries* before realising that the reality of South America in 2002/03 is very similar to that described by Ernesto Guevara in his book. The structural problems are pretty much the same, of bad distribution of land and wealth. I realised that our own adventure within the continent could somehow mirror what happened to them on a very small scale, and that improvisation was possible' (Andrew 2004).

16. This return to the original scroll also makes the journeying and the friendship with Dean partly about the search for a (lost) father.

17. Jack Kerouac was born Jean-Louis Lebris de Kerouac in Lowell, Massachusetts, to parents who had immigrated from rural Québec (Charters 1991: ix–x).

18. Carolyn Cassady met Neal in Denver when she was studying for an MA in Fine Arts and Set Design at the University of Denver (Cassady 2007: 4).

19. Indeed, Kristen Stewart talks about how she listened to hours and hours of tapes by Luanne Hendersen to understand better her motivations for travelling with Neal and Jack across America (Matheou 2012: 47).

20. This line comes from the novel and actually comes during the road trip south to New Orleans (1991: 121).

21. Salles staged a month-long beat 'boot camp' for the principal players in Montreal, Canada, before the shoot began. During this boot camp, Riley, Hedlund and Stewart were able to immerse themselves materials from the real individuals they would be portraying (O'Connor 2012).

ARGENTINA: INTRODUCTION

In June of 2016 at the Buenos Aires Museum of Latin American Art (MALBA), Argentina's National Film Institute, the INCAA (Instituto Nacional de Cine y Artes Audiovisuales) presented its *Anuario Estadístico de la Industria Cinematográfica y Audiovisual Argentina* (*Yearbook of Argentina's Film and Audiovisual Industry*) including the key successes of 2015 (INCAA – Anuario de la Industria Cinematográfica y Audiovisual Argentina Año 2015). Figures from the yearbook suggest that Argentine cinema is thriving. Domestic production is increasing: with 182 national films released in 2015, more than the 172 films released in 2014, the 167 films released in 2013 (INCAA – Anuario de la Industria Cinematográfica y Audiovisual Argentina Año 2015: 25) and considerably more than the thirty-eight films produced in 1996 when production began to pick up again after the crisis of the early 1990s (Rocha 2011: 20). The yearbook records that audience figures have also increased to over 52 million spectators, that the market share for national films is 14.49 per cent and that this is the best audience share of all Latin America's three significant film industries (in the same year Mexico's is 6.1 per cent and Brazil's is 13/12.7 per cent) (INCAA – Anuario de la Industria Cinematográfica y Audiovisual Argentina Año 2015: 5, 14). Although, as the yearbook also indicates, these figures are mitigated somewhat by the fact that the Argentine market is smaller in comparison to the other big industries in Latin America in terms of both population (43 million), screens (912) and rate of cinema attendance per capita (1.21 tickets) (Table 9, INCAA – Anuario de la Industria Cinematográfica y Audiovisual Argentina Año 2015: 46). The yearbook also offers figures on

Table 9 Total admissions for 2015 Argentina and other countries (INCAA – Anuario de la Industria Cinematográfica y Audiovisual Argentina Año 2015: 46)

PAÍS *Country* País *Pays*	ESPECTADORES (1) *Admissions (1)* Espectadores (1) *Spectateurs (1)*	POBLACIÓN (2) *Population 2015 (2)* Populacao 2015 (2) *Poulation 2015 (2)*	ENTRADAS POR HABITANTE *Tickets per capita* Ingressos por habitante *Entrées par habitant*
Argentina	52.125.925	43.131.966	1,21
Brasil	172.915.057	100.955.522	1,69
Chile	26.170.993	18.006.407	1,45
Colombia	59.519.309	48.203.405	1,23
España	97.883.957	46.423.064	2,11
Francia	203.392.663	66.380.000	3,06
Italia	112.306.084	60.795.612	1,85
México	286.000.000	121.005.815	2,46

how much state support national films received in 2015 including details on credits, and subsidies awarded for production, distribution and also launches. In 2015 fifty feature films were given credits and over 300 films given grants of some kind. In Argentina, most domestic productions receive some kind of funding from the state, including, controversially, high budget 'industrial' films like *El clan* (*The Clan*, Pablo Trapero, 2015) (INCAA – Anuario de la Industria Cinematográfica y Audiovisual Argentina Año 2015: 255; Falicov 2007b: 94) with additional funding coming from a variety of other different sources and not just from the state.

At the MALBA presentation ceremony awards were given to the director (Trapero) and actors (Guillermo Francella and Peter Lanzini) of the highest grossing national film for 2015, *El clan*, which attracted a domestic audience of 2.6 million (Anon. 2016b). *El clan*'s success, though remarkable, pales slightly in comparison with the highest grossing film of 2014, the Oscar-nominated *Relatos salvajes* (*Wild Tales* Damián Szifrón), which, with a historic total of 3.45 million spectators, beat its closest rival, the Disney animated film *Frozen* (Chris Buck and Jennifer Lee) by nearly 2 million spectators (INCAA – Anuario de la Industria Cinematográfica y Audiovisual Argentina Año 2015: x) and led to an 18 per cent annual share of the market for Argentine film (INCAA – Anuario de la Industria Cinematográfica y Audiovisual Argentina Año 2014: v).

In April of 2017, and also at the MALBA, the INCAA presented 2016's yearbook (Anon. 2017). As with the previous year, domestic releases are up, to 199, as are the number of screens (933). The presentation ceremony also involved awards for the director (Juan Taratuto) and actors (Adrián Suar and Valeria Bertucelli) of the highest grossing film *Me casé con un boludo*

Table 10 Top ten Argentine box office films 2016 (INCAA – Anuario de la Industria Cinematográfica y Audiovisual Argentina Año 2016: 64)

1	Me casé con un boludo		2.026.469	3,98%	3,98%	27,66%	27,66%
2	Gilda, no me arrepiento de este amor		944.755	1,86%	5,84%	12,89%	40,55%
3	El hilo rojo	España	713.964	1,40%	7,24%	9,74%	50,30%
4	El ciudadano ilustre	España	657.358	1,29%	8,53%	8,97%	59,27%
5	Inseparables		361.707	0,71%	9,24%	4,94%	64,21%
6	Cien años de perdón	España/ Francia	358.671	0,70%	9,95%	4,90%	69,10%
7	Permitidos		354.527	0,70%	10,64%	4,84%	73,94%
8	Koblic	España	308.733	0,61%	11,25%	4,21%	78,15%
9	Al final del tunel	España	282.792	0,56%	11,81%	3,86%	82,01%
10	Una noche de amor		219.913	0,43%	12,24%	3,00%	85,01%

(*I married a Dumbass* Taratuto 2015) (INCAA – Anuario de la Industria Cinematográfica y Audiovisual Argentina Año 2016: 12) (Table 10). However, market share for national films is down (to 14.4 per cent) and *Me casé con un boludo*'s domestic audience (2.02 million) represents a decline from those of *Relatos salvajes* and *El clan* (INCAA – Anuario de la Industria Cinematográfica y Audiovisual Argentina Año 2016: 12).

The figures in 2015's and similarly in 2016's yearbooks paint a mostly optimistic picture of an expanding Argentine industry that is able to not just compete with but, on occasion, also beat its closest rival, Hollywood. However, although annual production numbers are high, critics such as Leonardo M. D'Espósito and industry veterans such as filmmaker and former head of the national film institute Octavio Getino (1989–1990) point out the lack of a real film industry in Argentina (D'Espósito 2014; Getino 2007: 170). The success of the highest grossing national films of the last three years aside, figures offered in the yearbook show that all other Argentine films actually represent a very small portion of the market and that Argentina suffers as much as or potentially more than the other big Latin American industries with the same structural problems of poor distribution and unfair competition. For instance, there's a much bigger drop off from the highest grossing national film to the next best performing national film, even after taking into consideration the much smaller market that Argentina represents. In the 2015 top grossing national films, after *El clan* comes *Abzurdah* (Daniela Goggi), which attracted 808,135 spectators, which is then followed by *Relatos salvajes*, which attracted 516,786 spectators in its second year of release (INCAA Año 2015: 60). Similarly, in 2016 *Me casé con un boludo* is followed by *Gilda, no me arrepiento de este amor* (Lorena Muñoz), which attracted 944,755 spectators (Table 11) (INCAA – Anuario de la Industria Cinematográfica y Audiovisual Argentina Año 2016: 62)

In fact, the 2015 and 2016 yearbooks point to a very familiar picture of Hollywood domination in terms of exhibition. In 2016, of the top ten films, nine are produced by US studios and only one is Argentine – *Me casé con un boludo*. Together, the top ten films, including the most popular film overall, which was *Finding Dory* (Andrew Stanton) with an audience of 3 million, represent 40 per cent of the market (Table 11). That such high percentages of the Argentine market are represented by a small number of US films and by only one Argentine film means there is less exhibition space left for the majority of Argentine productions. In 2011, for instance, Pablo Giorgelli's *Las acacias* (*The Acacia Trees*) won prizes at the Cannes and San Sebastián film festivals but domestically the film was only able to secure distribution in thirteen theatres and only reach an audience of 24,000 (Falicov 2014: 19). These poor figures for a critically acclaimed film like *Las acacias* and the even worse figures of 8,000 spectators (in sixteen theatres) for the more recent and also critically acclaimed *Jauja* (Lisandro Alonso 2014) compare unfavourably, as Argentine critic Diego Batlle has recently pointed out, with the 80,000 and 70,000 spectators that early *nuevo cine argentino* (New Argentine Cinema) successes *Pizza, birra, faso* (*Pizza, Beer and Cigarettes* Bruno Stagnaro and Caetano 1997) and *Mundo grúa* (*Crane World* Trapero 1999) were able to record respectively when they were first released (2014).[1] In relation to these distribution problems, Batlle notes that whereas micro-budgeted films can get by with a 'few screenings at the Gaumont' (an art cinema in Buenos Aires), 'industrial films' made with professional union crews, a group in which he includes *Jauja*, struggle to find enough screens and to remain on the screens they can find.[2] This is what Batlle refers to as an 'in between cinema,' that is in between independence and the 'blockbuster' films of Trapero and others (2014). This situation is despite the protectionist measures set in place by the government to ensure the exhibition of national films: the screen quota brought in in June 2004, and the establishment of the Espacios INCAA (like the Gaumont), that are funded by the INCAA and dedicated to the exhibition of Argentine, Spanish language and global art cinema and of which 79 now exist across Argentina (INCAA – Anuario de la Industria Cinematográfica y Audiovisual Argentina Año 2016: 10). Directors and industry commentators have called for other measures to ensure the exhibition of Argentinian films in Argentina (and protection from Hollywood product), including the creation of a National Cinemateque (Cinemateca Nacional), like the one that exists in Mexico (Alonso, 2014).

Table 11 Top twenty box office films Argentina 2016 (INCAA – Anuario de la Industria Cinematográfica y Audiovisual Argentina Año 2016: 62)

#						
1	Buscando a Dory	Finding Dory	Estados Unidos	3.006.043	5,91%	5,91%
2	La era de bielo 5	Ice Age 5	Estados Unidos	2.608.457	5,13%	11,03%
3	La vida secreta de tus mascotas	The Secret Life of Pets	Estados Unidos	2.446.783	4,81%	15,84%
4	Me casé con un boludo	Me casé con un boludo	Argentina	2.026.469	3,98%	19,82%
5	Zootopia	Zootopia	Estados Unidos	1.833.440	3,60%	23,42%
6	El conjuro 2	The Conjuring 2	Canada/Estados Unidos	1.796.001	3,53%	26,95%
7	El libro de la selva	The Jungle Book	Estados Unidos	1.704.301	3,35%	30,30%
8	Capitan America: civil war	Capitan America: Civil War	Estados Unidos	1.548.948	3,04%	33,34%
9	Batman vs Saperman: el origen de la justicia	Batman vs Superman: Dawn of Justice	Estados Unidos	1.373.943	2,70%	36,04%
10	Escuadrón suicida	Suicide Squad	Estados Unidos	1.237.490	2,43%	38,48%
11	Gilda, no me arrepiento de este amor	Gilda, no me arrepiento de este amor	Argentina	944.755	1,86%	40,33%
12	Alicia a traves del espejo	Alica Through the Looking Glass	Estados Unidos	900.989	1,77%	42,10%
13	Deadpool	Deadpool	Estados Unidos	872.286	1,71%	43,82%
14	Angry Birds: la película	Angry Birds: The Film	Estados Unidos	853.011	1,68%	45,49%
15	Animales fantásticos y donde encontrarlos	Fantastic Beasts and Where to Find Them	Estados Unidos	810.747	1,59%	47,09%
16	Kung Fu Panda 3	Kung Fu Panda 3	Estados Unidos	807.630	1,59%	48,67%
17	X-Men: Apocalipsis	X-Men: Apocalypse	Estados Unidos	718.029	1,41%	50,08%
18	El bilo rojo	El bilo rojo	Argentina/España	713.964	1,40%	51,49%
19	El ciudadano ilustre	El ciudadano ilustre	Argentina/España	657.358	1,29%	52,78%
20	El renacido	The Revenant	Estados Unidos	655.464	1,29%	54,07%

However, as with Brazil and Mexico, the current situation of Argentine cinema is much more complicated than straightforward Hollywood hegemony. As John Hopewell points out, the Argentinian films that do outstandingly well in the national market and globally like *El clan* ($20 million) and *Relatos salvajes* ($24 million), do so in part because they are co-productions with Hollywood studios or their local subsidiaries and distributed by MPA member companies in and outside of Argentina (Hopewell 2016; Hopewell and Barraclough 2014).[3] *El clan* was co-produced by Fox International Productions and distributed by Twentieth Century Fox. *Relatos salvajes* was co-produced by Warner Bros. Pictures International and distributed by Warner Bros. As Luisela Alvaray indicates, other 'alliances and exchanges' made by the film industry with media conglomerates in and outside of Argentina – particularly Spain – are also key to the film industry's successes. *El clan* and *Relatos salvajes* are also co-productions with a transnational media conglomerate, the Spanish owned broadcast network Telefe (2011: 70).[4] The role of individual producers can also be key in the success of individual films. *El clan* and *Relatos salvajes* are co-produced by Spanish auteur Pedro Almodóvar through El Deseo S. A.[5] As the following section's historical overview will explore, Argentina's expanded film production (to numbers that are the highest in Latin America), the growth in total audiences, the increase in audience share for (individual) national films and global exposure of the domestic cinema, are the result of both changes in Argentine film legislation in the last twenty years and also the strategies of transnational media conglomerates (Alvaray 2008: 55).

Part of this picture of the situation of Argentine cinema is the role 'industry auteurs' have played in the growth of the Argentine industry. Used to primarily describe directors like Juan José Campanella (*El mismo amor, La misma lluvia/The Same Rain, The Same Love* 1999; *El hijo de la novia/Son of the Bride* 2001, *Luna de Avellaneda/Avellaneda's Moon* 2004; *El secreto de sus ojos/The Secret in Their Eyes* 2009), the late Fabián Bielinsky (*Nueve reinas/Nine Queens* 2001; *El aura/The Aura* 2005), and Marcelo Piñeyro (*Cenizas del paraíso/Ashes of Paradise* 1997, *Plata quemada/Burnt Money* 2000, *Kamchatka* 2002, *Las viudas de los jueves/The Thursday Widows* 2009) who make successful films within mainstream 'industry' contexts (most often transnational media conglomerates), 'industry auteur' is now also applied to directors formerly associated with independent cinema who have shifted into 'industry' films, like Trapero (*Mundo grúa*) director of *El clan* and *Carancho* (*Vulture* 2010) and Caetano (*Pizza, birra, faso, Bolivia* 2001, *Un oso rojo/A Red Bear* 2002), director of the thriller *Crónica de una fuga* (*Chronicle of an Escape* 2006).[6] In the Argentine context, and in addition to the institutional venues in which they make films, the terms 'industry' and 'auteur' are put together to indicate how these directors work within mainstream stylistic parametres (crime narratives, grifter-thrillers, detective films, romantic comedies) but refashion them to produce 'parallel plots involving identity or the political' (Aguilar 2011: 268, 16; Navitski 2012: 359). In addition to being the product of changes in how films are made in Argentina, these directors and their mainstream successes have also been instrumental in changing how films are made, by attracting MPA member companies into the Argentine production market (Alvaray 2013: 75).

Campanella is Argentina's most successful and globally well known 'industry auteur' and indeed director. Until *Relatos salvajes*, Campanella's Oscar-winning *El secreto de sus ojos* previously held the record for a domestic audience (2.4 million viewers) and made $34 million globally, and his Oscar-nominated *El hijo de la novia* and *Luna de Avellaneda* similarly performed well: both attracting over a million spectators domestically (Rocha 2011: 22–23; Falicov 2014: 20) with the former film also doing modestly well in Spain and the US (Alvaray 2008: 51).[7] Campanella's co-directed animated debut, *Metegol* (*The Underdogs* 2013), co-produced with Spain and The Weinstein Company, has achieved a global box office of $25 million and is now available in such mainstream contexts as a streaming service like, Netflix. Campanella's films also epitomise many of the changes in how films are made and distributed in Argentina and globally. Produced by MPA member companies, transnational media conglomerates and as international co-productions (most commonly with Spain), Campanella's films utilise mainstream genres (the thriller, the romantic comedy, the sports achievement film) that make them 'culturally legible both in Argentina and elsewhere' (Navitski 2012: 359–360), yet also rely on 'local' features (popular television actors, Argentina's recent history of dictatorship and political violence) that appeal to domestic audiences. Campanella's transnational intermedial history (work in 'quality' television and film in the United States) also plays a part in his ability to function as an 'industry auteur'. This section and its account of the significant changes in filmmaking in Argentine cinema in the last twenty-five years acts as a platform to the director-centred analysis of Campanella's films in Chapter 6, and situates Campanella and his filmmaking practice as typical of one vector of Argentina's changed filmmaking landscape.

Argentina's 'industry auteurs', like Campanella, are the product of the neoliberal reforms made to Argentina's film industry by President Carlos Saúl Menem (1989–1994, 1994–1999). The 1989 financial crisis in which hyper-inflation soared to 'previously unmatched heights' had dire implications for the film industry. As part of neoliberal measures to 'curb' inflation, funds for film production were reduced and the number of films released consequently fell to single figures and the low teens for much of the first half of the 1990s. However, during Menem's second term in office, whilst privatisations were increasing and the state was being 'downsized' the system of state-subsidy for film was actually 'strengthened' (Falicov 2007b: 88). The film industry was 'spared and even nurtured' in the 1994 New Cinema Law that imposed taxes on home video rentals, and television advertisements in addition to the already existing 10 per cent tax on box office receipts that was to be used for producing national cinema (Falicov 2007b: 88). Part of the law also mandated links between the national film institute (then the INC) and 'other audiovisual sectors' including cable, free television, and home video and the institute was consequently renamed to include audiovisual arts rather than just cinema, to reflect these new links (Falicov 2007b: 89). Not surprisingly, given the neoliberal mode of his presidency, the model Menem 'looked to' for the Argentine industry was the US film industry – profitable, big budget films with special effects – seeking to foster not the art cinema practices of national cinema from previous administrations but a cinema with 'industrial capabilities' (Falicov 2007b: 151–152).

In the mid-1990s, in addition to fomenting the production of 'higher budgeted commercial films' (Falicov 2007b: 115), the state also fostered low budget filmmaking through a number of measures. A state-funded short film competition produced the anthology *Historias breves* (*Short Stories* 1995) featuring shorts by recent film graduates who 'in the following decade' released what would become 'some of the most significant films of the *nuevo cine argentino*': Daniel Burman, Lucrecia Martel, Adrián Caetano, and Bruno Stagnaro (Ros 2011: 97). In 1996, after a 26 year 'hiatus', the Mar del Plata International Film Festival was revived and in 1997 the 'first' film of the *nuevo cine argentino*, Caetano and Stagnaro's *Pizza, birra, faso* won the special jury prize there (Falicov 2000: 329). In 1999 another film festival was established, the Buenos Aires International Festival of Independent Film – commonly known as the BAFICI – and *Mundo grúa*, another significant early film of the *nuevo cine*, was premiered there. Additionally, the state funded film schools both in the capital and across the regions (Falicov 2007b: 110; Aguilar 2011: 8).

Government strategies to foster the film industry began to bear fruit in 1997, 'a remarkable year for the Argentine film industry' when the success of Argentine films was so great that it eroded the market share of Hollywood films to 61 per cent (Falicov 2007b: 95, 96; Rocha 2011: 22). Three films attracted over a million spectators: the police drama *Comodines* (*Cops* Jorge Nisco), the animated film *Dibu la película* (*Dibu, the film* Olivieri and Stoessel), and *La furia* (*Fury* Juan Batista Stagnaro) whilst another, *Cenizas del paraíso*, attracted over 800,000 spectators (Rocha 2011: 22). These four successful films were Argentina's first 'blockbusters' and were all produced by transnational media conglomerates but, following the New Cinema Law, with financing from the state through a mixture of loans and subsidies, and in a model designed to reward success. *Comodines*, the highest grossing film of the year received 2.2 million pesos, the level of subsidy determined by its high audience figures. *Cenizas del paraíso* meanwhile received 875,000 pesos and *Dibu* 600,000 pesos (Falicov 2007b: 97).

These four successful films were all produced by two transnational media conglomerates that were formed in the wave of media de-regulation of the early 1990s and potentially encouraged into filmmaking, as Falicov speculates, in order to recoup the taxes media conglomerates had to pay that were earmarked for film production (2000: 332): Pol-Ka (*Comodines*) and Patagonik (*Comodines, Cenizas del paraíso, Dibu, la pelicula*) (Falicov 2008: 272). As Getino points out, Patagonik is part of a transnational conglomerate that involves media group Clarín (which includes Argentina's most read newspaper *Clarín*, the production company Artear, and the cable channel Cablevision), broadcast network Telefe (owned by the Spanish telecommunications giant Telefónica) and Miravista (subsidiary of Disney Studios) (2007b: 70). It produces films via a mixture of its own monies, state and co-production funds. Like other conglomerates in the other major national industries, Televisa in Mexico and Globo in Brazil, Patagonik/Clarín/Telefe/Miravista counts on the resources of its multimedia companies (Channel 13 for instance owns Artear) as well as the distribution network (of Disney's Buena Vista) to ensure its films are well-publicised (through its various television channels and print media outlets) and reach large audiences. In addition to these resources, the kinds of films Patagonik makes use 'sure fire methods for success': genres and narratives influenced by Hollywood cinema, screenplays that model televisual narratives, well-known television actors and high production values (Getino 2007: 169–170).[8] In 2007, as a result of these resources and features Patagonik was consequently responsible for 70 per cent of the box office takings for domestic films (Getino 2007: 170).

Patagonik/Clarin/Miravista/Telefe has had continued success from the 1990s onwards in the Argentine market including Campanella's *El hijo de la novia*, his *El secreto de sus ojos*, the highest grossing film of 2008, the romantic comedy *Un novio para mi mujer* (*A boyfriend for my wife* Juan Taratuto 2008), and several other high grossing romantic comedies by the same director including the highest grossing domestic productions of 2014, 2015 and 2016, *Relatos salvajes, El clan* and *Me casé con un boludo* respectively (Anon. 2008). Although many of these films may model themselves in part on Hollywood, as Getino (2007) and Batlle (2008a) point out, some scholars (Falicov, Navitski) also point out that their successes represent more than a simple case of imitation. Argentine films that do well at the box office, even if they emulate 'Hollywood styles' and are coproduced (in part) by Hollywood companies, also rely on what Courtney Brannon Donoghue has called, in relation to the Brazilian blockbusters 'local exceptionality'; television actors (Suar, who starred in *Comodines* and also in Taratuto's films, Ricardo Darín, who features in all of Campanella's live-action films), Argentine slang, and a particular local take on mainstream formats even from directors not considered 'industry auteurs' such as Taratuto (Falicov 2007b: 99; Navitski 2012: 59–60). Although some of these successful films are limited to the local market as a result of their local features, others are also designed to be successful, or (like *Nueve reinas*) have surprise success abroad, particularly in the Spanish market, to which they have distribution access through Telefe, and are often cast, as *Relatos salvajes* was, with Argentine actors (Darín, Darío Grandinetti, Leonardo Sbaraglia) who are also name actors in Spain, with this dual market appeal in mind (Hopewell 2013).

In independent filmmaking, the raft of measures introduced by the Government in the 1994 new cinema law were also successful. Critics began to welcome the 'new' kinds of films made by young directors in the mid- to late 1990s. In newly formed film journals (*El Amante Cine, Film*), these critics began to speak of a new movement *el nuevo cine argentino* (although the label itself is also highly debated), and to champion its directors who were graduates of the new state and private film schools (Garavelli 2011: 35). In addition to the movement's early manifestations *Pizza, birra, faso* and *Mundo grúa*, subsequent films began to attract attention and funding from foreign institutions, film festivals and their related funding bodies. Lucrecia Martel's *La ciénaga* 2001, Alonso's *La libertad* 2001 and a string of other films won production awards (Sundance/NHK, Fonds Sud, World Cinema Fund) and festival prizes (Berlin, Havana, Rotterdam, Oslo). Indeed, as explored in the Introduction to the book, although it had (limited) state support, the films of the *nuevo cine argentino* were also largely dependent on these exterior sources of funding for their international circulation and visibility, and also on a new generation of 'savy' producers who were capable of navigating the complex requirements of these foreign funding bodies (Aguilar 2011: 8).

In the period 1997–2006, and as Carolina Rocha and Falicov point out, Argentine cinema continued to produce local 'blockbusters' that attracted relatively large audiences. In addition to the standout films of 1997 already mentioned, Campanella's Argentinean feature-film directorial debut, *El mismo amor, la misma lluvia*, his *El hijo de la novia* and *Luna de Avellaneda*, Bielinsky's *Nueve reinas* and several other films all attracted over a million spectators (Rocha 2011: 22–23; Falicov 2007b: 143–144). The period also saw the feature film debut of Szifrón (*Relatos salvajes*), known for creating several popular Argentine television series (*Los simuladrones/The Pretenders*, [2002–2003] and *Hermanos y Detectives/Brothers and Detectives* [2009]) whose buddy film *Tiempo de Valientes* (*On Probation* 2005) attracted half a million spectators (Rocha 2011: 24–25). Production figures also continued to climb from twenty-seven films in 1997 to sixty-nine films in 2004 (although in 2005 they fell back to twenty-seven) (Aguilar 2011: 215–226). During this period the *nuevo cine argentino* consolidated its position on the international festival and art cinema circuit with films like *Bombón, el perro* (Carlos Sorín 2004), *Los muertos* (*The Dead* Alonso 2004) and *Tan de repente* (*Suddenly* Diego Lerman 2002) winning awards at major festivals.

Although overall this was a period of cinematic growth in Argentina in terms of production and international visibility, the worsening economic and social crisis effected the industry (Falicov 2007b: 112). On the one hand, spectatorship fluctuated dipping to its lowest numbers during the years of highest unemployment and financial insecurity (2001, 2002) when ticket prices on a par with the US (because of the pegging of the local currency to the dollar) made cinema going an unaffordable luxury for many (Rocha 2011: 19). On the other, the minimalist mode of production (location shooting, non-professional or not well-known actors) realist aesthetics (long takes, minimal camera set ups) and focus on the everyday of many of the films of the *nuevo cine argentino* responded creatively to, whilst also signifying, the crisis and its roots in the failures of Argentina's neoliberal project as well as the material results of those failures: unemployment, poverty and crime (Garavelli 2011: 35–36; Page 2009: 2). The critical financial crisis of December 2001 which resulted in the resignation of President Fernando de la Rúa (1999–2001), and is foreshadowed in the final scenes of *Nueve reinas*,[9] did not lessen the rate of production in the industrial and independent sectors (forty-seven films in 2001, forty-six in 2002 and fifty-four in 2003) – although it did lead to a period of more 'cost conscious' filmmaking due to the scarcity of subsidies and, in the independent and industrial sector, to a 'corpus of films directly influenced by the 2001 events' like *Cama adentro* (*Live-in Maid* Jorge Gaggero 2004), *Vida en Falcon* (*Life in a Falcon* Gaggero 2004) and Campanella's own *Luna de Avellaneda* (Falicov 2007b: 146; Garavelli 2011: 37; Aguilar 2011: 215–226).[10]

The rise in the number of cinema screens over this period and beyond thanks to increased multinational corporate investment and an 'influx of foreign owned theatre chains' (Cinemark, Village Cinemas, Hoyts) attracted by the 20 per cent growth in the box office of 1997–1998 has created more money for the production of Argentine films (via the 10 per cent tax on box office receipts, which goes into a development fund) (Falicov 2007b: 90, 109). Whilst industry veteran, distributor of Campanella's films and one-time interim head of INCAA Bernardo Zupnik laments the domination of these screens by Hollywood blockbusters, he also acknowledges the benefits their huge revenues bring to the Argentine industry via the 10 per cent box office tax (Zupnik 2015: 29–30). However, these revenues from US films do not solve the perennial problem of a lack of exhibition space for Argentine films.

The 2004 exhibition quota was brought in to precisely address the problem of exhibition of Argentine films. It stipulates the exhibition of one national film per movie theatre per quarter. A further measure was also introduced to ensure the duration of quota films on screens (Rocha 2011: 22). '[T]he continuity average' obliges film exhibitors to 'continue screening national films' if they fulfil a certain capacity for the week (between 6 and 25 per cent) (Falicov 2007b: 153). Commentators agree that in the absence of the big marketing campaigns affordable to Hollywood blockbusters, but not to the average Argentine production, the quota and continuity average have helped films like Campanella's *Luna de Avellaneda* gain good word-of-mouth publicity over a period of months and subsequently return decent box office receipts (Jorge Coscia qtd in Falicov 2007b: 153–154). In reality however, as Batlle points out in relation to the fate of veteran director Leonardo Favio's film *Anicieto* (2008b), which barely lasted a week on screens, exhibitors treat many Argentine films badly, removing them 'violently' as soon as they fail to meet the minimum number of spectators necessary for the 'continuity average' even if they are doing better than other films from overseas. Additionally, he suggests, exhibitors cheat the quota to clear up screens for Hollywood blockbusters (Batlle 2008b).

The contested effectiveness of the screening quota and continuity average aside, the INCAA has sought other ways to strengthen the exhibition of Argentine cinema, in particular, the Ventana Sur film market. Launched in 2009 – in partnership between the INCAA, the Marché du Film de Cannes and the San Sebastián Festival – it is designed to help in the development and sale of films from Argentina and across Latin America (Hopewell 2014). Although Batlle points out the success of the first instalment of Ventana Sur for Argentine productions, he also suggests *Variety* correspondent John Hopewell's evaluation of it as 'Latin America's premiere market for regional films' has to be taken with a 'pinch of salt' given the industry daily is actually the media sponsor for the event (Batlle 2009a). Additionally, and as Batlle also points out, the amount INCAA spent on the event in 2009 angered many filmmakers who were left waiting on promised INCAA subsidies for their films as a result (2009a).

In the past, Campanella has defended the screen quota and continuity average and tussled with critics who have maligned his work and its 'national' credentials and questioned his commitment to Argentine cinema (Minghetti 2005). Although Campanella works transnationally, and also, like other Argentine directors (Caetano) sometimes in television he has also underlined his commitment to the history and future of Argentine cinema by taking on the role of President of the re-founded (2004) Argentine Academy of Cinematography Arts and Sciences (*Academia de las Artes y Ciencias Cinematográficas de la Argentina, AACCA*) from 2010 to 2014 and is currently one of its vice-presidents. However, even in this role, he has drawn ire from other filmmakers for being too 'cosy' with the Government. For instance, he was criticised when a photograph appeared of him seated beside President Cristina Fernández de Kirchner (2007–2015) as she signed the agreement for the creation of a new National Cinemateque in 2010. The criticism of Campanella in particular relates to shifts in government policies towards cinema which make the dividing up of funds and who gets what from the INCAA a continued source of controversy (Panozzo 2009: 47). Many of the most applauded of the recent wave of directors of the *nuevo cine argentino* – for instance Mariano Llinás, who made *Historias extraordinarias* (*Extraordinary Stories* 2008) on a tiny budget of $50,000 – have chosen to 'forego' INCAA funding altogether and consequently seek exhibition outside its parametres. Llinás' film ran for a whole year at the MALBA (Losada 2010: 5; Diestro-Dópido 2011: 15). The funds for the National Cinemateque have yet to be found.

Campanella has, like Latin America's other transnational auteurs (Iñárritu, del Toro, Cuarón, Meirelles, Salles) worked with MPA member companies. Both directly, with Warner Bros. who co-produced *El mismo amor, la misma lluvia*, and also through conglomerates, who have produced all his other features in Argentina, including the Disney subsidiary Miravista. Like Latin America's other transnational auteurs, his own MPA involvement has not, however, prevented him from criticising some of the unfair practices Hollywood studios engage in to protect their own products. In 2013 for instance, he engaged in a Twitter war of words with Disney who, wanting to protect their own animation legacy, refused to carry advertising for his animated feature *Metegol* on their television channels.

Notes

1. *Jauja* won the FIPRESCI award when it was shown in the Un Certain Regard section of the Cannes Film Festival. It also won Argentina's Silver Condor award for Best Cinematography (Timo Salminen).
2. According to the yearbook, the Gaumont was the cinema that showed the greatest number of Argentine films in 2015 – eighty-eight titles (INCAA – Anuario de la Industria Cinematográfica y Audiovisual Argentina Año 2015: 206).
3. Box office figures from boxofficemojo.com
4. That the measure of success for Argentina's national cinema necessarily extends beyond its geographical boundaries – into a continental global arena – is something the yearbook acknowledges by recording top ten box office figures for Argentinian films in Spain (and Brazil, Colombia, Mexico and Chile), in difference to those of the two other big industries. In 2015 the yearbook records that *Relatos salvajes* (in its second year of release) and *El clan* attracted 69,903 and 83,330 spectators respectively in Spain. *Truman* (Cesc Gay), another Argentina/Spain co-production, topped Argentina's performance attracting 499,000 spectators in Spain (INCAA – Anuario de la Industria Cinematográfica y Audiovisual Argentina Año 2015: 51).
5. See the Introduction for more on Almodóvar's Latin American co-productions.
6. *Crónica de una fuga* was a co-production with Twentieth Century Fox.
7. *El secreto de sus ojos*' global box office is taken from boxofficemojo.com
8. *Comodines* was a conscious attempt on the part of its producers to reproduce the Hollywood police procedural film, complete with lots of explosions, chases and gun fights. But it was also designed around strong elements of locality. The film was based on the popular television series *Poliládron* which previously aired on the conglomerate's Channel 13, and featured actors from the series including

the star Adrián Suar. It also used typical Argentine Spanish (*lunfardo*), featured a soundtrack of Argentine rock bands and also has plot twists that are particular to Argentine police procedurals, such as some of the guilty escaping evasion at its closure (Falicov 2007b: 97).

9. At the end of the film, Marcos (Darín), the conman who unknowingly is being conned himself, has received the payoff in the form of a cashier's cheque. However, on arriving at the bank to cash it, he discovers the cheque is useless: the bank's doors are closed and there is turmoil outside from its customers 'clamouring' to get money the bank no longer has because the directors have fled the country and taken it with them (Copertari 2005: 287). Marcos' fate foreshadows the fate of many Argentines who lost money in the financial crash of 2001.

10. Ironically, the flow of external capital into Argentina for film production together with the collapse of the Argentine peso, central themes of the new Argentine cinema (*Nueve reinas*), also facilitated film production (Lee 2011: 44n12)

6. JUAN JOSÉ CAMPANELLA: HISTORICAL MEMORY AND ACCOUNTABILITY IN *EL SECRETO DE SUS OJOS (THE SECRET IN THEIR EYES* 2009)

As explored in the Introduction to the Argentine industry, Juan José Campanella's Argentine films are the product of 1990s neoliberal economic policies and related changes to the previously solely government-supported film industry. Working with transnational media conglomerates formed in the free trade oriented media de-regulation of the 1990s, Campanella's Argentine solo-directed features *El mismo amor, la misma lluvia* (1999), the Oscar-nominated *El hijo de la novia* (2001) and *Luna de Avellaneda* (2004), the Oscar-winning *El secreto de sus ojos* (2009) and *Metegol* (2013) controversially epitomise the shift away from an auteur/art cinema dominated model of state patronised national cinema of the 1980s and early 1990s towards a model of high-grossing, transnationally co-produced mainstream genre features which nevertheless still receive some funding from the state (Losada 2010: 4).[1] Campanella was already a television and feature film director in the United States before he began his solo directing career in Argentina with *El mismo amor, la misma lluvia*.[2] Unlike Iñárritu, Cuarón, del Toro, Meirelles and Salles, Campanella has, to date, not followed the international successes of his second (*El hijo de la novia*) or fourth (*El secreto de sus ojos*) features by making deterritorialised films outside of Argentina, but has simply continued working transnationally in other ways, moving between work as a director of 'quality' television series in the US including *House* (2007–2010), *Law and Order* (2000–2010) and *30 Rock* (2006), his own creative television projects in Argentina, including his co-written Argentina/Spain mini-series *Vientos de Agua* (*Winds of Water* 2006), and making more Argentine features. He has however, like the other transnational auteurs written about in this book, been the object of analyses that criticise the mainstream 'commercial' forms (melodrama, the thriller) and venues he works in (US television, transnational conglomerates) and consequently question the national credentials of his Argentine films (Andermann 2011; Losada 2010).

Despite being recognised as an 'industry auteur' – a term which carries with it a sense of 'quality' mainstream filmmaking and 'personal artistic vision' – amongst Argentine critics Campanella has many detractors (Copertari 2009: 10, 95). The most 'fervent', as Argentine critic Diego Batlle points out (2009b), are the critics from *El Amante Cine*, one of the journals that has most championed the *nuevo cine argentino* and most maligned Campanella's work (Kercher 2015: 334).[3] Many dismiss his films as 'overly sentimental and melodramatic' and compare them unfavourably with the 'minimalist, open narrative, [and] experimental style' of directors of the *nuevo cine argentino* (Lee 2011: 25). European critics similarly denigrate Campanella in favour of art cinema. Many were outraged when *El secreto de sus ojos* won the Oscar for Best Foreign Language Film over art cinema films *Un prophète* (*A Prophet* Jaques Audiard 2009) and *Das weiße Band* (*The White Ribbon* Michael Haneke 2009) in 2010 (Bradshaw 2010). Writing after its Oscar win, British critic Peter Bradshaw conceded that *El secreto de sus ojos* may be a 'good' film, but also suggested it was more like '[television] box-set quality drama than cinema'[4] (2010).

Academic writing about Argentine cinema, in English and Spanish, shows less interest in or less appreciation for the kind of 'industrial' cinema Campanella makes and more interest in the 'heterogeneous corpus of films and aesthetic projects that constitute the so-called "new Argentine cinema"' (Copertari 2005: 279). A plethora of monographs, chapters and articles that are predominantly about or implicitly more highly value the *nuevo cine argentino* have been published in English and Spanish since its emergence (Aguilar 2006; 2011; Andermann 2011; Andermann and Fernández Bravo 2013; Bernades, Lerer and Wolf 2002; Garavelli 2011; Gundermann 2005; Page 2009; Pena Pérez 2009; Rêgo and Rocha 2011; Ros 2011; Sosa 2009; in a list that is by no means exhaustive). A much smaller number of monographs, chapters and articles dedicated wholly or in part to mainstream filmmaking have appeared (Copertari 2005; 2009; Navitski 2012; Getino 2007; Rocha 2012) and only one monograph, an anthology and a handful of chapters or articles that attempt to give an overview of both (Copertari 2009; Falicov 2007b; Rêgo and Rocha 2011). One exception in the former, more plentiful, group of publications is Jaime Pena Pérez's *Historias extraordinarias: nuevo cine argentino 1999–2008* (*Extraordinary stories: New Argentine Cinema 1998–2008*) (2009), which includes the industrial filmmaking of Trapero and Caetano. Although these two directors have moved away from their artisanal beginnings in the *nuevo cine argentino* their industrial work is still examined in an auteurist anthology like Pena Pérez's in chapters that trace a strong authorial trajectory from Trapero and Caetano's early and seminal new Argentine films, *Mundo grúa*, *Pizza, birra, faso,* and *Bolivia,* through their subsequent industrial and television projects (Noriega 2009; Wolf 2009).

Another exception to the dominance of the *nuevo cine argentino* in scholarship is the analysis of certain mainstream films which draw a significant amount of attention because of their huge international box office and critical success: *Nueve reinas* (Bielinsky 2001), *Plata quemada* (Piñeyro 2004) and Campanella's four Argentine features, particularly *El secreto de sus ojos* (Copertari 2005; Navitski 2012; Hortiguera 2012; Shaw 2007; Rocha 2014; Choi 2013; Lee 2011; Moraña 2011; Andermann 2011; Solomianski 2011; Tandeciarz 2012). However, often the grounds on which mainstream films are studied is to emphasise disparities between them and the *nuevo cine argentino* and, on some occasions to critique them based on these same disparities (Andermann 2011; Moraña 2011; Losada 2010).

Some analyses of Campanella's second and third solo features in Argentina – *El hijo de la novia* and *Luna de Avellaneda* – are representative of this kind of comparative critique. In *El hijo de la novia* Rafael (Darín) is struggling to keep the family restaurant – started by his Italian immigrant father Nino (Héctor Alterio) – in business in the midst of the economic crisis and also struggling in his relationships with his girlfriend Naty (Natalia Verbeke), his daughter and his ex-wife. His father wants to give his mother Norma (Norma Aleandro), who is suffering from Alzheimer's, the church wedding she never had. After a heart attack that makes him re-evaluate his life, Rafael decides to; sell the restaurant (to the Italian consortium that has been trying to buy it), make up with his childhood friend Juan Carlos (Eduardo Blanco) with whom he has fallen out during the course of the film, give his parents a 'white' wedding, spend more time with his daughter, commit to his girlfriend and, at the film's denouement, buy another restaurant (the 'Buenos Aires') with the intention of starting again. In *Luna de Avellaneda* Román (Darín) is a life-time member of, and tireless volunteer at, a working class social club that is struggling with mounting debts. Founded in the 1950s when there was full employment, the club faces a severe financial crisis and a drastically reduced membership.[5] Presented with a new obstacle to its survival – a 40,000 peso fine levied by the local government – a local politician (and former member) Alejandro (Daniel Fanego) presents the possibility of a foreign consortium buy-out that would bring a Casino and 200 jobs to the area. The members vote to accept the deal and a defeated Román prepares to follow his son to Spain in search of a better economic future. At the end of the film, finding the Luna de Avellaneda club membership card he thought he had lost he asks his friend Amadeo (Blanco) how to go about setting up a new club.

It has been suggested that not only are *El hijo de la novia* and *Luna de Avellaneda* part of a host of films (including films of the *nuevo cine argentino*) addressing the 'crisis of the urban' but also, less appreciatively, different versions, with the same cast (Darín, Blanco) and same story (a small community to be defended against a 'hostile exterior'), of the same film (Andermann 2011: 38). Additionally, this analysis has suggested that '[r]ather than focusing on the margins of urban society', by which is meant the working class, the underemployed, the unemployed, or the immigrants focused on in key films of the *nuevo cine argentino* – Rulo (Luis Margani) in *Mundo grúa*, Freddy (Freddy Flores) in *Bolivia*, Jacinta (Hebe Duarte) in *Las acacias* – *El hijo de la novia* and *Luna de Avellaneda* focus on a 'more accommodated middle class threatened with financial decline' (Andermann 2011: 38; Aguilar 2011: 23–24). What is also critiqued in *El hijo de la novia* and *Luna de Avellaneda* is their classical form and particularly that they ultimately offer 'recomposition', 'sav[ing] the couple, the family and the nation through love, trust and patriotism' and that this makes them 'hardly subtle' 'political allegories' (Andermann 2011: 38, 42, 40, 42). The conclusion of this analysis is that both the form – 'plot structures that maintain an adherence to the rules of genre' – and the production model – 'a transnational production company' part owned by Spain – of *El hijo de la novia* and *Luna de Avellaneda* 'counteract [...] the affective nationalism they preach' (Andermann 2011: 43).

Although it is to be welcomed that this analysis includes Campanella's films in the corpus of films that are defined as Argentine cinema (some key studies which profess to analyse Argentine cinema barely mention them), it is also important to note how *El hijo de la novia*, *Luna de Avellaneda* and *El secreto de sus ojos*, are being implicitly devalued by a critical hierarchy that rates the features art of cinema (*el nuevo cine argentino*'s resistance to national allegories, genres and resolution of any kind as defined in Gonzalo Aguilar's key study of the movement [2011: 20]) above those of a 'commercial' cinema to suggest his films are based on a 'successful formula' 'emotional[] resol[ution]' and going through 'the motions of classical Hollywood style melodrama' (Andermann 2011: 41, 40, 41, 173; Losada 2010: 4). It is also suggested that the art cinema aesthetics of the *nuevo cine argentino* are much more (in relation to *El secreto de sus ojos* specifically) 'intellectually stimulating', fitting the exploration of national concerns (in the case of *El hijo de la novia* and *Luna de Avellaneda* the material results of the economic crisis) and intrinsically more national (Andermann 2011: 173). However, with respect to Jens Andermann's point about the nationality of Campanella's films in particular and, as this book's Introduction has noted, the *nuevo cine argentino* like the other 'home-grown' realist movements (Navitski

2012: 363) of contemporary Latin American independent cinema are potentially as textually and financially implicated in a transnational economy of representation (in its case determined by the European and North American art cinema circuit) as Campanella's and those of the other prominent transnational auteurs. Gabriela Copertari's analysis of *El hijo de la novia* on the other hand – in a book that also talks about the New Argentine Cinema (76 89 03 Cristian Bernard and Flavio Nardini 2000) does not, admirably, differentiate between the ability of mainstream films (like *El hijo de la novia*, and also *Nueve reinas*) and new Argentine films to speak for or to the nation (2009: 1–3, 95).

Despite historic shifts in film studies to recognise the resistive possibilities of mainstream filmmaking (particularly melodrama), in US (Brooks 1991; Elsaesser 1991; Gledhill 1987) and Latin American scholarship (López 1991, 1993; Tierney 1997), many analyses of Argentine cinema persist in maintaining a cultural hierarchy that values art cinema as automatically national and critical of the status quo and devalues what are often only very loosely defined 'Hollywood' or 'mainstream aesthetics' as supporting that status quo and concomitantly dominant (imperialist) ideology. Representative of this idea of loosely defined Hollywood aesthetics supporting dominant ideology is Andermann's overriding suggestion about *El hijo de la novia* and *Luna de Avellaneda*: that they function to shore up the 'traditional role [of cinema] as a dream factory capable of releasing viewers albeit temporarily, from the constraints and frustrations of everyday experience' (2011: 40). A significant issue with the 'dream factory' model espoused by Andermann, and similar arguments voiced in the Argentine press about other industrial Argentine films – director Raúl Beceyro's estimation that *Nueve reinas* 'has as its primary concern to leave the spectators soothed once the screening is over' (Beceyro qtd in Copertari 2005: 280) – is that it has been superseded by subsequent models of cultural analysis which, rather than suggest Hollywood or 'Hollywood-style' films produce passive consumers lulled into accepting things as they are, precisely value the critical potential of mainstream filmmaking forms to work politically in relation to 'everyday life' (Tierney 2007: 30–31; Dyer 1992: 24). Assertions like those of Beceyro and Andermann, which question the ability of Campanella's films to 'speak for nation' dismiss the incredible popularity of high grossing films as 'escapist' pleasures rather than explore why (beyond the benefits of the distribution and exhibition that they enjoy thanks to their transnational conglomerate producers and their mainstream formats) Argentine audiences are drawn towards them (Andermann 2011: 42; Kercher 2015: 332). They also fail to take into account a cultural studies narrative which stresses melodrama as a local Latin American form with a cultural pedigree dating back to the nineteenth century (Martín Barbero 1995: 277–281). When critics question a film's national credentials they also also fail to take into account Andrew Higson's idea that a national cinema, although partly determined by who (co)owns the means of production (which in the case of Campanella's films would be Spain and, via Disney subsidiary Miravista, the US), is also determined by consumption and exhibition, 'the question of which films audiences are watching' (Higson 1989: 37). Although as Higson also points out, because of the number of 'foreign films' particularly 'American' (read Hollywood) films consumed worldwide this approach is not without 'anxiety about cultural imperialism' (Higson 1989: 37). Gripped by this anxiety of 'cultural imperialism' these analyses do not speculate (as a more contemporary cultural studies model might do) that these films and the topics they explore may be speaking to popular audiences, or that their forms, in addition to being 'Hollywood style' might also connect strongly to local traditions of melodrama and, in the case of *El secreto de sus ojos*, local traditions of noir. They also forget that these films (with monies from Spain) in addition to speaking to the nation, might equally be speaking to the Spanish transnation(al audience); in the case of *El secreto de sus ojos* specifically, Spanish spectators invested in scenarios that offer symbolic reparation for the Spanish victims of Argentine military repression or a level of historical accountability (Tandeciarz 2012: 63), or who are drawn to films that echo Spain's similarly dictatorial and violent past.[6] Critics of mainstream films like Losada, Andermann and others also do not take into consideration how previous Argentine blockbusters (*Comodines*, *La furia*) which have similarly taken on a 'Hollywood form' have connected to elements of local culture (television actors, use of slang and televisual formats) (Falicov 2007b: 99). These analyses also do not explore or value as Copertari does, in her analysis of *El hijo de la novia*, how a mainstream film might dramatise scenarios of 'compensation' and 'reparation' for the 'injuries' and 'losses' experienced by Argentine society as a result of the processes of neoliberal globalisation (2009: 68) or speak to the 'national trauma' of Argentina's most recent dictatorship (1976–1983).

Copertari's analysis, is exemplary of how in the present moment of 'transnational practices', genre films like *El hijo de la novia, Luna de Avellaneda, Crónica de una fuga* and *El secreto de sus ojos*, could be viewed less as 'formula[ic]' (Andermann 2011: 41) or purely 'representative of conformist or mainstream ideology' and increasingly considered, as 'shortcuts to tell autochthonous stories' (Alvaray 2013: 69). Like Caetano's *Crónica de una fuga*, which is set during the years of the dictatorship, and successfully 're-inscribe[s]' features of the horror genre onto a true story of kidnapping, torture and escape of four detainees of the military forces during the dictatorship (Alvaray 2013: 74), *El secreto de sus ojos* re-inscribes the features of the melodrama and *noir* onto the narrative of a fictional crime that went unpunished because of the dictatorship. Both films' success in Argentina – *Crónica de una fuga* was the second highest grossing domestic film of 2006, *El secreto de sus ojos* was the highest grossing film of 2009 and in box office history in Argentina up to that point – indicate that the history the films explore 'resonate' strongly with both those who still had memory of the practices of the 'Dirty War' as well as those who only knew about it 'through reference' (Alvaray 2013: 74). The films also point, as Alvaray suggests in relation to *Crónica de una fuga*, to the fact that directors like Caetano and Campanella can use 'the language of cinematic genre without neglecting political content' (2013: 74).

Ultimately, oppositions between *el nuevo cine argentino* and Argentina's mainstream industrial filmmaking that denigrate the latter as simply 'imitative of Hollywood', whilst praising the politics of the former, are 'reductive' and problematic, and additionally so when in some cases the lines between the two modes have become increasingly blurred (Alvaray 2011: 80). Some of the pioneers of the *nuevo cine argentino* Caetano and Trapero have been partnering with transnational production companies to make a more 'industrial' (larger crews, higher production, genre) cinema, while other directors more loosely attenuated to the movement – like Martel and Alonso – are also now making more 'industrial' films. Martel's eighteenth century epic *Zama* (2017) is an international co-production involving many countries (Spain, Argentina, France, the US and the Netherlands) and production companies including transnational conglomerate Patagonik, Almodóvar's Deseo and Mexican independent production company CANANA. Alonso's nineteenth century epic *Jauja* (2015) was similarly made on a much grander scale to the micro-productions of his earlier films. *Jauja* is his first film to use professional actors (most notably Viggo Mortensen), not to be set in the present, feature a soundtrack and have scripted dialogue.

A less dichotomous and less hierarchical approach to mainstream Argentine films explores how Hollywood-style genre films may illustrate important aspects of locality through 'strategic cultural mixing' (Navitski 2012: 362). Rielle Navitski suggests Argentina's 'new *policiales*' (police/crime films) such as *Nueve reinas* and *Plata quemada* (a group to which we could easily add Campanella's *El secreto de sus ojos*) 'combine a use of self-conscious cinematic citation [of the *noir* and police film] with a keen attention to the rhythms of daily life and the realities of social exclusion that define contemporary Argentina' (2012: 360). It is also worth pointing out that Argentina has its own tradition of *noir* filmmaking, most notably the films of Carlos Hugo Christensen (*El ángel desnudo/The Naked Angel* 1946, *La trampa/The Trap* 1949, *Si muero antes de despertar/If I die before I wake* 1952). Although scholarship posits that Argentine *noir* draws on the tradition of American *noir*, it is also recognised that Argentine *noir* has some of its own 'autochthonous elements' (Janin 2015: 7; Ruétalo 2006).

Taking a cue from Navitski's ideas about 'strategic cultural mixing,' Alvaray's call for 'more work' on how 'regional film industries' like those in Latin America 'register and interpret the function of genre', and re-evaluations of melodrama in both US and Latin American scholarship, this chapter explores Campanella's *El secreto de sus ojos* and the work it performs on historical memory (Alvaray 2013: 69). It suggests *El secreto de sus ojos* uses melodrama and film *noir* to engage with both the legacy of the 'Dirty War' and of the period directly before it into which, the film shows, its practices extended, and also the contemporary moment and its attempt to deal with the twenty year-long period of impunity which followed. This chapter argues that melodrama and film *noir* are an effective means both to self-consciously stage the past and also pose key issues of historical memory and accountability of the crimes committed during Argentina's 'Dirty War'.

El secreto de sus ojos: Staging the Past

El secreto de sus ojos is an Argentina-Spain co-production, produced, like several of Campanella's other features, through the transnational conglomerate and Spanish-owned Telefe, with participation from Spanish state and private television channels (Televisión Española, Canal+) as well as Campanella's own production company 100 Bares Producciones and Argentina's national film institute, the INCAA. It attracted 2.4 million spectators in Argentina, and a global box office of $27.5 million and was nominated for and won multiple national and international awards in addition to the Best Foreign Film Oscar, including several awards at the Havana Film Festival, two Goyas (for Best Actress and Best Spanish Foreign Language film), eleven Condors in Argentina, and an Ariel in Mexico.[7]

El secreto de sus ojos' main narrative takes place in 1974–1975. Benjamín Espósito (Darín) is a deputy clerk in the Buenos Aires investigative courts, and Irene Menéndez Hastings (Soledad Villamil), his Cornell-educated superior, is a lawyer and assistant judge. Not long after Irene begins working there, Espósito investigates the violent rape and murder of Liliana Coloto (Carla Quevedo). When the main suspect for the murder, Isidoro Gómez (Javier Godino) escapes, the case is closed. A year later however, when Espósito finds the victim's husband Ricardo Morales (Pablo Rago) determinedly still looking for his wife's killer, he requests to re-open the case. He and his colleague Pablo Sandoval (Francella) track down Gómez, he confesses and is subsequently imprisoned. The frame narrative takes place in 1999, twenty-five years later. Espósito, now retired from the courts, attempts to write a novel about the Morales Case and to resolve, not just a brutal injustice at its conclusion, but also, his own issues; the love he has always felt for Irene (who is now a judge), but which he has never been able to openly express to her.

El secreto de sus ojos' winning of the Oscar for Best Foreign Language film, and the approbation this signals from the Hollywood Academy has been interpreted as an indication of the film's 'estilo Hollywoodense' ('Hollywood style'), its conventional aesthetics and its successful attempt to speak to a 'US audience' and 'a globalized Latin American public' (Moraña 2011: 382). The film's Oscar win is also mentioned in accounts that suggest its 'thriller mode' and 'story of impossible' love are '[un]productive' as a means of exploring the 'currently pressing question of the memory of the dictatorship and its crimes' (Losada 2010: 1–2). However, as this chapter will suggest, rather than detract from its exploration of 'the memory of the dictatorship and its crimes' *El secreto de sus ojos* noirish 'thriller mode' and melodramatic 'story of impossible love' are used self-consciously as tools to productively tackle this history.

Argentina's 1976–1983 dictatorship instigated 'The National Reorganization Process' (*El Proceso de Reorganización Nacional*), which employed kidnap, torture and disappearance to eradicate radical political movements and any kind of dissension. It is estimated that up to 30,000 people including teachers, lawyers and students were killed as a result of 'el proceso'. Trials that had begun in the aftermath of the 1983 democratic elections to bring those responsible for these murders to justice were stopped however 'because of growing military opposition' (Humphrey and Valverde 2016: 131). In the mid-1980s Amnesty laws – the Ley de Punto Final (The Law of Full Stop), which put an 'end to the possibility of further trials' and the Ley de La Obediencia Debida (the law of Due Obedience), which blocked prosecution of pending cases on the argument that perpetrators 'were merely obeying orders' – were passed, effectively ending any current or future proceedings against military personnel (King 2000: 265).[8] The 'final dismantling' of any legal proceedings against military personnel took place in 1990 when, under President Menem, six military leaders, including former military presidents Jorge Videla and Roberto Viola (who had been tried and found guilty of crimes before the amnesty laws) as well as some former leftist guerrilla leaders were pardoned and released from prison (King 2000: 265; Marx 1990). In 2003 the amnesty laws were repealed enabling, from 2006, the (re) opening of trials against the military including Videla and others who were subsequently tried and sentenced to life in prison (Humphrey and Valverde 2016: 131).[9]

El secreto de sus ojos, based on Eduardo Sacheri's 2005 novel *La pregunta de sus ojos* (*The Question in Their Eyes*), was produced in the context of these ongoing and restarted trials. It is significantly one of several contemporary Argentine films to deal with, not just the violence of the 'Dirty War' (and the period immediately proceeding it) but also the extended period of immunity which followed it. In Martel's *La mujer sin cabeza* (*The Headless Woman*

2008), a middle class woman, Vero (María Onetto) and her family in the Northern town of Salta are ultimately complicit in the covering up of Vero's involvement in the knocking down and murder of a child, although the deliberate ambiguities of the film's art cinema text never definitively reveal whether the accident actually took place. Trapero's *El clan,* the highest grossing film of 2015, depicts the true story of the climate of impunity in the early postdictatorship period in which a family kidnapping gang led by a former member of the security forces, Arquimedes (Francella), was able to operate. At one point Arquimedes visits a fellow kidnapper, Gordon, in jail who (in the film's gesture to the 'continued influence of the military over the justice process') fully expects to be released (Humphrey and Valverde 2016: 138). Referring to the new democratic government as 'just different bosses' Gordon says 'It will all be back to normal soon.'

El secreto de sus ojos, which was co-written by Campanella and Sacheri, sets its present day in 1999 (as in the novel), just as the 1990 pardons granted by President Menem were being challenged in the courts and consequently at what was the beginning of the end of the period of immunity.[10] The film also makes several alterations to the dates of the events recounted in the novel to tie the film much more forcibly to this present moment of accountability for the political and state-sponsored violence of the 'Dirty War', and before (Hortiguera 2012: 114; Colás 1994: 76). The film transposes the events of the book – Coloto's murder, Gómez's arrest, imprisonment and subsequent release – from the 1968 of Juan Carlos Onganía's dictatorship (1966–1970), the 1972 and the 1973 of President Cámpora's brief regime and pardon for political prisoners (Sacheri 2005: 31, 53, 179, 240) to 1974 and the short-lived presidency of María Estela Martínez de Perón (1974–1976), Juan Perón's widow, which immediately proceeded the military coup of March 1976. These shifts trace the beginnings of state repression from the death of Perón in July 1974, and the rise of the Alianza Anticomunista Argentina (The Argentinian Anti-communist Alliance, the Triple A) that became particularly active from the winter of 1974 (Solomianski 2011: 775). This has the effect, Alejandro Solomianski suggests, of derailing the myth that, before the coup Argentinians were a group of 'progressive partisans' and emphasising that, from 1974 there was already a 'powerful state terrorism' taking place at different levels of society and functioning with impunity (2011: 775).

Another aspect of the film's alteration of the novel to deal more closely with issues of accountability, are changes to the character of Espósito's love object, Irene who in the film is involved not only in the Morales Case in the past but also in Espósito's present day novelisation of it. In the course of his writing he brings her various drafts of his novel, the reading of which becomes the basis for several conversations about the past. The film also makes Irene an aristocratic Menéndez-Hastings and stresses Espósito's lower class status by changing his surname.[11] These two changes mean that issues of accountability, historical memory and the resolution of the case are tied up with Espósito's feelings for Irene and also their different class positions.[12] Irene's class status and privilege protect her but not Espósito from retribution by Romano and his Triple A death squad and enable her (via her father's contacts) to arrange transfer to, and subsequent protection for Espósito in, Jujuy where her cousins are 'feudal Lords'. In that she is, as Roman states, 'intocable' ('untouchable'), the film gestures towards the pact between those who were privileged (Irene's family) and the military, to keep quiet in order to escape retribution (Moraña 2011: 378–379). Irene's aristocratic class status also means however, that she is romantically 'untouchable', preventing Espósito from expressing his feelings for her.

The film also ties itself to issues of accountability and historical memory specific to the Argentine context through use of a particular vocabulary. When, in the frame narrative, a retired Espósito comes to visit Irene to tell her he wants to be a writer and that he wants to write about the Morales Case, he says: 'In reality we *never* spoke about that *again*. Why did we *never* speak about that *again?*'[13] The words Espósito repeats 'never' and 'again', are significantly those of the title of the published report produced by the National Commission into the Disappeared (Comisión Nacional sobre la Desaparición de Personas [CONADEP]) *Nunca Más* (Never Again 1984). The report documents the 'process of disappearance': abduction, secret detention centres, torture, mass graves and the details of victims and 'repressors' (Humphrey and Valverde 2016: 131). The first edition of *Nunca Más* presented a 'war' narrative which emphasised a struggle between two armed groups, the military and the guerrilla and a society in between that was 'oblivious to the whole clash' (Humphrey and Valverde 2016: 132; Hortiguera 2012: 122). This 'war' narrative, it has been suggested, effectively upheld by the transition to democracy, 'somehow cancelled the possibility of narrating what went on during [and before] the coup and during the military dictatorship' (Hortiguera 2012: 112). The film gestures towards this period of narrative '[im]possibility' and its passing, in dialogues that make an issue of why Espósito has been unable to write about the past until now.[14] On one level the film figures this not talking about the past as part of Irene and Espósito's personal drama – their unspoken love, which blossomed during the Morales Case but was curtailed by his enforced internal exile. On another level however, the film figures not talking about the past, as a politically enforced position established by the narrative of *Nunca Más*, the amnesty laws, and the pardons of culpable individuals. In the second edition of *Nunca Más* (2006), a new prologue 'resignified' those who were kidnapped, tortured and disappeared from the 'innocent victims' of the first edition, to a social group 'struggling for social justice', deliberately targeted by the military government imposing 'a neoliberal economic system'

Figure 31   *El secreto de sus ojos* (Juan José Campanella 2009)

and consequently resignified the human rights abuses that went on during the 'proceso' not as a 'war' but a 'genocide' waged through acts of state terrorism (Humphrey and Valverde 2016: 140–141).

Although there's no direct representation of the period of the dictatorship, it is this narrative of an in-place bureaucratic system of state organised extrajudicial violence that we see unfolding in *El secreto de sus ojos*. When Morales spots Gómez on television as a member of Estela Perón's presidential guard (Figure 31), Irene and Espósito discover that he has been freed from prison on executive order, and incorporated into the state security forces. They go to challenge their former colleague Romano at his new offices in the Ministerio de Bienestar Social (The Ministry of Social Wellbeing) (as announced by a bright poster behind his desk).[15] Irene and Espósito are made aware of the threat of state-sponsored violence towards themselves when, leaving the Ministry, they are forced to ride down in a lift with a smartly dressed (and now socially mobile) Gómez, who, shot from a low angle so as to appear larger and more menacing, ostentatiously takes out and loads his handgun in both a show of force and a threat of violence (Figure 32).

As much as *El secreto de sus ojos* places itself within the historical narrative of 'genocide' of the 'Dirty War', it also takes on a self-conscious exploration of how to represent that narrative in light of the contemporary moment of accountability and also the coming to terms with the historical memory of genocide.[16] For instance, the film has a number of openings each of which represent both the film's and Espósito's search for a suitable mode in which to

Figure 32   *El secreto de sus ojos* (Juan José Campanella 2009)

write (his)story/begin his novel. The film's three different attempts at beginning this story are pieces of 'self conscious cinematic citation' which exaggerate iconographic features of each respective genre (in the case of melodrama) or 'sensibility' (in the case of *noir* whose status as a genre is contested) (Navitski 2012: 360; Hirsch 1981: 70; Krutnik 1992: ix). The first beginning is highly melodramatic. It opens on a platform sign and then pans to an extreme close up of a pair of female eyes, whilst piano music plays on the soundtrack, signalling the emotive excess of a genre most commonly understood as a 'women's genre' (Gledhill 1987: 10) (Figure 33). In subsequent shots of a man and a woman (Espósito and Irene) saying goodbye at a railway station, the image is de-saturated of colour emphasising that this is the past. Irene and Espósito are shown initially in (soft) focus, whilst other people and the station itself are mostly out of focus as if to suggest that this is a memory that cannot be fully fixed upon. As the scene climaxes and she runs after his train and he runs down the train to watch her from its back window, they also appear out of focus. Adding to the sense of a highly emotive and slightly unreal opening, an absence of diegetic sound and a montage effect convey the sense that this is an impressionistic rather than realist depiction of the scene. This first attempt at starting the story, which we learn later is the moment Espósito went off to exile in the North of Argentina to escape being murdered by the Triple A, ends with a shot of a page on which written words describe the goodbye just as we have seen it. Unhappy with this opening and, it is suggested, its melodramatic excesses, Espósito scratches through the writing and then rips the piece of paper out of his notepad.

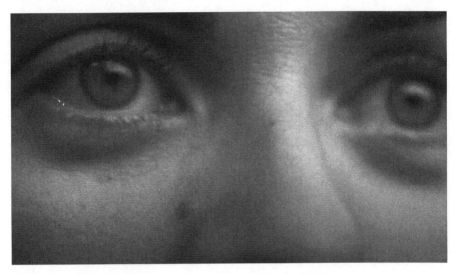

Figure 33   *El secreto de sus ojos* (Juan José Campanella 2009)

After a moment's pause in which we see Espósito in long shot at his desk, he begins writing in the notebook. We hear in a matter-of-fact voice-over the words he is writing: 'The 21st June, 1974.' This second beginning is strongly marked by a *noir* sensibility: Espósito's voice-over recounting the details of a past crime, the venetian blinds glimpsed at the right side of the frame, the small patches of light and the all encompassing darkness surrounding him as he writes are all aspects of *noir* style (Place and Peterson 1974: 30–32; Hirsch 1981: 78, 90) (Figure 34). In his attention to the details of 'the last day Ricardo Morales would have breakfast with his wife, Liliana Coloto', including what she was wearing, what they ate ('a sweet gooseberry jam') and drank ('tea with lemon'), Espósito is like the *noir* detective. But this attempt at a beginning is also cut short as Espósito now in a closer medium shot, but still framed by lamps, darkness and venetian blinds, groans with frustration (at potentially the emotional detachment of the hard-boiled voice-over, or the excessively flowery writing style he falls into at the end of the recounted scene about the 'ray of sunshine on her left cheek') and again rips out and scrunches up the sheet he has been writing on.

The third attempt at a beginning to the film/story, is the murder itself. We see Espósito start writing and then cut to images of a woman being attacked. We see Liliana with a bloodied face, her vest being grabbed and torn by a naked assailant and hear her desperate protestations and groans of pain. With the sound of Liliana's screaming carrying over, the shot then cuts to Espósito, in the present, closing his eyes, as if he is unable or unwilling to confront the violent murder directly, much less describe it in writing. He tears out the page,

Figure 34   *El secreto de sus ojos* (Juan José Campanella 2009)

folds it and, rather than destroy it, places it significantly to one side. We cut back to the long shot of him at his desk, surrounded by darkness, and framed by lamps and venetian blinds.

By shuttling between and discarding, in turn, melodrama, the *noir*/crime story, and a more straightforwardly violent depiction, *El secreto de sus ojos'* opening signals both the modes the diegesis will make use of throughout and also confronts the difficulty of how to speak about or remember the national past. In this respect, *El secreto de sus ojos* is like the films of the redemocratisation period – including Argentina's previous Oscar winner *La historia oficial* (*The Official Story* Luis Puenzo 1984), *Camila* (Maria Luisa Bemberg 1984), *Miss Mary* (Bemberg 1986) and *Hombre mirando al sudeste* (*Man Facing South East* Eliseo Subiela 1986) – all of which also explore self-consciously how to represent aspects of the past (violence, torture) that are, as Idelber Avelar suggests, in some way 'unmediable' (2001: 255).[17]

After this opening, *El secreto de sus ojos* continues with the flashback structure and other stylistic elements of *noir* (the crime, the processes of detection, a darkened *mise-en-scène*, night time exteriors), and also with the emotive and stylistic excesses of melodrama (Espósito's love for Irene, anguished close ups on his and her faces and eyes, the romantic piano theme). But it is always highly self reflexive about its use of these modes, sometimes cutting from scenes in the past back to the present where Irene comments on what we have just seen/what she has just read (in Espósito's novel drafts).

In that *El secreto de sus ojos* explores the act of representing and remembering the past, it shares a point of contact with the meta-documentary *Los rubios* (*The Blondes* Albertina Carri 2003) about the director's loss of her parents Roberto Carri and Ana Maria Caruso, left wing activists who were arrested and disappeared in 1977. It addition to featuring standard interviews, *Los rubios* also focuses on the apparatus of documentary filmmaking (video recorders, cameras and computers). It also fictionalises aspects of Carri's search for what happened to her parents. Carri's 'part' is played by an actress (Analia Couceyro) who sometimes wears a blonde wig (in order to resemble 'the blondes' of the film's title: Carri, her sisters and parents). We see 'her' speaking to the family's old neighbours and friends and visiting the clandestine detention centre where her parents were held. At times we see Carri coaching Couceyro on how to say 'her' lines (which are Carri's own testimony) to camera, as well as see that testimony unmediated. Another strand represents Carri's life as a child with Play Mobil characters: it represents the past and Carri's memories in a deliberately unreal and childlike way.

Los rubios, like *El secreto de sus ojos*, performs the work of memory whilst simultaneously questioning the means through which that memory work is being performed and represented. Like *Los rubios*, with its focus on the apparatus of filmmaking, *El secreto de sus ojos* questions its own status as representation with an emphasis not just on the process of writing but also on the genre/sensibility through which events are represented. This emphasis on the means of representation is notably one of film *noir*'s key modernist impulses (Jameson 1993: 33; Naremore 2008: 40–45). After the film's particularly self-conscious openings, Espósito's writing of his novel is significantly transferred to an old and broken typewriter (itself an important part of *noir* iconography) lent by Irene from a cupboard at the courts where he used to work and which imperfectly performs its job (Jameson 1993: 41). Because one of its keys is jammed Espósito has to write in all the missing letter 'A's.

Although the film contains several playful and self-aware references to classic *noir*,[18] the *noir* iconography and stylistics that feature throughout *El secreto de sus ojos* are not employed in the manner of 'pastiche' or 'blank parody' 'associated with the lack of historical consciousness manifest in the retro-aesthetic of the "nostalgia" film' (Navitski 2012: 358). The stylistics of film *noir* in *El secreto de sus ojos* – use of canted and oblique angles (Figure 35), the 'pervasive darkness' that often surrounds Espósito, the shadows from venetian blinds and, also, in the case of his apartment, slatted windows that throw lined shadows – function, historically and politically to point to a world that in the past and the present, was and is 'never stable' or 'safe', that 'jars' and 'disorients' (Navitski 2012: 358; Place and Peterson 1974: 31–32; Naremore 2008: 189). *Noir* stylistics are a marker of the film's self-conscious use of the genre to question both the past and the contemporary status quo (in the manner of classic films *noir*). Notably, in the past, line-like shadows fall across

Figure 35   *El secreto de sus ojos* (Juan José Campanella 2009)

Figure 36   *El secreto de sus ojos* (Juan José Campanella 2009)

the shoulder of the Triple A assassin (in Espósito's imagining of his friend's last moments alive) when he asks Sandoval '¿Vos sos Espósito?' ('Are you Espósito?') (Figure 36). In an identical deployment of the *mise-en-scène*, in the present day frame narrative, line-like shadows fall across Espósito's shoulder as he shows another draft of his novel to Irene (Figure 37). Referring to classic *noir* stylistics, Foster Hirsch suggests that these kinds of shadows, which in *El*

Figure 37   *El secreto de sus ojos* (Juan José Campanella 2009)

secreto de sus ojos feature in the present and in the past, 'create a prison-like aura, underlining the psychological and physical enclosure that is at the core of most *noir* stories' (1981: 90). What Espósito and also implicitly Irene are enclosed in, the film suggests, is a violent past that has not been fully accounted for and whose perpetrators (Gómez) have not been properly brought to justice. This lack of accountability and justice has caused Morales – and also Irene and Espósito, the dialogue implies – to lead lives that are unfulfilled or 'llena de nada' ('full of nothing').

Although, as if in a nod to Campanella's critics, the film contains a meta-cinematic critique of the stylistics of melodrama, it also uses melodrama, like *noir*, as a key part of its historical and political representation. In the scene which plays out after the shot of Irene and Espósito's 'psychological and physical enclosure' (Figure 36) for instance, Irene suggests that the highly melodramatic goodbye at the station as she has just read it in the draft of his novel and which we have just seen, (significantly for issues of memory, much more clearly and for the second time in the film) is not truthful or even credible. She continues:

> The bit where the guy is leaving for Jujuy and him crying like he was being torn apart and her running along the platform as if he were the love of her life and their hands on the glass as if they were one person and her crying as if she knew that the fate that awaited her was one of mediocrity and indifference, almost falling on to the tracks and wanting to scream out a love that she had never dared to confess.

Irene is disdainful of the melodramatic excesses of Espósito's rendering of the past. She also disputes his excessively emotional memory of it. Irene's comments are reminiscent of the ambivalent position melodrama once occupied in film studies and which it continues to occupy in many analyses of Argentine cinema, particularly analyses of Campanella's films (Kercher 2015: 8) or more broadly in analyses of other melodramatic films – like *La historia oficial* – which take on 'the traumatic experience of the dictatorship' (Gundermann 2005: 258).

Once dismissed for its (female) excessiveness and highly emotional context in favour of the (more manly) genres like westerns and even films *noir* by early film theorists, and for its 'colonizing tendencies,' and reduction of social problems to an emotional level complicit with the dominant ideology by Latin American theorists, (Colina and Díaz Torres 1972: 14–16), melodrama has been redeemed since the 1970s by feminism, psychoanalysis and a changed attitude towards the products of mass culture which have brought about a revalorisation of its subversive potential to question (rather than uphold) the norms of patriarchal bourgeois society (Landy 1991: 14, 20). In Latin America, restricted access to an official literary or institutional culture, has led theorists to proclaim melodrama as the privileged genre of regional identity that 'personalizes the political' and 'unifies' Latin America (Martín Barbero 1998: 181; Monsiváis 1994: 8).

El secreto de sus ojos harnesses the political potential of melodrama by personalising (what becomes, with Gómez's incorporation into the state security forces) a political story of the past. Although the film opens with a pair of female eyes, suggesting it will mostly be a woman's love story, it skews previous female associations of melodrama (Rocha 2014: 4) to emphasise that it is Espósito's story: his investment in the case largely stems from the love he sees in Morales' eyes for his (murdered) wife and his own (unspoken) love for Irene. Irene on the other hand, in the present, initially, rejects any emotional connection to the past, and the criminal state-sponsored violence that allowed Gómez to go free. She tells Espósito: 'My whole life has been looking forward. The past is not my jurisdiction. I declare myself incompetent'. Although Irene is talking on a personal level in relation to Espósito's novel and its version of their shared history, her use of the term 'jurisdiction' and 'incompetent' (and her frequent reference to Espósito's draft novel as a 'file') also point towards her professional position (in the present) as a judge. The film deliberately blurs the boundaries between the personal and the political to argue that an emotional connection to the past (melodrama) is necessary for there to be an adequate personal, political and juridical resolution to past crimes like the murder of Liliana and the crimes of the dictatorship.[19] The film also personalises the political through Espósito and Irene's cross-class love story: his 'subaltern professional [and class] position' (Rocha 2014: 12) prevents him from declaring himself to her but also means he has to go into internal exile because he cannot benefit from the same protection Irene's class affords her. At the end of the discussion of his draft novel's version of the goodbye at the railway station, the film also recodes melodrama as a kind of first-person testimony (Espósito's) and thus, within the terms of the historical allusions it makes (to *Nunca Más*, which largely consisted of first-person testimonies), as a truthful and credible way of dealing with the past. After protesting Irene's disdainful description of his novel's goodbye at the railway station, he insists: 'Didn't it happen like that?' Irene seemingly confirms his melodramatic account of the event: 'Well if it did happen that way' she says 'why didn't you take me with you?'

In *El secreto de sus ojos* melodrama and *noir* both have their usefulness for approaching elements of the political past and the issue of historical memory in the present. *Noir* figures the film's exploration of the crime narrative through a lens which suggests the characters are trapped by structures of denial, silence and immunity that were established in 1974 and which persist in the present. Melodrama functions to elucidate the emotional cost of that crime: Irene, Espósito and Morales' truncated and loveless lives.

ENDINGS AND RESOLUTIONS

In what is a broader criticism of its 'Hollywood' and mainstream industrial features *El secreto de sus ojo*'s ending has been described as a 'nullifying finish', and a 'fantasy fulfilment' that is too 'personal' and too 'commercial' to 'say [anything] about the present possibilities of dealing with the crimes of [Argentina's] past' (Losada 2010: 1–4). Setting aside the reductionism of these criticisms, or how a more current cultural studies model might explore the production of meanings in a mainstream and successful film like *El secreto de sus ojos*, it is important to point out that, the personal story of revenge presented at the end of *El secreto de sus ojos* is actually considerably problematised in the text and that this consequently disrupts any 'resolution' (Losada 2010: 6) it may offer. In fact, the film contravenes several tenets of classical form (whilst still remaining within the parametres of that form) with several endings, not just the one that turns out to be completely untrue, and this contravention has implications for what the film has to say about present day justice, historical memory and accountability for the crimes of the 'Dirty War'.

In an attempt to seek a resolution to the case, to his novel and to his life, Espósito tracks down Morales at his rural home. He tells Morales that he has to 'get' Gómez because it was the last thing his friend Sandoval promised they would do on the night he was killed by the Triple A. Morales then urges Espósito 'no le busques más' ('don't look for him anymore') and begins to recount how, not being able to pursue Gómez at the Ministry, he staked out Espósito's apartment. While Morales is speaking, the shot cuts to what appears to be a flashback as we see a much younger Morales at a café keeping watch over Espósito's apartment building and Gómez turning up there (with his paramilitary death squad colleagues just visible inside the car). Subsequent scenes show Morales following Gómez, kidnapping him and then shooting him in his car boot. Given that there has been no indication in the film's language that we should take Morales' account as anything but truthful, it is a considerable shock when, later, Espósito returns and discovers Gómez, feeble and prematurely aged, incarcerated by Morales in a makeshift prison behind his house.

Some critics suggest that this denouement, and the 'exchange of looks' between Gómez, Morales and Espósito make the protagonist, and indeed the audience watching the film, complicit in Morales' act of taking justice into his own hands and imprisoning Gómez (Hortiguera 2012: 118; Chauca 2015: 16; Tandeciarz 2012: 67). What critics perhaps do not take into consideration however, is that, by breaking the classical rules of the principles of narration (that a film's narration will always be 'knowledgeable about the fabula it presents'), the film text actually distances the audience (and Espósito too) from any kind of identification in Morales' actions (Bordwell 1985: 57). Having given Morales a story to recount that then turns out to be untrue, he becomes not just an unreliable narrator (a common generic feature in *noir* films) but, in terms of the film's narrative voice, also an unreliable character and therefore not someone whose actions are being condoned in any way by the text (Krutnik 1992: 129).[20] Additionally, it is not just Morales that has lied to us, but as with Hitchcock's *Stage Fright* (1950), the 'canonic case' of the false flashback, so has *El secreto de sus ojos* by not giving us any clues that what we were seeing was anything but true (Bordwell 1985: 61). Adding to these overarching doubts about Morales' solution to the lack of justice he was able to gain by proper channels, is the fade to black that follows Espósito's discovery – which signals in its duration that this is the end of the film, only for the film's narration to trick us again and the screen to fade from black into another image (of flowers).

The implications of Morales' false flashback and of the equally false cuing of the ending (the fade to a sustained black screen), is that the film is *not* positing a resolution to the problem of the past on individual terms, i.e. Morales taking his own action when the state has refused to act, although this is how some analysts have interpreted the film's denouement and the precise terms on which they have criticised it (Chauca 2015: 16–17; Solomianski 2011: 775). In these critiques, this ending, and equally Esposito's novelisation of it, envisages a privatisation of justice commensurate with a neoliberal world view, where an 'inexistent state' has relinquished its

Figure 38   *El secreto de sus ojos* (Juan José Campanella 2009)

responsibility and this is ultimately, in some critics' opinions, what makes the film so attractive to the market (i.e. 'commercial') (Chauca 2015: 18; Solomianski 2011: 775).[21]

Rather than advocating a privatisation of justice and memory (and seemingly a lack of public accountability), the film language and indeed Espósito rejects Morales' personal solution, that leaves him, the framing suggests, 'trapped' in the past and the prison which he has created for Gómez (Figure 38). This is indicated by the subsequent actions we see Espósito engaging in after he has left Morales' house which act as further endings to the film. First, having not felt able to do so before, Espósito takes flowers to Sandoval's grave. Secondly, he finishes his novel. We see him binding it with a needle and thread, in an act which also memorialises Sandoval (who used to do the same with legal files) – seated at the desk in his apartment, but significantly without the imprisoning noirish *mise-en-scène*. Thirdly, he picks up the notepad on which, at the beginning of the film, awakening from sleep, he had written 'Temo' ('I fear'). He is now able to see that, like the novel he has been writing on the broken typewriter, the phrase is missing the letter A. Adding it in the note now reads 'Te amo' ('I love you'). Fourthly he goes to the courts to finally tell Irene how he feels about her.

The film thus shows Espósito able, now that he knows what happened to Gómez, to begin the process of mourning for Sandoval. Once Espósito has begun this process he is able to finish his account of the case (contribute to the task of historical memory) and, recover (in a Freudian sense) that which was missing or repressed – his love for Irene. Writing the events down, partly testimonial style (from his own admittedly emotional and melodramatic perspective) and partly in a detective or empirical style (a noirish perspective) and binding that work (in the manner of a legal file) is figured as a way of remembering and accounting, that is not, in the contemporary context of the film, a 'privatisation of memory' as some critics have suggested, but like *Nunca Más* where the 'use [of] private memory (individuals) to produce public memory [can help in] the (re)constitution of the significance of the historical violent events' (Humphrey and Valverde 2016: 132) a politically significant act. It is to be remembered that *Nunca Más,* although not a legal document, did provide the groundwork for many of the cases brought in the immediate post-dictatorship moment.

When Espósito says to Irene 'I have to speak to you', her response, which again blurs the boundaries between the personal and the political is 'It'll be complicated.' 'It doesn't matter' Esposito responds. And she then urges him to 'Close the door', which is the final image of the film – what Irene and Espósito do in the office is not seen. Ultimately, this and the other multiple endings of *El secreto de sus ojos*, both false and 'real' within the terms of the diegesis, signal that the resolution of Argentina's violent past is not completed or simple and is still, in 2009, ongoing and 'complicated'.

The grounds on which industrial films like those of Campanella are maligned and *nuevo cine argentino* films are praised is more than film studies' traditional favouring of art cinema 'complexity' over the mainstream 'simplicity', or the favouring of a 'home grown' realist movement over the 'foreign' Hollywood model (Navitski 2012: 363). In the Argentine context this dismissal has also to do with the broader crisis of representation engendered by both the Dirty War and its practices, and also the failure of the narratives of nation engendered by the financial collapse of 2001. In the context of these twin crises, the allegories of the 1980s (*La historia oficial, Miss Mary, Camila, Hombre mirando al sudeste*) and their attempt to narrate the traumas of the dictatorship through displaced means fail, in the eyes of the advocates of the *nuevo cine argentino*, to acknowledge sufficiently 'the rips and breaks' in representation in the post-dictatorship period, or the 'lost object' that is part of the modernist Latin American literary tradition, and which will (must) always be lost (Avelar 2001: 253–254). Hence the rejection in *nuevo cine argentino* of allegories or overt political narratives of the 'old' cinema of the 1980s and early 1990s (Page 2009: 182), the favouring in film criticism of *Los rubios* as an exercise in the (non) narration of the traumatic past and the denigration of *El secreto de sus ojos* because of its (seeming) closure and resolution.

What this textual reading of *El secreto de sus ojos* highlights however, is that, although the film may end with the recovery of the 'lost object', (the missing 'A'), its false flashback and false ending also acknowledges the unreliability of its own representation. And rather than this just be a feature of the way *El secreto de sus ojos* ends, this unreliability is notable through the film's self-conscious use of *noir* and melodrama. *El secreto de sus ojos* acknowledges the crisis of representation that critics register and value specifically in the *new Argentine cinema* and more broadly as part of post-dictatorial representation in Argentina and the rest of the Southern Cone (Avelar 2001: 254). What this chapter seeks to emphasise in its textual analysis of how mainstream parameters function in one contemporary Argentine film, – in keeping with one of the key aims of this book – is the extraordinary 'breadth of the Hollywood paradigm' as displayed in Campanella's *El secreto de sus ojos*: able to register both the crisis in representation whilst at the same time contributing to the task of historical memory and accountability.

NOTES

1. Campanella co-directed a documentary with Fernando Castets, his later screenwriting partner in Argentina in 1984 *Victoria 392*.
2. Campanella directed two features in the United States *The Boy Who Cried Bitch* (1991) and *Love Walked In* (1997), and also directed several docudramas for the HBO series *Lifestories: Families in Crisis* (1993).
3. As of the beginning of 2017, the journal has ceased publication in print format. In a tweet from 22 January 2017, Campanella (@juancampanella) lamented the loss of *El Amante Cine* as a print publication, 'despite old enmities'.
4. Bradshaw's disparaging use of the term 'box-set' to equate Campanella's film with television drama series consumed in one sitting, is considerably out of step with current critical perspectives about television as the new source of 'serious drama,' and the number of critically revered contemporary directors (Soderberg, Campion, Scorsese, Cuarón) as well as those from history (Hitchcock, Godard) who work or have worked in this format (Miller et al. 2013: 20–32).
5. In the opening of the film we see the club in its heyday: a vibrant social space filled with members, laughter and music.
6. Judge Baltasar Garzón pursued justice for Spanish citizens who were victims of the 'Dirty War'. See Chapter 3 for an analysis of how Guillermo del Toro's *El espinazo del diablo* (*The Devil's Backbone* 2001) and *El laberinto del fauno* (*Pan's Labyrinth* 2006) also offer reparation for the unaccounted Republican victims of the Franco regime and the Nationalists during the Spanish Civil War (1936–1939) and afterwards.
7. Figures from boxofficemojo.com
8. President Raúl Alfonsín (1983–1989) was forced, under threat of a new military coup, to introduce the two laws to stop further trials of any more military, generals, or police culpable of crimes during the 'Dirty War'.
9. After Menem's pardon and his release in 1990, Videla remained a free man (except for a brief stay in prison in 1998). In 2007 his pardon was ruled unconstitutional and his conviction reinstated. He was put on trial again in 2010, found guilty of human rights violations leading to the deaths of 37 prisoners and died in prison in 2013 aged 87.
10. Having been pardoned in 1990, Videla was arrested on kidnapping charges in 1998 and accused of having organised the illegal adoption of babies born to those detained during the 'Dirty War' (López 2013).

11. The film names Benjamín, Espósito rather than Chaparro as in the novel, to empha-sise his lack of social standing. As Ana Moraña points out, Espósito was a common surname given to foundling children (2011: 382n3).
12. In the novel, Irene's class is not emphasised. What makes her inaccessible to Benjamín is her education. She gets a degree (unlike him) and is promoted over him.
13. 'En realidad nunca más hablamos de esto ¿Por qué nunca más hablamos de esto?'
14. In the frame narrative Irene and Espósito are in a café where he is showing her another draft of his novel in progress when she asks 'We never spoke about this case. Why not? [...] Why now?' When did you return from Jujuy?' 'In 1985' Espósito responds. It's important that he has been back in Buenos Aires for some time, but is only in 1999 beginning to write about the case/the past. Many critics incorrectly suggest he has just returned in 1999 and that this is the trigger for writing about the past.
15. Paramilitary death squads were organised from the Ministerio de Bienestar Social (Department of Social Welfare) by the then Minister José López Rega (Hortiguera 2012: 114; Tandeciarz 2012: 64).
16. This adds considerably to the self-consciousness of the novel, which shifts between first (recounting the events of the past) and third person (the present day/frame narrative).
17. One of the means of circumventing the problems of representation was the recourse to allegory and other forms of displacement, shifting representations of dictatorship and violence to previous time periods – Bemberg's *Camila* recounts the story of the scandalous elopement of a young woman from the aristocracy with a Catholic priest during the nineteenth-century dictatorship of Rosas – or to smaller self enclosed institutions; her *Miss Mary* is about Uruburu's dictator-ship of the 1930s, Subiela's *Hombre mirando al sudeste* where a man appears in a mental hospital claiming to be from outer space. Others took aspects of the reality (the children of the disappeared given to wealthy families) but also used the family itself as a metaphor for the country. Set in 1983 in the last days of the dictatorship, *La historia oficial* tells the story of Alicia (Aleandro), an upper class history teacher at a private boy's school with an adopted daughter, Gaby. Through a series of events (her students, newspaper stories, a woman from the Madres de la Plaza de Mayo and a friend recently returned from exile), Alicia becomes con-vinced that her daughter is in fact the child of 'disappeared' parents, 'obtained' by Roberto (Alterio) her wealthy husband through his links to the military junta. *El secreto de sus ojos* shares with *La historia oficial* melodramatic form and also an attempt to make sense of a mystery, the answer to which lies in the film's his-torical past.
18. In one of these, arriving at the building site to arrest Gómez, the foreman asks Espósito and Baez who they are. Responding to the question Baez shows him his police badge and asks: 'Who is it going to be, idiot? Mike Hammer?' in refer-ence to the fictional American hard-boiled detective from novels, comics, televi-sion and films, and most famously the *noir* film *Kiss Me Deadly* (Robert Aldrich 1955).
19. Similarly, there are times when Espósito is talking juridically (about re-opening the Morales Case, having witnessed Morales' dedication to finding his wife's killer) and Irene mistakes this for his personal feelings, expecting Espósito to declare himself to her romantically.
20. A feature of the German expressionist film *The Cabinet of Dr Caligari* (Robert Wiene, 1920), the unreliable narrator becomes a feature of *noir* (*The Locket* John Brahm 1946) and subsequently neo-noir films (*Memento* Christopher Nolan, 2000; *The Usual Suspects* David Fincher 1995).

21. It is also worth pointing out that the justice enacted in *Nueve reinas* is, as Copertari notes, also 'private' and 'alternative' with these latter two qualities not being considered problematic or too commercial. Marcos (Darín), the swindler, who has conned his younger siblings out of the inheritance of their grandparents, is, in turn conned out of his money by an elaborate scheme run by his sister Valeria (Leticia Brédice) and her boyfriend Juan/Sebastián (Gastón Paul). What's problematic about the justice for Copertari, is not that it is private and alternative (and not handled by the state) but that it is purely a simulation with no outside referent and therefore the reconstitution it offers the Argentine public (the film's audience) –for whom it is an imagined resolution to the national injury of fleecing of Argentina's resources through the wave of privatisations of national resources that took place throughout the 1990s – is also simulation and also ephemeral (2005: 289). As exemplified in the ring Sebastian gives to Valera and the lie/truth he tells her about its origins, illusion and deceit appear to continue at the film's end.

EPILOGUE: *GRAVITY* (ALFONSO CUARÓN 2013), *BIRDMAN* (ALEJANDRO G. IÑÁRRITU 2014), *THE REVENANT* (G. IÑÁRRITU 2015) AND *CRIMSON PEAK* (GUILLERMO DEL TORO 2015)

In many analyses of contemporary Latin American Cinema, the nation remains the principle site for both the production and reception of films. The use of the term transnational, and the study of films that overtly reflect the multiple processes of transnational filmmaking –engaging with popular (Hollywood) genre templates, receiving script development support from US-based institutions or partially US-owned companies, whole or partial funding from transnational or multinational companies, innovative marketing campaigns funded by US-based global distribution networks and global distribution through these same networks – is perceived to go against the broader and historical project of the region's national cinemas: to be culturally and economically resistant to Hollywood cinema and hegemony. This has resulted in the privileging of a, more easily theorised as national, art house model of filmmaking, the denigration or devaluing of commercial or popular filmmaking, and (in some cases) a lack of attention paid to the deterritorialised films made by Latin American directors outside the region.

What this book has attempted in its reading of the local and deterritorialised films of six transnational Latin American auteurs – Iñárritu, Cuarón, del Toro, Meirelles, Salles and Campanella – is a rethinking of the relationship between Hollywood, popular cinema and contemporary Latin America cinema, other than that of (resistance to) US cultural hegemony (Alvaray 2008; Thanouli 2008: 5). It has suggested that, rather than be 'effaced' when they work within mainstream, semi-independent or independent US infrastructure, models or genres, these directors (and often their Latin American core creative teams) function as 'interstitial auteurs' negotiating between their own national and in some cases continental cultures and authorial vision and that of an always diverse and diversifying Hollywood (Naficy 1996: 119). Hence the transnational films of these Latin American auteurs challenge what some critics perceive as the easy appropriation of Western models and reveal instead a model of dynamic 'cinematic exchange' (Newman 2010: 4). Through comparative approaches that prioritise industrial, auteurist, director-centred and genre analyses this book has developed ways of reading these directors' local and deterritorialised films alongside each other to reveal how they share many of the same visual, stylistic and narrative strategies and a marked ideological coherence. It has also emphasised the role independent or semi-independent financing structures have played in the production of these directors' films and as a source of support/oppositional aesthetics. At the same time, it has argued against the many critics that narrowly present Hollywood itself as a bad object and Hollywood genres as unremittingly conservative and hence unsuitable to the exploration of Latin American politics and identity. Hence, this book's analyses of del Toro, Cuarón, Meirelles, Salles and Campanella's use of popular genres and the conventions of commercial filmmaking have shown how (and will show in the case of Iñárritu's *The Revenant*) an understanding of the complexity and capacities of the genre system significantly enriches the understanding of these directors' films and their political and critical projects.

This Epilogue briefly analyses some of these auteurs' recent films – Cuarón's *Gravity*, Iñárritu's *Birdman* and *The Revenant*, and del Toro's *Crimson Peak* – some of which are wholly studio films embedded in the larger ideological, institutional and industrial complex of contemporary studio filmmaking (as the cumulative Oscar count between Iñárritu's and Cuarón's recent films attests)[1] and located narratologically and in production and financing terms for the most part in the Global North (or off planet) and with no overt peripheral or Ibero-American narratives or links. The Epilogue questions whether it is possible to continue to think of these directors within some of the same paradigms this book has used to look at their previous films. For instance, is it possible to think about situating Iñárritu's *The Revenant*, a western set in the American North East, as speaking politically from a position rooted in the Global South? And similarly, with *Gravity*, can we talk about a peripheral, Global South or Latin American perspective in outer space?

GRAVITY

Interestingly enough, *Gravity* begins with astronauts, Matt Kowalski (George Clooney) and Dr Ryan Stone (Sandra Bullock) over Mexico – the camera pans over to a shot of the Earth with Mexico and the Central American Isthmus visible after Kowalski remarks 'Can't beat the view.' She is performing a task related to her role as mission scientist. He is trying to break the record for the longest space walk. Like *Children of Men* and indeed most of Cuarón's previous genre films, *Gravity* both conforms to and frustrates many of the conventions of the genre and the subgenre it most resembles: the science-fiction/ (space) disaster film. Its plot has the necessary elements of both danger – Stone and Kowalski are stranded in space, after debris knocked out of orbit by a Russian missile targeting one of its own defunct satellites kills their colleagues and destroys their space shuttle – and survival – the rest of the film is a desperate attempt to find a way back to Earth. Stone, who we learn has previously lost her daughter in a tragic accident, is also very much the typical disaster/ science fiction film protagonist in need of rebirth. Her emergence from the lake where her re-entry vehicle has landed and shaky steps in the last few minutes of the film emphasise how she has been reborn through the struggle to return safely to Earth.

In as much as its basic plot conforms to the central aims of the science fiction/disaster film, and has goals, motifs, defined characters, careful set ups of upcoming action and other traits of the classical narrative, *Gravity* works within the Hollywood paradigm (Thompson 2013). But *Gravity* also differs in several ways both from the norms of classical filmmaking and the terms of the (space) disaster film. Unlike other films in the subgenre (*Apollo 13* [Ron Howard 1995], *Armageddon* [Michael Bay 1988] *Deep Impact* [Mimi Leder 1998] *The Martian* [Ridley Scott 2015]) there's no cross-cutting between mission control and the ongoing crisis in space (or on Mars). After the debris strike, and the media blackout it causes, there is no communication between Houston and the stranded astronauts at all, not until a brief radio message heard but not responded to when Stone has re-entered Earth's atmosphere. The only radio contact Stone does make with Earth is with Aningaaq – an Inuit fisherman who can be heard singing to a baby. *Gravity* never establishes who or where the man is, although the astute listener might guess from the sound of his dogs and his name that he is one of the native peoples of the Arctic Circle. An 'associated paratext', the short *Aningaaq* by Jonás Cuarón expands this episode (Mittell 2013). Unlike the (space) disaster film and specifically *Armageddon* there is also no romantic subplot. There is not even the thwarted expectation of a romantic subplot as there was in *Children of Men* – conversations between Kowalski and Stone although playful do not promise a possible future between them had they both survived. Defying expectations, the strong male character common to the disaster film dies, leaving Stone to continue the struggle alone.

Gravity also differs in its editing patterns and visual style from classical and generic norms. As Kristin Thompson points out, for many parts of the film, the continuity editing system and its spatial clues (which allow us to comprehend where characters are moving and where they are in relation to the space and other characters and hence understand the story) are totally 'eliminated' (2013). This disruption of the classical continuity system, is partly a result of the attempt to create a realistic sense of what it feels like to be untethered in zero gravity. Indeed, at different points in the narrative it is important to emphasise how Stone in particular cannot orient herself in relation to other characters or the significant spacecraft she is trying to get back to/enter. Additionally, as with Cuarón's previous films, but also in contrast to the conventions of the subgenre, where short shot lengths predominate, particularly during moments of peril or impact – Gravity is marked for its extraordinary long takes (Bordwell 2002b: 17).[2] For instance, during the 'epic' seventeen-minute opening long take, and after the debris strike, the shot continues to follow Stone as she detaches herself from the mechanical arm and spins away from the camera into space. The shot remains on her for several minutes without cutting, gradually moving from an extreme long shot into an extreme close up that then goes inside her helmet to look out from her point of view. The predominance of the long take mean other conventions of the space disaster film and indeed classical continuity patterns are also eschewed. Important plot points (the death of another astronaut, Shariff, for example) are seen only in the background, when classical convention would require a cut in to reveal this kind of event. Although these long takes are achieved digitally, as with Children of Men, they are not several takes 'stitched together' to make one long take. They were, as Thompson points out, created in special effects animation with the faces of the actors being 'jigsawed into them through a complex combination of rotoscoping and geometry builds' (2013). In constructing this realist perception of space, Cuarón and cinematographer Lubezki respect geographical realism – plotting lighting and colouring cues (the 'bounce light' and colour we see reflected on the characters' helmets for instance) according to the precise orbit of Earth below them or the position of the Sun, and shooting the actors faces to 'match an all digital environment' (Cohen and McNary 2013; Thompson 2013).

Another counter to the conventions of the science fiction/(space) disaster movie is Gravity's realist respect of the absence of sound in space.[3] Subjective sound, such as sound Stone would experience through her space suit or helmet including Kowalski's voice, her own heartbeat and her breath are heard. But there are no noisy explosions or crashes. Instead, because of the absence of carried sound the sound track carries the weight of emphasis in the film – punctuating the impact of the debris on the shuttle – including, significantly, the moment of Shariff being hit and killed.

This stripped down quality of Gravity's single plot line, editing patterns and sound design has led several critics to call it an 'experimental film' (Thompson 2013). In reality, the film is a mixture of both mainstream conventions (star casting, genre, big budget [$100 million]) and 'avant-garde' techniques (long takes, lack of spatial cues, contravening of classical plot, genre and editing conventions), which together have attracted the label of 'blockbuster modernism' (Hoberman 2013). Other critics have also pointed out how 'innovation' and 'experiment' on the level we see in *Gravity* can exist and indeed have always existed in Hollywood cinema as long as there is a classical story which motivates this 'strangeness' (Thompson 2013). *Gravity*'s win of seven Oscars in 2014, including the Oscar for Best Director for Cuarón, the first Latin American director to win the award, and with a film that carries over much of his auteurist style, points towards this sense of a Hollywood institution (Warner Bros.) capable of absorbing (but not co-opting) an experimental, modernist cinema.

But *Gravity*'s nod to the peripheries – beginning over Mexico and making contact with the Arctic Circle (Aningaaq) – and its refusal to refer back diegetically to a continental US (a Mission Control which is unusually visually absent for the entire film and present audibly for only eleven or so minutes at the beginning) or have the standard global montage (of people around the world waiting anxiously to hear the fate of the (stranded) astronaut(s) as in *The Martian, Armageddon* and other space disaster films) or have shots of the entire Earth which Langley suggests are key to the discourse of US hegemonic power and predominate in space disaster films, and in particular *Interstellar* (Christopher Nolan 2014), suggest that *Gravity* departs on a broader ideological level from 'the American story [...] writ large on a global campus' (Langley 2011).

In the way that it is studio made, spectacle based, with a large budget, classical narrative and huge box office gross ($723 million) *Gravity* is like many other conservative Hollywood (space) disaster films.[4] But in many terms of style and geopolitics, including not 'endors[ing] American global leadership' (Langley 2011), it is not. What *Gravity* shows is that there is 'space' in the Hollywood disaster movie for a range of different ideologies and positions. But this ability to be sometimes within and sometimes outside the dominant ideology is wholly reliant on the film being a part of the system itself.

BIRDMAN OR (THE UNEXPECTED VIRTUE OF IGNORANCE)

As Chapter 1 has explored, Iñárritu's first four features, *Amores perros, 21 Grams, Babel* and *Biutiful* are linked by the exploration of pain, death, and the inequities of neoliberalism in the developing and developed worlds. But *Birdman*, a comedy set in a New York theatre, initially seems to be a departure for Iñárritu.

The film follows Riggan Thomson (Michael Keaton) a Hollywood actor famous for playing the superhero Birdman in a Hollywood franchise of the same name. With his career in decline, he mounts his own adaptation of

Raymond Carver's collection of short stories *What We Talk About When We Talk About Love* (1981). The film is set during the play's preview week and in the run up to opening night. In between rehearsals and previews, in his dressing room, Riggan sits and muses about his washed-up career and the play which he hopes will give him artistic credibility. Listening to the dark voice of his inner Birdman, he practices telekinetic stunts worthy of his cinematic alter-ego.

Birdman displays a number of features which link it to the director's other work. It has, for instance, the cyclical format of *Biutiful*: images of a meteor flying to earth open and come near the end of the film. It also has a subtitle *The Unexpected Virtue of Ignorance* which, together with some opening quotations by Carver, give the film the meditative quality of Iñárritu's previous films.[5] Spanish even sneaks in at the margins of the film, when a few words of it are heard over black screen before the film proper begins.[6] Like all Iñárritu's previous films, *Birdman* has a core creative team of Latin Americans, some of whom have worked with him before including Argentinean screenwriters Bo and Giacobone (*Biutiful*), Mexican sound designer Hernández (all of Iñárritu's films to date), and some who have not, Mexican cinematographer Emmanuel Lubezki and Mexican drummer Antonio Sánchez. Like *21 Grams, Babel,* and *Biutiful* (in part), *Birdman* is financially and institutionally a product of the US independent sector, involving monies from New Regency and major specialty division Fox Searchlight.

Also strongly supporting the idea that *Birdman* represents a continuation for Iñárritu is the film's most salient formal feature; its seemingly unending single take. A characteristic of all Iñárritu's previous films, the mobile long take in *Birdman* is taken to an extreme. The camera follows characters in and out of rooms, up and down the stairs and corridors, on and off the stage and inside and outside the St James Theatre on Broadway. Hours and sometimes days pass between scenes and yet the shot never cuts.[7] The film's extended long take is more than a stylistic flourish. A cornerstone of Bazin's theory of cinema, the long take provides the cinematic credentials for a script that emphasises the importance of authenticity in stagecraft, in cinematography, in the film business, and in the job of simply being oneself.[8] And, it is on the charge of inauthenticity, that Iñárritu calls to account Hollywood's superhero franchises (*X Men, Avengers, Iron Man*) and the talented actors (Robert Downey Jnr, Michael Fassbender, Jeremy Renner) who, the film suggests, allow themselves to be subsumed by them. Casting Keaton to play Riggan (who also left a superhero franchise) is another seeming weapon marshalled in the film's armoury of art cinema authenticity.[9]

Despite all these auteurist and art cinema elements, there are aspects of *Birdman* in which Iñárritu distances himself from anything as serious as authenticity, and from what some reviewers call the 'miserablist agony' of his previous films (Bradshaw 2007).[10] Unlike any of Iñárritu's previous features *Birdman* is funny. More precisely, its humour often seems to be about punctuating the art cinema seriousness for which Iñárritu is known. At one point Riggan and method actor Mike Shiner (Edward Norton) carry on an intense conversation as they leave the theatre to walk to a bar. The sequence is accompanied by a jazzy drum solo which we presume to be on the soundtrack (by Sánchez). However, as Riggan and Shiner walk, a tracking shot reveals the drummer (Sánchez in cameo) is actually busking outside on the street. Riggan even gives him some money. This reveal punctures the seriousness of the moment and is used another time in similar bathos style inside the theatre itself to counter some of the intensity of the moment when Riggan is about to take to the stage on opening night. This playing with the percussive score and much of the dialogue[11] suggests *Birdman* makes fun of the features of its own artiness, and of its use of the always self-conscious mode of art cinema.

Also pointing towards *Birdman* as a departure is the change in the director's signature itself. Abbreviating his first surname (González) to the initial G for the first time, Iñárritu emerges as a slightly mainstreamed (and less 'other') manifestation of his former directorial self. Some might argue that this change in his signature has been accompanied by a similar mainstreaming/taming of his previous films' critique of Hollywood aesthetics and politics, although the critique of superhero franchises and his subsequent film *The Revenant*'s critique of the practices of white colonialism in the American West, suggests he has not left this position behind.

Another way of looking at Iñárritu's position within the institution can be gleaned from *Birdman*'s four Oscar wins in 2015 – Best Picture, Best Cinematography (for Lubezki), Best Original Screenplay, and Best Director – Iñárritu is the second Mexican and Latin American director, after Cuarón, to win this award. These confirm *Birdman* to be the favourite of an industry that likes nothing more than to see itself simultaneously critiqued *and* therefore aggrandised, hence the number of other meta-Hollywood insider-films that have also won Best Picture or multiple awards at the Oscars – *The Artist* (Michel Hazanivicius 2012), *Argo* (Ben Affleck 2013) and *The Bad and the Beautiful* (Vincente Minnelli 1952).

THE REVENANT

In 2016, as in 2015, the Academy was criticised for the lack of diversity in its award nominations. The Twitter hashtag #OscarsSoWhite[12] trended amongst commentators and industry personnel to signal dismay at the lack of nominations received by people of colour in front of and behind the cameras. In the midst of the controversy Iñárritu and *The Revenant*'s nomination in twelve major categories was a much commented upon exception.

However, despite the emphasis placed on Iñárritu's nationality and ethnicity in the press, it has been suggested that *The Revenant* unproblematically supports a narrative of white settler colonialism in the American North West, privileging the abilities of one white man to survive the harsh winter and a near death experience (Quayson 2016). Such readings, which posit that the film might have been more critical of white settler colonialism 'with more diverse voices in Hollywood' disavow not just Iñárritu's own position as a Mexican director (and his co-scriptwriter credit for the film), but also a body of work which, as this book has emphasised, criticises the racism and certainties of US modernity, its border controls, its foreign policy and its ideology. Iñárritu's epic is based on Michael Punke's novel (2002), which is in turn based on the true narrative of Hugh Glass (played by Leonardo Di Caprio in the film), an early nineteenth century fur trapper who was mauled by a bear, left to die by a fellow trapper Fitzgerald (played by Tom Hardy in the film) and yet survived.

Perspectives which fold the film into the 'white settler narrative' also disavow the changes Iñárritu and his co-screenwriter Mark L. Smith made to the novel – adding a number of indigenous/mixed race characters and plot lines: Hickuc (Arthur Redcloud) the Pawnee man who cures Glass and, the film emphasises, helps him survive; Glass's wife (Grace Dove) who we see in Glass's flashbacks, dreams and visions; Hawk (Forrest Goodluck), Glass's mixed race son killed by Fitzgerald, and Elk Dog (Duane Howard) the Arikara warrior searching for his daughter, Powaqa (Melaw Nakehk'o), who has been stolen by white men.[13] These perspectives also ignore the film's editing strategies and narrative construction which draw parallels between Glass's quest to avenge the murder of his son and that of Elk Dog to find his daughter. Indeed, far from the film being purely from a 'white settler' perspective, the opening ambush on the trapper encampment ends from the Arikara perspective with dialogue making clear that what has motivated the attack is not warlike aggression (as camera work at the beginning of the attack suggests), but the search for a lost child.

In many ways *The Revenant*, like other contemporary westerns 'with a strong Native American presence', could be called a revisionist western. Its graphic depictions of and frequent allusions to massacred Native American Indians (Hikucs's family, Glass's wife and her village, the village Fitzgerald and Tom [Will Poulter] come across) and conversations that underline the commodity value of the beaver pelts collected by the trappers also suggests it takes a revisionist position towards the history of the American West, casting the politics of 'western expansionism' as clear 'imperialism motivated by economic forces' (Carter 2014: 1). However, there are problems with the category of the revisionist western. The term 'revisionist western' projects an overwhelmingly Anglo United States as constantly moving towards an ever more enlightened and liberal perspective on its (still classed as) internal others. Furthermore, the Western has always been more complex than a straightforward projection of the myth of the American West

(Tierney 2011), and revisionist westerns themselves are not necessarily always socially progressive or ideologically contestatory (Carter 2014: 92–93).[14] Casting *The Revenant* as a revisionist western is also problematic because it folds the film within the norms of the Hollywood industry and does not take into consideration the position and previous work of its director.

Comparing *The Revenant* with Iñárritu's body of work, it becomes evident that it does indeed share many thematic and textual similarities with Iñárritu's previous films. Thematically it shares a focus on parents and children and indeed parents who lose children in some way. Cristina in *21 Grams*, Richard and Susan in *Babel*, El Chivo in *Amores perros*,[15] Valeria in *Amores perros*.[16] Like *21 Grams*, *The Revenant* is also about surviving after the death of a child/ children (Smith 2014: 80). Textually, *The Revenant*, like Iñárritu's previous films, displays a commitment to heightened realism. It does this most overtly in set pieces like the film's opening attack on the fur trapper encampment in which several, minute-long takes pan vertically and horizontally, tracking and moving as the characters move. Beyond film language, realism is also emphasised in the shooting style and acting technique. Lubezki's much talked about use of only available light together with other realist techniques such as location shooting (in sub-zero temperatures), as well as the overt shunning of the available facilitating film technology (apart from scenes involving the bear, the bison and the Elk crossing the river, all of which are digitally enhanced), Di Caprio's eating of raw fish and bison, and physical immersion in freezing water establish the credentials of a shoot which chooses not to compromise or fabricate its spectacle (a feat recognised by Lubezki's third Oscar, and Di Caprio's first for Best Actor) (Kermode 2016).

The Revenant is nevertheless a departure for Iñárritu in several ways. Whereas all his previous English language films were 'independent' films made by specialty houses (New Regency, Fox Searchlight, Focus Features, Paramount Vantage) belonging to the studios, *The Revenant* is his first with a major studio, Twentieth Century Fox. And yet, despite its institutional position the film resists many of the representational norms of the US industry and even approximates aspects of Mexican national ideology. As Iñárritu's own words during his acceptance speech for Best Director at the 2016 Oscars suggest, the film's central relationship is between Glass and his mixed race son, which positions *The Revenant* not just as a counter narrative of the American West and a purely Anglo point of view but also gestures towards Mexico's official racial ideology of *mestizaje*.[17]

CRIMSON PEAK

Unlike Iñárritu, for whom *The Revenant* marks a first foray into studio film-making, del Toro's work and the nature of his auteurist filmmaking continues to be defined through a range of different institutional venues – both independent and mainstream – and an ongoing interest in what have been perceived as genres of 'low' cultural value: science fiction (*Pacific Rim, The Shape of Water*), and horror, in *Crimson Peak*, his first English language horror film, made with Universal and Legendary Pictures.

Crimson Peak shares many points of contact with del Toro's Spanish language horror/fantasy trilogy. Like del Toro's *El espinazo del diablo* and *El laberinto del fauno*, *Crimson Peak* is based loosely around the gothic conventions of horror cinema: a scary house and a (youngish) girl.[18] Edith Cushing (Mia Wasikowska) is courted by English Baronet Thomas Sharpe (Tom Hiddleston) and taken to live with him and his sister Lucille (Jessica Chastain) at their remote and crumbling ancestral home (Allerton Hall). *Crimson Peak* also has several 'monsters'. Since her mother's funeral, Edith has seen her ghost twice. At Allerton Hall Edith is menaced by several ghosts. And like *El espinazo del diablo* and *El laberinto del fauno*, *Crimson Peak* uses the *mise-en-scène* of horror to explore political issues.[19]

Although, as in *El espinazo del diablo*, the film uses the conventions of horror to make the initial appearance of these ghosts terrifying and threatening, it also gradually reveals the ghosts (as *El espinazo* does with Santi) in ways that are less about the shock value intrinsic to horror's gothic dynamic of concealment and revelation, and more about the discovery of past crimes. For instance, Edith is led by ghostly sounds to the discovery of phonograph rolls in a cupboard and ultimately to a phonograph in the basement from which she learns the truth about her husband and sister in law. At the same time as this process of revelation goes on, it becomes clear that the ghosts are not trying to harm Edith but to help her, as Santi is trying to help the boys in the orphanage in *El espinazo del diablo*. In *Crimson Peak* the red skeleton in the bath with the cleaver lodged in its skull is the ghost of Thomas and Lucille's mother and its telling Edith to leave is not a threat but a warning. The ghost of Enola Scioti is similarly trying to warn Edith that Thomas and Lucille are lovers and planning to kill her (signaling to her that she should look upstairs in the nursery, where she discovers them having sex). During the climactic fight between Edith and Lucille, Thomas' ghost appears to help Edith. A key part of the film's revelatory scheme of representation is the way it visualises its ghosts. In continuity with Santi, the ghosts are fully revealed and given substantive presence, plumes of blood emanate from their wounds – and these can be touched and felt (as Edith finds out). Ghosts are presented as real, as Edith's *El espinazo del diablo*-like opening and closing monologue underlines, in ways that emphasise their physicality: 'Ghosts are real, this much I know.'

Crimson Peak's ambiguously threatening and sympathetic representation of its monsters evokes Wood's theory of the monster in the American horror film as a return 'of all that our [capitalist] civilisation represses or oppresses' in the interests of 'patriarchal, heterosexual, bourgeois monogamy' particularly in the case of this film: 'women' and 'children' (1985: 200–201, 205). *Crimson Peak* makes it clear that it is Thomas and Lucille's brutal childhood that has turned them into monsters. To a certain extent, this characterisation of the horror film's monster threat as the oppressed is made clear by the way Edith (and we the spectators) gradually come to see the ghosts (and even Thomas and Lucille), as Santi is eventually seen in *El espinazo del diablo*, as victims too. Several of the ghosts have been victims of Thomas and Lucille's scheme to marry and murder wealthy women and take their assets and Edith is next. *Crimson Peak*'s pervasive references to other cultural texts and films in the horror/gothic tradition – Alfred Hitchcock's *Rebecca* (1940) is evoked by Lucille's Mrs Danvers-like presence (1940) and Edith's own preference as an author to be likened to Mary Shelley (author of *Frankenstein*) rather than Jane Austen – point towards the film's critique of marriage as an instrument of patriarchal culture and authority that robs women of autonomy and financial independence.

Like *El laberinto del fauno*, *Crimson Peak* has a female-centric narrative. Edith and the ghosts are all female. And like *El laberinto del fauno* with the muddy tree root Ophelia has to enter to retrieve a key, *Crimson Peak* draws on the abject as a kind of seeping return of repressed femininity in response to patriarchal violence. In the basement and ground floor of Allerton Hall the damp and the red clay coming up from the mine below make it look as if the walls and the floor are oozing blood. It is significantly in the basement that Edith finds clues to the murders committed by her husband and sister-in-law, and where the skeleton of one of their victims is hidden.

Although *Crimson Peak* suggests that it is the mother who emotionally and physically abused Thomas and Lucille through abandonment and beatings, it is also suggested that it is the broader context of an emotionally repressed patriarchal British aristocracy that is to blame for Lucille and Thomas' monstrosity, it is suggested that their father was neglectfully distant and largely absent from their lives. That this institution and its financial underpinnings is falling apart is suggested by the house crumbling into the mine which had previously provided the family's money and position.

Crimson Peak therefore mobilises the conventions of the horror film in similar ways to del Toro's Spanish language horror trilogy. Del Toro even characterises the acceptance of ghosts as being 'real' (from Edith's opening speech) as not an Anglo Saxon but specifically a Mexican and Latin belief (Diestro-Dópido 2015), which is useful to note given that lots of criticism (including this analysis) draws on the film's links to Anglo culture including Charlotte Brontë's *Jane Eyre* (1847).

In this study of six Latin American transnational auteurs and the broader transnational filmmaking apparatus in Latin America and the United States, the impetus has been to open up new areas of investigation and new per-spectives on commercial transnational filmmaking in the region. As for the implications of this study, it hopes to draw more attention to contemporary popular cinemas made both by the Latin American directors it has focused on and others who are working transnationally both in film (Pablo Larraín's *Jackie* [2016], Claudia Llosa's *Aloft* [2014], del Toro's *The Shape of Water* [2017], Cuarón's *Roma* [2018]), in television (del Toro's animated children's series *Trollhunters* [2016–], and new FX channel series *The Strain* [2017–] Cuarón's *Believe* [2013], José Padilha's *Narcos*) and virtual reality (Iñárritu and Lubezki's *Carne y Arena*, which was screened in the Official Selection of the Cannes Film Festival 2017). This book also hopes to contribute to the larger study of comparing genres across cultures. Ultimately, it is hoped that this book will help to expand the idea of (transnational) Latin American cinemas beyond the geospatial limits of the continent and art cinema-defined aesthetic hierarchies.

Notes

1. It is because the Epilogue situates the most recent films of the transnational auteurs within the industrial and genre context of Hollywood studio filmmaking that these directors' Oscar wins feature so prominently: as much as a marker of quality filmmaking and industry approbation, they function as a measure of these directors' position within the institution. Oscars are, in a way, Hollywood's award to itself.
2. In another space disaster film *Armageddon* the average shot length is 2.3 seconds.
3. For all its realism in cinematographic terms, the feats *Gravity* proposes have been debunked by NASA scientists.
4. Box office figures and budget from boxofficemojo.com
5. The subtitle turns out to be the title of the complimentary review written by Tabitha Dickenson, a theatre critic who had previously shown great dislike for Riggan's attempt to be a 'real' actor.
6. Spoken by the soundtrack composer Antonio Sánchez, who is asking Iñárritu a question.
7. *Birdman* of course does have masked edits which take place, like they do in another famously 'single take' film *Rope* (Alfred Hitchcock 1946), in moments where the camera focuses on darkness, usually corners.
8. When spectacular computer generated imagery including explosions, a huge bird/monster and tanks, common in the superhero franchise does appear in the film towards the end it deliberately clashes with the realist diegesis that has already been established.
9. Keaton played Batman in Tim Burton's *Batman* (1989) *and Batman Returns* (1991).
10. Indeed, one of Riggan's most memorable monologues about the abuse he suffered as a child turns out to be deliberately put on to show Shiner just how *method* and convincing he can be.
11. At one point, Riggan's inner Birdman says in reference to the action of the super-hero franchise films he used to appear in 'That's what people want, not this talking philosophical bullshit.'

12. Coined by Broadway Black (<http://broadwayblack.com>) managing editor April Reign in 2015, the hashtag became a way of calling attention to the Academy's overlooking performances and achievements of actors, directors, screenwriters and other film personnel of colour.

13. Unlike Punke's novel, which is almost exclusively told from the perspective of the white fur trappers and other white Europeans. Furthermore, the novel portrays the Arikara as attacking 'without provocation' (2002: 9–10), and gives almost no subjectivity to the American Indians it portrays (except for a couple of lines from the perspective of a Mandan Indian who brings Glass back to his village to be cured [2002: 172–173] and the thoughts of some boys about to steal horses from Glass and his fellow travellers).

14. Carter suggests that Kevin Costner's *Dances with Wolves* (1990) re-visions one tribe (the Lakota Sioux, who are given full characteristics and histories) only to polarise another (the Pawnee, who are portrayed as 'natural savages') (2014: 92–93).

15. El Chivo, the ex-university lecturer turned guerilla fighter and now contract killer becomes a revenant of sorts returning (awkwardly) to his daughter and to society and acting as a kind of ghost and conscience of Mexico's violent past.

16. She loses her Richie who, it is suggested, is her child replacement, under her floor boards.

17. *Mestizaje* or racial mixing is the official racial ideology in Mexico. In this discourse, *mestizaje* is the 'fruitful coming together of two separate cultures, the Spanish culture and the indigenous culture' (Tierney 2007: 73). Although there is more to be said about the gap between this ideology and racial politics in Mexico both contemporaneously and historically. I thank Paul Julian Smith for pointing out this aspect of *The Revenant* to me.

Inarritu's other words during the speech also commented obliquely on the institutional racism of the Hollywood Academy and the #OscarsSoWhite controversy by paraphrasing Dr Martin Luther King Jr:

> So what a great opportunity to our generation, to really liberate ourself from all prejudice and this tribal thinking and make sure for once and forever that the color of the skin become as irrelevant as the length of our hair.

18. Edith is not a child, but childlike smallness is emphasised at different times through oversized *mise-en-scène* (a bed, a chair, a teacup) which make her appear small and childlike (Diestro-Dópido 2015: 22).

19. There are also continuities between *Crimson Peak*'s imaginary and the décor. The bathtub Edith bathes in is similar to the one Ophelia bathes in *El laberinto del fauno*. The 'clay tubs' down in the basement – which hide one of Thomas's previous wives – resemble the pool in the basement of the orphanage in *El espinazo del diablo*. There are also links to other films which del Toro has referenced elsewhere – Erice's *El espíritu de la colmena* in the focus on the magnified sound of insects although *Crimson Peak* focuses on ants and butterflies and *El espíritu* focuses on bees – and del Toro's own *Mimic*, which he initially disavowed because of the difficulties he had during its production, but which he now embraces as part of his oeuvre.

SELECT FILMOGRAPHY

8 Mile (Curtis Hanson 2002)
11'09'01–September 11 (Alejandro González Iñárritu et al. 2002)
21 Grams (Alejandro González Iñárritu 2003)
25th Hour (Spike Lee 2002)
28 Days Later (Danny Boyle 2002)
33, The (Patricia Riggen 2015)
76 89 03 (Cristian Bernard and Flavio Nardini 2000)
127 Hours (Danny Boyle 2010)
360 (Fernando Meirelles 2011)
2012 (Roland Emmerich 2009)
Aloft (Claudia Llosa 2014)
Abril Despedaçado/Behind the Sun (Walter Salles 2001)
Abzurdah (Daniela Goggi 2015)
Acacias, Las/The Acacia Trees (Pablo Giorgelli 2011)
Amelie (Jean Pierre Jeunet 2001)
Anicieto (Leonardo Favio 2008)
Apollo 13 (Ron Howard 1995)
Artist, The (Michael Hazanavicius 2011)
¡Asu mare!/Oh Mother! (Ricardo Maldonado 2013)
Así / Like This (Jesús Mario Lozano 2005)
Albert Nobbs (Rodrigo García 2011)
American Pie (Paul Weitz 1999)
American Pie 2 (J. B. Rodgers 2001)
Amores perros/Love's a Bitch (Alejandro González Iñárritu 2000)
Angel desnudo, El/The Naked Angel (Carlos Hugo Christensen 1946)
Ano em que Meus Pais Saíram de Férias, O / The Year My Parents Went on Vacation (Cao Hamburger 2006)
Angel de fuego (Dana Rotberg 1992)

Antônia (Tata Amaral 2006)
Aquarius (Kleber Mendonça Filho 2015)
Argo (Ben Affleck 2013)
Armageddon (Michael Bay 1998)
At Play in the Fields of the Lord (Héctor Babenco 1991)
Até que a sorte nos separe/Til Luck Us Do Part (Roberto Santucci 2012)
Até que a sorte nos separe 2/Til Luck Us Do Part 2 (Roberto Santucci 2013)
Até que a sorte nos separe 3/Til Luck Us Do Part 3 (Roberto Santucci 2016)
Aura, El / The Aura (Fabián Bielinsky 2005)
Automóvil gris, El/The Grey Car (Enrique Rosas 1919)
Avatar (James Cameron 2009)
Avengers, The (Joss Whedon 2012)
Babel (Alejandro González Iñárritu 2006)
Bad and the Beautiful, The (Vincente Minnelli 1952)
Baile Perfumado/Perfumed Ball (Lírio Ferreira and Paulo Caldas 1999)
Bajo California (Carlos Bolado 1998)
Bastardos, Los/The Bastards (Amat Escalante 2008)
Batalla en el cielo/Battle in Heaven (Carlos Reygadas 2005)
Batman vs Superman (Zack Snyder 2016)
Band à part/Band of Outsiders (Jean-Luc Godard 1964)
Beavis & Butthead (Mike Judge 1996)
Bienvenido/Welcome (Gabriel Retes 1994)
Bienvenido Mr Marshall/Welcome Mr Marshall (Luis García Berlanga 1953)
Big Sleep, The (Howard Hawks 1946)
Birdman (Alejandro G. Iñárritu 2014)
Biutiful (Alejandro González Iñárritu 2010)
Blackout (Rigoberto Castañeda 2008)
Blade II: Blood Hunt (Guillermo del Toro 2002)
Blair Witch Project, The (Daniel Myrick and Eduardo Sánchez 1999)
Blindness (Fernando Meirelles, 2008)
Boi Neon/Neon Bull (Gabriel Mascaro 2015)
Bolivia (Adrián Caetano 2001)
Boda Secreta/Secret Wedding (Alejandro Agresti 1991)
Bombón, el perro (Sorín 2004)
Bonnie and Clyde (Arthur Penn 1967)
Book of Life, The (Jorge R. Gutierrez 2014)
Bourne Ultimatum, The (Paul Greengrass 2007)
Brokeback Mountain (Ang Lee 2005)
Brood, The (David Cronenberg 1979)
Buenos Aires Vice Versa (Alejandro Agresti 1996)
Bulto, El/Excess Baggage (Gabriel Retes 1992)
Burning Plain, The (Guillermo Arriaga 2008)
Bye Bye Brasil (Carlos Diegues 1979)
Cabinet of Dr Caligari, The (Robert Wiene 1920)
Calle Mayor/Main Street (Juan Antonio Bardem 1956)
Callejón de los milagros/Midaq Alley (Jorge Fons 1995)
Cama adentro/Live-in Maid (Jorge Gaggero 2004)
Camila (Maria Luisa Bemberg 1984)
Captain America – Civil War (Joe and Anthony Russo 2016)
Carancho/Vulture (Pablo Trapero 2010)
Carandiru (Héctor Babenco 2003)
Carlota Joaquina, princesa do Brazil / Carlota Joaquina (Carla Camurati 1995)

Carrie (Brian De Palma 1976)
Casa de Areia/House of Sand (Andrucha Waddington 2005)
Casa muda, La/The Silent House (Gustavo Hernández 2010)
Cat People (Jacques Tourneur 1942)
Cenizas del paraíso/Ashes of Paradise (Marcelo Piñeyro 1997)
Central do Brasil/Central Station (Walter Salles 1998)
Céu de Suely, O/Love for Sale (Karim Aïnouz 2006)
Children of Men (Alfonso Cuarón, 2006)
The Chronicles of Narnia: The Lion, the Witch and the Wardrobe (Andrew Adamson 2005)
The Chronicles of Narnia: Prince Caspian (Andrew Adamson 2008)
The Chronicles of Narnia: The Voyage of the Dawn Treader (Michael Apted 2010)
Chungking Express (Kar Wai Wong 1994)
Cidade Baixa/Lower City (Sérgio Machado 2005)
Cidade de Deus/City of God (Fernando Meirelles and Kátia Lund 2002)
Cidade dos Homens/City of Men (Paulo Morelli 2007)
Ciénaga, La/The Swamp (Lucrecia Martel 2001)
Cilantro y perejil/Recipes to Stay Together (Rafael Montero 1995)
Cinema de Lágrimas/Cinema of Tears (Nelson Pereira dos Santos 1995)
Clan, El/The Clan (Pablo Trapero 2015)
Clown, El (Pedro Adorno and Emilio Rodríguez 2006)
Cloverfield (Matt Reeves 2008)
Club sándwich (Fernando Eimbcke 2013)
Cobrador: In God We Trust, El (Paul Leduc 2006)
Como agua para chocolate/Like Water for Chocolate (Alfonso Arau 1992)
Comodines/Cops (Jorge Nisco 1997)
Constant Gardener, The (Fernando Meirelles 2005)
Contagion (Steven Soderbergh 2011)
Conversation, The (Francis Ford Coppola 1974)
Coronel no tiene quien le escriba, El/No one writes to the Colonel (Arturo Ripstein 1999)
Cosas insignificantes/Insignificant Things (Andrea Martínez 2008)
Crash (Paul Haggis 2004)
Cría cuervos/Raise Ravens (Carlos Saura 1975)
Crimen del padre Amaro, El/The Crime of Father Amaro (Carlos Carrera 2002)
Crimson Peak (Guillermo del Toro 2015)
Chronic (Michel Franco 2015)
Crónica de una fuga/Chronicle of an Escape (Adrián Caetano 2006)
Cronos (Guillermo del Toro 1993)
Danzón (María Novaro 1991)
Day After Tomorrow, The (Roland Emmerich 2004)
Day the Earth Stood Still, The (Robert Wise 1951)
Dark Water (Walter Salles 2005)
Deep Impact (Mimi Leder 1998)
Déficit (Gael García Bernal 2007)
De la calle/Streeters (Gerardo Tort 2001)
De Pernas pro Ar 2/Legs in the Air 2 (Roberto Santucci 2012)
Después de Lucía/After Lucia (Michael Franco 2012)
Deus e Brasileiro/God is Brazilian (Carlos Diegues 2003)
Deus e o diabo na terra do sol/Black God, White Devil (Glauber Rocha 1964)
Der leone have sept cabeças/The Lion Has Seven Heads (Glauber Rocha 1971)
Diarios de motocicleta/Motorcycle Diaries (Walter Salles 2004)
Días de Santiago/Days of Santiago (Josué Méndez 2004)

Dibu, la película/Dibu: the Film (Carlos Olivieri and Alejandro Stoessel 1997)
Dirty Pretty Things (Stephen Frears 2002)
Dois Filhos de Francisco/Two Sons of Francisco (Breno Silveira 2005)
Do the Right Thing (Spike Lee 1989)
Domésticas/Maids (Fernando Meirelles 2000)
Don't Be Afraid of the Dark (Troy Nixey 2010)
Dona Flor e seus Dois Maridos/Dona Flor and Her Two Husbands (Bruno Barreto 1976)
Dracula (Tod Browning 1931)
Dude Where's My Car? (Danny Leiner 2000)
Easy Rider (Dennis Hopper 1969)
Election (Alexander Payne 1999)
Elejidas, Las/The Chosen Ones (David Pablos 2015)
Elysium (Neil Blomkamp 2013)
Espinazo del diablo, El/The Devil's Backbone (Guillermo del Toro 2001)
Espíritu de la colmena, El/Spirit of the Beehive (Víctor Erice 1973)
Estômago/Estomago: A Gastronomic Story (Marcos Jorge 2007)
Eu Tu Eles/Me You Them (Andrucha Waddington 2000)
Exorcist, The (William Friedkin 1973)
Exposure/A Grande Arte (Walter Salles 1991)
Fase 7/Phase 7 (Nicolás Goldbart 2011)
Fast and Furious 6: The Game (Scott Blackwood 2013)
Ferris Bueller's Day Off (John Hughes 1986)
Fraude/Fraud (Luis Mandoki 2007)
Frankenstein (James Whale 1931)
Frida (Julie Taymor 2002)
Furia, La/The Fury (Juan Batista Stagnaro 1997)
Furtivos/Poachers (José Luis Borau 1975)
Gallo con muchos huevos, Un/Little Rooster's Egg-cellent Adventure (Gabriel y Rodolfo Riva Palacio Alatriste 2015)
Goodfellas (Martin Scorsese 1990)
Grande Família – O Filme/The Big Family – The Film, (Maurício Farias 2007)
Géminis, Los/The Twins (Albertina Carri 2005)
Girl in Progress (Patricia Riggen 2012)
Gone (Heitor Dhalia 2012)
Gravity (Alfonso Cuarón, 2013)
Great Expectations (Alfonso Cuarón 1998)
Guantanamera (Tomás Gutiérrez Alea and Juan Carlos Tabio 1995)
Guantes mágicos, Los/The Magic Gloves (Martín Rejtman 2003)
Guerra de Canudos/The Battle of Canudos (Sérgio Rezende 1997)
Harry Potter and the Sorcerer's Stone (Chris Columbus 2001)
Harry Potter and the Chamber of Secrets (Chris Columbus 2002)
Harry Potter and the Prisoner of Azkaban (Alfonso Cuarón 2004)
Harry Potter and the Goblet of Fire (Mike Newell 2005)
Harry Potter and the Order of the Phoenix (David Yates 2007)
Harry Potter and the Half-Blood Prince (David Yates 2009)
Harry Potter and the Deathly Hallows, Part 1, Part II (David Yates 2010, 2011)
Halley (Sebastián Hofman 2012)
Halloween (John Carpenter 1978)
Hellboy (Guillermo del Toro 2004)
Hellboy II: The Golden Army (Guillermo del Toro 2008)
Heli (Amat Escalante 2013)
Hero (Yimou Zhang 2002)

Hijo de la novia, El/Son of the Bride (Juan José Campanella 2001)
Historias breves/Short Stories (Daniel Burman, Lucrecia Martel, Adrián Caetano, Bruno Stagnaro 1995)
Historias extraordinarias/Extraordinary Stories (Mariano Llinás 2009)
Historias mínimas/Intimate Stories (Carlos Sorín 2002)
Historia oficial, La/The Official Story (Luis Puenzo 1984)
Hobbit, The: An Unexpected Journey (Peter Jackson 2012)
Hobbit, The: The Desolation of Smaug (Peter Jackson 2013)
Hobbit, The: The Battle of the Five Armies (Peter Jackson 2014)
Hombre mirando al sudeste/Man Facing Southeast (Eliseo Subiela 1986)
Hora de los hornos, La/The Hour of the Furnaces (Fernando Solanas and Octavio Getino 1968)
House of the Flying Daggers (Yimou Zhang 2004)
Independence Day (Roland Emmerich 1996)
Invasion of the Body Snatchers (Don Siegel 1956)
Invasor, O/The Trespasser (Beto Brant 2002)
Iron Man (Jon Favreau 2008)
Iron Man II (Jon Favreau 2010)
Iron Man III (Shane Black 2013)
It Happened One Night (Frank Capra 1934)
Jackie (Pablo Larraín 2016)
Japón (Carlos Reygadas 2002)
Jauja (Lisandro Alonso 2015)
Jia Zhanke: A Guy from Fenyang (Walter Salles 2014)
Kamchatka (Marcelo Piñeyro 2002)
KM 31 (Rigoberto Castañeda 2006)
KM 31-2 (Rigoberto Castañeda 2016)
Kiss Me Deadly (Robert Aldrich 1955).
Kiss of the Spider Woman (Héctor Babenco 1985)
Kony 2012 (Jason Russell 2012)
Laberinto del fauno, El/Pan's Labyrinth (Guillermo del Toro 2006)
Lake Tahoe (Fernando Eimbcke 2008)
Lake House, The (Alejandro Agresti 2006)
Leonera/Lion's Den (Pablo Trapero 2008)
Lemonade Mouth (Patricia Riggen 2011)
Lengua de las mariposas, La / Butterfly's Tongue (José Luis Cuerda 1999)
Libertad, La/Freedom (Lisandro Alonso 2001)
Life Somewhere Else (Walter Salles 1995)
Linha de Passe (Walter Salles and Daniela Thomas 2008)
Little Princess, A (Alfonso Cuarón 1995)
Liverpool (Lisandro Alonso 2006)
Locket, The (John Brahm 1946)
Lola (María Novaro 1989)
Lord of the Rings, The: The Fellowship of the Ring (Peter Jackson 2001)
Lord of the Rings, The: The Two Towers (Peter Jackson 2002)
Lord of the Rings, The: The Return of the King (Peter Jackson 2003)
Loucas pra Casar/Mad to Marry (Roberto Santucci 2015)
Luna de Avellaneda/Avellaneda's Moon (Juan José Campanella 2004)
Madeinusa (Claudia Llosa 2006)
Madam Satã (Karim Aïnouz 2002)
Mama (Andrés Muschietti 2013)
Mars Attacks (Tim Burton 1996)

Martian, The (Ridley Scott 2014)
Masculin Féminin (Jean-Luc Godard 1966)
Me casé con un boludo/I married a Dumbass (Juan Taratuto 2015)
Memento (Christopher Nolan 2000)
Menace II Society (Hughes Brothers 1993)
Menino Maluqinho 2/The Nutty Boy 2 (Fernando Meirelles 1998)
Message in a Bottle (Luis Mandoki 1998)
Metegol/The Underdogs (Juan José Campanella 2013)
Misma luna, La/The Same Moon (Patricia Riggen 2007)
Mimic (Guillermo del Toro 1997)
Mismo amor, la misma lluvia, El/The Same Rain, The Same Love (Juan José Campanella 1999)
Miss Bala (Gerardo Naranjo 2011)
Miss Mary (Maria Luisa Bemberg 1984)
Mother and Child (Rodrigo García 2009)
Muerte de un ciclista/Death of a Cyclist (Juan Antonio Bardem 1955)
Muertos, Los/The Dead (Lisandro Alonso 2004)
Mujer del puerto, La/The Woman of the Port (Arturo Ripstein 1991)
Mujer sin cabeza, La/The Headless Woman (Lucrecia Martel 2008)
Mujeres al borde de un ataque de nervios/Women on the Verge of a Nervous Breakdown (Pedro Almodóvar 1988)
Mundo grúa/Crane World (Pablo Trapero 1999)
Mystery of the Wax Museum (Michael Curtiz 1933)
Neutrón contra el Dr. Caronte/Neutron vs Dr Caronte (Federico Curiel 1963)
Niña santa, La/The Holy Girl (Lucrecia Martel 2004)
Night of the Living Dead (George A. Romero 1968)
¡No! (Pablo Larraín 2012)
No eres tú, soy yo/It's not you, it's me (Alejandro Springall 2011)
No manches Frida/WTH Frida Nacho (G. Velilla 2016)
No se aceptan devoluciones/Instructions Not Included (Eugenio Derbez 2013)
Nosotros los Nobles/The Noble Family (Gary Alazraki 2013)
Nostalgia de la luz/Nostalgia for the Light (Patricio Guzmán 2011)
Not Another Teen movie (Joel Gallen 2001)
Noticia de uma Guerra Privada/News from a Private War (Kátia Lund and João Salles 1999)
Novia que te vea/Like a Bride (Guita Schyfter 1994)
Novio para mi mujer, Un/A boyfriend for my wife (Juan Taratuto 2008)
Nueve reinas/Nine Queens (Fabián Bielinsky 2001)
Octubre/October (Daniel and Diego Vidal Vega 2010)
Ojos de Julia, Los/Julia's Eyes (Guillem Morales 2010)
Orfanato, El/The Orphanage (Juan Antonio Bayona 2007)
Orfeu/Orpheus (Carlos Diegues 1999)
On the Road (Walter Salles 2012)
Ônibus 174/Bus 174 (José Padilha 2002)
Oso rojo, Un/A Red Bear (Adrián Caetano 2002)
Others, The (Alejandro Amenábar 2001)
Pacific Rim (Guillermo del Toro 2013)
Painting Lesson, A (Pablo Perelman 2011)
Pixote (Héctor Babenco 1981)
Pizza, birra, faso/Pizza, Beer, and Cigarettes (Bruno Stagnaro and Adrián Caetano 1997)
Plata Quemada/Burnt Money (Marcelo Piñeyro 2000)

Post Tenebras Lux (Carlos Reygadas 2012)
Post Mortem (Pablo Larraín 2010)
Possibility of Hope, The (Alfonso Cuarón 2006)
Pretty In Pink (Howard Deutch 1986)
Primeiro Dia, O/Midnight (Walter Salles and Daniel Thomas 1998)
Prisioneiro da Grade de Ferro, O/The Prisoner of The Iron Bars (Paulo Sacramento 2004)
Profundo carmesí/Deep Crimson (Arturo Ripstein 1996)
Prophète, Un/A Prophet (Jaques Audiard 2009)
Pulp Fiction (Quentin Tarantino 1994)
Quincas Berro d'Água/The Two Deaths of Quincas Wateryell (Sérgio Machado 2010)
Quatrilho, O (Fábio Barreto 1995)
¿Qué culpa tiene el nino? (*Don't Blame the Kid* Gustavo Loza 2016)
Que é Isso Companheiro, O/Four Days in September (Bruno Barreto 1997)
Raise the Red Lantern (Yimou Zhang 1991)
Rapado/Skinhead (Martín Rejtman 1992)
Relatos salvajes/Wild Tales (Damián Szifrón 2014)
Reservoir Dogs (Quentin Tarantino 1992)
Revenant, The (Alejandro G. Iñárritu 2015)
Revolución 'La Séptima y Alvarado'/Revolution 'La 7th Street and Alvarado' (Rodrigo García 2010)
RoboCop (José Padilha 2014)
Roma (Alfonso Cuarón 2018)
Rope (Alfred Hitchcock 1949)
Rubios, Los/The Blondes (Albertina Carri 2003)
Rudo y Cursi/Rudo and Cursi (Carlos Cuarón 2008)
Sangre/Blood (Amat Escalante 2005)
Santo en el museo de cera/Santo in the Wax Museum (Alfonso Corona Blake 1963)
Scream (Wes Craven 1996)
Scream 2 (Wes Craven 1997)
Scream 3 (Wes Craven 2000)
Secreto de sus ojos, El/The Secret in Their Eyes (Juan José Campanella 2009)
Se Eu Fosse Vôce/If I Were You (Daniel Filho 2006)
Se Eu Fosse Vôce 2/If I Were You 2 (Daniel Filho 2009)
Serra Pelada/Bald Mountain (Heitor Dhalia 2013)
Sexo, pudor y lágrimas/Sex, Shame and Tears (Antonio Serrano 1999)
Shape of Water, The (Guillermo del Toro 2017)
Shrek Forever After (Mike Mitchell 2010)
Si muero antes de despertar/If I die before I wake (Carlos Hugo Christensen 1952)
Sin dejar huella/Without a Trace (María Novaro 2000)
Sin nombre (Cary Fukunaga 2009)
Slumdog Millionaire (Danny Boyle 2008)
Sólo con tu pareja/Love in a Time of Hysteria (Alfonso Cuarón 1991)
Somos lo que hay/We are what we are (Jorge Michel Grau 2010)
Stage Fright (Alfred Hitchcock 1950)
Stellet Licht/Silent Light (Carlos Reygadas 2007)
Stranger Than Paradise (Jim Jarmusch 1984)
Sudor frío/Cold Sweat (Adrián García Bogliano 2010)
Syriana (Stephen Gaghan 2005)
Tan de repente/Suddenly (Diego Lerman 2002)
Tangos, el exilio de Gardel/Tangos, the Exile of Gardel (Fernando Solanas 1985)
Temporada de patos/Duck Season (Fernando Eimbcke 2004)

Tenemos la carne/We are the Flesh (Emiliano Rocha Minter 2016)
Terra en Transe/Land in Anguish (Glauber Rocha 1967)
Terra estrangeira/Foreign Land (Walter Salles and Daniela Thomas 1996)
Tesis/Thesis (Alejandro Amenábar (1996)
Teta asustada, La/The Milk of Sorrow (Claudia Llosa 2009)
Texas Chain Saw Massacre, The (Tobe Hooper 1974)
The Three Burials of Melquiades Estrada (Tommy Lee Jones 2006)
Them! (Gordon Douglas 1954)
Things You Can Tell Just By Looking at Her (Rodrigo García 2000)
Tiempo de valientes/On Probation (Damián Szifrón 2005)
Tieta do Agreste/Tieta (Carlos Diegues 1998)
Todo el poder/Gimmie Power (Fernando Sariñana 2000)
Traffic (Steven Soderbergh 2000)
Trainspotting (Danny Boyle 1996)
T2 Trainspotting (Danny Boyle 2017)
Trampa, La/The Trap (Carlos Hugo Christensen 1949)
Trance (Danny Boyle 2013)
Trois couleurs: Blue/Three Colours: Blue (Krzysztof Kieslowski 1993)
Trois couleurs: Blanc/Three Colours White (Krzysztof Kieslowski 1994)
Trois couleurs: Rouge/Three Colours Red (Krzysztof Kieslowski 1994)
Tropa de Elite/Elite Squad (José Padilha 2007)
Tropa de Elite 2: O Inimigo Agora é Outro/Elite Squad: The Enemy Within (José Padilha 2010)
Two-Lane Blacktop (Monte Hellman 1971)
Usual Suspects, The (David Fincher 1995)
V for Vendetta (James McTeigue 2005)
Vampiro y el sexo, El/Sex and the Vampire (Rene Cardona 1969)
Vai que Cola/What if Something Happens (César Rodrigues 2015)
Ventanas al mar/Windows on the Sea (Jesús Mario Lozano 2012)
Viaje, El/The Voyage (Fernando Solanas 1992)
Vida en Falcon/Life in a Falcon (Jorge Gaggero 2004)
Videodrome (David Cronenberg 1983)
Vicky Cristina Barcelona (Woody Allen 2008)
Viva Cuba (Juan Carlos Cremata 2005)
Voces Inocentes (Luis Mandoki 2004)
Volcano (Ben Fogg 2007)
Walk in the Clouds, A (Alfonso Arau 1995)
Wall Street: Money never Sleeps (Oliver Stone, 2010)
War of the Worlds (Stephen Spielberg 2005)
We bought a Zoo (Cameron Crowe 2011)
Weiße Band, Das/The White Ribbon (Michael Haneke 2009)
When a Man Loves a Woman (Luis Mandoki 1994)
Whiskey (Juan Pablo Rebella and Pablo Stoll 2004)
Wrath of the Titans (Jonathan Liebesman 2012)
X-Men: Apocalypse (Bryan Singer 2016)
Xala (Ousmane Sembene 1976)
Xingu (Cao Hamburger 2012)
Yawar Malku/Blood of the Condor (Jorge Sanjinés 1969)
Y tu mamá también/And your mother too (Alfonso Cuarón 2001)
Zama (Lucrecia Martel 2017)
Zoom (Pedro Morelli 2015)

BIBLIOGRAPHY

Acevedo-Muñoz, E. (2008) 'Horror of Allegory: *The Others* and its Contexts', in J. Beck and V. Rodríguez Ortega (eds), *Contemporary Spanish Cinema and Genre*, Manchester: Manchester University Press, 202–218.

Acevedo-Muñoz, E. (2004) 'Sex, Class and Mexico in Alfonso Cuarón's *Y tu mamá también*', *Film and History*, 34.1, 39–48.

Aguilar, G. (2011) *New Argentine Cinema: Other Worlds*, London and New York: Palgrave Macmillan.

Aguilar, G. (2006) *Otros mundos: Un ensayo sobre el nuevo cine argentino*, Buenos Aires: Santiago Arcos Editor.

Alemán, G. (2009) 'Epilogue. At the margin of the margins: contemporary Ecuadorian exploitation cinema and the local pirate market', in V. Ruétalo and D. Tierney (eds), *Latsploitation, Exploitation Cinemas and Latin America*, London and New York: Routledge, 261–274.

Almodóvar, P. (2010) 'Cultura contra impunidad', YouTube, <http://www.youtube.com/watch?v=Xf8oZKEejD8> (last accessed 15 March 2012).

Alonso, L. (2014) 'Por una Cinemateca Nacional', 'Crisis del cine de autor industrial en la Argentina: Desafíos y propuestas', *Otros Cines*, 16 December, <http://www.otros-cines.com/nota?idnota=9282&idsubseccion=157> (last accessed 29 November 2016).

Alvaray, L. (2013) 'Hybridity and Genre in Transnational Latin American Cinemas', *Transnational Cinemas*, 4.1, 67–87.

Alvaray, L. (2011) 'Are we global yet? New challenges to defining Latin American Cinema', *Studies in Hispanic Cinema*, 8.1, 69–86.

Alvaray, L. (2008) 'National, Regional, and Global: New Waves of Latin American Cinema', *Cinema Journal*, 47.3, 48–65.

Amago, S. (2010) 'Ethics, Aesthetics, and the Future in Alfonso Cuarón's *Children of Men*', *Discourse*, 32.2, 212–235.

Amaya, H. and L. Senio Blair (2008) 'Bridges between the divide: The Female body in *Y tu mamá también* and *Machuca*', *Studies in Hispanic Cinemas*, 4.1, 47–62.

Ames Ramello, N. (2017) interview with the author.

Ames Ramello, N. (2012) 'Analysis of the Representation of the logic of race in *Madeinusa* (Claudia Llosa 2006)', unpublished essay.

ANCINE, (2016) *Anuário Estatístico do Cinema Brasileira*, <https://oca.ancine.gov.br/sites/default/files/publicacoes/pdf/anuario_2015.pdf> (last accessed 9 September 2017).

ANCINE, (2015) *Anuário Estatístico do Cinema Brasileira*, <http://www.ancine.gov.br> (last accessed 28 August 2016).

ANCINE (2010) 'Informe de Acompanhamento de Mercado', <http://www.ancine.gov.br/media/SAM/Informes/2010/Informe_Anual_2010.pdf> (last accessed 12 September 2012).

Andermann, J. and A. Fernández Bravo (eds) (2013) 'Introduction', *New Brazilian and Argentine cinema: Reality Effects*, London and New York: Palgrave Macmillan, 1–9.

Andermann, J. (2011) *New Argentine Cinema*, London and New York: I. B. Tauris.

Andrés Del Pozo, M. N. (2010) 'Dealing with an Uncomfortable Relative: The Silent Mass Graves in *The Orphanage*', More Than Thought, Fall, 1–14.

Andrew, D. (2006) 'An Atlas of World Cinema', in S. Dennison and S. H. Lim (eds), *Remapping World Cinema: Identity, Culture and Politics in Film*, London: Wallflower Press, 19–29.

Andrew, G. (2004) 'Walter Salles' Interviewed at the National Film Theatre, 26 August, <http://www.theguardian.com/film/2004/aug/26/features> (last accessed 12 October 2014).

Anon. (2017) 'Hubo más público para el cine nacional en el ejercicio 2016' *Diario de Cultura* 7 April No 2727, <http://www.diariodecultura.com.ar/estadisticas-culturales/hubo-mas-publico-para-cine-nacional-en-el-ejercicio-2016/> (last accessed 14 September 2017).

Anon. (2016a) '"El Renacido", la más taquillera de Iñárritu en México', *La Jornada* Espectáculos, 25 January, <http://www.jornada.unam.mx/ultimas/2016/01/25/el-renacido-la-mas-taquillera-de-inarritu-en-mexico-6723.html> (last accessed 27 June 2016).

Anon. (2016b) 'Se presentó el anuario estadístico de la INCAA', <http://www.incaa.gob.ar/novedades/se-presento-el-anuario-del-incaa-2015> (last accessed 29 November 2016).

Anon. (2015) 'Ibermedia mueve fichas y depura recursos', *El telégrafo*, 30 July, <http://www.telegrafo.com.ec/cultura1/item/ibermedia-mueve-fichas-y-depura-recursos.html> (last accessed 12 October 2014).

Anon. (2008) 'Un novio para mi mujer, imparable en la taquilla', *La Nación*, 23 September, <http://www.lanacion.com.ar/1052522-un-novio-para-mi-mujer-imparable-en-la-taquilla> (last accessed 29 November 2016).

Anon. (2007) 'Instituto Mexicano de Cinematografía: Informe de Labores 2007', <http://www.imcine.gov.mx> (last accessed 20 October 2011).

Anon. (2006) 'Children of Men: Brilliant but Expensive', *The Hollywood Reporter*, <http://reporter.blogs.com/risky/2006/11/children_of_men.html> (last accessed 17 October, 2009).

Appadurai, A. (1996) *Modernity at Large: Cultural Dimensions of Globalization*, Minneapolis: University of Minnesota Press.

Archibald, D. (2004) 'Reframing the Past: Representations of the Spanish Civil War', in A. Lázaro-Reboll and A. Willis (eds), *Popular Spanish Cinema*, Manchester: Manchester University Press, 76–91.

Avelar, I. (2001) 'Five Theses on Torture', *Journal of Latin American Cultural Studies*, 10.3, 253–271.

Ayala Blanco, J. (2014) *El cine actual, confines temáticos*, Mexico D. F.: Centro Universitario de Estudios Cinematográficos, Universidad Nacional Autonoma de Mexico.

Bacon, S. (2014) '"This Is Something New ... or – Something Very, Very Old": The Strain Trilogy in Context', in A. Davies, D. Shaw and D. Tierney (eds), *The Transnational Fantasies of Guillermo del Toro*, London and New York: Palgrave Macmillan, 63–82.

Baer, H. and R. Long (2004) 'Transnational Cinema and the Mexican State in Alfonso Cuarón's *Y tu mamá también*', *South Central Review*, 21.3, 150–168.

Barrow, S. (2013) 'New configurations for Peruvian cinema: The rising star of Claudia Llosa', *Transnational Cinemas*, 4.2, 197–215.

Barrow, S. and S. Dennison (eds), (2013) 'Latin American Cinema Today: Reframing the National', *Transnational Cinemas*, 4.2, 143–145.

Batlle, D. (2014) 'Introducción: Cifras y estado de situación', 'Crisis del cine de autor industrial en la Argentina: Desafíos y propuestas', *Otros Cines*, 16 December <http://www.otroscines.com/nota-9279-introduccion-cifras-y-estado-de-situacion> (last accessed 29 November 2016).

Batlle, D. (2009a) '¿Valió la pena hacer Ventana Sur?', *Otros Cines*, December 8, <http://www.otroscines.com/nota?idnota=3649> (last accessed 30 November 2016).

Batlle, D. (2009b) '*El secreto de sus ojos*, de Juan José Campanella: De cómo casi me gustó de una película de Campanella' *Otros Cines*, <http://www.otroscines.com/nota?idnota=3106> (last accessed 10 December 2016).

Batlle, D. (2008a) 'Un novio para mi mujer, de Juan Taratuto', *Otros Cines*, <http://www.otroscines.com/nota?idnota=1777> (last accessed 30 November 2016).

Batlle, D. (2008b) 'Reflexiones sobre el presente y el futuro del cine: Leonardo Favio, otra víctima del Mercado (y de los errores)', *Otros Cines*, <http://www.otroscines.com/nota?idnota=1602> (last accessed 30 November 2016).

Bazin, A. (2005) 'The Evolution of the Language of Cinema', *What is Cinema?* Trans. H. Gray, Berkeley and Los Angeles: University of California Press, 23–41.

Beaty, B. (2011) 'In Focus: Comic Studies Fifty Years after Film Studies: Introduction', *Cinema Journal*, 50.3, 106–110.

Bedoya, R. (2011) 'Páginas del diario de Satán', <http://paginasdeldiariodesatan.blogspot.co.uk/2011/05/el-fin-de-la-autonomia-de-conacine.html> (last accessed 20 May 2012).

Begin, P. (2015) 'Empathy and Sinophobia: Depicting Chinese Migration in *Biutiful* (Iñárritu, 2010)', *Transnational Cinemas*, 6.1, 1–16.

Behlil, M. (2016) *Hollywood is Everywhere: Global Directors in the Blockbuster Era*, Amsterdam: Amsterdam University Press.

Benjamin, B. (2011) 'Letting Go', *American Cinematographer*, January, 1–3, <http://www.ascmag.com/ac_magazine/January2011/Biutiful/page2.php> (last accessed 15 October 2011).

Berg, C. Ramírez (2000) '*El automóvil gris* and the advent of Mexican Classicism', in C. Noriega (ed.) *Visible Nations Latin American Cinema and Video*, Minneapolis: Minnesota University Press, 3–32.

Bermúdez, N. (2011) *Latin American Cinemas Local Views and Transnational Connections*, Calgary: University of Calgary Press.

Bernades, H., D. Lerer and S. Wolf, (2002) 'From industry to independent cinema: are there "industry auteurs"?', *New Argentine Cinema: Themes, Auteurs and Trends of Innovation*, Buenos Aires: FIPRESCI/Ediciones Tatanka, 2002, 119–132.

Bentes, I. (2013) 'Global Periphery: Aeshetic and Cultural Margins in Brazilian Audiovisual Forms' in J. Andermann and A. Fernandez Bravo (eds), *New Brazilian and Argentine cinema: Reality Effects*, London and New York: Palgrave Macmillan, 103–117.

Bentes, I. (2003) 'The *Sertão* and the *Favela* in Contemporary Brazilian Film', in L. Nagib (ed.), *The New Brazilian Cinema*, London and New York: I. B. Tauris, 121–137.

Binelli, M. (2016) 'Alejandro G. Iñárritu: Hollywood's King of Pain. How the director of "The Revenant" pushed his stars and crew to the edge of sanity – and created a modern epic', *Rolling Stone*, February 17, <http://www.rollingstone.com/movies/features/alejandro-g-inarritu-hollywoods-king-of-pain-20160217> (last accessed 28 February 2016).

Biskind, P. (2000) *Seeing is Believing: How Hollywood Taught Us to Stop Worrying and Learn to Love the Fifties*, New York: Henry Holt.

Blasini, G. (2016) '*Recorriendo las Americas*: Cars, Roads and Latin American Cinema', in V. Gariboto and J. Pérez (eds), *The Latin American Road Movie*, London and New York: Palgrave Macmillan, 97–120.

Bloom, H. (2005) *José Saramago*, Philadelphia: Chelsea House Publishers.

Bonfil, C. (2007) '¿Hay cine mexicano después del Oscar?', *La Jornada*, 28 January, <http://www.jornada.unam.mx/2007/01/28/index.php?section=espectaculos&article=a09a1esp> (last accessed 15 February 2007).

Bordwell, D. (2002a) 'The Art Cinema as Mode of Film Practice', in C. Fowler (ed.), *The European Cinema Reader*, London: Routledge, 94–102.

Bordwell, D. (2002b) 'Intensified Continuity: Visual Style in Contemporary American Film', *Film Quarterly*, 55.3, 16–28.

Bordwell, D. (1985) *Narration in the Fiction Film*, Madison: University of Wisconsin Press.

Bosley, R. K. (2006) 'Forging Connections', *American Cinematographer*, 87: 11, <http://www.theasc.com/ac_magazine/November2006/Babel/page1.php> (last accessed 7 October 2007).

Boyle, K. (2009) '*Children of Men* and *I am Legend*: the disaster-capitalism complex hits Hollywood', *Jump Cut*, 51, <http://www.ejumpcut.org/archive/jc51.2009/ChildrenMenLegend/text.html> (last accessed 12 October 2012).

Bradshaw, P. (2010) Review, 'The Secret in Their Eyes', *The Guardian*, 12 August, <https://www.theguardian.com/film/2010/aug/12/the-secret-in-their-eyes-review> (last accessed at 20 December 2016).

Bradshaw, P. (2008) '*Blindness*', *The Guardian*, 15 May, <http://www.guardian.co.uk/film/2008/may/15/cannesfilmfestival.france> (last accessed 11 October 2008).

Bradshaw, P. (2007) Review, '*Babel*' *The Guardian*, 18 January, <https://www.theguardian.com/film/2007/jan/19/drama.thriller> (last accessed 20 January 2015).

Brandellero, S. (ed.) (2013) *The Brazilian Road Movie: Journeys of Self Discovery*, University of Wales Press: Cardiff.

Brontë, C. (2006 [1847]) *Jane Eyre*, London and New York: Penguin Classics.

Brooks, P. (1991) 'The Melodramatic Imagination', in M. Landy (ed.), *Imitations of Life: A Reader on Film and Television Melodrama*, Detroit: Wayne State University Press, 50–67.

Brooks, X. (2002) 'First Steps in Latin', *The Guardian*, 19 July, <http://www.guardian.co.uk/film/2002/jul/19/artsfeatures> (last accessed 28 November 2008).

Bueno, E. (2007) '"Motorcycle Diaries": the myth of Che Guevara in the twenty-first century', *Confluencia*, 23.1, 107–114.

Butcher, P. (2016) email correspondence with the author, October.

Butcher, P. (2006) 'The Re-birth of Brazilian Cinema', *Cinemas of the South* (FIPRESCI) <http://controling.fipresci.org/world_cinema/south/south_english_brazilian_cinema_contemporary.htm> (last accessed 20 January 2010).

Caballero, J. (2011) 'Menos películas, mayor calidad y más autocrítica, pide Alejandro Ramírez', *La Jornada*, Espectáculos, 21 October, <http://www.jornada.unam. mx/2011/10/21/opinion/a10n1esp> (last accessed 15 July 2016).

Caine, J. (2006) *The Constant Gardener: The Shooting Script*, New York: Northam.

Cajueiro, M. (2016), 'Fernando Meirelles' O2Filmes puts "Suria" Into Production', <http://variety.com/2016/film/global/rio-content-market-fernando-meirelles-o2filmes-suria-1201729181/> (last accessed 20 September 2016).

Calhoun, J. (2003) 'Heartbreak and Loss', *American Cinematographer*, 84: 12, <http:// www.theasc.com/magazine/dec03/cover/index.html> (last accessed 15 December 2007).

Campos, M. (2013) 'La América Latina de "Cine en Construcción": Implicaciones del apoyo económico de los festivales internacionales', *Archivos de la Filmoteca*, 71, 13–26.

Campos, M. (2012) 'El circuito de financiación de los cines latinoamericanos'/'Le circuit de financement des cinémas latino-américains', *Cinémas d'amerique latine*, 20, 172–180.

Cantú, M. J. (2016) 'Van a Cannes con apoyo de Cuarón e Iñárritu', *Milenio*, 10 January, <http://www.milenio.com/hey/cine/Tenemos_la_carne_Cannes-Cuaron_ Inarritu-Emiliano_Rocha_Tenemos_la_carne-cine_mexicano_0_731926813.html> (last accessed 22 July 2016).

Carneiro, G. (2012) 'Os Desafios do Cinema Brasileiro para se Chegar ao Público', *Revista de Cinema*, 29 August, http://revistadecinema.uol.com.br/index.php/2012/08/ os-desafios-do-cinema-brasileiro-para-chegar-ao-publico/ (last accessed October 2012).

Carroll, L. (1992 [1865]) *Alice in Wonderland*, New York: Norton.

Carter, M. (2014) *Myth of the Western: New Perspectives on Hollywood's Frontier Narratives*, Edinburgh: Edinburgh University Press.

Carver, R. (1981) *What We Talk About When We Talk About Love*, New York: Vintage.

Cassady, C. (2007) *Off the Road: Twenty years with Cassady, Kerouac and Ginsberg*, London: Black Spring Press.

Chan, F. and V. Vitali (2010) 'Revisiting the "realism" of the cosmetics of hunger: *Cidade de Deus* and *Ônibus 174*', *New Cinemas: Journal of Contemporary Film*, 8.1, 15–30.

Chang, J. (2010) 'Biutiful', *Variety*, 17 May, <http://www.variety.com/review/ VE1117942786/> (last accessed 20 November 2012).

Charters, A. (1991) 'Introduction' *On the Road*, London: Penguin, vii–xxix.

Chauca, E. (2015) 'Comunidades imaginadas imposibles: derechos humanos y neo-liberalismo en el cine y la literatura latinoamericana', *Alternativas* 5, 1–23, <http:// alternativas.osu.edu> (last accessed 9 September).

Choi, D. (2013) 'In Praise of Difficulty: Notes on Realism and Narration in Contemporary Argentine Cinema', in J. Andermann and A. Fernández Bravo (eds), *New Argentine and Brazilian Cinema: Reality Effects*, London and New York: Palgrave Macmillan, 173–184.

Clover, C. (1992) *Men, Women and Chainsaws: Gender in the Modern Horror Film* Princeton, NJ: Princeton University Press.

Cohan, S. and I. R. Hark (eds), (1997) *The Road Movie Book*, London and New York: Routledge.

Cohen, D. S and D. McNary (2013) 'Alfonso Cuarón Returns to the Big Screen After Seven Years', *Variety*, 3 September, <http://variety.com/2013/film/news/alfonso-cuaron-returns-to-the-bigscreen-after-seven-years-with-gravity-1200596518/> (last accessed 20 January 2017).

Colás, S. (1994) *Postmodernity in Latin America: the Argentine Paradigm*, Durham: Duke University Press.

Cole, T. (2012) 'The White Savior Industrial Complex', *The Atlantic*, 21 March, <http://www.theatlantic.com/international/archive/2012/03/the-white-savior-industrial-complex/254843/> (last accessed 11 March 2013).

Colina, E. and D. Díaz Torres, (1972) 'Ideología del Melodrama en el Viejo Cine Latinoamericano', *Cine Cubano*, 74, 14–26.

Copertari, G. (2009) *Desintegración y justicia en el cine argentino contemporáneo*, London and New York: Tamesis.

Copertari, G. (2005) '*Nine Queens*: A Dark Day of Simulation and Justice', *Journal of Latin American Cultural Studies*, 14.3, 279–293.

Corrigan, T. (1991) *A Cinema Without Walls: Movies and Culture After Vietnam*, New Brunswick, NJ: Rutgers University Press.

Creed, B. (1999) 'Horror and the Monstrous Feminine: An Imaginary Abjection', in S. Thornham, (ed.), *Feminist Film Theory*, New York: New York University Press, 251–266.

Cuarón, A. (2006) *The Possibility of Hope* DVD Extra, *Children of Men*, Universal Pictures.

Cunnel, H. (2007) 'Fast This Time: Jack Kerouac and the Writing of *On the Road*', *On the Road: The Original Scroll*, London: Penguin, 1–52.

Davies, A., D. Shaw and D. Tierney (2014) *The Transnational Fantasies of Guillermo del Toro*, London and New York: Palgrave.

Davies, A. (2008) 'Guillermo del Toro's *Cronos*: The Vampire as Embodied Heterotopia', *Quarterly Review of Film and Video*, 25.5, 398–403.

Davies, A. (2006) 'The Beautiful and the Monstrous Masculine: The Male Body and Horror in *El espinazo del diablo* (Guillermo del Toro 2001)', *Studies in Hispanic Cinemas*, 3.3, 135–147.

De la Garza, A. (2009) 'Realism and National Identity in *Y tu mamá también*: An Audience Perspective', in L. Nagib and C. Mello (eds.), *Realism and the Audiovisual Media*, London and New York: Palgrave Macmillan, 108–118.

De la Mora, S. (2006) *Cinemachismo: Masculinities and Sexuality in Mexican Film*, Austin: University of Texas Press.

De la Mora, S. (2003) 'A Star is Born: Neo-liberal Mexican Cinema Rising', Catalogue: 10th San Diego Latino Film Festival, March 13–23, 9–10.

Deleyto, C. and G. López (2012) 'Catalan Beauty and the Transnational Beast: Barcelona on the Screen', *Transnational Cinemas*, 3.2, 157–175.

Deleyto, C. and M. del Mar Azcona (2010) *Alejandro González Iñárritu*, Champaign: University of Illinois Press.

Del Toro, G. (2002) 'Director's Commentary', *El espinazo del diablo*, DVD Sony Pictures Home Entertainment.

Del Toro, G. (2008) 'How I Made *Hellboy* in My Image', *The Observer*, Film Quarterly, July 27, 38–41.

De Marco, C. (2016) 'Italy joins Ibermedia', 25 October, <http://cineuropa.org/nw.aspx?t=newsdetail&l=en&did=319019> (last accessed 20 December 2016).

Denby, J. (2007) 'The New Disorder', *New Yorker*, March 5, <http://www.newyorker.com/arts/critics/atlarge/2007/03/05/070305crat_atlarge_denby?currentPage=all> (last accessed 12 August 2010).

Dennison, S. (2016) 'Rio's green Olympic Games get underway with low budget, high-spirited opening ceremony', *The Conversation*, <http://theconversation.com/rios-green-olympic-games-get-underway-with-low-budget-high-spirited-opening-ceremony-63620> (last accessed 16 August 2016).

Dennison, S. (ed.) (2013) *Contemporary Hispanic Cinema: Interrogating the Transnational in Spanish and Latin American Film*, London: Tamesis.

De Pablos, E. (2015) 'Brazil launches New Latin American Co-Production Fund', *Variety*, 22 May, <http://variety.com/2015/film/spotlight/cannes-brazil-ancine-manoel-rangel-incaa-1201506209/> (last accessed 20 September 2016).

D'Espósito, L. M. (2014) 'Los cuatro elementos del cine argentino' *El Amante Cine* 266 <http://www.elamante.com/criticas/los-cuatro-elementos-del-cine-argentino/> (last accessed 15 September 2017).

Deveny, T. (2012) *Migration in Contemporary Hispanic Cinema*, London: Scarecrow Press.

Diestro-Dópido, M. (2015) 'Ghost Hunter', *Sight & Sound*, 25.11, 22–26.

Diestro-Dópido, M. (2011) 'The new new Argentine Cinema', The *S&S* blog, <http://old.bfi.org.uk/sightandsound/newsandviews/festivals/blog/lff-2011-11-02-new-new-argentine-cinema.php> (last accessed 15 September 2017).

Dixon, W. W. (2000) 'Fighting and Violence and Everything, That's Always Cool', in (ed.) *Film Genre 2000: New Critical Essays*, Albany: State University of New York Press, 125–143.

D'Lugo, M. (2003a) 'Authorship, globalization, and the new identity of Latin American cinema: From the Mexican "ranchera" to Argentinian "exile"', in W. Dissanayake and A. Guneratne (eds), *Rethinking Third Cinema*, London and New York: Routledge, 103–125.

D'Lugo, M. (2003b) '*Amores perros/Love's a Bitch*', in A. Elena and M. Díaz López (eds) *The Cinema of Latin America*, London: Wallflower Press, 221–229.

Donoghue, C. Brannon (2014a) 'Sony and Local-Language Productions: How Conglomerate Hollywood Is Changing Localization Strategies and Its Approach to the Global Film Market', *Cinema Journal*, 53.4, 3–27.

Donoghue, C. Brannon (2014b) 'The Rise of the Brazilian Blockbuster: How Ideas of Scale, Exceptionality, and Neoliberal Logic Shape A Booming Cinema', *Media, Culture & Society*, 36.4, 537–550.

Donoghue, C. Brannon (2011) 'Globo Filmes, Sony, and Franchise Film-making: Transnational Industry in the Brazilian *Pós-retomada*', in C. Rêgo and C. Rocha (eds), *New Trends in Argentine and Brazilian Cinema*, Bristol: Intellect, 51–66.

Durbin, K. (2002) 'Film; Comedy of a Sexual Provocateur', *New York Times*, 17 March, <http://www.nytimes.com/2002/03/17/movies/film-comedy-of-a-sexual-provocateur.html?src=pm> (last accessed 1 July 2011).

Ďurovičová, N. (2010) 'Preface', in N. Ďurovičová and K. Newman (eds), *World Cinemas: Transnational Perspectives*, New York and London: Routledge, ix–xv.

Dyer, R. (1992) 'Entertainment and Utopia', *Only Entertainment*, London and New York: Routledge, 17–34.

Ebert, R. (2005) '*The Constant Gardener*', <http://www.rogerebert.com/reviews/the-constant-gardener-2005> (last accessed 15 February 2010).

Elena, A. (2008) 'La *nueva* era del cine mexicano: Virtudes y paradojas', *Afuera. Estudios de crítica cultural*, 5, 1–12, <www.revistaafuera.com/NumAnteriores/print.php?page=05.Articulos. Elena.htm> (last accessed 20 September 2011 [site no longer available]).

Eliot, T. S. (2016[1922]) *The Waste Land and Other Poems*, London: Wisehouse Classics.

Elsaesser, T. (1991) 'Tales of Sound and Fury: Observations on the Family Melodrama', in M. Landy (ed.) *Imitations of Life: A Reader on Film and TV Melodrama*, Detroit: Wayne State University Press, 68–91.

Ezra, E. and T. Rowden (2006) 'General Introduction: What is Transnational Cinema?' *Transnational Cinema: The Film Reader*, London and New York: Routledge, 1–11.

Falicov, T. (2014) 'Spotlight on the Argentine Film Industry', in B. Urraca and G. Kramer, (eds), *Directory of World Cinema: Argentina*, London: Intellect, 18–21.

Falicov, T. (2010) 'Migrating from South to North: the Role of the Film Festival in Funding and Shaping Global South Film and Video', in G. Elmer, C. Davis, J. Marchessault and J. McCullough, (eds), *Locating Migrating Media*, Lanham, MD: Lexington Books, 3–22.

Falicov, T. (2008) 'Latin America: How Mexico and Argentina Cope and Cooperate with the Behemoth of the North', in P. McDonald and J. Wasko (eds), *The Contemporary Hollywood Film Industry*, Oxford: Wiley-Blackwell, 264–275.

Falicov, T. (2007a) 'Programa Ibermedia and the Cultural Politics of Constructing an Ibero-American Space', *Spectator*, 27.2, 21–30.

Falicov, T. (2007b) *The Cinematic Tango: Contemporary Argentine Film*, London: Wallflower Press.

Falicov, T. (2000) 'Argentina's Blockbuster Movies and the politics of culture under neoliberalism, 1989–1998', *Media, Culture and Society* 22.3, 327–342.

Fein, S. (1998) 'Transnationalization and Cultural Collaboration: Mexican Film Propaganda during World War II', *Studies in Popular Latin American Culture*, 17, 105–128.

Filme B. (2017) Evolução do Mercado: '*Ranking* nacional 2000–2016 (público) Top 20', <http://www.filmeb.com.br/estatisticas/evolucao-do-mercado> (last accessed 12 September 2017).

Filme B. (2016a) Estatísticos: 'Lançamentos', <http://www.filmeb.com.br/estatisticas> (last accessed 12 September 2016).

Filme B. (2016b) Evolução do Mercado: 'Evolução do market share nacional', <http://www.filmeb.com.br/estatisticas/evolucao-do-mercado> (last accessed 12 September 2016).

Finnegan, N. (2007) 'So What's Mexico Really Like? Framing the Local, Negotiating the Global in Alfonso Cuarón's *Y tu mamá también*', in D. Shaw (ed.), *Contemporary Latin American Cinema: Breaking into the Global Market*, New York: Rowman and Littlefield, 29–50.

Flory, D. (2008) *Philosophy, Black Film, Film Noir*, University Park, PA: Penn State University Press.

Fonds Sud (2016) 'Overall Objective' < http://www.filmfrasor.no/sorfond/about> (last accessed 14 October 2016).

Fordham, J. (2007) 'The Human Project', *Cinefex*, 110, 33–44.

Foster, D. W. (2004) 'Motorcycle Diaries', *Chasqui*, 33.2, 192–195.

Fowks, J. (2016) 'Los cinco años de parto del cine peruano: Los cineastas sudamericanos invierten gran parte de su tiempo en la búsqueda de fondos' *El País*, Cultura, 16 August, <http://cultura.elpais.com/cultura/2016/08/14/actualidad/1471193590_409298. html> (last accessed 20 August 2016).

French, P. (2012) '*On the Road* Review', *The Guardian* 14 October, <http://www. theguardian.com/film/2012/oct/14/on-the-road-review> (last accessed 12 November 2013).

Freud, S. (1991 [1900]) *The Interpretation of Dreams*, London: Penguin.

Galt, R. (2011) *Pretty: The Decorative Image in Film*, New York: Columbia University Press.

García Canclini, N. (1997) 'Will there be a Latin American Cinema in the Year 2000? Visual culture in a Postnational Era', in A. M. Stock (ed.), *Framing Latin American Cinema: Contemporary Critical Approaches*, London and Minneapolis: University of Minnesota Press, 246–258.

García Canclini, N. (1995) *Hybrid Cultures: Strategies for Entering and Leaving Modernity*, translated by C. L. Chiappari and S. L. López, Minneapolis: University of Minnesota Press.

García Espinosa, J. (1997 [1969]) 'For an Imperfect Cinema', in M. Martin (ed.), *New Latin American Cinema* Vol. 1, Detroit: Wayne State University Press, 71–82.

García Tsao, L. (2001) 'Sólo con tu pajero', *La Jornada*, 22 June, <http://www.jornada.unam.mx/2001/06/22/15an1esp.html> (last accessed 27 June 2011).

Gariboto, V. and J. Pérez (eds) (2016) *The Latin American Road Movie*, London and New York: Palgrave Macmillan.

Garavelli, C. (2011) 'Post-crisis Argentina films: De-localizing daily life through the lens of Jorge Gaggero', *Studies in Hispanic Cinemas*, 7.1, 35–46.

Gelb, D., F. Meirelles and P. Morreli (2008) 'A vision of *Blindness*', Making of documentary, Rhombus Media, O2Filmes and Bee Vine Pictures.

Getino, O. (2007) 'Los desafíos de la industria del cine en América Latina y el Caribe', *Zer*, 22, 167–182.

Getino, O. and F. Solanas ([1969] 1997) 'Towards a Third Cinema', in M. Martin (ed.), *New Latin American Cinema*, Vol. 1, Detroit: Wayne State University Press, 33–58.

Gilbey, R. (2009) 'The Truth Behind a Revolutionary Road Movie', *The Sunday Times*, 18 October, 10–11.

Gilchrist, T. (2006) 'Interview: Alejandro González Iñárritu', <http://uk.movies.ign.com/articles/742/742071p2.html> (last accessed 21 December 2007).

Gledhill, C. (1987) 'The Melodramatic Field: An Investigation,' in C. Gledhill (ed.), *Home is Where The Heart Is: Studies in Melodrama and the Women's Film*, London: British Film Institute, 5–39.

González Iñárritu, A. (2011) 'Flip Notes', *Biutiful*, Focus Features International/Roadside.

Granado, A. (2008) *Con el Che por sudamérica*, Buenos Aires: Editorial Marea.

Grant, C. (2008) 'Auteur Machines? Auteurism and the DVD', in J. Bennet and T. Brown (eds), *Film and Television After DVD*, London: Routledge, 101–115.

Grant, C. (2000) 'www.auteur.com?' *Screen*, 41.1, 101–108.

Guevara, E. (2003 [1993]) *Motorcycle Diaries: Notes on a Latin American Journey*, Minneapolis: Ocean Press.

Gundermann, C. (2005) 'The Stark Gaze of the New Argentine Cinema: Restoring Strangeness to the Object in the Perverse Age of Commodity Fetishism', *Journal of Latin American Cultural Studies*, 14.3, 241–261.

Gutiérrez, C. (2013) '*Asu Mare!* Breaks All Time Records in Peruvian History', *CinemaTropical*, 4 May, <http://www.cinematropical.com/Cinema-Tropical/iasu-mare-breaks-all-time-records-in-peruvian-history.html> (last accessed 4 May 2014).

Haddu, M. (2007) *Contemporary Mexican Cinema, 1989–1999: History, Space and Identity*, Lampeter: Edward Mellen Press.

Hark, I. R. (1997) 'Fear of Flying: Yuppie critique and the buddy-road movie in the 1980s', in I. R. Hark and S. Cohan (eds), *The Road Movie Book*, London: Routledge, 204–229.

Hart, S. (2004) 'Introduction', *Contemporary Latin American Cinema*, London: Tamesis.

Hewitt, C. (2010) 'Del Toro Won't Direct The Hobbit' *Empire*, May 31, <http://www.empireonline.com/movies/news/del-toro-direct-hobbit/> (last accessed 20 March 2014).

Higbee, W. and S. Hwee Lim, (2010) 'Concepts of transnational cinema: towards a critical transnationalism in film studies', *Transnational Cinemas* 1.1, 7–21.

Higson, A. (2011) *Film England: Culturally English Filmmaking Since the 1990s*, London and New York: I. B. Tauris.

Higson, A. (2000) 'The Limiting Imagination of National Cinema', in M. Hjort and S. MacKenzie (eds), *Cinema and Nation*, London and New York: Routledge, 63–74.

Higson, A. (1989) 'The Concept of a National Cinema', *Screen*, 30.4, 36–46.

Hind, E. (2004) 'Post-NAFTA Mexican Cinema, 1998–2002', *Studies in Latin American Popular Culture* 23, 95–111.

Hinojosa, M. (2006) 'Making of *Children of Men*', *Children of Men* DVD, Universal Pictures.

Hirsch, F. (1981) *The Dark Side of Film Noir*, Cambridge, MA: Da Capo Press.

Hjort, M. (2010) 'On the Plurality of Cinematic Transnationalism', *World Cinemas, Transnational Perspectives* (eds), N. Ďurovičová and K. Newman, New York and London: Routledge, 12–33.

Hoad, P. (2012a) 'Foreign-Language Oscar: why border control restricts the selection process', 21 February, *The Guardian*, filmblog, <http://www.guardian.co.uk/film/filmblog/2012/feb/21/foreign-language-oscar-selection-process> (last accessed 20 November 2012).

Hoad, P. (2012b) 'Whatever Happened to Non-Linear Films?', *The Guardian*, 21 March, <http://www.guardian.co.uk/film/2012/mar/21/non-linear-film-narrative-con traband> (last accessed 20 November 2012).

Hoberman, J. (2013) 'Drowning in the Digital Abyss', <http://www.nybooks.com/blogs/nyrblog/2013/oct/11/gravity-drowning-digital-abyss/> (last accessed 15 August 2016).

Hoefert de Turégano, T. (2004) 'The International Politics of Cinematic Coproduction: Spanish Policy in Latin America', *Film & History: An Interdisciplinary Journal of Film and Television Studies*, 34.2, 15–24.

Hopewell, J. (2016) 'Argentina Approves $61 Million Promotion Plan for Cinema', *Variety*, 2 October, < http://variety.com/2016/film/global/argentina-approves-61-million-promotion-plan-cinema-1201875941/> (last accessed 20 December 2016).

Hopewell, J. (2014) 'Ventana Sur Market Works to Fuel Biz in Latin America, Europe', *Variety*, 30 November, <http://variety.com/2014/biz/global/argentinas-ventana-sur-market-works-to-fuel-indie-biz-in-latin-america-europe-1201361516/> (last accessed 3 November 2015).

Hopewell, J. (2013) 'Spain reaches out for Amigos to Partner in Film production', *Variety*, <http://variety.com/2013/film/global/spain-looks-looks-partners-in-film-pro duction-1200391619/> (last accessed 3 November 2015).

Hopewell, J. (2012) 'Spain to overhaul incentive system', *Variety*, 5 November, <http://variety.com/2012/film/news/spain-to-overhaul-incentive-system-1118061722/> (last accessed 8 November 2012).

Hopewell, J. (2010) 'Studio Canal, VideoFilmes team on two', *Variety*, Feb 10 <http://variety.com/2010/film/markets-festivals/studiocanal-videofilmes-team-on-two-1118 015002/> (last accessed 20 October 2016).

Hopewell, J. and L. Barraclough (2014) 'Warner Bros to distribute Wild Tales in France, Spain and Latin America', *Variety*, 12 May, <http://variety.com/2014/film/global/warner-bros-to-distribute-wild-tales-in-france-spain-and-latin-america-12011 78166/> (last accessed 15 December 2016).

Hortiguera H. (2012) 'Perverse Fascinations and Atrocious Acts: An approach to Campanella's *The Secret in Their Eyes*', *Studies in Latin American Popular Culture*, 30, 110–123.

Humphrey, M. and E. Valverde (2016) 'From Private to Public Memory: Transitional Justice and the Revision of Official Memory of the Dirty War in Argentina', in C. Andrews and M. McGuire (eds), *Post-Conflict Literature: Human Rights, Peace, Justice*, London and New York: Routledge, 130–146.

IMCINE (2017) *Anuario Estadístico de Cine Mexicano* <http://www.imcine.gob.mx/cine-mexicano/anuario-estadistico>(last accessed 9 September 2017).

IMCINE (2016) *Anuario Estadístico de Cine Mexicano* <http://www.imcine.gob.mx/cine-mexicano/anuario-estadistico> (last accessed 13 July 2016).

INCAA (2016) *Anuario Estadístico de la Industria Cinematográfica y Audiovisual Argentina*, Buenos Aires: Instituto Nacional de Cine y Artes Audiovisuales, INCAA.

INCAA (2015) *Anuario Estadístico de la Industria Cinematográfica y Audiovisual Argentina*, Buenos Aires: Instituto Nacional de Cine y Artes Audiovisuales, INCAA.

INCAA (2014) *Anuario Estadístico de la Industria Cinematográfica y Audiovisual Argentina*, Buenos Aires: Instituto Nacional de Cine y Artes Audiovisuales, INCAA.

Irwin, R. and M. Ricalde (2013) *Global Mexican Cinema: Its Golden Age*, London: British Film Institute.

Jafaar, A. (2006) 'Border Crossing', *Sight & Sound*, 16(7), 14–16.

James, P. D. (1992) *Children of Men*, London: Faber & Faber.

Jameson, F. (1993) 'The Synoptic Chandler', in J. Copjec (ed.), *Shades of Noir: A Reader*, London and New York: Verso, 33–56.

Jameson, F. (1986) 'Third World Literature in the Era of Multinational Capitalism', *Social Text*, 15, 65–88.

Janin, A. H. (2015) 'Hombres de negro. Masculinidad y *film noir* en *La trampa* (Carlos Hugo Christensen, 1949)', *Imagofagia: Revista de la Asociación Argentina de Estudios de Cine y Audiovisual*, 11, 1–20.

Johnson, R. (2007) 'The Brazilian *Retomada* and Global Hollywood', in G. Lillo and W. Moser (eds), *History and Society: Argentinian and Brazilian Cinema Since the 80s*, Ottowa: Legas, 87–100.

Johnson, R. (2006) 'Post-Cinema Novo Brazilian Cinema' *Traditions in World Cinema*, in L. Badley, R. Barton Palmer and S. J. Schneider (eds), Edinburgh: Edinburgh University Press, 117–129.

Johnson, R. (2005) 'TV Globo, the MPA, and Brazilian Cinema', in S. Dennison and L. Shaw (eds), *Latin American Cinema: Essays on Modernity, Gender and National Identity*, London: McFarland, 11–38.

Kantaris, G. (2000) 'The Repressed Signifier: The Cinema of Alejandro Agresti and Eliseo Subiela', *Identity and Discursive Practice*, F. Domínguez, (ed.), London: Peter Laing Publishers, 157–173.

Kawin, B. (1999) 'The Mummy's Pool', in L. Braudy and M. Cohen (eds), *Film Theory and Criticism: Introductory Readings*, 5th ed., Oxford: Oxford University Press, 679–660.

Keane, S. (2001) *Disaster Movies: The Cinema of Catastrophe*, London: Wallflower Press.

Kercher, D. (2015) *Latin Hitchcock: How Almodóvar, Amenábar, De la Iglesia, Del Toro and Campanella became Notorious*, London: Wallflower Press.

Kermode, M. (2016) '*The Revenant* Review – A Walk on the Wild Side', *The Guardian* 17 January, <https://www.theguardian.com/film/2016/jan/17/the-revenant-review-leonardo-dicaprio-alejandro-gonzalez-inarritu-tom-hardy-domhnall-gleeson> (last accessed 20 January 2016).

Kermode, M. (2006) 'Girl Interrupted', *Sight & Sound*, 16.12, 20–24.

Kerouac, J. (2007) *On the Road: The Original Scroll*, London: Penguin.

Kerouac, J. (1991) *On the Road*, London: Penguin.

Kerr, P. (2010) '*Babel*'s network narrative: packaging a globalized art cinema', *Transnational Cinemas*, 1.1, 37–51.

Kinder, M. (1993) *Blood Cinema: The Reconstruction of National Identity in Spain*, Berkeley: University of California Press.

King, G. (2009) *Indiewood, USA: Where Hollywood Meets in Independent Cinema*, London and New York: I. B. Tauris.

King, G. (2004) 'Weighing Up the Qualities of Independence: *21 Grams* in Focus', *Film Studies: An International Review*, 5, 80–91.

King, J. (2004) 'Cinema in Latin America', in J. King, (ed.) *Cambridge Companion to Latin Modern Latin American Culture*, Cambridge: Cambridge University Press, 282–313.

King, J. (2000) *Magical Reels: A History of Cinema in Latin America*, London: Verso.

Klein, N. (2007) *The Shock Doctrine: The Rise of Disaster Capitalism*, New York: Picador.

Kolker, R. P. (2011) *The Cinema of Loneliness*, Oxford: Oxford University Press.

Kraniauskas, J. (1998) 'Cronos and the Political Economy of Vampirism: Notes on a Historical Constellation', in F. Barker, P. Hulme and M. Iversen (eds), *Cannibalism and the Colonial World*, Cambridge: Cambridge University Press, 142–157.

Krutnik, F. (1991) *In a Lonely Street: Film Noir, Genre, Masculinity*, London and New York: Routledge.

Labanyi, J. (2007) 'Memory and Modernity in Democratic Spain: The Difficulty of Coming to Terms with the Spanish Civil War', *Poetics Today*, 28.1, 89–115.

Laderman, D. (2002) *Driving Visions: Exploring the Road Movie*, Austin: University of Texas Press.

Landy, M. (ed.) (1991) 'Introduction', *Imitations of Life: A Reader on Film and Television Melodrama*, Detroit: Wayne State University Press, 13–30.

Langley, R. (2011) 'American Un-Frontiers: Universality and Apocalypse Blockbusters', </vimeo.com/32288942> (last accessed March 2012).

Lawrenson, E. (2002) 'Interview with Alfonso Cuarón', *Sight & Sound*, 12.4, 19.

Lawrenson, E. (2001) 'Pup Fiction', *Sight & Sound*, 11.5, 28–30.

Lázaro-Reboll, A. (2012) *Spanish Horror Film*, Edinburgh: Edinburgh University Press.

Lázaro-Reboll, A. (2008) ' "Now Playing Everywhere": Spanish Horror Film in the Marketplace', in J. Beck and V. Rodríguez Ortega, (eds), *Contemporary Spanish Cinema and Genre*, Manchester: Manchester University Press, 65–83.

Lázaro-Reboll, A. (2007) 'The Transnational Reception of *El espinazo del diablo* (Guillermo del Toro)', *Hispanic Research Journal*, 8.1, 39–51.

Le Carré, J. (2006) *The Constant Gardener*, London: Sceptre.

Lee, R. L. (2011) 'National Belonging in Juan José Campanella's *Luna de Avellaneda*', in N. Bermúdez (ed.), *Latin American Cinemas: Local Views and Transnational Connections*, Alberta: University of Calgary Press, 25–46.

Lefere, R. and N. Lie, (2016) *Nuevas perspectivas sobre la transnacionalidad del cine hispano*, Leiden: Brill.

Locke, C. (2016) 'Why *City of God*'s Director Took on Tonight's Opening Ceremony', *Wired*, <http://www.wired.com/2016/08/olympics-2016-opening-ceremony-director/> (last accessed 7 August 2016).

Long, R. (2006) 'Sex, Lies and Mariachis', DVD notes, *Sólo con tu pareja*, Criterion Collection.

López, A. M. (2000a) 'Crossing Nations and Genres: Travelling Filmmakers', in C. Noriega, (ed.) *Visible Nations: Latin American Cinema and Video*, Minneapolis: Minnesota University Press, 33–50.

López, A. M. (2000b) 'Early Cinema and Modernity in Latin America', *Cinema Journal*, 40.1, 48–78.

López, A. M. (1998) 'From Hollywood and Back: Dolores Del Rio, A Trans(National) Star', *Studies in Latin American Popular Culture*, 17: 5–32.

López, A. M. (1996) 'Greater Cuba', in A. M. López and C. Noriega (eds), *The Ethnic Eye: Latino Media Arts*, Minneapolis: Minnesota University Press, 3–21.

López, A. M. (1993) 'Tears and Desire: Women and Melodrama in the "Old" Mexican Cinema', in M. Alvarado, J. King and A. López, *Mediating Two Worlds: Cinematic Encounters in the Americas*, London: British Film Institute, 147–164.

López, A. M. (1991) 'The Melodrama in Latin America: films, telenovelas and the currency of a popular form', in M. Landy (ed.), *Imitations of Life: A Reader on Film and Television Melodrama*, Detroit: Wayne State University Press, 596–606.

López, E. E. (2013) 'Jorge Videla, Jailed Argentine Military Leader, Dies at 87', *New York Times*, 17 May, <http://www.nytimes.com/2013/05/18/world/americas/

jorge-rafael-videla-argentina-military-leader-in-dirty-war-dies-at-87.html> (last accessed January 2017).

Losada, M. (2010) '*The Secret in Their Eyes*: Historical Memory, Production Models and the Foreign Film Oscar', *Cineaste*, 36.1, 1–7.

MacLaird, M. (2016) interviewed by the author.

MacLaird, M. (2013a) *Aesthetics and Politics in the Mexican Film Industry*, London and New York: Palgrave Macmillan

MacLaird, M. (2013b) 'Documentaries and celebrities, democracy and impunity: thawing the revolution in 21st-century Mexico', *Social Identities*, 19.3–4, 468–484.

MacLaird, M. (2011) 'Funding and the Auteur: Comparing the Objectives of National, Regional, and International Production Grants', Society for Cinema and Media Studies Annual Conference, March, New Orleans.

MacLaird, M. (2010) '*Y tu mamá también*', in C. Gutiérrez (ed.), *The Ten Best Latin American Films of the Decade*, Bethesda M. D.: Jorge Pinto Books, 47–53.

MacLaird, M. (2008–2009) 'Co-producing IberoAmerican Culture: *Sólo Dios sabe*'s Transcontinental Journey', *Lucero: A Journal of Iberian and Latin American Studies*, 18.19. 51–59.

Mafe, D. A. (2011) '(Mis)Imagining Africa in the New Millennium: *The Constant Gardener* and *Blood Diamond*', *Camera Obscura*, 25.3, 69–99.

Mariátegui, J. C. (2007 [1928]) *7 Ensayos de Interpretación de la Realidad Peruana*, Caracas: Biblioteca Ayacucho.

Martí, J. (1977 [1891]) *Nuestra américa*, Caracas: Biblioteca Ayacucho.

Martín Barbero, J. (1998) *De los medios a las mediaciones: Comunicación, cultura y hegemonia*, Mexico: Ediciones Gili.

Martín Barbero, J. (1995) 'Memory and Form in the Latin American soap-opera', in R. C. Allen (ed.), *To be Continued ... Soap Operas around the World*, London and New York: Routledge, 276–285.

Martin-Jones, D. and M. S. Martínez (2013) 'Uruguay Disappears: Small Cinemas, Control Z Films and the Aesthetics and Politics of Auto-Erasure', *Cinema Journal*, 53.1, 26–51.

Martínez, G. (2008) 'Cinema Law in Latin America: Brazil, Peru and Colombia', *Jump Cut: A Review of Contemporary Media*, 50 <www.ejumpcut.org/archive/jc50.2008/LAfilmLaw/text.html > (last accessed 2 September 2010).

Marx, G. (1990) 'Argentina's President Pardons Leaders of "Dirty War" and Leftists', *Chicago Tribune*, 30 December, <http://articles.chicagotribune.com/1990-12-30/news/9004170832_1_pardoned-two-former-military-presidents-dirty-war> (last accessed 12 December 2016).

Marzon, M. I. (2009) *Cinema e Políticas de Estado da Embrafilme à Ancine*, São Paulo: Escrituras Editora.

Massood, P. (1999) 'An Aesthetic Appropriate to Conditions: *Killer of Sheep*, (Neo) Realism and the Documentary Impulse', *Wide Angle*, 21.4, 20–41.

Matheou, D. (2012) 'The Beat Goes On' *Sight & Sound*, 21.11, 44–47.

Matheou, D. (2010) *New South American Cinema*, London: Faber.

McClennen, S. (2011) 'From the Aesthetics of Hunger to the Cosmetics of Hunger in Brazilian Cinema', *Symploke*, 19.1–2, 95–106.

McGowan, T. (2008) 'The Contingency of Connection: The Path To Politicization in *Babel*', *Discourse*, 30.3, 401–418.

McIntosh, D. (2008) 'Waiting for Hollywood: Canada's Maquila Film Industry', *Canadian Dimensions*, 29 October, <https://canadiandimension.com/articles/view/waiting-for-hollywood-canadas-maquila-film-industry> (last accessed October 2013).

Meleiro, A. (2010) 'Finance and Co-productions in Brazil', given at Brasilian Studies Association (BRASA) 2010, <http://www.cenacinema.com.br/wp-content/uploads/brasa.pdf> (last accessed 11 October 2011).

Middents, J. (2013) 'The first rule of Latin American cinema is you do not talk about Latin American cinema: notes on discussing a sense of place in contemporary cinema', *Transnational Cinemas*, 4.2, 147–164.

Middents, J. (2009) *Writing National Cinema: Film Journals and Film Culture in Peru*, Dartmouth, NE: Dartmouth College Press.

Middents, J. and P. Fernández (2013) 'Vengancha: How Mexican Filmmakers Accent the Margins of Dominant Cinema', <https://vimeo.com/78128737> (last accessed 18 August 2016).

Miles, R. J. (2011) 'Reclaiming Revelation: *Pan's Labyrinth* and *The Spirit of the Beehive*', *Quarterly Review of Film and Video*, 28, 195–203.

Miller, H. K. et al. (2013) 'Home Cinema', *Sight & Sound*, 23.9, 20–32.

Miller, T. and R. Stam (2000) *Film And Theory: An Anthology*, Boston: Blackwell.

Minghetti, C. (2005) 'El director de "Luna de Avellaneda" promedia el rodaje de la miniserie "Vientos de agua"', *La Nación*, 1 September, <http://www.lanacion.com.ar/734777-campanella-de-asturias-a-la-argentina> (last accessed 29 November 2016).

Mittell, J. (2013) '*Gravity* and the Power of Narrative Limits', 16 October, *JustTV*, <https://justtv.wordpress.com/2013/10/16/gravity-and-the-power-of-narrative-limits/> (last accessed 10 January 2016).

Modleski, T. (1999) 'The Terror of Pleasure: The Contemporary Horror Film and Postmodern Theory', in L. Braudy and M. Cohen, (eds), *Film Theory and Criticism: Introductory Readings*, 5th ed., New York: Oxford University Press, 691–700.

Moisés, J. A. (2003) 'A new policy for Brazilian Cinema', in L. Nagib (ed.), *The New Brazilian Cinema*, London and New York: I. B. Tauris, 3–22.

Monsiváis, C. (1994) *A través del espejo: el cine mexicano y su público*, México: Ediciones el Milagro.

Morales, E. (2012) 'Oscar Contender "On the Road" Burns the Candle on Both Ends', *ABC News*, 26 December, <http://abcnews.go.com/ABC_Univision/Entertainment/walter-salles-film-version-road-politics-race/story?id=18063722> (last accessed April 15 2016).

Moraña, A. (2011) 'Memoria e impunidad a través del imaginario cinematográfico: "La mujer sin cabeza" (Lucrecia Martel 2008) y "El secreto de sus ojos" (Juan José Campanella 2009)', *Revista de Crítica Literaria Latinoamericana*, 37. 73, 377–400.

Naficy, H. (2001) *An Accented Cinema: Exilic and Diasporic Filmmaking*, Princeton: Princeton University Press.

Naficy, H. (1996) 'Phobic Spaces and Liminal Panics: Independent Transnational Film Genre', in R. Wilson and W. Dissanayake (eds), *Global/Local: Cultural Production and the Transnational Imaginary*, Durham and London: Duke University Press, 119–143.

Nagib, L. and C. Mello (eds) (2013) *Realism and the Audiovisual Media*, London and New York: Palgrave Macmillan.

Nagib, L. (2006) 'Going Global: the Brazilian scripted film', in S. Harvey (ed.) *Trading Culture: Global Traffic and Local Cultures in Film and Television*, New Barnet: John Libbey & Co, 95–103.

Nagib, L. (2004) 'Talking Bullets: The Language of Violence in *City of God*', *Third Text*, 18.3, 239–250.

Nagib, L. (ed.) (2003) *The New Brazilian Cinema*, London and New York: I. B. Tauris.

Naremore, J. (2008) *More Than Night: Film Noir and Its Contents*, Berkeley: University of California Press.

Navitski, R. (2012) 'The Last Heist Revisited: Reimagining Hollywood Genre in Contemporary Argentine Film', *Screen*, 53.4, 359–380.

Newman, K. (2010) 'Notes on Transnational Film Theory: Decentered Subjectivity, Decentered Capitalism', in N. Ďurovičová and K. Newman (eds), *World Cinema: Transnational Perspectives*, New York and London: Routledge, 3–11.

Noble, A. (2005) *Mexican National Cinema*, New York and London: Routledge.

Noriega, G. (2009) 'Israel Adrián Caetano/Adrián Israel Caetano', in J. Pena Pérez (ed.), *Historias extraordinarias: nuevo cine argentino 1999–2008*, Madrid: T&B Editores, 109–119.

O'Connor, J. (2012) 'Walter Salles on Filming the Unfilmable', *The Guardian*, 7 October, <http://www.theguardian.com/film/2012/oct/07/walter-salles-interview-on-road> (last accessed 12 November 2013).

O2Filmes (2017) 'Nova Temporada de Cidade dos Homens' <http://www.o2filmes.com/entretenimento/cidade-dos-homens--nova-temporada> (last accessed 8 September 2017).

Ogrodnik, B. (2014) 'Focalisation Realism and Narrative Asymmetry in Alfonso Cuarón's *Children of Men*', *Senses of Cinema*, 71, <http://sensesofcinema.com/2014/feature-articles/focalization-realism-and-narrative-asymmetry-in-alfonso-cuarons-children-of-men/> (last accessed 20 April 2015).

O'Malley, I. (1986) *The Myth of the Revolution: Hero Cults and the Institutionalization of the Mexican State, 1920–1940*, New York: Greenwood Press.

Oubiña, D. (2009) 'La vocación de alteridad (Festivales, críticos y subsidios del nuevo cine argentino', in J. Pena Pérez (ed.), *Historias extraordinarias: nuevo cine argentino 1999–2008*, Madrid: T&B Editores, 15–23.

Overhoff Ferreira, C. (2013) 'Losing sight in the globalized city: *Estorvo/Turbulence* (2000) by Ruy Guerra and *Ensaio sobre a Cegueira/Blindness* (2008) by Fernando Meirelles' *Migracion(es) e identidad(es): Transgresiones en el cine y en la televisión de América Latina*, Dossier coordinado por V. Berger y G. Jonas Aharoni, *Imagens, Memorias e soms*, 1–19.

Page, J. (2009) *Crisis and Capitalism in Contemporary Argentine Cinema*, Durham: Duke University Press.

Panozzo, M. (2009) 'El mainstream que nunca estuvo', in J. Pena Pérez (ed.) *Historias extraordinarias: nuevo cine argentino 1999–2008*, Madrid: T&B Editores, 47–57.

Pena Pérez, J. (ed.) (2009) *Historias extraordinarias: nuevo cine argentino 1999–2008*, Madrid: T&B Editores.

Perkins, V. F. (1990) 'Film Authorship: The Premature Burial', *CineAction*, Summer/Fall: 57–63.

Phillips, D. (2017) 'Brazil's ex-President Sentenced to Nearly Ten Years in Prison for Corruption', *The Guardian* 12 July <https://www.theguardian.com/world/2017/jul/12/brazil-president-lula-convicted-corruption> (last accessed 14 September 2017).

Piglia, R. (2008) 'Ernesto Guevara: The Last Reader', *Journal of Latin American Cultural Studies*, 17.3, 261–277.

Pinazza, N. (2014) *Journeys In Argentine and Brazilian Cinema*, London and New York: Palgrave Macmillan.

Place J. and L. Peterson, (1974) 'Some Visual Motifs of Film Noir', *Film Comment*, 10.1, 30–35.

Poblete, J. (2004) 'New National Cinemas in a Transnational Age', *Discourse*, 26.1&2, 214–234.

Podalsky, L. (2011) *The Politics of Affect and Emotion in Contemporary Latin American Cinema*, London and New York: Palgrave Macmillan.

Podalsky, L. (2003) 'Affecting Legacies: historical memory and contemporary structures of feeling in *Madagascar* and *Amores perros*', *Screen*, 44: 3, 277–294.

Preston, P. (2012) *The Spanish Holocaust: Inquisition and Extermination in Twentieth-Century Spain*, New York: W. W. Norton.

Punke, M. (2002) *The Revenant: A novel of Revenge*, New York: Picador.

Quayson, A. (2016) 'What lies beneath *The Revenant*', *The Guardian*, 22 Feburary, <https://www.theguardian.com/commentisfree/2016/feb/22/the-revenant-oscar-nominated-film-america> (last accessed 28 February 2016).

Rêgo, C. and C. Rocha (eds) (2011) *New Trends in Argentine and Brazilian Cinema*, Intellect: London.

Rêgo, C. (2011) 'The Fall and Rise of Brazilian Cinema', in C. Rêgo and C. Rocha (eds), *New Trends in Argentine and Brazilian Cinema*, Bristol: Intellect, 35–50.

Rêgo, C. (2005) 'The Fall and Rise of Brazilian Cinema', *New Cinemas: Journal of Contemporary Film*, 3, 85–100.

Roberts, S. (1997) 'Western Meets Eastwood: Subtext, Genre and Gender on the Road', in S. Cohan and I. R. Hark (eds), *The Road Movie Book*, London and New York: Routledge, 45–69.

Rocha, C. (2014) '*El secreto de sus ojos*: An Argentine male melodrama', *New Cinemas: Journal of Contemporary Film*, 12.1 & 2, 3–14.

Rocha, C. (2012) *Masculinities in Contemporary Argentine Popular Cinema*, London and New York: Palgrave Macmillan.

Rocha, C. (2011) 'Argentine Cinema during Neoliberalism', in C. Rêgo and C. Rocha (eds), *New Trends in Argentine and Brazilian Cinema*, Intellect: London, 17–35.

Rocha, G. (1994[1965]) 'An Esthetics of Hunger', in M. T. Martin (ed.), *The New Latin American Cinema* Vol. 1, Detroit: Wayne State University Press, 59–61.

Rodríguez Isaza, L. (2012) 'Branding Latin America Film Festivals and the International Circulation of Latin American Films', submitted in accordance with the requirements for the degree of Doctor in Philosophy, University of Leeds.

Rohter, L. (2009) 'The Three Amigos of Cha Cha Cha', *New York Times*, April 23 <http://www.nytimes.com/2009/04/26/movies/26roht.html?pagewanted=all> (last accessed 20 May 2009).

Romero, S. (2016) 'Brazilian Politics Smother a Film's Oscar Ambitions', *New York Times*, 27 September, <http://www.nytimes.com/2016/09/28/world/americas/brazilian-politics-smother-a-films-oscar-ambitions.html?_r=0> (last accessed 1 October 2016).

Ros, A. (2011) 'Leaving and Letting Go As Possible Ways of Living Together in Jorge Gaggero's *Cama Adentro/Live-In Maid*', in C. Rêgo and C. Rocha (eds), *New Trends in Argentine and Brazilian Cinema*, London: Intellect, 97–116.

Ross, M. (2011) 'The Film Festival as Producer: Latin American Films and Rotterdam's Hubert Bals Fund', *Screen*, 52.2, 261–267.

Rouanet, A. (2013) '*God is Brazilian*: A Re-Examination of *Cinema Novo* and Self', in S. Brandellero (ed.), *The Brazilian Road Movie: Journeys of Self Discovery*, Cardiff: University of Wales Press, 116–144.

Ruétalo, V. (2009) and D. Tierney (eds), *Latsploitation, Exploitation Cinemas and Latin America*, London and New York: Routledge.

Ruétalo, V. (2006) 'Intersections: Latin America in Film Noir, Film Noir in Latin America' Society for Cinema and Media Studies, Vancouver, March.

Ruétalo, V. (2001) 'Fernando Solanas' Post-Dictatorial Journey into the Hollows of the Image', *Quarterly Review of Film and Video*, 18.4, 413–423.

Ryall, T. (1998) 'Genre and Hollywood', in J. Hill and P. Church Gibson (eds), *The Oxford Guide to Film Studies*, Oxford: Oxford University Press, 327–341.

Sacheri, E. (2005) *The Secret in Their Eyes*, trans. J. Cullen, New York: Other Press.

Sadlier, D. J. (2007) 'Leaving Home in Three Films by Walter Salles', *Symploke*, 15, 1–2: 125–139.

Saldaña-Portillo, M. J. (2002) 'On the Road with Che and Jack: Melancholia and the Legacy of Colonial Racial Geographies in America', *New Formations: A Journal of Culture/Theory/Politics*, 47 (Summer), 87–108.

Saldaña-Portillo, M. J. (2005) 'In the Shadow of NAFTA: *Y tu mamá también* Revisits the National Allegory of Mexican Sovereignty', *American Quarterly*, 57.3, 751–777.

Salgado, W. (2014) 'Eficine, panacea fílmica mexicana', *Milenio*, <http://m.milenio.com/hey/cine/Eficine-panacea-filmica-mexicana_0_306569353.html> (last accessed 25 July 2016).

Salles, W. (2003) 'Preface', in A. Elena and M. Díaz López, *The Cinema of Latin America*, London: Wallflower Press, xiii–xv.

Sampaio, S. (2011) Film Review '*Blindness*', *Scope: an online journal of Film and TV studies*, 16, <http://www.scope.nottingham.ac.uk/filmreview.php?issue=16&id=1207> (last accessed 5 August 2012).

Sánchez, F. (2002) *Luz en la oscuridad: Crónica del cine mexicano*, Mexico City: Cinemateca Nacional.

Sánchez Prado, I. (2014) *Screening Neoliberalism*, Nashville University of Vanderbilt Press.

Santaolalla, I. (2005) *Los 'Otros': etnicidad y 'raza' en el cine español contemporáneo*, Zaragoza, Spain: Prensas Universitarias de Zaragoza.

Sconce, J. (2002) 'Irony, nihilism and the new American "smart" film', *Screen*, 43: 4, 349–369.

Shary, T. (2005) *Teen Movies: American Youth on Screen*, London: Wallflower Press.

Shaw, D. (2013a) *The Three Amigos: The Transnational Filmmaking of Guillermo del Toro, Alejandro González Iñárritu and Alfonso Cuarón*, Manchester: Manchester University Press.

Shaw, D. (2013b) 'Walter Salles', in N. Pinazza and L. Bayman (eds), *Directory of World Cinema: Brazil*, London: Intellect, 27–28.

Shaw, D. (2011) '*Babel* and the Global Hollywood Gaze', *Situations: Project of the Radical Imagination*, 4.1, 11–31.

Shaw, D. (2007) 'Playing Hollywood at Its Own Game?: Bielinsky's *Nueve Reinas*', *Contemporary Latin American Cinema: Breaking Into the Global Market*, New York: Rowman and Littlefield, 67–85.

Shaw, L. and S. Dennison (2007) *Brazilian National Cinema*, London and New York: Routledge.

Shaw, M. (2005) 'The Brazilian *Goodfellas*: *City of God* as a Gangster Film', in E. P. Vieira (ed.), *City of God in Several Voices: Brazilian Social cinema as Action*, Nottingham: Critical, Cultural and Communication Press, 58–70.

Simkins, M. and B. Woods (2003) *Dying for Drugs*, Channel Four.

Smith, N. M. (2016) ' "Brazil is Divided" Aquarius Star Sonia Braga and Director Address Protests', *The Guardian*, 18 May <https://www.theguardian.com/film/2016/may/18/brazil-is-divided-aquarius-sonia-braga-cannes-protests> (last accessed September 2016).

Smith, P. J. (2016) 'Behind the Money: Iñárritu as Career Director' Keynote Address, 9th Contemporary Directors Symposium, Sussex University, 23 May,

Smith, P. J. (2014) *Mexican Screen Fiction: Between Cinema and Television*, London: Polity Press.

Smith, P. J. (2008a) 'Transnational Cinemas in Latin America: The Cases of Mexico, Argentina and Brazil', lecture at the British Academy, 26 November.

Smith, P. J. (2008b) review of '*Blindness*' <https://sites.google.com/site/pauljuliansmith-filmreviews/Home/blindness--dec--2008> (last accessed August 2013).

Smith, P. J. (2007) '*Pan's Labyrinth*', *Film Quarterly*, 60.4, 4–9.

Smith, P. J. (2003a) 'Transatlantic Traffic in Recent Mexican Films', *Journal of Latin American Cultural Studies*, 12.3, 389–400.

Smith, P. J. (2003b) *Amores perros*, London: British Film Institute.

Smith, P. J. (2003c) Review '*City of God*' *Sight & Sound*, 13.1, <http://old.bfi.org.uk/sightandsound/review/1483> (last accessed October 2012).

Smith, P. J. (2002) 'Heaven's Mouth', *Sight & Sound*, 12.4, 16–19.

Smith, P. J. (2001) 'Ghost of the Civil Dead', *Sight & Sound*, 11.12, 38–39.

Solomianski, A. (2011) Review '*El secreto de sus ojos*', *Hispania*, 94.4, 774–775.

Solomianski, A. (2006) 'Significado estructural, historia y tercer mundo en *Amores perros*', *Contracorriente*, 3.3, 17–36, <www.ncsu.edu/project/acontracorriente> (last accessed 4 December 2011).

Solomons, J. (2008) 'In the director's chair: Fernando Meirelles', 20 November, <http://www.guardian.co.uk/film/video/2008/nov/20/fernando-meirelles-on-blindness> (last accessed 8 June 2013).

Sontag, S. (1966) 'The Imagination of Disaster', *Against Interpretation and Other Essays*, New York: The Noonday Press, 209–225.

Sosa, C. (2009) 'A Counter-Narrative of Argentine Mourning: *The Headless Woman* by Lucrecia Martel', *Theory, Culture and Society*, 26.7–8, 25–62.

Stam, R. and L. Spence (1983) 'Colonialism, Racism and Representation: An Introduction', *Screen*, 24.2, 2–20.

Stock, A. M. (1999) 'Authentically Mexican? *Mi Querido Tom Mix* and *Cronos* Reframe Critical Questions', in J. Hershfield and D. R. Maciel, (eds), *Mexico's Cinema: A Century of Film and Filmmakers*, Wilmington, DE: Scholarly Resources, 267–286.

Stursberg, R. (2016) 'The Secret Canadian Life of Jack Kerouac' *Macleans*, 12 June, <http://www.macleans.ca/culture/books/the-secret-canadian-life-of-jack-kerouac/> (last accessed 29 June 2016).

Syder, A., and D. Tierney (2005) 'Mexploitation/Exploitation: Or How a Mexican Wrestler Almost Found Himself in a Sword and Sandal Epic', in S. J. Schneider and T. Williams (eds), *Horror International*, Detroit: Wayne State University Press, 33–55.

Taibo, P. I. II (2008) *Ernesto Guevara: También conocido como el Che*, Barcelona: Editorial Planeta.

Tandeciarz, S. (2012) 'Secrets, Trauma, and the Memory Market (or the return of the repressed in recent Argentine post-dictatorship cultural production)', *CINEJ Cinema Journal*, 1.2, 63–71, <http://cinej.pitt.edu/ojs/index.php/cinej/article/view/43> (last accessed 30 December 2016).

Thanouli, E. (2008) 'Narration in World Cinema: Mapping the Flows of Formal Exchange', *New Cinemas: Journal of Contemporary Film*, 6.3, 5–15.

Theidon, K. (2012) *Intimate Enemies: Violence and Reconciliation in Perú*, Philadelphia: University of Pennsylvania Press.

Thompson, K. (2013) 'Gravity, Part 2: Thinking Inside the Box', 12 November, <http://www.davidbordwell.net/blog/2013/11/12/gravity-part-2-thinking-inside-the-box/> (last accessed January 2014).

Thornton, N. (2007) 'Travelling Tales: Mobility and Transculturation in Contemporary Latin American Film', *Film & Film Culture*, 4. 30–40.

Tierney, D., A. Davies and D. Shaw (eds) (2014) 'Introduction', *The Transnational Fantasies of Guillermo del Toro*, London and New York: Palgrave Macmillan.

Tierney, D. (2012) 'Latino Acting on Screen: Pedro Armendáriz Performs Mexicanness in Three John Ford Films', *Revista Canadiense de Estudios Hispánicos*, 37.1, 111–134.

Tierney, D. (2011) 'Emilio Fernández "in Hollywood": Mexico's postwar Inter-American Cinema, *La perla/The Pearl* and *The Fugitive*', *Studies in Hispanic Cinemas* 7.2, 81–100.

Tierney, D. (2007) *Emilio Fernández: Pictures in the Margins*, Manchester: Manchester University Press.

Tierney, D. (2004) 'José Mojica Marins and the Cultural Politics of Marginality in Third World Film Criticism', *Journal of Latin American Cultural Studies*, 13.1, 63–78.

Tierney, D. (2002) 'El Terror en *El beso de la mujer araña*', *Revista Iberoamericana*, 68.199, 355–365.

Tierney, D. (1997) 'Silver Sling-Backs and Mexican Melodrama: *Salón México* and *Danzón*', *Screen*, 38.4, 360–371.

Triana-Toribio, N. (2013) 'Building Latin American Cinema in Europe: Cine en Construcción/Cinema in construction', in S. Dennison (ed.) *Contemporary Hispanic Cinema: Interrogating the Transnational in Spanish and Latin American Film*, London: Boydell & Brewer, 89–112.

Triana-Toribio, N. (2003) *Spanish National Cinema*, London: Routledge.

Tudor, A. (1974) *Image and Influence: Studies in the Sociology of Film*, London: Allen and Unwin.

Turan, K. (2002) *Sundance to Sarajevo: Film Festivals and the World They Made*, Los Angeles: University of California Press.

Tzioumakis, Y. (2012) *Hollywood's Indies: Classics Divisions, Speciality Labels and American Independent Cinema*, Edinburgh: Edinburgh University Press.

Udden, J. (2009) 'Child of the Long Take: Alfonso Cuarón's Film Aesthetics in the Shadow of Globalization', *Style*, 43.1, 26–44.

Vargas, J. C. (2005) 'Agonia Postindustrial: 1990–2005', *Proceso*, September, Special Edition, 17, 16–18.

Vertiz de La Fuente, C. (2016) 'En 2015, más cinema mexicano pero menos espectadores', <http://www.proceso.com.mx/432737/en-2015-cine-mexicano-menos-espectadores> (last accessed 17 July 2016).

Vieira, E. R. P. (2010) '*City of God*: Eight Years Later', in C. A. Gutiérrez (ed.), *The Ten Best Latin American Films of the Decade*, Bethesda, MD: Jorge Pinto Books, 27–36.

Vieira, E. R. P. (2007) '*Cidade de Deus* Challenges to Hollywood, Steps to *The Constant Gardener*', in D. Shaw (ed.), *Contemporary Latin American Cinema: Breaking into the Global Market*, New York: Rowman and Littlefield, 51–66.

Villazana, L. (2009) *Transnational Financial Structures in the Cinema of Latin America: Programa Ibermedia in Study*, Saarbrücken: VDM Verlag.

Villazana, L. (2008) 'Hegemony Conditions in the Coproduction Cinema of Latin America: The Role of Spain', *Framework: The Journal of Cinema and Media*, 49.2, 65–85.

Vlessing, E. (2011) 'Guillermo Del Toro's Pacific Rim at Pinewood Studios', *The Hollywood Reporter*, 7 May, <http://www.hollywoodreporter.com/news/guillermo-del-toros-pacific-rim-208026> (last accessed 15 March 2014).

Von Busack, R. (2007) 'Making the Future: Richard von Busack talks to Alfonso Cuarón about filming "Children of Men"', *Metroactive*, <http://www.metroactive.com/metro/01.10.07/alfonso-cuaron-0702.html> (last accessed 10 August 2010).

Williams, C. (2007) '*Los Diarios de Motocicleta* as Pan-American Travelogue', in D. Shaw (ed.), *Contemporary Latin American Cinema: Breaking into the Global Market*, Lanham, MD: Rowman & Littlefield, 11–27.

Williams, L. (1989) *Hardcore: Power, Pleasure and the Frenzy of the Visible*, Berkley: University of California Press.

Wolf, S. (2010) 'No Turning Back', *Sight & Sound*, 20.9, 14–17.

Wolf, S. (2009) 'Pablo Trapero: Pasaje a Otros Mundos', in J. Pena Pérez (ed.), *Historias extraordinarias: nuevo cine argentino 1999–2008*, Madrid: T&B Editores, 121–128.

Wood, J. (2006) *Faber Book of Mexican Cinema*, London: Faber & Faber.

Wood, R. (2003) *Hollywood From Vietnam to Reagan ... and Beyond*, New York: Columbia University Press.

Wood, R. (1985) 'An Introduction to the American Horror Film', in B. Nichols (ed.), *Movies and Methods*, Vol. 2, Los Angeles: California University Press, 195–226.

Zakarin, J. (2012), 'How Walter Salles Did the Impossible and Made Kerouac's "On the Road" Into a Movie', *The Hollywood Reporter*, 14 November, <http://www.hollywoodreporter.com/news/on-the-road-walter-salles-kerouac-390425> (last accessed November 2012).

Žižek, S. (2006a) DVD commentary, *Children of Men*, Universal Pictures.

Žižek, S. (2006b) 'The Clash of Civilizations at the End of History', <edelen.bengalenglish.org/wp-content/uploads/.../children-of-men.doc> (last accessed 30 November 2009).

Zupnik, B. (2015) 'Bernardo Zupnik', in INCAA *Anuario Estadístico de la Industria Cinematográfica y Audiovisual Argentina*, Buenos Aires: Instituto Nacional de Cine y Artes Audiovisuales, INCAA.

INDEX